THUS SPAKE
THE CORPSE

AN EXQUISITE
CORPSE READER
1988-1998

VOLUME I—POETRY & ESSAYS

*Edited by ANDREI CODRESCU
& LAURA ROSENTHAL*

BLACK SPARROW PRESS
SANTA ROSA—1999

Black Sparrow Press books are printed on acid-free paper.

LIBRARY OF CONGRESS CATALOGING-IN-PUBLICATION DATA

Thus Spake the Corpse : An Exquisite Corpse Reader, 1988-1998 / edited by Andrei Codrescu & Laura Rosenthal.
    p.   cm.
    Contents: v. 1. Poetry & Essays
      ISBN 1-57423-100-6 (paperback)
      ISBN 1-57423-101-4 (cloth trade)
      ISBN 1-57423-102-2 (signed cloth)
    I. Codrescu, Andrei, 1946–   . II. Rosenthal, Laura, 1958–
III. Exquisite corpse.
AC5.T45   1999
808.8—dc21

99-32586
CIP

TABLE OF CONTENTS

POETICS & POETRY

INTRODUCTION
CORPSE READERS, TAKE HEART

Andrei Codrescu moved *Exquisite Corpse: A Journal of Books & Ideas* to Louisiana in 1984 when he came to teach at LSU in Baton Rouge. Since its founding in January 1983 in Baltimore, the *Corpse,* as the aficionados intimately call it, has delighted not-so-innocent readers and catered to the craven complexes of overeducated esthetes, while also pleasing the autodidact lumpenproletariat on those long American afternoons by the Kerouakian railroad tracks now known as Starbucks and PJ's Coffee. In other words, we fed the souls of both the jaded and of those too young to drink. We also enraged the literary establishment, garnering resentment, jealousy, damnation, and three threats of never-materialized lawsuits. From the very first issue, the *Corpse* attracted an energetic and sophisticated cadre of writers united by a kind of suicidal fearlessness specific to eighties America. In 1983, American literature had settled into a cozy bubble of MFA-program McWriters buttered with postgraduate NEA fellowships. American poetry was increasingly going back to the esthetics of the 1950s under the tutelage of impressionist critics like Helen Vendler of Harvard. Alongside prosaic confessional drivel in "free verse," throwback versification calling itself "the new formalism" captured the workshops and the university quarterlies. American fiction began returning to psychological realism and sentimental autobiography. The fury of the establishment at having its nap disturbed by experimental writers in the sixties and seventies (and by modernism, surrealism, and post modernism before that) resulted in the return to a literary landscape H. L. Mencken had once called "the Sahara of the Bozarts."

Taking potshots at this new status quo would have been like shooting fish in a barrel, but for the fact that the new reaction was (and is) huge. This was just fine by the *Corpse,* which relishes a fight the way academics crave prizes. It turned out, however, that fighting was not what the *Corpse* turned out to be about. After the initial skirmishes with some of the more visible capos of the new retrenchment, it became evident that a community of terrific writers existed in pristine disdain of the mainstream, and their works made the *Corpse* an important literary magazine. These writers embraced a variety of esthetics and were part of different scenes: New York school and Black

ANDREI CODRESCU & LAURA ROSENTHAL

13

Mountain poets, West Coast surrealists and eco-surrealists, ethnic accentualists, Iowa actualists, midwestern abstractionists, southern minimalists, and San Diego maximalists. The editor's eclectic pleasures were further enhanced by the absence of biographical notes. From the beginning, *Exquisite Corpse* was conceived as a newspaper, to be read for the news within, not for the glamorous bios of recent conquerors of the Amy Lowell Traveling Fellowship plus glam shot. We began on page one with debate and controversy and moved, like Don Quijote, from windmill to windmill. Each issue had its own story pieced together by its contributors exactly like a "cadavre exquis," the collaborative form that the French surrealists had enjoyed in the 1920s, from which *Exquisite Corpse* got its name. The *Corpse*, like Don Quijote, or perhaps Pantagruel, was also dedicated to the blurring of genres, demolishing distinctions between poetry and prose, lyric and reportage, essay and manifesto. In addition to poetry and a sprinkling of fiction (there was an inexplicable editorial bias against fiction), essays, letters, and art, the *Corpse* published "bureau" reports from various parts of the world, and a great many translations.

The *Corpse* in Louisiana (1984–1998) had two distinct periods: the first (1984–1990) was more or less an extension of the Baltimore *Corpse*, tropicalized by the environs; the second (1990–1998) was the era of the Body Bag. In its first Louisiana stage, the *Corpse* drew its energy from early contributors to the magazine and material solicited by the editor, with less than twenty percent of its contributions coming over the transom. There was also a nameless and invigorating force emanating from the diffuse hostility of the academic environment which, in those days was (and weakly still is) a bastion of New Criticism reincarnated as Southern-boy hickism.

In the second stage, with the addition of Laura Rosenthal's column "Body Bag," which answered would-be contributors directly in the pages of the magazine, there was a sudden influx of young, new, hip voices into the *Corpse*. We were discovered by another generation of literary revolutionists who found in the tone of the magazine a perfect medium for their pop-culture-informed skepticism, violence, and humor. During this time, more than ten thousand literate, amused, hungry readers took the *Corpse*. The audience widened from just writers to readers interested in culture and, to some extent, the *Corpse* became a general culture magazine. *Corpse* essays were reprinted in *Harper's, Utne Reader, Playboy,* and other mass-circulation magazines, and *Corpse* poets started winning awards (!), such as Pushcart Prizes, and inclusion in anthologies like *Best American Poetry*. We didn't feel that such successes created any painful dilemmas, preferring to believe instead that "grownup" culture had finally tired of academic pieties and found the *Corpse* tonic and necessary. The initial critical attitudes of the *Corpse* became an inspiration for dozens of small magazines, zines, and newsletters. The world was catching up. At this time, more than seventy percent of our material came over the transom from writers unknown to us, but who had caught perfectly the *Corpse je-ne-sais-quoi*. Five years ago we changed the name of the publication to *Exquisite Corpse: A Journal of Letters & Life*, because we felt that it more accurately reflected our turn toward topics of wider interest.

Academic hostility continued unabated, however, because the retros in charge of the pathetic literature pie resented having any part of their wobbly conformism questioned. The problem with the wimps, Jim Gustafson once said, is that there are so many of them. You said it, Jimbo. Every year they multiply to the point where they cover the sky like a locust plague, leaving room only for their own reproduction. No matter. We have our own sky. And it's a cybersky. In 1998, tired of mountains of paper, but also fearful of inevitable institutionalization, ossification, poetry fatigue, and literary ennui, we suspended publication of the paper *Corpse*, taking it into cyberspace. *The Cybercorpse* can be found at: http://www.corpse.org. *The Cybercorpse* is still the *Corpse*, but it is more fluid, subject to instant change and, above all, not so labor- and time-intensive for us. And the trees are ecstatic.

In 1998, City Lights Books published *The Stiffest of the Corpse: An Exquisite Corpse Reader, 1983–1988*. This anthology represented our first five years well, so that we did not feel the need to include here any material covered by that book. The present successor anthology, a gathering of the best contributions to *Exquisite Corpse* since 1988, will be published in two volumes: the first will contain poetry, poetics, and essays; the second will contain fiction, "bureaus," translations, and essays on translation.

Exquisite Corpse would not have been possible without the help of a number of bright and enthusiastic graduate assistants. The editors hereby proffer a kiss-shaped lillyrose (a new flower) to: Matt Clark, Mark LaFlaur, Dave Racine, Kathy Crown, Lisa McFarren, Josh Russell, Dan Olson, Mark Yakich, and the indefatigable perfectionist Jean C. Lee. Particular thanks are in order to Mark Yakich, our current assistant, for working fiendishly on this anthology.

THUS SPAKE
THE CORPSE

1
ESSAYS

KEITH ABBOTT

LECTURE

JACK COLLOM

Scientific tests in poet-Chomskyan generative linguistics have demonstrated conclusively that beyond the splurge of consciousness we pass from a pure logic & phenomenology to physiology if we wish to maintain an equivalence between concept & remembered image, & within that shifting morphology the suprasegmental accuracy of represented metamorphosis may well be reduced via narratology by what Daniloff calls "the partially digested subjective." In lay terms, for the would-be artist:

FORGET YOURSELF. Do not take yourself seriously, including Ideas, no matter how achingly ultimate they seem, nor how their cloudiness turns into a Noah's Flood of clarity.

Become a beakful of mud with hands & ears & eyes, a mouth to drink coffee with, & memory. No more. It's amazing how difficult & deceptive the task of divorcing care & self is. We are all aware, with a sort of painful, gay laughter suspended in boredom, how artists inferior to or more naive than ourselves display everywhere, blatantly but unknowingly, a childish need to put themselves in a good light. Even when they're putting themselves down, they're semiconsciously crying out for adoration. It's *this* distraction that makes most art less thrilling than a dying squirrel.

We, as mature artists, feel we have transcended ego-taint in our work. But in fact the entire world-interface of *anyone* in every tiny detail is *interwoven* with piranha swarms of image need.

Children carry this like another few inches of transparent flesh. Then it sinks in, & the more adult we become the more it's part of our Very Fiber. It takes a thousand guises, emerges under masks of unvarying virtue.

"My heart reaches out to these poor people. They're figurines of Sorrow. Let's go home."

"I know a place of peace & beauty, faraway, some day."

"I adore her. That's all that matters."

These poor objects of love don't get to *exist*, except as puppets of mealy-mouthed fingers. What exists is falsified pastels of the self sloshing all available receptors.

OR: "Sittin' in the kitchen." All of *my* poems begin with these four words. & I stole them from my friend Richard. Too beautiful to think up. By means of them, I constantly wish to image forth these things, about myself:

21

1. I'm direct, no-nonsense.
2. I'm a keen observer ("sittin'").
3. I'm colloquial, folksy, colorful, down-home. Sittin' in the kitchen.
4. I'm economical, with words & life.
5. I'm musical.
6. I'm in tune with the warm, feminine center of things. Sittin' in the kitchen.
7. I'm humorous.
8. & I'm hungry.

Well! This winds up to be watered-down Br'er Rabbit. Desperation patches on blue hollow.—Could be worse. Art's inconvenient.

Artists have studied out positions wherein they can have a little fun with their backs to the wall; dance about with kitchen doors glued to their shoulders blades. Their whole deal is to be a step ahead of laughter, play The Fool via planned obsolescence. A total idiot, whether the condition be *natural* or gained by means of much study, as in the religions, can't do *things*, which is what artists do. That is, things. Purity never moves.

You might, at this point, go half-blind by feeling your face light up, not too much but just right, at the prospect of *compromise*, but that's just a bad word. Forget it. Unless it's a matter of multidimensional interexisting spheres. Unworldliness, which is what compromise leads to, is just a Gothic happy-face of zombie-white sentimentality. Black Hole of sugar. An artist has to be integral but nonrepeating, all-of-a-piece like a starfish.

Artists are like unpredictable Wall Street pirates who hack around with some genuine pigiron but protect, *inside,* this snow white egg-shaped synapse town of beautiful retardism so it's unhurt by the gorgeously cruel world & yet functions in every string of their Thing, sometimes. This is getting hard to picture, which may be because it's all wrong. It's certainly hard to do. Artists whine a lot, but they seek novel whines.

You really need a 3-D computer screen for this, & that's why nobody ever digs the graphics well enough to get a further insight. Meanwhile, this tender, icy synapse-egg is maintained, in terms of ordinary hydraulics, & functions like a thermostat. Its humanoid shell is both more & less human than the average, depending on what "human" means.

All language emits the metallic stench of statement. The statement is invariably the person of the statement-maker. So you might as well just start playing around, & *play hard.* This is nobility.

Charity is a cheap shot. It's as if by throwing 86 cents on the ground you have a brick. Or by saying "Brick" you become one. The magic of names is much more expensive. You may become electrically connected to a brick by forgetting the name. You may become electrically connected to a poem by keeping the name & forgetting what it means. You may pick up a brick & throw it. At me. I need the attention. But *don't worry*, because all these insights are perfectly sound.

These insights are boiled in a selfless hot ether, painstakingly plucked from the wisdom surrounding decades of sincerity, & dressed in a clever motley.

I have a dream.

I mean, y'know what I mean? I mean, I've been making choices here, forsaking my food and exercise, on the basis of a perfect crystal of goodness, which you didn't realize. But now it's time to reveal this as a personal essay. But *don't worry*, I *know* what I'm doing. *Don't worry*. It's not that I can't practice what I preach & forget myself. I can. I just don't *want* to right now, because I'm willing to sacrifice *my* dignity for *your* edification, & besides I have another, perfect dignity just below the one I'm tossing away now.

Actually, what I'm doing, in a sense, is cunningly bucking the tide of your latest perception of the intentional fallacy's borders by jumping *right into it*. Know what I mean? Like, the intentional fallacy's where sincerity makes liars of us all. *You* know, declaration runs us stone-blind. But if you just turn around & get double sincere, then you *fool* the system because you use something that got blocked off, which is good (sincerity, y'know), but you're outside *too* so you don't partake of its preachy crap. It's kinda like the camp appreciation of "White Christmas" jingling back into a yellow haze. So, anyway, that's what I'm doing.

Sure, I'm not the first, I'm just *in* the breeze. Opposites are alike, uh-huh, but it's the twist of the knife that cuts the mustard. I *really* know what I'm doing. But *doesn't* this make you just a trifle nauseous? When I *say* that? Sure, & I *know* that. That's what I'm doing. & the way I stay on top of your nausea is this: by telling you about it! I know what you're thinking. Like sticking the bridal pair on top of the wedding cake. What can you do (don't tell me)? Like, chattering like an idiot savant in the five-&-dime. Stupidity has its beauty (which gets old because it's so damn eternal), but when you get into *off*-stupid, like falling off a rope, you're approaching *sub*-stupid. Aha, the alpha state. Right? But when I *tell* you this, I mean, it falls right into Ezra Pound, &, y'know,

23

rhythm can go *any*where. The whole purpose is to get into what you know. Basic chatter.

Let's take a breath. An attractive version of knowledge, poetically now, would be in the field of ranching tips, or community finance. *Textural acts* as beautiful as cellular fission, slicing then from now. But all these varieties of barbwire fence & Brooklyn Dodger candy bars are attempts to *paint yourself up* so as to resemble the off-white solidity of a hospital bed. Yes. I wanna cut *right through* that. I was born, & I'm twice-divorced but it wasn't my *fault*. In fact, in the last analysis, these divorces were all a beautiful adventure. I've actually extracted gristle, from fake wood, in a living graph that whispers "beautiful adventure," like a telephone line to your dream's bathroom, because I'm a bloody beautiful guy. My hand would be steadier castrating a pig, but that, & the breakfast afterwards, & the old beige farmhouse, are all categorized by now. *True* truth lies in what's ordinarily swept under the bridge & called "pettiness," really curved light when you just take a minute of your time & look at it.

So, articulation never builds its own floor. You might as well give that up. I mean, history is nice if you just want to be a sideshow type like Metternich.—But let me tell you some more about myself.

I'm idealistic in a sort of golden way that I cherish because of its sheer nobility, but I'm also vividly colorful & as realistic as a brown bear, in a *very* attractive total melange. I understand everything. The fact that I haven't attracted an unruly cadre of slavish cognoscenti, or even *one fan*, is simply due to the fact that I'm ultra-subtle & ahead of my time, & I pad beautiful lost trails in my lone-wolf sorta way.

I'm also very youthful & vigorous, basically, but at the same time old & wise, not to mention "in the middle," which is very balanced & *good*. I'm even sorta crippled & not crippled, like Lord Byron, depending on my mood. I mean, it's *totally* real, & I can back it up, but if you were to ask me about it, which nobody ever does, I'd answer in a kindly but objective manner which certainly wouldn't exceed 3 or 4 hours, include some medical terms. I've been very heroic about it & I never speak of it, because all I care about is positive things. It's *very* interesting though. Also I'd like to mention frankly that I'm good in bed, take my word for it, I'm referring to *fucking* y'know—at least I used to be before being melodramatically "mugged" by my tragic illness, which had nothing to do with drinking. *Nothing* goes to my head. My shit has a rather pleasant farm aroma.

Don't misunderstand me & crowd around wanting to touch me & suck my brains, I *really* don't have much time, but that's all *part* of it. Y'know I have a lot of courage, y'know, to stand up here & talk like a Beautiful Fool (but not the *specious* kind) so you all can learn to find happiness in your lives.

Am I happy myself? Oh yes, yet in a way that *includes* deeply post-up-to-date gut sorrow.

However, my delicate sense of modesty, resembling in many ways the italianate shapeliness of ultimate light & shadow, draws me away from this frank discussion. Back to *art*, not that this only *seeming* digression wasn't, in its blend (but *not* blend in the *homogeneous* sense) of outrage & buried eu*clid*ishness, a vegetarian spaceship looking down on the postmodern. It was.

Art, it has been amply demonstrated, is the justification, in flipped hindsight, of civilization. Might as well try it. It's almost as pretty as everything else. Now. You're *gonna* have ego "problems." So just *deny* them! Present-day psychology has amassed just enough knowledge that its recommendations are all ass-backwards. It's like the discovery of pus.— Oh wow, it's real, let's turn the whole body into this stuff! Forget that. They're at that *stage* where you act free by *precepts*, the quivering light-green edge of age 13. The only thing that saves hipness is the breathtaking beauty of its lies. Here are my recommendations. Let your need to wallow in self-pity (*which* is just another chemical) emerge in convoluted petty ways that *really* make people work to halfway pigeon-hole because they're so simple. *That's it!* You lay eggs on people's hands while they're holding on to something. Simplicity *itches* to become complex. I *could* just spit on the floor & tell you about geranium seeds &/or artificial colors but you're probably not ready for that. You've got a wire through your throat. *Nothing* is what we think it is: a big zilch. Can't tell where it's coming from. Take my "word" for it.

So back to forgetting self in art, you realize of course that my *apparent* trumpeting of self is in fact a *real trumpet*, golden brass & spit & bell-motion, much more self-transcendent than the pretensions of Objectivism, since I *knowingly* cast myself into the perspective of a whiff of comic figure, which in turn is *pure atoms*.

Forget yourself in art. Exceptions prove the rule because they're like weird faces that pop & swirl up when you're not looking. You may think you know this, but it's dumb of you to think like that. I've discovered that to be so, like a diamond. I discovered it in Western Springs, Illinois, on a roller-coaster hall of mirrors, the *very first day*. I was the center of the universe then, thinking about sex with a package of hot dogs. Going Hey bop a lula boppa spiffety bam dee bop a lula bop a libbidy-do.

Thank you.

REVOLUTIONARY PROPOSAL

Proposal to the National Endowment for the Humanities
for a Working Class Revolution

REQUEST

The Party is requesting $978,150 in support from the National Endowment for the Humanities for a new initiative designed to serve a broad constituency including serfs, workers, plebeians, wage-laborers and the wretched poor. The goal of the revolution is to iden-tify class antagonisms and foster the class consciousness of the oppressed currently under-represented by the State. If this pilot program is successful, the Party would like to continue the Revolution until the State is overthrown or funding is eliminated.

THE NEED

To say the Emperor has no clothes is to pander to bourgeois culture which is, after all, mere training to act as a machine; however, to rephrase this in the language of class conflict: the old boy is buck-ass naked.

The need for a workers' revolution is part of the larger historical picture which foresees the inevitable decline of late capitalism or K-Martification. Everywhere the exploited masses are made to scurry to the ever-receding beacon of the Blue Light Special while the tottering bour-geoisie crouches precariously on its well-larded haunches, sucking the sweet syrupy life-blood of a seemingly endless supply of Slush Puppies and feeding the masses the cold crushed ice. The opportunity of a revolu-tion will unite the fettered masses and forcibly imprison the bourgeoisie into the Betty Ford Clinic of History.

THE PROGRAM

We call for immediate and staggering action! There can be no substitute. To this end, the Party has developed a highly explosive Seminar and Study Program to launch emergent revolutionaries into the rhetorical melée. The aim is to link some of the most incendiary and well-paid scholars in Revolutionary Studies with bona fide lumpen proletariats. (This is not to recapitulate the false dichotomy between physical and cul-tural work but simply to recognize that some workers—the oppressed mechanic, for instance—crank wrenches, while others—the embattled professorate—wrench cranks.) In a series of really strident collo-quia, the seminar group will focus their attention on several

26

volatile issues including the relation of intellectual capital to monetary capital and consequent salary hikes among academics, the rise of the intelligentsia to senior-level bureaucratic posts, and the need for these posts to garner private incentives such as mobile phones, private physical fitness trainers and off-shore banking. And, if there is time, we will also discuss strategies for mobilizing the slumbering populace—no obstacle is so great that it can't be theorized!

Within the program year, or directly following it, we foresee issuing a highly provocative monograph or series of white papers (the format to be determined in trenchant debate) which might fan the flames of revolution and uncover the need for new funding to support additional seminar groups, thinktanks and round tables around the colonized globe. In subsequent program years, and in keeping with our commitment to involve the workers at every level, we will issue highly inflammatory rhetoric in class-specific mediums: fortune cookies, box tops, food stamps, beer labels, as well as condom and feminine hygiene packaging. (This carries the additional benefit of creating a synergistic link between revolutionaries and the guild masters who produce and are alienated from these fine products.)

IN CONCLUSION

If we are to use the master's tools to take apart the master's house, we must never forget the spiralling costs of hardware and building supplies. Thus it is the goal of the Party to support all insurgents at all stages of their intellectual and financial development. And we will continue to identify emergent revolutionaries in an attempt to make them more profoundly aware of the grant cycle and the full range of support available through matching honoraria, Fulbrights, pledge drives and celebrity golf tournaments.

The Party respectfully and earnestly requests the National Endowment for the Humanities to become its partner in this revolution and lurk in ambush against the brutal capitalist stooge.

FUNDRAISERS OF ALL COUNTRIES, UNITE!

IS LITERATURE USEFUL?

translated by Kirby Olson

Nothing is more ordinary today than political poetry. It developed during the war clandestinely, and now it proposes to survive.

GEORGES BATAILLE

27

I would like to articulate a first principle.

There is no possible human being who should not have put themselves to the test, who deserves not to try, or who could not have done so happily.

I have before me an unpublished poem from the insurrection: everything that the rage for liberty causes in the head of an eighteen-year-old cries out in these verses: *We will throw our heads to the corners of the outer limits*, they say. The remainder is of a fiery inspiration. It has such a true violence, I cannot help myself from rejoicing.

That said, I cannot see any reason not to underline a second principle: which touches in particular on this war.

This war is being fought against a system of life of which the literature of propaganda is the key. The fate of fascism is slavery: among others the idea is to reduce literature to mere usefulness. What does useful literature signify other than to treat human beings as raw matter? For this sad work, in fact, literature is necessary.

This does not mean the condemnation of any genre more than the party line, the orders from above. I only write authentically on one condition: to not give a damn for anything or anybody, to stomp on my orders with both feet.

That which spoils the game, which makes a writer weak is the concern that he should be useful.

Every woman and man should be useful to her or his pals, but becomes disgusting if there is nothing in her or him above Utility.

The fall into utility, through shame, when divine liberty, uselessness, has a bad conscience, is the beginning of a desertion. The field is left free to the clowns of propaganda ...

Why not accuse in these circumstances the place from which every truth springs, the fact that literature in a fundamental fashion refuses to be useful. Being the expression of man, of the essential part of mankind, it cannot be useful, in that man, or at least what is essential in him, cannot be reduced to utility. Sometimes a writer falls, tired of solitude, letting his voice mix with the mob's. However he cries with theirs if he wishes, if he only can—whether he does it through fatigue, through self-disgust, it is still only a poison to him, but he communicates to others this poison: fear of liberty, need for servitude! His true task is the opposite: to reveal in solitude the intangible part that no one can ever enslave. A single political goal corresponds with his essence: the writer can only engage in the struggle for liberty, announcing the free part of ourselves that cannot be defined by formulas, but only through the emotion and poetry of harrowing works. Instead of fighting for it, the writer should use liberty, incarnate as a minimum every liberty in whatever it is that he or she says. Often it is this liberty which destroys him: it is this which makes it the most difficult. But it is this that he is obliged to love, this proud and fierce liberty, hardy and limitless, which sometimes leads to death, which even loves death. It is this that the true writer teaches— through the authenticity of his writings—the refusal of servility (and especially the hatred of propaganda). It is for that reason that he refuses to go along with the mob and that he meets death in solitude.

First Published in Combat, *1944*

THE REVOLUTION AT ST. MARK'S CHURCH

ELIOT WEINBERGER

[In May 1994, the Poetry Project at St. Mark's Church in New York held their annual symposium; the topic that year was "Revolutionary Poetry." On the opening night there were four "keynote" speakers: Erica Hunt, an African-American poet and labor organizer; Eileen Myles, poet and gay activist; Amiri Baraka; and, inexplicably, myself.

The evening began strangely: as I entered the church, a young woman from the Poetry Project said, "Oh, we got your package and paid for it." She handed me a large and bulging jiffy bag that had been sent to me c/o the church, C.O.D. for $27. I hesitated to open it, but curiosity always conquers. The package was filled with trash.

Hunt spoke first; in the subsequent chaos I'm afraid I forgot what she said. Then I spoke; the reception was not particularly hostile. Myles gave a very funny "I'm a lesbian" rap. Baraka got up, talked for five minutes, then whipped out his notebook, said, "And now I'd like to reply to the gentleman who preceeded me," and launched into a fifteen minute tirade, pointing his finger at me. No one expresses rage like Amiri Baraka. When he turned to Eileen, shouting that lesbianism has nothing to do with the revolution, she began yelling back. Things fell apart, and the night ended.

A few months later, *Poetry Flash* ran an account of the symposium by Tim Griffin. He wrote: "Everyone seemed to be hating Eliot Weinberger, who attempted to derail the notion of an effective 'witness poetry,' and espoused what scholar Walter Lew would in a panel discussion the next day call 'an incredibly outdated liberal, Cold War demonization of China.' Baraka had kicked his two cents in against Weinberger as well, saying that revolution never consisted of 'an endowed chair in a concentration camp.'" (Anti-Semitic vapors aside, I am not sure what this last remark means, but it should be noted that Baraka has been a Professor for years; I don't teach.)

29

This was followed by a report in the Poetry Project newsletter by Douglas Rothschild on my "now legendary talk." Rothschild held up Jackson Mac Low as "living proof" against "Mr. Weinberger's claim that politically radical views & allegiances lead you to stop writing." (Obviously!) And he wrote that "Mr. Baraka had taken very careful notes on what Mr. Weinberger had just said & launched a full scale barrage; effectively scuttling Mr. Weinberger's thesis (the likes of which we have not seen since the Potempkin) [sic]." (Rothschild—Mr. Rothschild—seemed to have forgotten that the Potemkin sailors were the Good Guys.]

I wrote to the newsletter in an attempt to salvage what I'd actually said, and wondered why neither of the correspondents had been alarmed by, among other things, Baraka's condemnation of the "pornography" of rap lyrics, and his defense of the imprisonment of the utterly apolitical but gay writer Reinaldo Arenas as a "counter-revolutionary." (The St. Mark's crowd may not be what it used to be, but one would expect them, at least, to be against censorship in any form, against government persecution of any writer for any reason, and for gay rights.) This led to a letter in a subsequent issue from Baraka, who repeated three times in seven sentences that "bourgeois intellectuals like Weinberger lie." (Perhaps this is the place to mention that the publication by Marsilio of Baraka's *Transbluency: Selected Poems* is a project that began at my suggestion to the publishers.)

I thought I'd let the whole thing drop, but reading my speech again a year later, it's curious that this corner of Po-World was scandalized and thought they were hearing neocon ravings—one person called it the "Pentagon version of world poetry"—when actually I had uttered a series of banal commonplaces. Most of them were infants during the Vietnam War. It was disheartening that they had grown up to adopt uncritically certain dreams and models of Revolution that are now—particularly in the countries where they once occurred—almost kitsch.

The speech was meant to be spoken, not read, and I hadn't intended to publish it at all. The reaction to it is probably more interesting than the speech itself, but one needs both to understand what went down. It should be mentioned again that this is May 1994: a nationally eventless time, before the ascension of Gingrich (to call him Newt is to insult our salamander friends), the passage of Proposition 187, the Republican feeding frenzy on the poor, and the Oklahoma bombing. Also it is remarkable how, in only a year, the government and the corporations have taken over the Internet: Just a few weeks ago, a man in L.A. was arrested for receiving "salacious materials" over the net in his own home on his own computer. Anyway, this is, unedited, what I said.]

Lenin to Maxim Gorky: "I can't listen to music too often. It affects your nerves, makes you want to say nice stupid things and stroke the heads of people who could create such beauty while living in this vile hell. These days you mustn't stroke anyone's head—you might get your hand bitten off. You have to hit them on the head, without any mercy."

There is something nostalgic and quaint, and something sickening, about a conference now, in 1994, on revolutionary poetry. [My first thought, on being invited here, was to recall the least prophetic line uttered in my lifetime: "The revolution will not be televised."] And yet the subject is more pertinent than ever. I want to clear through the first, to get to the second.

First a matter of definitions, the classic difference between revolt and revolution. Revolt is an uprising of some kind against some aspect of the existing order. Revolution is the struggle, nearly always, but not necessarily, a violent struggle, to replace one form of society and state with another. Most important, the form of the new society is usually fairly fixed in the minds of the revolutionaries. In this sense, nearly all of us in the generation of 1968—except Bill & Hillary—were engaged in some form of revolt; but only a few were revolutionaries. It's always a mistake to confuse one with the other, particularly as revolutionary societies tend to suppress any further revolt.

In talking about revolutionary poetry—in its political sense—I also want to draw a line between it and political, "socially aware" poetry. The poetry that bears witness to, or expresses outrage at, or is the product of, the enormous horrors and injustices of the historical moment is not necessarily revolutionary. It is only revolutionary when it serves, in some way, the destruction of the old order, and carries within it a formed image of the new order. Traditionally, revolutionary poetry presents the horrific details of present existence, excoriates or lampoons those who are responsible for the misery, rallies its readers or listeners to struggle against injustice, exalts certain individual heroes of that struggle, and offers a vision of the paradise that will follow the victory of the revolutionary forces.

Politically revolutionary poetry only sometimes coincides with aesthetically revolutionary poetry. When it does, we have some of the great poetry of the century: Hikmet, Neruda, MacDiarmid, Brecht, Mayakovsky, to name a few. When it doesn't—as is obvious when one reads old issues of *The New Masses* or any anthology of guerrilla poetry—it can produce some of the worst poetry, some of it written by these same poets: a poetry where the message is the medium.

But the real problem with revolutionary poetry is the Revolution. With certain exceptions—Mexico, Spain, Iran, among them— nearly every important revolution of the 20th century has

31

been fought under the inspiration of Karl Marx. [Though interestingly, none of these revolutions were imagined by Marx, and were, in fact, specifically denied by him: He believed that the revolution would be led by the urban proletariat in countries like England and Germany, and thought that a revolution led by the rural peasantry, in a place like Russia, would be impossible. Furthermore, he assumed an internationalism to the revolutionary proletariat, quite unlike the nationalistic Marxist revolutions that actually occurred.]

I happen to think that all of us as writers, like any good union members, must judge the merits of a state first according to what it does for (or against) us as writers. And there is no question that, in this respect, all of the Communist states were, or continue to be, disasters. On the one hand, Communism brought nearly universal literacy to its masses and produced millions of inexpensive books for them to read; it created writers' unions where the state essentially paid writers to write. On the other hand, these same states all enforced strict censorship, and tended to execute, imprison, exile or silence most of their best writers. The writers who flourished were either supporters who were famous before the revolution, achieving a kind of Grand Old Man status (such as Nicolas Guillen or Alejo Carpentier in Cuba) or else they were the kind of utter mediocrities—familiar to us in the U.S. or any capitalist country—who thrive in arts bureaucracies.

How thrilling it once seemed that Chairman Mao wrote poetry in classical Chinese—even though no one else was allowed to do the same, a kind of poet's dream. In China, the revolution wiped out a thriving modernist movement that had begun in the 1920's and 30's. The poets who were not killed were essentially required to write useful paeans to the boiler plate factories. Only in the crevices could something new or aesthetically radical be published: translations of foreign poets with impeccable political credentials, such as Neruda, Eluard, or—because of his death—Lorca, or considered too remote in time to be dangerous, such as Rimbaud and Baudelaire. It was these translations that inspired the young poets who came of age in the Cultural Revolution and rejected social realism to write what were, at first, simple, highly subjective imagist poems. In the 1970's, a whole generation of students was exhilarated by a line of poetry most of us in the West would be too embarrassed to write: Bei Dao's "I—do—not—believe!" For in a collective society, what is more subversive than the first-person singular, a negative and a verb? Targeted by the "anti-spiritual pollution" campaign, these poets were imprisoned, silenced, or forced to publish underground. Since the Tiananmen Square massacre in 1989, most of them are in exile.

How thrilling it once was that Che carried a copy of Neruda's *Heights of Macchu Picchu* in his knapsack in Bolivia. Meanwhile, in Cuba, a poet as great as Neruda, Jose Lezama Lima, was under a form of house arrest, and forbidden to publish. Today, when I think of Cuba, it is not all the beautiful books published by Casa de las Americas. It is one writer among the many exiles: Reinaldo Arenas, who spent a few years in prison for the crime of being homosexual, who wrote novels that were confiscated and then wrote them again, and who was finally let out of the country with the mentally retarded and the violent criminals in the Mariel boat exodus. It is Arenas, some years before he began dying of AIDS, in a tenement in Times Square, telling me, with serious intensity, that the KGB had some sort of death ray aimed at his apartment, and that it had exploded a glass of water on his windowsill.

How thrilling it was to read about Nicaragua under the Sandinistas, proclaimed here as a "land of poets," with a well-known poet, Ernesto Cardenal, as its Minister of Culture, who had opened hundreds of poetry workshops around the country for the campesinos. No one seemed to remember that Cardenal had started out as the youngest member of the Nicaraguan poetry vanguardia, fascists who supported Franco, Mussolini, and the first Somoza, and that Cardenal himself wrote love poems to one of the Somoza girls. That his conversion to both Marx and the Church had led to some strange conjunctions, as when, in one of his many poems against the Vietnam War, he compared napalm to abortion. Of all the American poets who trooped down to Nicaragua in those years, how many reported back that in the workshops only a certain kind of poetry, called "exteriorism," could be written, and that, among other things, traditional prosody and all metaphors were strictly forbidden? How many reported back that gays and lesbians who had fought for the revolution were interrogated and sometimes imprisoned in an attempt to purge the Sandinista ranks of deviants?

I need hardly speak of the Soviet Union and Eastern Europe, where, as Mandelstam said, they took poetry seriously. But it is revealing that those poets who maintained a life-long devotion to the Party tended to live in countries that never had a Communist government—Neruda, Vallejo, Aragon, Eluard, MacDiarmid, Césaire, among many others—or else, like Brecht and others in Eastern Europe, had never experienced a revolution. For what Communism has never understood—or perhaps it understood it too well—is that a collective builds a dam, but a book can only be the result of solitude.

The landscape of the revolution is filled with doomed young people. Here is Roque Dalton, the guerrilla saint of Latin America:

The Party must train the poet as a good militant Communist, as a valuable cadre for mass revolutionary action. The poet must contribute in the utmost to the cultural education of all members of the Party. The Party, specifically, must help the poet develop into an effective agitator, a soldier with expert marksmanship—in a word, a fit cadre. The poet must acquaint all his comrades with Nazim Hikmet or Pablo Neruda, and give them a clear concept of the role of cultural work within the context of general revolutionary activity. He must also make sure that the Administrative Secretary of the Central Committee, for example, loves St. John of the Cross, Henri Michaux, or St-John Perse.

Dalton joined the People's Revolutionary Army (ERP) in his native El Salvador. In 1975, unattracted by possible discussions of *Anabasis* or *Miserable Miracle*, he was executed by his own people as a CIA spy. (This is now attributed to a "militarist" or "adventurist" or "Maoist" faction.) A few years later, the EPP formed the Roque Dalton Cultural Brigade.

Doomed young people: The great unwritten history in 20th century American poetry is the black hole into which the young poets vanished in the 1930's. In 1931, Louis Zukofsky attempted to launch a new generation of American modernist poets with his "Objectivists" issue of Poetry and subsequent anthology. The fate of four of these "Objectivists" is well known: Zukofsky would not publish his first pamphlet of poetry for another ten years; Oppen's second book came 28 years after his first; Rakosi took 26 years between books; Reznikoff, who was not a young man then, essentially gave up poetry during the late 30's and 40's to write prose (like William Carlos Williams and the young poet Kenneth Fearing). These four survived, after long periods of not writing or not publishing, but most of the other young poets included as "Objectivists" were never heard from again. Other anthologies from the period are similarly filled with the disappeared. In fact, the only significant poet to start publishing in book form in the 1930's and keep publishing was Muriel Rukeyser—with Kenneth Patchen a distant second—and Rukeyser, throughout her career, inhabited a no-man's zone between the avant-garde and the establishment, modernism and agit-prop.

[This was also true of prose writers: We know that some of the most prominent, such as Dos Passos and James T. Farrell, ended up as disillusioned cranks in the pages of the *National Review*. As for the others: in an interview just a few weeks ago, Henry Roth—who himself stopped publishing for 60 years—wondered what happened to the scores of writers he knew as a young radical.]

This was the period in America when the Party dominated intellectual life. I don't mean to suggest that all of the poets, like Oppen, joined the Party and gave up writing for organizing, though some undoubtedly did. Rather I think it was the general discourse fostered by the Party that discouraged young poets from going on. This was the era—to take Camus' example—when young people hotly debated whether one served the people best by being Shakespeare or a shoemaker, whether a pair of sturdy shoes was worth all the plays of Shakespeare, and whether, in Brecht's famous formulation, it was a crime, in times like these, to talk about trees. Who could write poetry when one had to defend both the utilitarianism of poetry and the murder of poets for the greater good? Only the stubborn, the oblivious, or those who had begun writing before Stalin. And who can keep writing, who can age gracefully, as it becomes apparent that there is nothing more unreal than yesterday's realism?

In retrospect, there is perhaps only one major world poet who managed to keep his commitment to Communism, keep writing, and never write a line of doggerel: Cesar Vallejo. His solution was to churn out colorless Party-hack prose and keep the poetry utterly uncontaminated, free to do whatever he wished: a prose to serve the people, and a poetry to serve poetry. Not coincidentally, it may be the most political, and the most revolutionary, poetry ever written by a Latin American—a poetry not only written out of extreme poverty and the trashheap of history, but one that dismantled and reinvented the received language of the conquistadors.

Three fundamentalisms have dominated the revolutions of this century: Marxism, fascism, and Islam. (The fundamentalisms of the other two monotheisms have created states, but not modern revolutions.) Because of this, it has become impossible to talk about revolutionary poetry, or the revolution itself, without reference to them. And the fact remains that, from Franco's Spain to Iran to Kampuchea—or, right at this moment, from Algeria to North Korea—they have murdered, imprisoned or silenced hundreds, probably thousands of poets, as the so-called secular capitalist states, with all their injustices, have never done. No amount of revolutionary romanticism, of the kind that is still being written, can obscure this. Now matter how thrilling, how inspiring to the poets revolution can be, the message is plain: After the revolution, you'd better move somewhere else.

What we need is a revolution of revolutions, a revolution to crush the dreams of the old revolutions and construct new ones, a revolution that will tear down the monoliths and not build prisons in their place, a revolution that will honor continual revolt, a revolution where the poets can live in their own homes. Who knows what that revolution could be? For the moment, it may only be possible to imagine what it will be pitched against.

Two specters haunt the next century. One is the secularism, nationalism, and ethnocentricity, the psychological apartheid that is paradoxically erupting as the world moves toward a single consumer culture. The other is the very real possibility of the extinction of the human race, following the extinction of countless other species.

Overpopulation, deforestation, the nuclear weapons that are still very much with us, the rotting canisters of plutonium on the ocean floor—I need hardly recite the list. We are at a moment in history when it is a crime not to talk about trees.

A revolution against these demons would require the kind of Internationale that Marx dreamed of, and Communism never saw—a rising of the humans of the world. It would depend on a transition to a global economy that is simultaneous to a dismantling of the multinational corporations. And it must begin with us talking to each other—more important, listening to each other—in ways that have never occurred before. Significantly, with the new information technology, the means are there—as long as we are able to keep those means democratic, and out of monopolistic control, which won't be easy. The new generation of revolutionaries will not begin as a ragged band in the sierras—it will be individuals and small groups thousands of miles from each other and neighbors in cyberspace.

And where are the poets in all this? First, as has been often said, revolutionaries are connoisseurs of the apocalypse and visionaries of the terrestrial paradise. Poets, though not lately in America, have always excelled at both. So we need poets to challenge received notions, tell us what we don't know, ask the questions we can't answer, and wake us up to both doom and Utopia.

Second, poetry has always traveled on its own Internet of underground channels from country to country. These must multiply, especially in the United States, which seems more self-preoccupied than ever. The 90's, beginning as they did in 1989, have brought extraordinary changes all over the world—many of them exhilarating, and many of them achieved without violence. Meanwhile, as you've probably noticed, absolutely nothing is happening here, in Anno 14 of Reagan America. We'd be better off if every member of the government resigned tomorrow, and was replaced by a citizen picked at random. And the left, such as it is, is obsessed with a new form of nationalism called multiculturalism—which is healthy insofar as it brings more Americans into the dialogue, and sick in that it still excludes everyone else: Chinese-Americans and no Chinese, African-Americans and no Africans, Mexican-Americans and no Mexicans. Only one contemporary Chinese poet has had books published in the U.S., no Indians, one or two Africans, maybe half a dozen Latin Americans, one Arab poet, a few from the Caribbean. The current poetry of 85% of humanity is represented in this country by a one-foot shelf of books. Americans, and American poets specifically, may be the last people to get the word that it's global time. Even the speakers and panelists all weekend here, at this symposium on an international theme, are a United Colors of strictly Americans.

Finally, I think we have to assert, over and over, that the

revolution of the world requires many revolutions of the word, and that poetry does indeed make something happen, no matter how slowly it moves from reader to reader. Zbigniew Herbert has written that the fire in the poem is one thing, and the town in flames another. In a sense, of course, it's true, but in another sense, it is the fire in the poem that helps us to see the town in flames, whether it is a town in history, or our own town tomorrow. Poetry is a way—not the only way, but for most of us here, our way—into the enormous events of history. Only bad poetry talks to itself, or tells us what we already know. Above all, only bad poetry is not subversive. The revolution will not only be televised, it will be published and read.

RAKOSI TO WEINBERGER

Dear Eliot:

I stumbled on to your piece, "The Revolution at St. Mark's Church," in *Exquisite Corpse* 56 and had to write you that I couldn't agree with you more, especially when you say, "The great unwritten history in twentieth century American poetry is the black hole into which the young poets vanished in the 1930s." I was one of those to whom it happened.

Why me? Remember this was during The Great Depression. There were no jobs, no matter what line of work you were in, and public welfare was just beginning to be organized to deal with people's relief needs on a scale never before even imagined. People were desperate and angry. In Chicago a welfare worker was stabbed to death by a desperate relief applicant. In San Francisco welfare offices were being stormed. And when it finally hit Wall Street, great fortunes were lost overnight and the victims were jumping out of windows to their death. There were signs everywhere that the system had collapsed and was incapable of reviving, all the more since the government was denying what was happening. The only group that was paying serious attention and had a program to deal with it was the Communist Party.

I was working in New York in those years and found that, as I put it later, everybody who had a brain and a conscience was joining the Party. I held back for a while, telling myself that I was a writer, not an activist, but I could do that only so long. In the end my conscience wouldn't let me simply gripe from the sidelines. So I joined the Party, thinking that I would be able to satisfy my curiosity about this secret organization at the same time.

To get in, however, you had to have a sponsor, someone

37

who vouched for your character and the genuineness of your commitment to social change. Leon Serabian, an Armenian poet whose family had perished in the Turkish massacres and who had become a dear friend, had been urging me to join for a long time. For him, the problem in society was simple: there were the rich guys who were always screwing us, and there were us poor guys who were always being screwed ... which was true enough, but not enough. He was happy to be my sponsor and went all out recommending me to the committee in his street cell (the Party was organized in small units called cells) with all the lyrical enthusiasm of his poetry. Once in, I found its mission was to march in May Day parades and protest marches of all kinds. I did do this and found it exhilarating. At last I was doing something useful, no matter how small.

Occasionally someone from the Central Committee ... I'm not sure of the name ... would come in and expound the Party line, which was made necessary because the Soviet Union kept changing its policies. These were guys who talked in the inexpressibly dry language of Higher Theory, always so sure of what they were saying that to question them ... actually very few had the nerve to do it ... was to put yourself immediately on the spot, either as a dumbbell or a secret enemy. They would accept questions about what they meant but not challenges. That was the underlying assumption ... a part of the atmosphere. These expounders of Higher Theory (Communist theory, of course) left a dead pall on everybody's spirits. Where did they come from? And where did they go when they left us? etc. At the same time I have to add that the day to day members of the Party whom I came to know were the most intelligent, the most ethical, the most idealistic people around.

After a year I was transferred to a social work cell in the large agency in which I was employed. Our sole mission there, it turned out, was to figure out ways to convert the other social workers to the Communist mission. This was interesting for a while, like a game in psychology, but for a good cause. But after a while I realized that I was not that committed to the task and simply stopped coming to meetings. Nobody noticed that I was gone, maybe because I had relapsed into my writing self, an observer, a listener.

The real action for me as a poet came not there, however, but in the pages of *The New Masses* where Mike Gold rode herd with his Bolshevik cowboys over any poetry that was simply lyrical or aesthetic. That poetry was branded bourgeois, the ultimate in scorn at that time, and elitist, which nobody at all sympathetic to The Party wanted to be caught dead with then. So when the attack came against such poetry, the savagery of it stunned its author. The poetry was not simply criticized, it was demolished and to make sure that it registered, the poet himself was demolished. I fell into the black hole because lyric and aesthetic poetry was the only kind I could write, and I wouldn't write propaganda poetry, so the only thing I could do was to withdraw from the scene. Although this was not the only reason I stopped writing, it entered into it. Had I not myself been divided in my mind, a part of me thinking that maybe *The New Masses* was right, I would have reacted the way I did when William Ellery Leonard, a poet as admired as Carl Sandburg in the 1920s, made fun of my poetry in a class at The University of Wisconsin in Madison. He didn't demolish me. On the contrary I said to myself, "What the hell does he know?" But I couldn't do that with the Communists. I had too much inner conflict about it and I was too much of an idealist.

In any case you have my testimony. You were dead right. You should have been given a bouquet, not attacked as bourgeois and a liar, for revealing the black hole, as you put it. And to think that the word bourgeois is going to demolish you today is to be in a time warp. It's funny.

So here we are in 1996 and we've had lots of time to wonder who these characters were who rose to the top in the Communist hierarchy. They were obviously the most ambitious, the most aggressive, the most single-minded, and hence the most repressive, who craved to be in control and admired. That left us commoners who were more modest, who didn't crave to be leaders, who were quite willing to leave that responsibility to others because there were other things they were more interested in. That relationship tends to get frozen, because it is comfortable for both parties... one reason why needed social reform comes so slowly.

All this is long past now, and with the demise of Communism the circumstances for revolutionary poetry no longer exist. Some old questions remain, perhaps unanswerable to everyone's satisfaction, but the attempt needs to be made nevertheless, because how we view the question will determine what we do about it. One of them is what our role in society is. This differs with time, place and circumstance... too much to bite off here. The other is what value does poetry have for society?

I do not hold the view, passionately held by some, that its value depends in some way on the proportion of its value to society. To believe this is to fall into the Communist trap. Trotsky himself, that fiery revolutionist, understood this. Literature, he said, was a different thing. It should be left alone to go its own way and not be expected to be another organ of the state.

Not to do this, in my view, is to mistake the nature of poetry. Writing poetry and reading it are ways of living, and like life itself need no other justification. Its value is therefore existential. This is not to say that poetry has no social value... it often does, but not always and not necessarily. Only in this view does poetry have the freedom to be fully itself, to go in whichever direction its poetic judgment chooses, revolutionary if that is it. And only in this view will poetry free itself of guilt about social action.

One other thing. I do not share the view, dear to many, that the world needs the vision of poets to save it, or that poets have some special vision to offer. To me that's self-serving egotism. Indeed, one could argue that vision is what the world does NOT need, that vision has caused great suffering and misery. Vision is not realism, and what the world needs is something much less vague and high-falutin'. What it needs is honesty and compassion and tolerance and a clear perception of the consequences to people of global capitalism's breakneck rush into the future, for although capitalism is now irreversible, it can be humanized if enough people demand it. Poets have something to contribute on this matter, of course, but to claim that this takes vision is silly.

THE WIDER EDUCATION OF STUDENTS: CADAVERS, COMPOSITION, AND THE PRESS

WILLIAM PALMER

When *The Wall Street Journal* and *Reader's Digest* reported that I took students in my composition classes to learn and write about cadavers, they ridiculed what was a profoundly educational experience. Because of the way the press distorted the project, I had to discontinue it.

My college's public relations staff and I did not foresee what would happen with this unusual teaching activity. Although the publicity helped Alma College achieve its goal of attaining national visibility, the low point came when *Reader's Digest* labeled us "Ghoul School."

For three years I had been taking my students in English 101 College Rhetoric to Alma's human anatomy laboratory. The experience enabled them to bridge science and the humanities, one of the goals of my course. I wanted students to make connections between what happens in a writing course and what happens in a human anatomy lab: observing distinctive details and engaging in inquiry. I wanted students not to focus on death but to realize life.

Although the excursion was voluntary, all but one or two students in each class attended—with anxiety and wonderment. My colleague Dr. John Davis, a professor of exercise and health science and director of the lab, conducted each session and treated the cadavers with respect. After explaining how the college obtains and uses human specimens in science courses, Dr. Davis unveiled three bodies of old people. He discussed how he encourages his students to look for anything abnormal—

40

such as a large liver full of cirrhosis caused by excessive alcohol. After answering questions, he invited students to inspect the bodies more closely and to ask him further questions, which students did.

My assignment for students was to write an objective summary of what Dr. Davis said and a personal reaction to the experience of seeing cadavers. The field trip motivated students to go beyond the information given, which psychologist Jerome Bruner has argued education should enable students to do. Here are two excerpts from students' papers:

When Dr. Davis held up a half of one cadaver's brain, I thought of my own brain, of Albert Einstein's brain, and my friends' brains, and how many mysteries there are within the brain. The brain controls our every movement, yet we do not even realize it; we do not think about how many muscles we are using when we smile briefly or when we write down a simple journal entry. When Dr. Davis held up that brain, I began to appreciate that my brain was intact enough to realize my innermost feelings and thoughts.

» «

The biggest question in my head was who were these people? What were they like when they were my age? Who did they love? What were their priorities? What made them happy? ... The most admirable thing is that after these people experienced life, they chose to "extend their life" by contributing to others. This way, their existence not only benefited them and their families but also total strangers. I find this noble, not morbid.

Students benefited from the experience. They not only learned about human anatomy and scientific inquiry but also discovered how it feels to face death. One student said, "It was ironic. There was that dead body, and all I could think about was being alive. It really made me analyze my life."

John Davis and I also tried our cross-disciplinary project with a few creative writing classes. Students wrote poems about the experience.

Then we told the media about our project. In the summer of 1992 Alma College hired Campus Crossroads, an academic news service from Keene, New Hampshire, to help us gain national recognition. After I met with our consultant from Campus Crossroads, he sent my article "Cadavers and Composition" (published in *The Language Arts Journal of Michigan*, Spring 1991) to print and electronic media around the country.

On October 20, 1992, when *The Wall Street Journal* ran the first article on us, I discovered how easily the press can distort a story. The *Journal* piece was titled "So Where Do Mortuary

Instructors Turn to Inspire Their Students?" This headline set the tone for misunderstanding. The article also referred to "the creative-writing program at Alma College," not English 101 College Rhetoric, which was the primary context for the project.

To sensationalize his story, the reporter, Dave Kansas, cited two extreme quotes from critics of the project. He quoted a creative-writing professor at Sarah Lawrence College: "I think it's probably the most untoward assignment for a writing class that I've ever heard of... The larger meaning of life doesn't have anything to do with looking at a cadaver." But surely, John Davis and I thought, the larger meaning of life has everything to do with death and the soul.

The most surprising quote came from Thomas Oram, chief medical examiner of Schenectady County, N.Y.: "I think what this teacher is doing is odd and doesn't help anyone. You have to worry about the potential for necrophiliacs and that kind of thing." Oram's quote angered many students at Alma. One wrote in our campus paper, "So what are you saying, Tom? That English majors have lusty fantasies about mounting the dead more so than pre-medical students? Is that why people sometimes look at me funny when I say I am an English major?"

At the end of his *Journal* article, Mr. Kansas omitted an important piece of information. He wrote that I had "invited a writer to read from behind a cadaver that had been wheeled on stage. At one point the writer held the cadaver's heart high above his head while reading about a heart. Says Mr. Palmer: "It was a beautiful, illuminating experience.' " Why did Mr. Kansas not name the writer?

I told him it was Dr. Richard Selzer, one of our country's best prose stylists, author of *Mortal Lessons: Notes on the Art of Surgery* (and *Raising the Dead*, a chronicle of his own near death). Selzer, a former surgeon at Yale University, had visited Alma College in March of 1992. During his three-day visit he gave a remarkable reading which we called "A Scientific and Literary Tour of the Human Body." He began this tour by explaining that it is important for students to confront death. "Many are virginal about death," he said. "But it's not good to distance ourselves from it. Doing so increases its power over us."

The cadaver remained veiled during the reading which took place in a large science classroom, not on a stage. Two hundred students and several faculty attended. A science student assisted Dr. Selzer. As Selzer read an excerpt about a heart, the student held the cadaver's heart, opening it for the audience to see. Like a poet, Selzer used the heart and the cadaver's right arm to represent the whole body. As I told the reporter, I found the reading "beautiful" and "illuminating" because Dr. Selzer shared personal stories about his encounters with death, culminating with a poignant account of the death of his mother.

By withholding Dr. Selzer's name, *The Wall Street Journal*

made the reading sound ridiculous. Mentioning Selzer's name, however, would have given the reading more credibility.

Although the cadavers and composition project received fair and mostly accurate coverage in *The Detroit Free Press* (Oct. 21, '92), *The Saginaw* (Mich.) *News* (Oct. 21, '92), and *The Chronicle of Higher Education* (April 7, '93), the *Reader's Digest* condemned it. This surprised me because a reporter had interviewed me twice over the phone and I had faxed her information about the project and about Selzer's reading.

In the June 1993 issue, the *Reader's Digest* version appeared in a column called "That's Outrageous" with a legend stating, "Spotlighting absurdities in our society is the first step toward eliminating them." To fit the aim of that column, *Reader's Digest* condensed *The Wall Street Journal* article, perpetuating its distortions. To top it off, the *Digest* titled its piece "Ghoul School."

That the press told the cadavers and composition story is not surprising. Abnormality generates inquiry. Much as my colleague John Davis encourages his students to look for abnormalities in human bodies, the media seek stories that are unusual. This is natural.

However, the media are responsible for being accurate and truthful. When they are not, we must challenge their accounts. I know firsthand that too many readers believe what they read. After the distorted coverage in *Reader's Digest*, I received hate mail. Even my mother—who was a supporter—suddenly preferred not to discuss the subject.

The most unfortunate consequence of the press covering the cadavers and composition project was that Michigan State University, which provides Alma with human specimens, mandated that we discontinue it. Officials at MSU's Department of Anatomy were concerned that the publicity might dissuade people from donating their bodies for medical education. Not wanting to jeopardize our human anatomy lab for Alma's science students, we suspended the project.

From the beginning of our national coverage, Alma's President Alan J. Stone has been strongly supportive, telling our campus paper, "I don't think all the attention is bad. It is good press; it shows we are on the cutting edge of liberal arts education." He pledged to find an additional source for cadavers so English and art students—especially those in medical illustration—can learn from them. But after three years, we have not found an additional source.

As a composition teacher committed to classroom research, I experiment with pedagogy. Periodically I try to take students out of the regular classroom, to engage them in thought-provoking activities not dependent on written texts. Learning about cadavers affected students in deeply personal and intellectual ways. The experience was meaningful and real. Although the media coverage helped to shut down the project, John Davis and I demonstrated that science majors are

43

not the only students who can benefit from entering a human anatomy laboratory.

After *The Detroit Free Press* article appeared, I received a letter of support from Marie Snell, a stained-glass artist from Oak Park, Mich., whose husband had died and donated his body to a university. She wrote, "I would be glad to know that, in addition to adding to medical knowledge, my husband (and I when my turn comes) could have also contributed to the wider education of students other than future doctors."

When I wrote to Dr. Richard Selzer about Alma College's experience with the media, he also vowed his support:

> Having suffered mightily over the years at the hands of the Press, I shudder at coming under their pitiless gaze again. But I would to defend you and your work at Alma. As far as the cadavers are concerned, the Medical Profession does not own death. It belongs to us all. To Leonardo, Vesalius, and to the students of Alma.

Similarly, the truth belongs to us all. It is not the property of the press to manipulate to their purposes.

Sharing a pedagogical innovation with the press is a gamble, especially if it challenges taboos such as death or traditions such as medical education. Although national visibility has been good for Alma College, much of it has been negative. Yet public relations experts claim that what matters is that a college's name is publicized and spelled correctly: readers do not remember a negative or positive story about a school—they remember the school's name. Maybe this is true.

However, for three years now I have been unable to take students in English 101 to Alma's human anatomy laboratory. I can no longer provide this profound experience that bridges science and the humanities that students would never forget.

SO LONG, RODGERS AND HART

ART HILGART

Those of us who favor free speech are often in the position of defending the right to publish stuff like "Sex Lives of Venusian Cheerleaders" which we are unlikely to encounter in our own libraries. Late last year, however, the Pennsylvania legislature illustrated the difference between freedom and democracy by going after the great American popular song. The proposal, which has been passed by the House, is an amendment to an anti-drug bill—apparently narcotics have been legal in Pennsylvania until now. It would require fluorescent yellow labels with black type (at least twelve point) to be affixed to records and tapes warning customers and their parents of dangerous lyrics. A retailer selling an unlabelled record with proscribed lyrics would pay a $300 fine and get ninety days in the slammer. The law thoughtfully identifies the forbidden topics that a lyric may not describe, advocate or encourage. The range is broad enough to cut a wide swath through the core repertoire of American music.

Suicide is out, so your local record connection is at risk if he slips you a copy of "Gloomy Sunday" by Billy Holiday, Artie Shaw, Josh White, or Paul Robeson. The Bill Harris version is okay, since it has no vocal.

A ban on reference to excessive use of alcohol would take out "Cocktails for Two," a large fraction of country music, and most of the recordings of the Clancy Brothers. A landmark case gives us the right to read James Joyce's *Ulysses*, but the Pennsylvania prohibition would deny us the English music hall tune that inspired his other major work. *Finnegans Wake* includes these lines:

> Tim had a sort of a tippling way,
> With a love for the liquor poor Tim was born.
> To help him on with his work each day
> He'd a drop of the creature every morn.

Sexual activity is a problem for the saintly legislators. What would they make of these lines of Lorenz Hart?

> Lots of kids for a poor wife are dandy.
> Girls of fashion can be choosy.
> Birth control and the modus operandi
> Are much too good for the average floozy!

Sodomy is forbidden, and so is Tom Lehrer's reference to the fellow "who was majoring in animal husbandry until they caught him at it." Perhaps Pennsylvania cops would overlook the implication in Ira Gershwin's claim that *all the sexes from Maine to Texas* want Wintergreen for President. Noel Coward and Cole Porter would earn yellow badges respectively for "Mad About the Boy" and "Love for Sale"—both deal sympathetically with prostitution. Porter's "Miss Otis Regrets" is a triple threat, covering adultery, murder, and for good measure, lynching.

Murder is found all through Sondheim's *Sweeney Todd*, as well as Stanley Holloway's version of the music hall number about this legendary barber. Both also deal with necrophagia, which is spared proscription in Pennsylvania, probably through a shortcoming in the drafter's vocabulary.

Sadomasochism is on the list, which gets the rest of country music, along with "My Man" (He isn't true; he beats me too) and "Body and Soul" (My life a hell you're making). *Porgy and Bess*

45

comes under the rape proscription thanks to Bess's line: Take your hands off me ... Your hands ... Your hands ... Most grand opera would be in trouble except maybe in the original languages. Wagner's *Ring* is riddled with incest, for example, and *Madame Butterfly* has adultery and ethnic intimidation, both banned.

The use of illegal drugs may not be described, so Harry the Hipster's immortal "Who Put the Benzedrine in Mrs. Murphy's Ovaltine" will be but a memory. The same fate awaits Fats Waller's *dream about a reefer five feet long, it's mighty mezz but not too strong.* "Mezz," by the way, entered the language as a synonym for cannabis because of the legendary quality of the product purveyed by clarinet player Mezz Mezzrow. Since he was an instrumentalist, Mezz's name on the label would probably not earn his own records a yellow sticker.

Regarding Tipper Gore, Donald Wildmon, the Pennsylvania legislature, and others who would purify our record collections, let us conclude with these lines from Rodger's and Hart's "The Boys from Syracuse":

> She was so chaste that it made her very nervous
> He loved to go to the vicarage for tea.
> And when they died and went to heaven
> All the angels moved to hell.
> And that is he and she!

LETTERS

These letters are excerpted from the forthcoming book by Hunter S. Thompson, The Proud Highway: Saga of a Desperate Southern *Gentleman, 1955–1967, edited by Douglas Brinkley.*

October 22, 1960
San Francisco
Editor
Time Magazine

Dear Sir,

Immediately after election day, if not sooner, the nation's press will render its judgement on the greatest spectacle in the history of politics—the Nixon-Kennedy "Great Debate." If the fifth encounter is as meatless as the first four have been, the judgement will in all probability be a harsh one.

Some of us will be surprised, however, if the blame falls where most of it belongs—on the shoulders of the press, itself.

Cub scouts could have asked more penetrating questions than the journalists have offered thus far, and no amount of grumbling about rules and regulations laid down by campaign managers and the television industry can obscure the fact that the representatives of the press have behaved like trained seals. The questions to the candidates have been, for the most part, nothing more than harmless cues, devoid of weight, meaning or perception. When you realize all the questions that could have been asked, all the fraud, quackery and evasion that might have been held up to merciless inspection before 17 million viewers, it raises the question that perhaps the press is no longer capable of fulfilling or even recognizing its responsibility to the nation it serves.

Never before have two presidential candidates been placed in such a vulnerable position, and never before has the press had such a golden opportunity to hack away the sham and expose the basic issues. When the time comes, as it will, to belabor the television industry for staging a political batting-practice instead of a world series, let the press remember who served up the soft floaters and the "fat ones" down the middle. It was a sad performance, and the sound of many snickers may be heard in the land when the pot starts calling the kettle black.

November 19, 1963
Woody Creek, CO
Postmaster General
Washington, DC

I would appreciate knowing if you mean to continue the stupid, vicious "Zip code" system, instituted by your predecessor. If so, I would also appreciate an explanation of same. Is it, in fact, any more or less than governmental harassment dreamed up by an anti-social pervert?

Also, will my letters continue to reach their destination without bearing such codes? I have no way of finding out the wretched numbers for any address I might write to, and no intention of using such numbers even if they were made available.

I voted for Kennedy in the last election, but the first time one of my letters comes back to me for lack of a "Zip code," he can count on one less vote in 1964.

July 3, 1958
New York

Dear Larry,
Well, I've finally managed to sit down at the typewriter: it's been a long, hard month. It's one that I'm going to have to

write off as a total loss, work-wise; and a hellish experience, living-wise. I've consumed an ungodly amount of liquid spirits, given in completely to the sexual spirit, and thrown all the other spirits to hell. There are sweet little southern girls here too, but they seem to be a little different here than they are in their natural setting. I thought I was a pretty hardened lecher, but even I have paled more than once at the sight of the "sweet little ole southern (or midwestern) mask" slipping off a gin-inflamed bitch in heat. Carry me back to the womb, Taddy, just like you done with so many others!

But as Scott Fitzgerald must have said to himself more than once: "now is the time to get a grip." I have to pay the rent with this paycheck, so my task will be that much easier. No more buying a fifth of McCarthy Square gin each night, no more dawn cab races to the Plaza fountain or the East River for a morning "dip," no more five course dinners on the balcony, or cocktails on the roof, or all-night orgies, or theatres: in short, the squeeze is on us; the party is over—at least for two weeks. Then I'll have money again. (Over-indulgence, thy name is Hunter!)

But even though all these are pretty overt signs of galloping dissipation, they really aren't my main source of concern. The real difference between this latest binge and all the others of the past two years is that I seem to have lost what I think is the most important thing a writer can have: the ability to live with constant loneliness and a strong sense of revulsion for the banalities of everyday socializing. It just doesn't seem very important anymore that I write. I can understand this, I think, in light of what I call "the psychology of imposition." This theory holds that the most over-riding of all human desires is the need to amount to something. I'm not talking about the old Horatio Alger gimmick, but the more basic desire to know that your life means something. As Faulkner says, writing is his way of saying "Kilroy was here," of imposing himself, however briefly, on reality. If only for an instant, the image of the man is imposed on the chaotic mainstream of life and it remains there forever: order out of chaos, meaning out of meaninglessness. Just as some people turn to religion to find meaning, the writer turns to his craft and tries to impose meaning, or to sift the meaning out of chaos and put it in order.

But—and here is where I'm going to try to justify my reason for not feeling the need to write—there is a school of thought which has (Spengler) classified men in one of two categories: the action men and the thought men. These are vague terms and Spengler's were unquestionably better—but you should know what I mean, even if you don't agree with me. So we look at people like Joyce or Proust or Pound, or for that matter, almost any of history's best writers; and we find virtually the same personality type (of the two, anyway). But they were all people who depended on their writing to give them the meaning or the satisfaction, if you will, that they sought.

And then we have Rabelais and Hemingway and to some extent Fitzgerald and certainly a host of others I'm not going to take the time to think about right now. Certainly the example of Hemingway should be enough.

Pause for re-location and abstract commentary of sorts... ... I've just been reading *Time*'s biographical file on Kingsley Amis (*Lucky Jim*) and the new British intellectuals. Somerset Maugham has a beautiful comment which I'm not at all surprised to have missed in many another article on the "angry young men." He says, and I quote: "it (*Lucky Jim*) describes a new class, the white-collar proletariat... which does not go to the university to acquire culture, but to get a job, and when they get one, scamp it. (scamp?) Their idea of a celebration is to go into a public house and drink six beers. They are mean, malicious, envious... they are scum."

Good old Maugham: it's good to see the sledge-hammer coming down from the top for a change, instead of striking up at the belly of society from the bottom.

Of course you're so far out of it up there that you probably don't realize that the "beat generation" is taking over American literature, while the "angry young men" are the driving force in Britain. And although I'm neither beat nor necessarily angry, I'm glad to see somebody taking a stand for a change. It's the first real "movement" in literature in many a year: a point of reference, if nothing else. The writing world seems at least to have settled into two very definitely opposing camps: the pedants and the hobos. Most of the best writers fit in neither camp, of course, but then very few of them ever have. A good writer stands above movements, neither a leader nor a follower, but a bright white gold ball in a fairway of wind-blown daisies. (If you've never played gold, you won't understand how pleasant it is to walk down a fairway and see forty or fifty balls where yours should be—and then to come a little closer and recognize the ball, a little rounder and little whiter than the rest, and a hell of a lot more solid. (The moral of this story is: Play golf!)

But I forgot that you're Iceland's answer to Jane Austen, so I'll close this harangue and get back to my original thesis.

I was talking about the need to impose oneself on reality and the difference between action men and thought men. (I think that statement makes the whole thing more clear and concise than my entire first page succeeded in doing.)

But it's obvious that the need is there and that the two categories of men have two different ways of doing it. And it seems that the ones who are either unable or unwilling to impose themselves on life through their actions are the ones who succeed most significantly in

49

the thought (or writing, in this case) category.

Now Hemingway seems to have done it from both angles: he's not even bothered—or possibly not been able—to create his own world in his books (a la Joyce, James, Faulkner, Proust, etc.) but he's mastered reality and still managed to become one hell of a good writer as well. (There are others, of course, but Hemingway serves as such a good example because his life and times are so familiar as to still apply in our day.)

But Fitzgerald tried and Fitzgerald failed and Fitzgerald didn't learn to think until it was too late. He was probably one of the great natural talents of any age and he could make a typewriter sound like a piano when he was in form, but was not a thinker—and neither was (or is) Hemingway. And yet they're both—from the point of view of natural facility with words—two of the best writers of the century, anyway.

So the difference, I think, boils down to this: you can either impose yourself on reality and then write about it, or you can impose yourself on reality by writing.

It's time to go now: I have to go down in the Village and destroy some furniture. This is merely the first of a series of lectures on "subjects Thompson needs to get straight in his mind." I find that writing is the best way. So until later, it's cheerio ...

January 15, 1960
Hyde Park, Puerto Rico
Distribution Manager
Brown-Williamson Tobacco Co.

I regret to inform you that Salems have all but swamped Kools in the Puerto Rico cigarette market. I don't know if this makes much difference to you or not, but let me tell you that it bothers the mortal hell out of me. I've been smoking Kools for close to ten years, but down here I'd have an easier time getting a steady supply of reefers. There are god knows how many cigarette machines in San Juan, and in only three of them can I find king-size Kools. This is working a tremendous hardship on me, and I'm writing you in hopes that you'll do something about it.

I'm quite willing to do my part. If you lack a competent distributor down here, then consider me at your service. Nothing would make me happier than to drive Salems off the market for good and ever. It's without a doubt the foulest cigarette in the history of tobacco-addicted man—a tasteless mish-mash of paper and dry weeds.

But I have yet to run across a cigarette machine that doesn't have *two racks* of Salems. And as I said before, only three that I've found contain the filter Kools.

There's no excuse for this kind of negligence on your part. If Kools are deemed too strong for the Puerto Rican taste, then get that hustling huckster Ted Bates on the ball and have him educate these people. He's not paid to ignore new markets.

As a native of Louisville, and as one of a long line of Brown-Williamson customers—and primarily as a man who *will* have Kools—I deplore this great vacuum in your distribution. As I said before, I will be glad to help in any way I can. At the moment I'm an associate editor of a new sports magazine here and I'll be glad to sell you a full-page ad to begin the campaign. Personally, I don't give a damn if you want the ad or not, but contact me if it interests you.

My primary concern is the frustrating lack of Kools in Puerto Rico. Whatever action you decided to take on this, please let me hear from you.

December 8, 1960
Big Sur
Mr. Donleavy:

I've been waiting since the *Ginger Man* for your next effort, a thing the grapevine led me to believe would be called *Helen*. But all I've seen is your short farce in *The Beat Gen. & Angry Young Men*.

Is *Helen* out? If so, where is it? And if it isn't, have you done anything big since the *Ginger Man*?

The *GM*, by the way, had real balls, a rare thing in these twisted times. I heard the priests gave you a rough time with the stage version, but to hell with them. The church is on its last legs and if we deal them blow for blow I think we may prevail.

At any rate, let me know if you have anything new in the bookstores. I'm stuck out here, writing the great Puerto Rican novel, and I'd like to know if anybody's running interference for me.

If you get to Big Sur, stop in.

NAN AND WARREN

CONGER
BEASLEY
JR.

Nan and Warren were lovers. She was a lowly seamstress. He was President of the United States. They consummated their passion regularly on the floor of a downstairs cloakroom in the White House. A secret service agent brought

51

Nan in the back door, while Mrs. Harding (the "dragon," as Warren affably called her) was upstairs supervising the domestic help.

Warren told his secretary he had an appointment in another part of the house, and slipped out of the Oval Office. Late morning was the optimum time for their trysts, before Warren had lunch. Warren ate big lunches, washed down with bottles of beer. He liked to doze off afterward, slumped in a comfortable chair, his feet propped up on an ottoman.

The cloakroom was a large, walk-in space, commodious enough to hold several people. Warren flung coats on the floor to make a pallet. There in the dark, with only a sliver of light leaking under the door, he fumbled for Nan, called her name, groped for her breasts with his pudgy fingers.

It was no place for a leisurely bout of coy arousal. Nan, who'd already removed her hat and unbuttoned her dress lurched toward him. Pawing blindly, they clunked together like railroad cars on a lonely siding in the late-night dark of a Midwestern town. The first kiss was electric. They tugged at their clothes, clawing at buttons, hooks, and stays. Warren, a big gouty man, peeled off his coat and vest and trousers. Nan pulled up her dress, loosened her corset, settled back against the pallet of coats. Warren's heart chattered like a squirrel. Pivoting on one knee, he settled his bulky hips between Nan's thighs and eased the Presidential member inside her. Nan—an Ohio hoyden with a knack for gratifying big-time politicians—received his thrust with an endearing grunt. Warren began to wheeze like a locomotive up the slope of the Sierras. Together they rasped out little avowals, trying not to titillate the ears of the agent standing guard on the other side of the door, yet longing to make some kind of confession, a verbal accompaniment to the spastic hunch of their bodies.

Nan and Warren. The ultimate illicit conjunction at the nexus of American power... with telephones ringing, secretaries typing, decisions pending, important politicos waiting for an audience. Hot, raunchy, subversive.

Isn't that fantastic? Don't you just love it? Isn't that better than Dick Nixon and his cronies smearing the walls with vituperation and hate? Or Ronnie and Nancy counting ball gowns and watching old movies? (Even Republicans can boogie when the itch hits their loins.) Nan and Warren humping like gerbils in the cloister of their little cage. Good for them. They must have really wanted one another. All the scheming they had to do. All the risks they took. All the clothes they had to remove.

I hope they had a good time. I hope they had deep, satisfying orgasms. I hope, when they parted, their cheeks glowed with good health and their hearts boomed like bass drums in a Beethoven symphony.

J. EDGAR HOOVER AND JULIUS LULLEY

J. Edgar Hoover, high school classmate of Julius Lulley, dined at Harvey's Restaurant three times weekly. The restaurant, continuously in operation for 95 years, was on Connecticut Avenue next to the Mayflower Hotel. Hoover and Lulley were long-time good pals, and Hoover liked to play practical jokes on his restaurant owner friend.

Julius picked up a young lady named Lillianne who was dining alone at the restaurant one evening. Taking several bottles of champagne from the wine room, he escorted Lillianne next door to the Mayflower, where he reserved a suite for the love tryst.

Hoover had one of his crack undercover FBI counterespionage teams film and record Julius's amorous revels. Once done, he confronted the culprit and threatened to expose him to his wife, Birdie. HA! HA!

Hoover was good at this. He later did the same to Dr. Martin Luther King. Sandy Smith, *Life* reporter, got the story from the FBI. The next week it was in *Life* magazine.

Lillianne later told us, J. Edgar's masculinity was beyond reproach. Her basis in fact: "I sat on his lap."

Cecil B. DeMille was filming the movie, *The Big Top* with Dorothy Lamour and Betty Hutton in Washington when the circus was still under canvas. Julius and Birdie invited Ruthie and me, J. Edgar and Clyde Tolson to a matinee performance. Mr. DeMille was perched high in a cherry picker following and filming Dorothy Lamour riding on the back of an elephant. When Dorothy passed us she tossed some smoked shrimp to Julius and J. Edgar which she had brought from Harvey's Restaurant and gave us a few HA-HA's.

In the 1890s, Diamond Jim Brady, a legendary lobbyist for the railroads and the lover of Lillian Russell, would take the train from New York and travel to Washington for lunch at Harvey's to dine on Chesapeake Bay diamond-back terrapin and Chincoteague oysters, consuming six dozen at a sitting. Julius, inspired by the many trenchermen, gourmands, gourmets, and fine-schmeckers who were part of Harvey's long history of fine dining, strove mightily to perpetuate the Harvey tradition of great food.

Julius told me of his Uncle George Hillman, also a noted gobbler and guzzler. He would only eat foods at their seasonal peaks, whether peaches, corn on the cob, asparagus, canvas-back ducks or shad and shad roe. He consumed enough to satisfy himself until the season would come around again in the following year.

Julius worked for his Uncle George before becoming involved in Harvey's Restaurant. Hillman was the builder and operator of the Ambassador Hotel in Atlantic City. Julius practiced and perfected his culinary skills there. Hillman later built and operated the George V Hotel in Paris.

Julius would close his restaurant at midnight and drive home to his farm in Bowie, Maryland. He often stopped at August Vasio's A.V. Italian Restaurant on New York Avenue. This still popular Italian bistro stayed open until 4:00 A.M . Julius would get together with August in the kitchen and the pair would check the day's larder and prepare either young goat, octopus, skate, rock fish, tripe or snails, and Julius would have his second dinner.

Julius lived on a 200 acre farm in Bowie. At Bowie race track Hoover had an announcement made over the loudspeakers inviting all to Julius's birthday party that evening. Many came.

Farmer Lulley not only smoked shrimp on the farm, but raised pheasants. The family of Polish peasants he had working the farm failed to wire over the top of the pen, alas, and the birds, when grown, flew away. A Polish joke, not a Hoover joke.

J. HILLMAN ON J. EDGAR: FOOD & FINGERPRINTS

JAMES HILLMAN

On page 11, Issue 32, 1992 you've got a piece "J. Edgar Hoover and Julius Lulley" by Milton Beyer. Julius was my father's cousin. I knew him in my years up to twenty. I lived in Washington, 1943 & '44. Julius and my father ran Harvey's awhile together; previously my grandfather, Joel (married to a Lulley), ran it; later on my brother (1947–1949) worked there for and with Julius.

So, I want to correct some errors in Beyer's text and add this and that.

Not "George" Hillman, gobbler and guzzler, but Joel (my grandfather) who started his career in food by sweeping blood in the Chicago stockyards and slaughter pens, then owned the Breakers (not Ambassador) and Chelsea in Atlantic City with my father, Julian, and were the American partners who built the George V in Paris.

J. Edgar Hoover ate almost every night when he was in D.C. at Harvey's. I met him there when I was a kid, and had the Great and Fearsome Honor of touring the FBI building under his auspices in the 1930s, time of Ma Barker, Pretty Boy Floyd, Babyface Nelson, Dillinger, etc. I watched G-men shoot machine guns at paper targets that outlined humans, and—O so naïve—excitedly had my fingerprints taken by the FBI. Memory images: I see J. Edgar Hoover at a table by the window, eating with another man; I see him with a red sort of fattish face behind a desk in an office. I feel myself tiny. I don't know what J. Edgar Hoover ordered to eat. I do know the waiters were all black, extraordinarily able, balancing trays on their heads and both hands. The coatcheck woman was Hattie; she had been born a slave. We always stopped to talk with her as if she were a Wonder.

Julius, according to my brother, may have stopped at Vasio's Italian restaurant but mainly ate Chinese regularly, mostly fried rice. Julius was fat and sweaty. Julius did not raise pheasants as Beyer says, but Guinea Hens.

If you wish to pursue any of this further, try me or better my brother.

SECRETS

It was getting late on a sultry evening during the summer of 1959. In larger, more costly houses, air conditioning units hummed in the dark behind banks of bushes. Their white noise masked the private functions of the wealthy and the powerful. On the outskirts of Washington D.C., in a neat and deceptively large Georgian style brick home, painted white and bristling with discreet security, J. Edgar Hoover, Director of the Federal Bureau of Investigation, yawned behind a dainty hand. He blinked once in the direction of his friend and life-long confidant Clyde, and in an uncharacteristically robust move, tossed off his brandy. After the briefest exchange of eye contact, Hoover announced he would now shower and retire for the evening. As he rose resolutely from his chair, tied off his robe and moved to the carpeted stairway, a suddenly exhilarated Clyde expressed a desire to brush his teeth. Through cozy yellow lamplight, Clyde followed his confidant and employer up the stairs.

In the bathroom, J. Edgar Hoover, pleased that his coded message had been received, ran the shower to a tolerable steaminess. He hummed and uh-huhed in agreement with his associate's banter. At the shower door, the director backed out of his slippers. Stripped from his robe and boxer shorts, he briefly flashed an intensely white and low-hung moon and a short, slightly swollen penis angling from under his belly like a kickstand. Except for weekends at Virginia Beach and a certain summer at Gibraltar, J. Edgar had never seen Clyde naked. The Director nude was resplendent, his authority was cloak enough. Out of his customary pinstripes, he was neither vulnerable or changed, only more himself.

J. Edgar stepped into the shower and closed the pebbled glass door behind him. In a voice raised over the shower splash, the Director mentioned an early appointment for the next day. Clyde recognized the gambit and reaffirmed his presence with an enthusiastic rinse and spit. He cleared his mouth a final time and leaned a hip against the sink.

"Tomorrow we'll have an early start, there's a meeting with the Attorney General at ten, his staffers are disorganized, I think you got my memo, so we'll hear what he has to say but I don't think we'll have to respond." Clyde didn't expect an answer from the shower, he knew The Director liked to listen.

J. Edgar Hoover, director of the Federal Bureau of Investigation, listened to his best friend's eager and entertaining voice echo off the octagonal white tiles of the large bathroom. The warm pressure of chemically softened water pelted his chest. His right hand gripped a gently curved bar of hornblend colored glycerin soap. Clyde knew this expensive soap was the only soap the Director used; they bought it in quantity on their trips to London.

Starting with his pubic hair, Mr. Hoover soaped his crotch thoroughly, raising a creamy tuft of lather. He turned from the shower head to face the pebbled glass door, and got a blast of spray in his ear. For a moment Clyde's cheerful voice drowned under water. The Director's erection slipped from its flaccid tray along the seam of his scrotal sac.

" ...so his secretary calls *me* and asks for an appointment. I couldn't believe it but that shows you how they run their operation, the kind of people we're dealing with doc..." This is the only time Clyde calls the Director "Doc." Usually he called him Edgar or when they were alone, John Edgar.

Hoover's penis pointed directly at the glass door of the shower behind which, five, possibly six feet away, his best friend and confidant stood by, recounting in measured tones a particularly humorous error in protocol committed that day by a young presidential staffer.

Over the years Clyde's voice, solicitous and eager, had developed into the most tantalizing facet of the sexual charade. His self absorbed tone was meant ostensibly to ignore the Director while at the same time cheering him on. They never touched. The men had turned over thirty years of friendship and confidence into an art form. Their sex life, for it truly belonged to both of them, had grown into a dance of intuition and consent. The Director knew the shower spray masked slaps and silences and that the pebbled glass offered only a creamy silhouette to his friend, and then only if he chose to observe carefully.

That Clyde did or did not stare at the shower door to discern his friend and confidant, J. Edgar Hoover, Director of the Federal Bureau of Investigation, engaged in an act of onanism was, for the Director, an aching pleasure, the secret at the core of the fantasy. Their sexual relationship was the summit of plausible deniability, the flawless secret.

"...these jokers don't know we've had them under

surveillance for the past eighteen months. And with what we've got from the IRS they'll be paralyzed, absolutely paralyzed." Clyde continued his spiel. Edgar slowly rubbed the soap into his pubic mound with his left hand while slowly and evenly stroking his rigid penis with the right. Every muscle slowly tensed. The Director triumphed as he prepared to unleash the crimson head of his penis, the head of his state, regal shiny and cruel as a weapon. Unsheathed from his body in one strong motion, the tip of his dick ran cleanly through the glass, followed by hand and arm then omnipotent and sexless body, to stand on the bathmat before his lifelong friend and confidant, Clyde.

"... but we can never really know what they're up to, day to day, and they know that, that's why they're so damn arrogant. But they also know we've got more authority than their boys, and you understand this beautifully, we need to step up, turn it on a little bit, so they have some doubts, so they will be looking over their own shoulders, you see, policing themselves."

J. Edgar Hoover drew a quick breath as his terrible swift sword spit a white fire, all consuming and benign, against the pebbled glass of the shower door. Shuddered out of his fevered sexual reverie back into the presence of his friend Clyde, the Director was again J. Edgar Hoover. J. Edgar Hoover, was once more pure and good.

Again, as it had been once a week for years, Clyde spoke faster and faster, always in the affirmative, about some trifle. He continued to talk while rubbing his own erection with the knuckles of his fist through the thin cloth of his grey trousers. Clyde was confident the Director would continue bathing until both their erections, and all trace of their copulation, had vanished.

For the thousandth time Clyde stared at the pebbled glass door of the shower stall, trying to identify the dense white spatter of jism that he, and no one else, had drawn from the obscurest physical regions in the loins of his friend and life long confidant, J. Edgar Hoover, Director of the Federal Bureau of Investigation. He stared at the glass hoping to discern a gob of the absolute power that he shared with his friend. He looked for semen as it mingled with the suds and splash of the shower sliding and sown into the drain, secret. The true glory of their lives together would remain secret. Their positions as maximum men defending an entire nation from an evil they could taste, the real work would stay hidden. Their lives were secure behind walls of the most secret plans and goals. The deepest work of government, control, and the trickiest repression would die with them, forever buried under layers of quiet.

WHAT I LEARNED FROM TV

PETER WEVERKA

When no one can identify it, a dead body is taken to the police station morgue and placed in a refrigerated filing cabinet. A name tag is tied around the dead body's big toe. If a person is found to identify the body, he or she is brought into the morgue. It is a stoic occasion. The identifier, with a tilt of the head, says, "That's him" or "That's her."

In the 1950s, all boys wore cuffed blue jeans, white shirts, and duck-tails. Girls wore pleated shirts, pony-tails and saddle shoes. Classroom discipline was at an all time low, even by today's standards.

After a horse is born, it must stand on its spindly legs within the first five minutes of life. If it fails to do so, its mother abandons it and it dies.

All criminals had acne in their youth. At night, under the glare of a streetlight, the scars look especially bad.

A homosexual undercurrent exists in the fire house. Firemen are burly, have well-groomed moustaches and all sleep in the same room.

When a man and woman are in bed together for the first time and have reached the point of abandoning themselves to ecstasy, the man will look in the woman's face and say, "God, I've wanted this for so long."

Children form tight, intimate friendships. They usually have a special, secret place to play in, and if one child dies the other will eventually return to the secret place, have a flashback, and then cry his or her eyes out until a feeling of inner peace ensues.

Cops and criminals have one thing in common—both are good at leaping chain-link fences.

You can tell who the really hip teachers in the high school are. Instead of standing behind the podium to deliver a lecture, a really hip teacher straddles a chair. Sometimes when he gets carried away, he jumps up to write on the blackboard and knocks his chair over.

There is only one way to escape from bloodhounds who are chasing you: find water. By wading in the shallows of a creek or river you can make the dogs lose your scent.

Detectives like visiting the forensics lab. Lab boys are helpful. They are good at explaining things. They know everything there is to know about hair, blood, and semen. Lab boys are a little eccentric too, which makes them fun to visit. They become eccentric because, unlike detectives, they don't mix with the populace. They work in seclusion deep inside the police station.

Old Black people are very wise. Young Black people are very spontaneous.

Even the most restrained, reticent, tight-lipped human being can become a master of eloquence at the airport—provided the airplane is about to take off. The person suddenly finds the words to say everything just right. Airport partings do that to people.

There are good cops and there are bad cops. Every cop knows instinctively where to draw the line between the good and the bad. When a good cop drifts across the line to the other side he is lost forever. He can never come back.

Every prostitute has a tough-as-nails veneer and an interior heart of gold.

In medieval Europe people lived in walled cities. When invaders attacked, everyone retreated behind the walls. Drawbridges were raised. The invaders attacked with catapults and battering rams. Sometimes, using ladders, they tried to scale the walls, and the defenders poured cauldrons of hot boiling oil on top of them.

Going on a first date with a girl is perhaps the most traumatic experience a high school boy will have. First he has to go to her house to meet her dad, who suspects him of being a rapist. At the hamburger stand he encounters his friends, who make fart noises whenever he opens his mouth to speak to the girl. Finally he takes her back to her house. This is the hardest part of all: he must kiss her at the front door. Does his breath stink? Will she slap him? They make small talk for a while, and gradually move closer together. Now he can almost taste her lips, but then her dad says from just inside the window, "Don't you think it's getting late?" She gives him a quick bird peck on the chin and rushes inside.

The people who live in the rusty decay of the inner city know a million shortcuts for getting from place to place. Besides alleys and corridors, they can jump from rooftop to rooftop, slide down fire escapes, or sprint through sewer drains.

THE AMERICAN MALE

"The greatest foe of the American male was Mr. Gillette, the inventor of the safety razor," a male friend said to me at lunch today. "The decline in prestige of the American male," he went on, "began the day he shaved off his whiskers.

"Foreigners retain their beards and their independence," my friend continued bitterly, "The beard is the prized plumage of the male, and the American male began molting about forty years ago. Mormons held out the longest. Only a man with a beard could uphold bigamy as a religious principle, and at the same time manage a household of wives. Beards are still a common enough sight in France, Italy, and England, countries where the power of woman is held moderately in check. As one moves toward the east, beards grow longer and more luxuriant, and the finest examples are always to be found where women are the most subservient. A man with a beard," he said with feeling, "would never be seen using the vacuum cleaner or drying a dish."

The finality of this seemed to me conclusive, but there was one more thought to come.

"Look how Santa Claus keeps the situation in hand," my friend said. "Do you ever see Mrs. Santa Claus' picture in the paper as serving on a committee or raising funds for aging gnomes or deer? Would this be the case if Mr. Claus had shaved his beard off? Never!"

Was it possible, I asked myself, that here, on my own soil, the relation between the sexes is in a state of crisis? I left that luncheon a troubled woman, determined to ask the men of my acquaintance what they thought of American manhood.

"The American male is disappearing. He is almost extinct," said the first man I put the question to. He was a literary agent, unbearded, married, with tragedy written in his eyes. "He will soon be a rare specimen, preserved behind bars at the zoo, and spoken of in the same hushed accents as are the bison and the whooping crane. And how will this thing have come about?" he asked. "Because whatever he does, his wife can do it quickly and more efficiently. Those are our two great national standards, set by women, let me point out, never by men. If it were not for the pressure of the American female, the American male would take it all more easily. He is as obsolete as the Model T Ford. In this twilight of the male, his function after dinner is to have a drink or two and then go to bed," said the literary agent quietly.

I did not wish to see the American male go, so I hastened to the home of a painter who had lived and studied in Europe, and who was infinitely wise.

"Oh, he is fighting for his preservation all right, the

American male," my friend said, standing before an easel with a paint brush in his hand. "But I'm not sure what his chances are. It's probably too late in the day for him to escape, as Gaugain did, but he's working hard to find his own South Sea. It was no accident of fate that the Wright Brothers were American. The American male has always sought to fly, and with good reason. His obsession with the jet, the instant get-away, it's all part of his desperate plan. He's got to get out of the female orbit if he's to survive. And the atom bomb, the tests they're making in Nevada for military use, you think? Absurd! They're seeking the special formula that will single out women for annihilation, the American woman, specifically. Time is short, and the American woman grows more determined every day."

I determined then to go to the office of a doctor whom I knew well, a man who is not old, but whose face is deeply engraved with lines. I had never thought to put the burning question of the American woman to him, but I now wondered if those lines could be the scars of domestic combat.

"I have run out of ammunition. My lances are broken," he said to me. "To the industry of the American woman can be attributed gastric ulcers, heart disease, and the highest divorce rate in the world. Nurtured on orange juice, proteins, and vitamins, which we doctors, alas, have prescribed, she is charged with an energy that knows no parallel. The American male has been forced into the arms of the psychoanalyst as the men of other countries are forced into the arms of mistresses. We are on the threshold of artificial insemination as a general practice, with the American woman specifying her favorite Hollywood star or TV actor as the father of her child by remote control. Beds will all be single, for the American female can get enough sleep under the hair dryer while at a beauty shop as her nails are being painted the color of blood and her eyebrows plucked into shape. When I was in the army," he finished bitterly, "my wife was unfaithful to me in the way only an American wife could be: she took over my medical practice and doubled it! She is now the vice-president of the Affiliated Doctors, Surgeons, and Midwives of America. I am about to retire to the country with my coronary thrombosis."

After that, I must have wandered for some time in a daze, for it was almost evening when I stopped a lean, be-spectacled gentleman as he came down the steps of the Columbia University Library.

"I am interested in your opinion of the American woman, Professor," I said, and behind the steel-rimmed lenses his eyes lit fanatically.

"Let us sit down here," he said, indicating the stone worn smooth by the feet of the learned. He took from under his arm the three volumes and the loose-leaf note book that he carried, and placed them with care on the cold stone of the steps. Then he sat quickly down on them. "Perhaps you thought I put them there for you?" he said, and he gave a cackle of laughter. "I fooled you, didn't I? I am the one man in America who believes that whatever is wrong with the American female is the fault of the American male. When I am not in the lecture hall demonstrating to class after class the ignominious role woman has played in history, I am in drug stores, subway trains, and other public places taking the seats that women were just about to sit down on, snatching the last ham sandwich off the counter, the last copy of the paper off the news stand, even wrenching these things, when necessary, out of their hands. Women hate litter, so I litter," he said. "I tear out pages from my notebook, and strew it before them, and when they stoop to pick the pieces up, I grind my heel as if by accident, into their toes."

"But, Professor," I managed to articulate, "has the situation always been as intense as it is now?"

"I would say it is increasing in intensity every semester," he stated unequivocally, and as he stood up and retrieved his books, he stepped back absent-mindedly on my foot.

I was weary and close to tears when I reached home. Was it possible, I asked myself, that American women were indeed like this? Was this consensus of male opinion true? I opened the front door and called out my husband's name.

"I'll be right with you as soon as I get the dish towels on the line to dry," he called back from the kitchen. "The chicken's ready to pop into the oven, and the potatoes are peeled." When he came from the kitchen carrying a tray with the cocktail shaker and two glasses on it, he was smiling his welcome. "How was your day at the office, dear?" he asked.

I think it was then that I began to cry.

HERMAPHRODITE, MON AMOUR

I. BEFORE I HAD A NAME FOR IT I HAD A NIGHTMARE

In the loft of a barn, among baling hooks and bat dung, I was seduced by Ann-Margret in her prime. She tumbled back into the hay, pulling me on top of her and let her breasts out of their halter, an Oxford shirt tied Calypso-fashion with a knot between them, one by one. I was greedy and clumsy. One of her nipples poked me in the eye. She laughed.

Then she raised her hips beneath me and unbuttoned her jeans which were cut off so high that the white pockets hung down beneath the ragged fringe. She took them off and flung them down into the horses' stalls. Slowly she then slipped off her panties to reveal the largest penis I had ever seen.

RICHARD COLLINS

I had not yet read Ovid or Plato or the Kabbalah. How could I have known that I wasn't dealing with a peculiarity of my own psychology but with an archetype older even than the two sexes?

2. TRUE HERMAPHRODITISM DOES NOT EXIST IN MAN

So the doctors and scientists tell us. Among plants and insects, especially mosquitoes, it is not uncommon, and in worms and fish it can almost be considered a third sex. Men and women must choose, either one or the other, but not both. André Breton said he would like to change his sex as he changed his shirt. But that is against the law. You can change your sex once, like my cousin Michael who is now my cousin Linda, but it's forbidden to change back again. As Dr. Rance says, in one of Joe Orton's plays, "There are two sexes. The unpalatable truth must be faced. Your attempts at a merger can end only in heartbreak."

3. I COULDN'T HAVE BEEN MORE THAN SIX OR SEVEN YEARS OLD WHEN I HAD TWO FRIGHTENING VISIONS

It was in Upland, California in the doorway of the Bank of America. On the marble slab of the doorway, just off the sidewalk, it was something the size and consistency of a large oyster. A pink, hairless, wrinkled sac with two ovals inside, the size of pigeons' eggs. There was no blood, but I could have sworn it was a scrotum.

It was about that time that I ran out of the Grove Theatre a block away from the bank, during a matinee showing of *The Attack of the Fifty-Foot Woman*. I walked home down the broken white line in the middle of the street, afraid to walk on the sidewalk under the trees, for fear that She would appear over the roofs of the houses.

4. TEN YEARS LATER I HAD ANOTHER DISTURBING DREAM

I was a court jester entertaining a group of eighteenth-century women with white Marie-Antoinette wigs and billowing champagne bosoms in a plush drawing-room with chandeliers and spindly-legged gilded furniture. After each of my tricks they would titter and clap their hands or snap their fans and blush beneath their powder and patches. At last it was time for my masterpiece, the magic trick for which I was world-renowned. A hush fell on the little audience with a muffled rustle of silk petticoats. I placed my hands on either side of my head and began to work my skull from side to side and back and forth until it came loose from my spine. Then I lifted my head high to the ooohs and aaahs of my audience and placed my head under my arm like a helmet. The applause of their admiration was prodigious, and I prolonged this little antic longer than usual for their enjoyment. It was an exhausting performance and could not be done often or for longer than a few moments at the most. Then I heard a petticoat behind me and turned my head upward to look at my headless shoulders, where I saw that one of the women had stolen up behind me and was looking down into my neck. This was expressly forbidden, along with flash photography. "No!" I said. "Don't look in there!" But it was too late. The woman shrieked and fainted. I knew what it was. She had seen the nothingness of a deep abyss and it was too much for her. I tried to lift my head onto my shoulders, but I had expended so much energy during the trick and so much adrenaline at the sound of her scream, that I just barely got the head up and onto the neck. But I could not snap it, like a doll's head over the lip of the neck, and the head fell onto the pink and green flowered carpet. And the room went black and red, black and red, and I felt the rough pile of the carpet on my cheek as I lost consciousness.

5. I MET CONCHA IN LINE AT THE IMMIGRATION OFFICE IN LONDON IN 1980

She was from Salamanca and was working as an *au pair* for a family in St. John's Wood while studying to perfect her English.

Mornings and evenings she spent taking care of the children, getting them ready for school or baby-sitting while the parents entertained. We would meet in the afternoons around Oxford Street or Piccadilly because she liked to look at men's clothes in the shop windows. "I like those shoes," she would say. "I don't like those shirts. Those trousers are too American." I began to wonder why I was with her. I should have been spending my afternoons in the British Library, looking up the skirts of hermaphrodites, reading Pater and Swinburne on the "toy of double shape," studying alchemical treatises and neo-Platonic encomia on androgyny. But then she would stop in the middle of the street and wrap her arms around my waist and say, "I feel so stupid. I would like to talk with you. But all I know how to say is I like this, I don't like that. I like it when you talk, it makes me feel like I am talking too. I don't like feeling so stupid." Slim and boyish in her wool shirt, pleated corduroys and polished oxblood penny loafers, she would pull me to her then and her boy's clothes and boyish manner and boy's figure made me feel a little depraved as I sank into her kisses and felt her teeth sink into my lips, and I was aware of the black umbrellas going up all around us and the rain coming down.

6. ONCE SHE WAS ABLE TO GET AWAY FOR THE ENTIRE NIGHT

We went to the Marquee, a club in Soho, and then back to my flat. In bed, after hours of slow undressing and mutual procrastination, I was wondering why she would not open her legs to me.

"Do you prefer women?" she asked abruptly. It seemed an odd question. "Yes," I said, "do you?" She shrugged her shoulders, then asked, "Have you ever slept with a man?" I told her that I once had a distant crush on a man I found irresistibly beautiful. And that I had once kissed another man in a booth in a darkened restaurant and had even felt him underneath the table. But I didn't like it. "It was like groping in the dark and finding myself, and I could feel myself but my self couldn't feel me. Like masturbating on anesthesia." Whereas touching a woman had the opposite effect, like plugging my fingers into an electric socket, like touching an extension of myself. I tried to explain it in terms of the difference between the myths of Narcissus and Hermaphroditus, but she shook her head and said I talked too fast.

"Do you have some cream or oil?" she asked. I said I didn't think that would be necessary; she had been physically ready for hours. "I don't like it that way," she said. "It makes me feel like a machine. I like it the way the Greek boys do it." But my experience was limited and I had never done that on a first date. I felt innocent and naive and callow, and part of me lost interest in the whole procedure. She tried to arouse my interest, but everything she tried was to no avail. At least the sun was beginning to rise. "You don't like me?" she asked. "It's not that," I said. "It's all right," she said, crawling on top of me. "Can I sleep here like this? I like to sleep like this." I lay there beneath her, stifling, struggling to breathe normally and not to show that I would never be able to fall asleep with her body on top of mine like that. She fell asleep and seemed to gain fifty pounds. I watched the blue grey dawn turn into the steel grey of the London morning and let her sleep there, like a tombstone, on my body.

7. THE NEXT DAY I LEFT FOR PARIS

In the Louvre I followed the crowds to the room which houses the Venus de Milo. But it was another statue I had come to see. A Hellenistic marble restored by Bernini, a slightly less than life-size figure half-reclining on a stone pillow. At first you see a beautiful woman's face resting on her arm, a breast revealed by her raised shoulder, and the curve of her sinuous waist and buttocks. But as you circle the statue to the other side, you find a diminutive penis, slightly erect, as though stirred in sleep by an erotic dream.

I spent hours in front of Bernini's *Sleeping Hermaphrodite* watching people's reactions as they discovered the secret of Hermaphroditus.

I recalled a performance piece erected in a California gallery. An expanse of white sheet stretched for the height and breadth of a wall. Through a slit in the sheet protruded a penis. All alone and apparently disembodied the small naked thing looked vulnerable and ridiculous, silly and innocuous, like a root in a landscape of snow. The title of the piece was "Touch a Penis," and that's what everyone was supposed to do, men, women and children, as flashbulbs caught them in the act.

I could not help but think that the artist behind the sheet was— like the Hermaphrodite behind the veil of sleep, and perhaps like all artists who dare to expose themselves behind the veil of artistic anonymity—aware of the hands that touch them so tentatively, and with such an ambiguous reaction of comic fascination and fear.

I remember in particular a Spanish family in the Louvre, well-dressed, well-behaved, bourgeois, who could not keep their hands off Bernini's Hermaphrodite, running their palms over the pillows to admire the realistic portrayal of softness in stone, over the buttocks to admire the curve of the creature's hip, and especially over the little stone penis, which had grown black and yellow from the oil of so many fingers paying homage to something monstrous and mysterious they could not touch.

TWENTY SEVEN IN A ROW OR A BLOW

Yesterday a woman told Deborah she had 27 consecutive orgasms. Deborah did not believe the woman. Insisted it was a mere case of hypothetical ecstasy. She knew. The evidence of falsehood: the woman was counting.

Still we imagined a row of 27 erect penises, arriving on a conveyor belt. Like sheep, the penises were counted. And viewed as a kind of delicacy. Perhaps in Technicolor. Large pink plants. Some were light pink, and some were dark pink. Mom always said well fed tulips produce a deeper color. Factory plants, grown in fluorescence, are never satisfying. They remind Mother of cafeteria foods that taste dank. And need butter.

Did the woman play leap frog? Was it a multi-penis man? One man suggested at least five penises. Waving like a hand. Another wondered what brand it might have been. A body builder suggested a mere muscular tongue. But Deb insisted it was just a singular penis and a woman who counted during sex. A singular penis. We don't know where it lives. Besides, it might have burnt out by now.

One young gentleman worried. He questioned the feminine potential for excessive climaxing. Couldn't it be harmful? He argued the woman of 27 orgasms must have been a ravaging woman, not a nice ordinary next door girl. No, she was a greedy, conquering sexual Napoleonette. We could hear her like a low wind against the house, irreverently howling, moaning louder, throbbing dangerously. We held our ears.

The scientist was unafraid. He had other ideas and an analytic mind. Perhaps the woman was hooked to an array of pulsing wires. Her naked body displayed on a medical table, covered only by a thin white sheet of paper. She rested, shivering in the sterile air on this contemporary altar as doctors watched. The experimental results could be sold in a new and startling book on the female potential. Did the doctors despair? Now with electricity there were no limits. And certainly no need for male appendages. But what did they discover? Perhaps it was sorcery. A black magic. A spiral dance into a woman without end.

AMERICAN PRINCESS

CAROL BERGÉ

Vanna White's knees show compassion. She expresses feelings for the gamblers. She is never found in a gray business suit. She is not in a family way, Pat says, though everyone knows she does marry. Vanna makes up her own name and the hair-do. She will have a doll made in her image. She thinks that Pat Sajak smells metallic. She notices that he parts his hair in the middle and she knows why. Vanna is never sarcastic. She is a princess earning her own way, just like Di. While she is away, someone appoints a substitute to turn the letters as they are guessed. Guest. The new woman stumbles and fumbles and proves how irreplaceable Vanna is. Vanna never hesitates. She knows which side of the board to move to. She pats her husband three or four times on the back when they hug in greeting or affection in the new American version of the abrazo. She is squeaky clean and she is not Squeaky Fromme. She has some secrets. She has a strong handshake. She is as strong-breasted as Artemis. Like Linda Evans, she has a beautiful "poitrine" (chest area), as the French say. She never says "different than" when "different from" is correct. Her high school teachers noticed her. She is somewhat smarter than (smarter from?) Tama Janowitz and a lot blonder. She is a lot smarter from Erica Jong. She never do paisley anything. She never do books. Figure of American form/American grace, she be female clothed in dreams. If she shrug a certain invisible way, her shoulder poufs fall, as if by. If a gambler be losing or fall into an accidental trap, she show compassion by the turn of her knee. In her sleep she clap her hands. She give away the gifts and miracles. She buy her own. She earn her own. Anyone by Pat/ surely have to. She knows

67

which side of the board has the butter. She better, like us/we. In her sleep she clap her hands to dream of Christmas every night, a awful reality compromise. A paean to her tailored image, it fashioned to fashion its curves part of today history. Of the attainable, given the gibbons. Of being and becoming America. She know there be an arrangement. Who leave empty-handed and who win. Attached to her compassionate right knee there be a string to pull the low numbers when needed. She be Winnie Mandela in blonde drag. She be proof of luck and skill to design the life pull the big numbers when needed. In the face of stars (of stage screen & radio) she shine and shimmer of a slimmer supple sort, she have a niche nobody can scratch. She be the supper idol, all she got to do is be nice like a good girl. Swing her hand upward toward the marvels to indicate. If you play the game right you got the secrets, the bucks. Vanna Whitebread she speak American. Dusty Polish immigrants tell the neighbors, That be my girl, you believe it, and nobody do. What White used to be or still is under a veneer. Turn her upside out she be drag Bukowski, smoothed of Polish. Not a smidge of bitter, she make the bed, they lie in it and spin. Forms and formal as at the first prom. All the promises. Any girl who dream can come there. Be a winner not a whiner. She be proof like a first coin. Profile of compassion.

TWO BY EDOUARD RODITI

A PROGRAM FOR SELF IMPROVEMENT

In the mirror of my bathroom door, I see myself as nature and the fleeting years have made me. In a brief moment of self-contemplation, I consider what improvements I might still undertake in order to offer, to the world at large, a more striking appearance.

I might begin, of course, with a mild diet that would rid me at a low cost of some superfluous blubber. Without too much expense, I could also take up jogging or go regularly to a local gym so as to tone up my muscles. Without yet being a Narcissus or a Hercules, I might then cease, at least, to be turned down as often by the few candidates that I still dare approach in my more amorous moments.

But even these slight improvements might fail to assure me the kind of spectacular successes that I need in order to bolster up my low morale, and this leads me to realize that I really must do something to make myself quite unique, if only so as to satisfy the secret desires of the one person in the world whose frustrated dreams are haunted by premonitions of what I now plan to become.

Grafted into my upper jaw, two long jade-green tusks

protruding over my lower lip and my chin would certainly do the trick, especially if I were also to dye my hair and eyebrows a bright red. Tattooed around my whole body, a scaly boa constrictor would also be an improvement, guaranteed to attract a lot of attention on the beach.

A twenty-carat diamond set in the lobe of each ear might not be in the best of taste, especially in these days of massive unemployment and frequent street-muggings. In any case, such expensive baubles would be part of my wardrobe rather than of my own physical beauty. I can begin later to think of how best to dress on various social occasions so as to set to its full advantage my improved face and figure.

Choices become more difficult, however, when I begin to consider how to improve my mind. There seem to be, for instance, so many different ways of becoming a genius or a saint.

IN PRAISE OF THE STATUS QUO

> Jack Spratt
> Would eat no fat,
> His wife would eat no lean.
> Between the two
> When their meal was through
> They'd licked the platters clean.
> —*English nursery rhyme*

Now that it has become relatively easy to change one's sex, we've begun to consider also ways and means of changing one's species. My wife has always resented being so petite and is seriously thinking of undergoing all the necessary surgical grafts and other treatments in order to become a Percheron mare, whereas I have never liked to attract much attention and might consider allowing myself to be pared down to the size of a mouse.

Fortunately, the various scientists whom we have so far consulted have assured us that their art has not yet reached the point where they might be able to satisfy our respective demands. For the time being, our marriage continues to be relatively happy, in spite of our frustrations. But these are nothing, I suspect, compared to those that I would probably experience as a tiny mouse married to a huge mare, or to my wife's hysterical behavior as a mare were she suddenly to find herself assaulted by a male mouse in her stable. After all, we're not too badly matched as matters now stand.

KEITH ABBOTT

ABBOTT ON RODITI

It was with sorrow that I read of Edouard Roditi's passing. I met Edouard during one of my stays at the Djerassi Foundation. He was writing his memoirs and each afternoon at lunch he would read to the assembled artists the next installment of his scandalous and hilarious epic. During this stage of composition, his writing at times was curiously circumspect, as if Edouard's fine-tuned politesse were the controlling factor. But when he talked, this would be cast aside, and he'd detail further complications and ramifications of each episode—and there were always more. "Edouard, you have to put that in there," we would urge him on, "don't leave that out." The next day the revisions would be gratifyingly expanded, and history ("our deep gossip") served. I hope that Edouard's memoir does get published so the rest of the world can enjoy how Andre Gide instructed the street hustler in French Grammar and who courted the Parisian traffic cop on his Asphalt Isle. Edouard was a great raconteur, a kind and sympatico elder, and a true man of letters.

DEBORAH SALAZAR

MY ABORTION

The procedure itself was the easiest part. A friend had told me to close my eyes and think about anything, think about Donald Duck— sweet and useless advice I thought at the time it was given—but when I heard the machine come on and I heard the doctor say, "The cervix is slanted at a right angle, this could be a problem, OK honey, relax," I thought Donald Duck, Donald Duck, Donald Duck, Donald Duck. I will never be able to watch another Donald Duck cartoon again without thinking about my abortion, but I went through the experience feeling pretty calm and entitled. Twenty-seven years old and pregnant for the first time in my life. God bless America, I thought, I sure as hell want a cheap, legal, safe abortion. I started practicing a necessary detachment. The Webster decision came through, the usual mobs of protesters around women's clinics were doubling in size, I got up at before dawn on the fifteenth of June and packed a paper bag with a sweater and socks (because the receptionist said it would be cold inside the clinic) and maxi-pads. I wanted to get there as soon as the doors opened, before most of the cross-waving, sign-carrying, chanting, singing Christians showed up. I used to work as a volunteer escort at this very clinic where I'm going to get my abortion. When my friend Beth pulled into the clinic parking lot, I saw only two people standing on the curb. A woman, all dressed in black, and a man. As we got closer, I saw that the woman was about the same age as me, with straight black hair and pale eyes like a girl I'd grown up with, a friend who became a fundamentalist Christian and occasionally came here to protest abortions. But I'd never seen this woman before. Her pale eyes were turned skywards, and she was moaning. She was moaning the words, "Don't kill me, Mommy, don't kill me." Beth said, "I'll drop you off at the door and go park in the back. See you in a little bit." And so I didn't have to walk very far. There was only the man and the woman to face. They followed the car until it stopped at the door. I stepped out, and the man was standing in front of me. He was tall, wearing a suit and tie and singing, "Jesus loves the little children..." I laughed in his face. Strange. Three years ago when I was working as an escort I'd been so solemn with these people. I never would've expected to laugh today. The man obviously hadn't expected me to laugh either. He got angry. "Lesbian!" he called after me as I walked into the clinic. "You're a lesbian! That's why you hate babies!" Another tall young man wearing an official clinic escort T-shirt was standing at the threshold. "Sorry about this," he muttered as I passed by. I was still laughing. "I wish I were a lesbian," I said a little hysterically. "I wouldn't be pregnant." And then I was inside the clinic. The receptionist recognized me right away. She smiled as I signed in. "What are you doing back here?" "About to pee into a cup," I said. I knew the routine. I took my forms and my plastic cup. I went directly to the bathroom before the receptionist could point the way. I could hear them while I was in the bathroom. I could hear them the whole time I was there. The chanting was discontinuous, but it was louder every time it started up. "Murderers! Murderers!" I could hear them in the bathroom, in the dressing room, in the weigh-in room, in counseling, in recovery, I don't remember if I could hear them in the procedure room itself. I was told later that my encounter with the protesters had been relatively undramatic; one escort said that these days he was seeing things like protesters who try to hold car doors shut while women try to get out. He was seeing women harassed to tears. He was seeing fistfights break out between angry husbands and passionate Christians. After I turned in my urine cup, I sat back in the waiting room and started filling out forms. A woman sitting next to me was chiding her boyfriend under her breath because he was mumbling something about going out there and giving those holy rollers a piece of his mind. One of the forms was a personal questionnaire that included the question, "What method of birth control were you using at the time you got pregnant?" I thought about lying for a second before I checked the box beside "none." One of the protesters outside had started playing a tape of a baby crying. I signed my name over and over, yes, I understand the risks involved, yes, I understand that the alternatives to abortion are birth and adoption. I wanted to do more—I wanted

71

to fill out a page or so explaining why I had chosen to do this. I wanted to explain to someone that I was a responsible person, you see, ladies and gentlemen, I never had sex without condoms unless I was on my period, I got pregnant during my period, isn't there something I could sign swearing to that? I had a three day affair with a friend, I'm broke and unemployed, I can't give up a baby, I can't afford for my body to be pregnant while I look for a job ... In the weigh-in room, where blood was taken and ibuprofen pills were given, where you were handed a dressing gown with little blue flowers all over it and a big white shopping bag to put your clothes in, in this little room full of all the friendly, obligatory, very sanitary-looking glass jars of cotton balls, thermometers, and tongue depressors, a woman asked me if I knew what the pain-killing shot "down there" would be like, did I know if it would hurt? I said probably so, it would hurt. "But not as much as having a baby would," I said, and she laughed. In counseling, I was asked why I'd gotten off the pill, and I didn't hesitate to respond, "I can get rid of an accidental pregnancy. I can't get rid of cancer." In the lounge room where you sat in your gown before going to see the doctor, there was a tiny television (Pee-Wee Herman was on) and a table with magazines (*Cosmopolitan, Vogue, American Baby*). The room was already filled to capacity, all twelve chairs taken, when the little bowhead came in. She couldn't have been over seventeen, wearing only her gown and a very big white satin bow in her hair. She was a beauty. She looked like she belonged on a homecoming float. She had been crying. "I hate them," she announced, dropping her shopping bag of clothes on the floor. "They don't have to say the things they say. Makes me want to go out there and shoot them with a gun." "You can't hear them that well in here, honey," one of the older women said. "You can watch the cartoons." "They're the cartoons," the beauty said. "You know what one of them said to my mama? Called her a slut, an unchristian woman. My mama yelled back at them that I got raped by a priest, that's how come I'm here." Stares. The bowhead picked up her shopping bag of clothes and leaned against the wall. She spoke again in a quieter voice. "I didn't really get raped by a priest. My mama just said that." The doctor was late that morning. It was in this room that I heard the stories, about boyfriends who were going through sympathetic pregnancies, fainting and puking, about a mother rejected by her own daughter because she, the mother, had decided to have an abortion, about a distraught boyfriend who was refusing to ever speak again to a young woman because she had chosen to "kill their baby." Outside, the chants were getting louder, to the point of competing with Pee-Wee Herman who was on full blast. Maybe, I thought, the protesters were actually helping some of the women re-channel some of their natural nervousness about the abortion procedure into a strong, healthy defiance. One of the women started grandstanding. "They can't

72

take this right away from us," she said. "And then something like the RU486 pill comes along—something that would almost make abortions obsolete—and these people don't want us to have that either. I don't know how many times they have to hear the plain facts before they understand. Before 1973, one in every ten women who had an illegal abortion died. I don't know what the statistics are about infections and sterilizations resulting from those awful unsafe operations, but they're there. You can look them up. Whether or not a fetus at seven weeks is a real person is an issue that will probably never be decided. But if Roe vs. Wade is overturned—god, a lot of very real persons, a lot of live women, are going to die. I want to yell "Murderers!" right back at those people out there." The protesters were singing when my name was called, some hymn I didn't recognize. I walked down a very short hallway in my bare feet, and then liquid Valium injected directly into a vein in my left arm made everything else after that feel like it was taking place on another planet. I remember that the doctor was wearing a dark red surgical outfit and that it looked pretty gruesome—I wished he'd worn the traditional pale blue or green. I remember that the Valium made me want to laugh and I didn't want to laugh because I was afraid I'd wiggle and I'd been warned not to wiggle unless I wanted my uterus perforated. I'd been at the clinic six hours already, preparing for this little operation that would only take five minutes. I remember that after the machine came on, it seemed like less than five minutes. I remember that it hurt and that I was amazed at how empty, relieved, and not pregnant I felt as soon as it was over. I thought for a second about asking the doctor if I could see what was in the tub, but then I changed my mind—he would think I was being macabre. The cramps that followed the abortion were painful but not terribly so; I could feel my uterus contracting and trying to collapse back to its former size. I was led by a nurse into a dark room where I sat on a soft mat in a soft chair and bled for a while. I closed my eyes. The woman in the seat next to me was sobbing softly. I knew it was the blonde with the white bow in her hair. I reached over and took her hand in mine. The Valium made me feel as though we were both wearing gloves. The hand in mine was so still, I wondered if she knew I was here for her, but the sobbing grew softer and softer and eventually it just stopped.

MASTURBATION AS SOCIAL REVOLUTION

KIRBY OLSON

In all the theory coming out on masochism and sadism and such, there is precious little theory of auto-erotics. This is deeply disturbing. Along with the new departments of Gay and Lesbian

Studies, a new breed must step out of the closet and into the classroom: the masturbator. Are there not more masturbators in the world than sexual practitioners of any other kind?

Diogenes speaks euphorically of the way the Creator arranged it so that our hands fall naturally to our genitals. And yet, what we do with our hands is not always reflected by what we say with our mouth.

The simple how-to-go-about-it is not worth the candle, so to speak, so I will leave it to you whether you cut a hole in a canteloupe, as did Henry Miller, or whether you use a sock as did my college room mate. More important than how, is the teleology of masturbation: more important than raising the next generation or running around after fur coats and diamond necklaces, jerking off must be seen as donning a rhino costume in the high school play, and then dreaming of snow falling as horses' hooves clatter over cobblestones (ah, romantic claptrap of the unique sign), and from there one can imagine four-leaf clover, Mrs. Rhino, until all the stars of libidinous joy shout like doves from the cannons at West Point, returning love to God on soft wings.

Willie Smith's *Oedipus Cadet* (Black Heron, 1990) is built on masturbation cycles: the rage of joy followed by profound lassitude and regret as feminazis parachute into Smith's mental hospital; the deep structure of self-love is disturbed into a union with unacceptable humans; one's parents; a profound mistake sponsored by the groovy nuclear family.

Jerking off can re-eroticize the universe which has been shrunk to a single partner; think of trash cans, think of the new Ferrarri with its "hub-cap diamond star halo" (Bolan), think of pink towels on soft green astroturf. "Only connect" (Williams), and the seething poetry of self-love will become a love as vast as the exploding and frivolous enigma of the Milky Way.

WAS NARCISSUS A NARCISSIST? AN ALTERNATIVE READING OF THE ANCIENT MYTH

DENISE NOE

The ancient Greek myth of Narcissus—he who fell in love with his own reflection in a river and pined to death from unrequited love—has come down to us as a parable about vanity. His name is synonymous with self-conceit.

But in the usual reading a vital aspect of the tale is overlooked: Narcissus fell in love with an image *he did not know was himself.*

Believing he saw a "beautiful waterspirit," he was disappointed because the loved one fled when he tried to kiss it/him. Had Narcissus realized he was admiring his own reflection he could have hugged and kissed himself (albeit not face-to-face). Not love of self but delusion of "otherness" killed Narcissus.

This failure to recognize the self *as self* is characteristic of schizophrenia. The schizophrenic hears voices that s/he cannot recognize as thoughts from within his/her own mind. This "I-Thou" confusion, not knowing where the "self" leaves off and the "other" begins, is a classic symptom of this mental illness.

Thus, the myth of Narcissus is a parable about the unrecognized self of schizophrenia rather than a warning against vanity.

GENESIS OF A QUIP

WILLIAM LEVY

"Three hundred homosexuals rule the world. And I know every one of them" are lines I created circa 1977-78. Who to assign them to was not an easy task. The requirements were it had to be someone who would lend it a modest degree of verisimilitude, who was openly gay and well known. At first I thought to give this witticism to William Burroughs, but anyone who knows Bill knows he doesn't feel comfortable in society. Then I considered Pier Paolo Pasolini, discarding him as not sufficiently famous at the time to an Anglo-American public. Since I had dined recently with David Hockney in Paris and felt he wouldn't really mind being designated as author of this quip he became my choice and "Table Talk" my source. Actually I didn't completely make it up. The lines are a paraphrase from Louis-Ferdinand Céline's *Bagatelles pour un massacre* (1937). "Le monde entier est gouverné par 300 Israelites que je connais" he writes and sarcastically ascribes it to "Rathenau, Juif, Ministre Allemand." That is to say Dr. Walther Rathenau the social democratic philosopher and post-World War I foreign minister of Germany who was assassinated in 1922. But I believe the origin of this quote is from Benjamin Disraeli's novel *Coningsby* (1844) where the words "Jew" or "homosexual" are not used in this context. "Three hundred homosexuals rule the world. And I know every one of them" I used as an epigraph to a poem "Nihilism in the Netherlands" which was first published in *Het Gewicht*, an Amsterdam literary newspaper. Subsequently the poem (with its epigraph) was published in a privately produced book of my verse *Jeremiad Chants* (Amsterdam/Genoa 1979). This joke was published also in my book *Natural Jewboy* (Ins and Outs Press 1981—widely reviewed in the States—as well as the German (Volksverlag 1981) and the Dutch (Uitgeverij

Bert Bakker 1982) language editions of that work. Because it was printed in the *Corpse* as filler, uncredited and out of context, that gullible sentimentalist Victor Bockris has now taken this absolutely apocryphal wisecrack as true, credited it to the wit and wisdom of David Hockney and used it in his book *Warhol: The Biography* (1989) attributing his source to where? None other than *Exquisite Corpse*, vol. 6, Nos. 10–12, Oct–Dec 1988! Cultural glory was invented for the use of school children studying for exams. The true artist creates things which lead an independent life.

SMOKERS IN THE HANDS OF AN ANGRY GOD

There are black clouds of God's wrath now hanging directly over your heads ...

—JONATHAN EDWARDS,
"SINNERS IN THE HANDS OF AN ANGRY GOD"

From Jonathan Edwards's famous sermon in 1741 until now, not much has changed in American society: We must unite to purify the sin from our midst, which would contaminate us and send us straight to hell. The form has varied, but it's the same old Puritan vinegar in new bottles. The Salem witch trials were only emblematic of the successive purges that erupted in colonial religious communities. These were, after all, God's children in the "devil's territories," and they had to be eternally protective of their purity in a contaminating environment.

Puritan theology died out, but its passion to purge became a permanent part of American culture. Purity and contamination have continued as a national obsession. In the early 19th century, for instance, it was "proven" that Irish Catholic immigrants contracted cholera from their own wickedness, and convents were burned to prevent the contagion of Papist perversion. In the South, toward the end of the century, it was then "proven" that syphilitic Negroes would contaminate the magnolia-blossom of the white race, and so as a "health measure," bathrooms, drinking fountains and restaurants were segregated. In the 1920s we learned, beyond the shadow of a doubt, that whiskey corrupts youth and destroys the family, and Prohibition laws were enacted. And in the '50s we rallied against the Communist-under-every-bed, and peered out between blinds wondering, as a pamphlet of the day pondered: "Is Your Neighbor a True American?"

In the 60s the Baby Boom generation, in a spurt of

vengeful hedonism, thought that we burned the Puritan heritage along with our bras and draft cards. Nobody wanted purity in any form, sexual, racial or physical, particularly the joyless patriarchal kind with its pinched lips and somber Thanksgiving tophat. In the early '80s, however, on our thirty-fifth birthdays perhaps, we woke up one morning with the shocking realization that one day soon we're going to die. We suddenly remembered that we forgot to have a baby, we forgot to become rich and powerful, we forgot about a future that would inevitably end in a coffin. The universal factor that determines all human endeavor had been swept under the carpet of a youth-marketed culture: the corruption of the flesh, death, the mouth of hell itself. "Virtue is terror," wrote Robespierre, "and terror, virtue." We reconnected with those Puritans trembling in pews under the terrifying shadows of Jonathan Edwards's gesturing hands.

Yet there were no clergy to turn to: this was part of the past we burned. So we, who grew up with Ronald Reagan chanting on General Electric Theater that "progress is our most important product," postponed middle-age, gave him a decade-long rerun as president and turned to the medical scientists for a progress report. They said to jog and eat your vegetables, to stop smoking, drinking and sleeping around. Yes, we would still die but later, maybe at 100 if we were good. "Clean living" is what was taught in Sunday school but coming from the mouths of research scientists, from laboratories with graphs, percentages and tumorous rats—it was a religious revelation. We were saved—or at least, those of us in the know were—and unleashing the judgmental self-righteousness of four centuries of Puritanism we turned upon those in our midst who weren't, those who would contaminate us with their fumes and flab, their sin and mortality: their death. Not ours.

In Shirley Jackson's story "The Lottery," every year in a New England village a different neighbor is randomly selected to be stoned to death in the town square to purge group anxiety. The ferocity with which adults and children attack their neighbor ends in a peaceful smugness that evil has been evicted for another year. In the past Americans have turned against witches, Catholics, Jews, blacks, drinkers, communists and homosexuals, all elements that, at one time or another, were seen to corrupt the village purity. Today a black Catholic lesbian witch in recovery could probably successfully run for the city council in any large city—unless she were photographed with a cigarette in her mouth. Now it's the smoker's turn.

The historical irony should escape no one, but I'm afraid it does. The first commercial colonies founded in North America were by Dutch and English tobacco-trading companies. The invention of tobacco as a product and of the United States as a nation were simultaneous and contingent. The early history of the U.S. is closely tied to the marketing of an indigenous herb used by native peoples for medicinal and ceremonial purposes. By the 18th century much of Europe was already hooked on cigar and pipe smoking, as well as chewing tobacco and snuff. It was the main cash crop of the United States until displaced by king cotton. In the past tobacco has meant to the economy of the United States what marijuana now means to Mexico and coca to Peru and Bolivia. All three native plants, first used ritually by American Indians, were later farmed, industrialized, fetishized and abused in ways unimaginable to their original cultivators, no doubt the revenge of ancestral ghosts upon the progeny of their colonizers.

Legally or illegally, nevertheless, these plants have become a cornerstone of the New World economy and identity. Just as the maple leaf appears as a symbol on the Canadian flag, perhaps the tobacco leaf should be emblazoned on the American, the marijuana leaf on the Mexican and the coca leaf on the Peruvian flags as a link between indigenous horticulture and modern economics.

Fanny Trollope, the novelist's mother, observed during her travels in the 19th century United States that dining cars, steamship compartments and public recreational areas were segregated by sex because of tobacco. For as long as I can remember, my grandparents had separate bedrooms because my grandfather not only smoked cigars but chewed them, and in parts of the house he was not allowed to light up—or to spit. A Southern gentleman from the Gilded Age, he traced the decline of American culture to the disappearance of brass spittoons from your better hotels and restaurants.

The smell of tobacco traditionally represented a male domain, as in the "smoke-filled rooms" of ward politics. If marijuana is a yin herb, associated with agreement and unity, then tobacco is a yang herb, smelling of assertion and authority. Smoking or chewing tobacco together was, from earliest times, a rite of male-bonding, off-limits to women until the 20s, when flappers and suffragettes expressed their equality by defiantly smoking cigarettes in public. Like most women of her generation, my grandmother abhorred the smell of tobacco. But she was finally overruled not by my grandfather, who courteously puffed, chewed and spat in his bedroom or among other men, but by her younger sister, an unmarried teacher with bobbed hair who smoked cigarettes freely throughout the house, even lighting up at the dining room table. Both of these tobacco-users, by the way, lived almost two decades longer than my abstemious grandmother, whose only vice was a piece of wine-cake every Christmas Eve.

Europeans are constantly chiding me that it was American movies and advertising that, from the 20s on, changed world smoking habits from gentlemanly cigar and pipe puffing to the sexy uni-sex glamour of chain-smoking cigarettes, à la Bogart and Bette. These are inevitably Europeans who have suffered a summer vacation in the United States, lighting up on the sly in alleys and backyards like junkies, when they had come to live out black-and-white celluloid fantasies with the flick of a silver lighter. That the main purveyor of a product could about-face into its lone outspoken opponent is inconceivable to them. Yet the United States has switched products, as any moviegoer can see, and gone from pimping booze and cigarettes to a far more dangerous duo: cars and guns. The urbane cocktail and cigarette of the American cinema of the 30s and 40s have been replaced by the obligatory metal-smash chase-scene and gut-splatter gun-massacre of the "health-minded" 80s and 90s. And what do we now sell to the world? Why, cars and arms. And, for conscience's sake, American cigarettes now bear a warning that they are dangerous to your health, whereas our cars, assault rifles and Scud mis-siles do not.

The Calvinist Dutch, chief world-traders both in wicked spices and in slaves during the 16th century, at home would periodically purge themselves of guilt by religious revivals that weeded out menial sinners from their congregations. While the American-generated petroleum and arms industries are tearing up the world with irreversible destruction to the ozone layer and interminable small-scale wars, we remain aloofly righteous by purging smokers, and paternalistically advising the world that, for their own good, they should stop puffing our herb. Don't smoke American: It's bad for your health. But by all means drive and shoot American: Rambo replaces Bogart. And slathered with sunscreen, cower-ing in bulletproof vests inside guarded compounds, we'll all live to cele-brate our 100th birthdays ... if we can only stop smoking.

Smoking, of course, is a dirty habit, and along with alcohol, red meat, deep-fried oysters, coffee, Sacher torte, wild sex and the fattening immo-bility imposed by TV and cars, is not particularly good for your health. Millions of laboratory rats didn't have to die to prove that. The ideal would be to subsist on fruits and nuts on an exercise treadmill, as those perfect, strong-willed hamsters among us already do. The compulsive self perfection of the Calvinist temperament—"every day a little bit better in every way"—is an inheritance from a theology in which you must *earn* salvation. Once saved, you are then like a heterosexual AIDS patient, an "innocent victim" to whatever calamities might befall you, more to be pitied than censured.

For the Puritan, it is essential not only to be pure, but also that everyone else in the inner-circle of the elect be pure, so as to not conta-minate those of true faith. An American rock star recently visiting

Europe announced that not only is she a vegetarian, but she wouldn't even sit next to anyone who eats meat. The carrion smell in the perspiration of another would ruin her tofu-burger: We must purge carrion-eaters from our fat-free midst.

Smell is the most basic mammalian sense, and often the nose is the agent through which the pure are contaminated: The Other stinks. Puritans were warned that the devil could be detected by a sulfurous odor. Nazis and white supremacists ascribe to the Jew and African a particular smell, a whiff of which contaminates their racial purity. Misogynists say the same about women, and in certain societies the smell of menstrual blood is said to contaminate food. Food is another chapter: The Irish immigrant smelled of cabbage, the Italian of garlic, and ever since the body-odor industry has marketed assimilation as an *essence du WASP*.

Contamination phobias go much further. Even before AIDS, homophobes felt their sexual purity contaminated by the mere presence of a homosexual, and that it was best to take a bath after inadvertently sitting next to one. But not take a bath with one: American soldiers now feel that showering or sharing quarters with gay soldiers would make them less than men. In the old South, whites were raised with a morbid horror of "colored spit." Dishes the black maid ate from were kept under the kitchen sink, along with cleansers and plungers, and a dish was considered contaminated should she accidentally eat or drink from one that wasn't "hers." Such irrational contamination phobias are at the core of all exclusive group identities, whether they be racial, linguistic, religious or dietary. As with animals, groups are formed along often invisible territorial lines that set limits to belonging.

The latest olfactory tribal taboo is against perfumes and aftershaves. "Scent-free" follows inexorably in the wake of "smoke-free." When group restrictions are tightened, the elect are resanctified. The issue of secondhand tobacco smoke, therefore, goes far deeper than whether it has or hasn't been proven to be unhealthy. The smell of tobacco smoke means an outsider is in our midst, one who is not saved, reminding us of our mortality: in short, a sinner. It amazes that the tallest and healthiest crop of Americans ever produced, raised in a 50s haze of Camel and Chesterfield smoke, would feel mortally jeopardized now by even the lingering smell of tobacco around them. I've known Californians to send their own parents to the backyard to smoke when they visit, as if the baby formula that formed their bones hadn't smelled like mama's or daddy's Lucky Strikes. I've seen people cross a cavernous bus terminal to ask fellow passengers to put out their cigarettes, with the same disdain with which a "lady" addresses a prostitute, as if the whore's very presence were a smirch, an insult to her purity, a contamination.

The lady's self-righteousness before the whore is heightened, of course, if the lady happens to be carrying on an affair behind her husband's back. Hypocrisy is an essential Puritan characteristic. And in terms of stench, health and pollution, I've never been able to understand how fossil-fuel junkies, that is, anyone who drives a car, could possibly criticize someone who smokes tobacco. An automobile puts five tons of carbon dioxide into the air every year, not to mention the chemicals added to gasoline. The disastrous climatic and environmental results are well known, yet it's more than encouraged—it is incessantly propagandized—that we should buy more and more cars. Public transportation budgets are being slashed by the same "environmentally-concerned" city council members who ban smoking. For now, and for generations to come, the environment is poisoned with fossil-fuel wastes and petroleum-derived plastics. Most Americans work and live inside sealed synthetic bubbles furnished with toxic acrylics, breathing fifth-hand air that circulates through sieves of moldy fibers. The windows don't open; there are no sidewalks. This is the culture of fresh-air fanatics?

People in shock often focus on some detail in order to simulate control over a devastating situation. And like a family watching their house burn to the ground, gripped by a panicky obsession to save the goldfish bowl inside, we have focused on "smoke-free"—meaning not petroleum but tobacco—as the symbolic solution to environmental apocalypse. The same resident of Los Angeles who drives an hour and a half through the yellow smog of gridlocked freeways to reach a restaurant, will insist that it be "smoke-free." But we don't drive in your living room, drivers protest. And I point to my windows opened over a packed row of parked cars and reply, oh yes you do. You do indeed.

The moment has come for me to march to the front of the church to declare before the beady eyes of the congregation that I am a sinner. I smoke. I live in Barcelona, a city where almost everyone smokes. My trips home have become nonstop polemics, like a Papist-convert returning to the Puritan village. The scarlet letter that sets me apart is an "S" for Smoker. The evangelical tape-loop is unrelenting: "There's still time to repent, I got the patch and look, now I'm saved." Praise the Lord, I say, and pass the ashtray.

I humbly occupy my place as a smoker, like Hester Pryne invited in for tea by a deacon's wife. People stare. I feel their wrath and condemnation. My little niece rushes up to inform me what she's learned in catechismal health classes, that because I smoke I'm going to die. That we're all going to die is what she'll learn in the next grade, I would hope. If the alternative were immortality, I'd give smoking a second thought.

A cousin gushes about an acquaintance, "She's really nice even though she's a smoker." You used to be able to fill-in-the-blank in this stock sentence with Jew, black, Catholic, lesbian or gay. In at least lip-service to a newfound tolerance, we have embraced all the elements of diversity, even what is euphemistically called "the leather community," or sadomasochists who hold potlucks just like Methodists. So I assumed the worst was over with my conservative New Orleans family—until I lit up. For years I was the black sheep, a Civil-Rights commie, pansexual hippy and no-account poet. "Perverted," as my father once put it, "by *The Communist Manifesto.*" Yet after all the battles we've been through—long hair, integration, Viet Nam, free love and revolution—all forgiven and forgotten in a rosy media-induced amnesia, now it's my cigarettes that mark me as the enemy, literally driving me outside to fume as my ideas once did. Funny, but back in 1968 smoking was the only thing we seemed to have in common.

Of course, back then the people in high school who wouldn't talk to me unless I had a Marlboro in my hand have become the very ones who won't talk to me now if I do. Yes, I started because of peer-pressure, and I'll be damned if I stop because of it: The same trendy morons aren't going to get me twice. Once you give in to the transitory satisfactions of peer-pressure in the United States, your life's work is cut out for you. Today it's decaf lattes and body-piercing; tomorrow you'll be eating bird seed and walking around on stilts.

Friends who virtuously clamped their hands over their glasses as I went to pour wine in the early 80s—"Do you have Perrier?" was the arch response—have learned that for years the Perrier springs were contaminated by carcinogenic wastes and that red wine fights dreaded cholesterol. The Mediterranean diet is now touted as the key to longevity, and Americans dutifully eat their pasta and sun-dried tomatoes. Yet Spaniards, who live on the average three years longer than Americans and are notably more attractive, do everything wrong by American standards: They smoke like chimneys, guzzle grease and alcohol, and stay up all night in noisy, smoke-filled cafes. The secret ingredients to the recipe are that they work as little as possible, stroll for hours every day, sleep the afternoon away, have affairs, sing out loud while they hang wash in the sun, take six-week vacations and generally enjoy life. This is the profoundly un-American basis for the success of the Mediterranean diet: not calamari and olive oil but a life lived for pleasure.

This pleasure is not the manic fever we experienced in the 60s and 70s, the flipside of a competitive Calvinist greed in which we set out to overdose on everything prohibited in the least amount of time. Like the proverbially wild minister's son, when the Puritan does enter the garden of earthly delights, he generally makes a big pig of himself and spends the rest of his life repentant, admitting that Father Knows Best. Mediterranean pleasure, on the other hand, is ritualized, relaxed, moderated by tradition, and tolerant of the failures of the flesh, to which we all, with a knowing wink, occasionally succumb.

Every time I board a flight from Barcelona back to San Francisco, I think of Flannery O'Connor's "The Lame Shall Enter First," because on these flights smokers board first to occupy the back rows. There we're seated next to the black box, stored in the plane's tail, best designed to survive a crash. I'm generally seated among Spaniards, smoking up a storm, drinking all the free wine we can get, standing in the aisles talking and laughing. Towards the front of the plane, in the nonsmoking section, are the American tourists, solemnly sipping canned fruit juice. Haunted by the cabin's "safety features," I inevitably picture the plane bursting into flames and splitting in two, going down over the Atlantic.

And in the Catholic Mediterranean version, it's rather like another O'Connor story, "Revelation," in which a self-righteous white Southern woman is granted a vision while hosing down her pigpen. Above her in the sky, she sees white trash, black share croppers, freaks and lunatics skipping into heaven singing and clapping, radiant and blessed, while behind them in grim procession march people like herself, "accountable as they had always been for good order and common sense and respectable behavior. They alone were on key. Yet she could see by their shocked and altered faces that even their virtues were being burned away."

In my vision, we smoking, drinking and flirting sinners in the smoking section are catapulted into the sea, where dogpaddling on our flotation devices we're rescued by a passing Club Med cruise ship. Shivering and dripping, we're then escorted into the bar for a complimentary Piña Colada. Whereas those in the nonsmoking section of the doomed aircraft, the perfect people, sin-free and most deserving of a long and healthy life, spin in fiery spirals down into everlasting darkness, clutching charred juice cans amid the rending of garments and gnashing of teeth.

THE LUDDITE DEVOLUTION

I recently received a letter from Les Smith, who co-edits a little fiction magazine called *Pangolin Papers* out of Marrowstone Island, Washington. In it, he described the operations of his associates, two "60ish women (which from my lofty plateau looks young)...who have the hardware and software, including a perfect binder, to produce just about anything."

Without another thought, I filed the operations of Turtle Press under the copious testimony to the conspicuous decentralization of the means of production brought on by the tool we know as the personal computer.

JIM NISBET

Two nights after receiving Les' letter, having jacklighted a prowler at about 2:30 a.m., I was sitting out the adrenal afterburn with *Utne Reader*'s l0th anniversary issue. Therein, I discovered a digest of Wendell Berry's infamous "Neo-Luddite" lament about how he's never going to get a computer. He stopped short of calling poor Computer a nefarious bane on creativity; but, as an alternate means of production, Berry's bottom line is that "Wife" ("my critic, my closest reader, my fellow worker") does all the typing around Berry's house—on a manual machine, it so happens—which frees the Boss to write exclusively by pencil. He further claims to write by daylight, which, aside from embroidering the notion of a stump leveled to desktop specs by a double-handed nuptial saw, thoroughly at a stroke dissociates the work of its author from the venerable tradition of midnight literature, certainly a great deal if not all of which, a hundred if not twenty years from now, must arguably eclipse Mr. Berry's own heliotaxical efforts entirely.

Aside from the idea that the glint of sunbeams off tapered graphite must somehow palliate the beast that is Mr. Berry's intellectual Em Cee Squared, the contrast between Les Smith and his partners with Wendell Berry and his wife continues to fascinate me.

I first read about Berry's outburst, as Virtually Addled Thinking, in the letters column of *Harper's*, which featured an ongoing uproar about it for several issues. I guess I still haven't read the original but, faulting my recent wee hours, I've read a digest version now, and I've not witnessed a rant longer in tooth since Reverend Wildmon cut loose his chipped marble over PBS' production of Amistead Maupin's *Tales of the City*. To be fair, Berry makes the Wildmon's caviling read like the back of a box containing morally competitive breakfast cereal.

(I might note, in passing irony, and by way of feebly bolstering my own neo-Luddite credentials, that I haven't owned a television for twenty-something years. What can I say, you ask? I say: It's a cross and I bear it.)

Mr. Berry's essay, however, can only have been penciled out of otiose, self-isolated cogitation, an attempt by one man to invert an idle peeve into generalized fear or, worse, reactionary hatred, of change, what we might term Bucolic Misoneism, the product of a man who lays claim to a smoothly graded enlightenment unwashboarded by dissent or even startling exceptions. That's fine, to a certain extent we all should get to do it, although the resulting paranoia is perhaps more useful when thermally converted into science fiction novels by Philip K Dick. What's upsetting about Berry's attitude is not that he insists on living by it himself. Really, who cares how he lives? By all the available (trumpeted, really) evidence, he lives better than most of us —if a century or so in arrears.

But that Mr. Berry insists on codifying his misoneism into

so-called standards for technical innovation would be laughable if it weren't for the fact that so many New Age ciphers apparently hang on this guy's every word. (Recently confirmed by Random Party Experience. If there is an Anglicized Arabic word for "absence of quantity," there must be one for "absence of quality.") Berry's attitude is that if something is insufficient unto himself it must be, therefore, insufficient unto others—if not all others, then at least those others bovine-balletic enough to dodge while embracing his falling sky. By the credit in *Utne Reader,* his caveat originally appeared in the *Breadloaf Quarterly,* a publication, I believe, of the noted writing colony. "Ah," observed Gore Vidal in a slightly skewed context, "the awakening at Breadloaf."

The Berryatricism fairly ululates, fairly wantonly, for rebuttal. It may have already received such buffeting as it deserves. Certainly, many readers wrote *Harper's* to decry Mr. Berry's rather Leatherstocking, not to say Dickensian, approach to the labors of his own wife, of which *Utne's* excerpt likely delivers a mere taste: "My wife types my work on a Royal standard typewriter bought in 1956 and as good now as it was then. As she types, she sees things that are wrong and marks them with little checks in the margin." (Timid emendations! She should see the margins of my copy. All quotes verbatim from "The computer revolution," reprinted in *Utne Reader* No. 62, March/April 1994, p. 74. Apparently, the lower cases used in the title reflect an adjustment in perspective.) While the feminist issue is obvious, if belaborable, the balance of Berry's argument is as full of holes as a purse seine in a sea lion sanctuary. Following the chain of illogic backwards as Mr. Berry teaches us to do, one is surprised some Uncial scribe hasn't slipped into the cabin while Mr. Berry and his wife were at the farrier getting their felloes riveted, and embalmed the Royal standard in oak gall sqeezings. One good anachronism begets a blizzard of them, taking the sun with them, darkening the New Age.

But while a great deal of artillery has descended upon his domestic arrangement, I've not seen a rebuttal of Berry's nine point list of "standards for technological innovation," which, in *Utne's* excerpted essay, follow immediately upon the heels of this interesting paragraph: "My final and perhaps my best reason for not owning a computer is that I do not wish to fool myself. I disbelieve, and therefore strongly resent, the assertion that I or anybody else could write better or more easily with a computer than with a pencil."

Other than to suggest that, judging by the sheer quantity of Mr. Berry's effusion, it would be hard to believe that anybody could write more easily, and harder to resent that anybody could write better, than Mr. Berry; and other than to riposte his lament with a saw much older than his double-handed one, that it's a poor craftsman who blames his tools before he's even attempted to do anything with them, we postpone spearing the meat out of his menudo until, in due course, it floats to the surface.

Berry's "standards for technological innovation in my own work" (farming, writing, and teaching, presumably), and categorical rebuttals follow.

THE NINE PILLS OF WENDELL BERRY

"1. The new tool should be cheaper than the one it replaces."

It is only as a computer user that I have found this stricture, if such it is, to be true. But as a cabinet maker, I have never found it to be true. Take the hand plane, for instance. I own several, and I use them. But when I have to plane a door, or taper the selvedge on a cabinet carcass, or achieve a certain uniform board thickness? For these and many other occasional uses, I own and inevitably employ an electric hand planer or an electric thickness planer. Their manual cognates—the jack plane, the slick plane, the block plane—stay in their box.

Although it is quite possible to spend twenty to three hundred percent of the price of a Makita 3″ electric hand planer (about $110) on any of a number of the finer hand planes—from Record, Anant, Stanley, etc.—the thickness planer cost me four or five times any hand plane I've ever been interested in owning. In terms of their cost versus labor and time involved, I've got one thing to announce: I'll pay. Such a powerful and practical tool reimburses its owner in its first week or two of use, and that's neither lie nor joke. In terms of productivity, quality of work and conservation of Labor, who the hell is this guy Berry kidding? Does he really work a farm? And if he works it, does he make a living off it?

The satisfaction of producing a well-made yet commercially viable piece of cabinetry or furniture is in no way diminished by the employment of "innovative" tools. Their utility makes them welcome. Such tools and many, many others enable me to make interesting pieces of cabinetry or furniture that I can afford to build and that other people can afford to buy. I might also note that the leaders of a recent revolution in electric hand tools were the Japanese, who, as a culture, have one of the most continuously venerable woodworking traditions in the world.

Why is it a surprise that innovation costs money? The people who get into a particular trend of innovation do so because they think they've found a demand and a way to meet it, they are the sort who don't mind taking a chance, they are dreamers, they are crazy, they are losers, they are desperate or clever, they are hopelessly behind or far ahead of a game played for keeps that forces millions of other people to go to a shitty job every day. Few succeed and many fail. A lot of innovators deserve to get paid and some of them do. But from one end to the other the risk-fraught endeavor of innovation beats the enslavement, man-killing labor, starvation, and totalitarianism that infest the environment from which innovation is excluded. Though I have worked all my life, I personally never saw much advantage to getting dragged behind a mule's ass up and down a field all day. The same went for my father, who grew up on way more of a farm than I did. Of course, as soon as he saw he had a couple of sons around his own place, that is to say, when suddenly there was labor available for nothing or cheap, he began to rethink the idea of minimizing his farm. But if a mule provides Mr. Berry a kick, let him receive it. That he chooses to disseminate his misoneism through the medium of his craft (not that I read him, or smoke his organic tobacco, or study Ned Ludlam under his tutelage at U. Kentucky) is nothing less than offensive, and wants for rebuke as much as it does for common sense.

As for the price of the usurper being less than the price of the usurped, I have a perfectly good KayPro 2x under my desk that I'll gladly give, not to Mr. Berry, but to Mrs. Berry, along with the guarantee that, if she really is a typist and editor, or keeps the books on their farm, or likes to play a diverting game once in a while, even this retro machine will blow her mind. Not only that, it will still permit her husband to give his wife some pencillations to redact around their industrious cottage. And, after a while, we, she and I, will point out to him that, whereas the 17 lb. 8 mhz. 64k KayPro cost $2000 in 1984, for half that amount of money in 1994 he could buy her a machine 1/4 the weight, 1000 times as powerful, and five times as fast.

Oh, yes. Mr. Berry writes that while he is "hooked into the energy corporations, which I do not admire," he hopes "to become less hooked into them." Consider this little chart comparing three computers I've owned:

Year Brand	Price ($k)	Weight (lbs)	Speed (mhz)	RAM (kb)	Power (watts)
1982 KayPro	2.0	17	8	64	65
1986 NEC3	1.5	12	16	640	44
1993 BCC	0.95	4.5	25	4,000	39

Out of all the technological innovations Mr. Berry might have picked on, Computer is the one, and perhaps the only one, that fulfills his own Primary Pill: that the newer tool be cheaper than the one it replaces.

Moreover, note that the KayPro draws 65 watts. How much does that yard light over the hog lot suck, Mr. Berry?

"2. It [the "new tool" aka technological innovation, in case your mind has wandered] should be at least as small in scale as the one it replaces."

Back to the chart, Wendy. Look under Weight. How much does your Royal Standard weigh? How big is it? Computers are orders of magnitude smaller than everything they have come to replace—including themselves, and they show no sign of letting up the pace. They're going to get smaller yet. The only practical limit on the spiral of their downsizing is the bluntness of the human fingers it generally takes to run them. But they'll probably get past that. Soon there will be a computer that can enter your home and keep a multifaceted eye on you 24 hours a day, barely noticed, like a mouse, and then a roach, and then a dust mite. After those machines will come a machine capable of entering your bloodstream undetected, like a spirochete...

Of course, another way to regard Pill No. 2 is to consider that perhaps Mr. Berry wishes things to remain just as small as they are, and no smaller. He probably needs bifocals. And lest some shithead cries ageism, I need them too—along with health insurance.

But while we're on the subject, since when is the typewriter smaller and cheaper then the pencil? Did I miss something here?

"3. It should do work that is clearly and demonstrably better than the one it replaces."

More muddled thinking, to which the quoted paragraph at the head of this list is a murkily expansive corollary and red herring. First of all as any fool knows, a tool does work no better than that dictated through it by the skills of the person wielding it. Charitably, if equivalent, it is conceivable that Mr. Berry is blaming the tool—the computer—for what *others* are doing with it. The inversion of Pill No. 3, retaining the logic and its sense, is to postulate the assertion that Berry or anybody else could write better or more easily with a pencil than with a computer. Nobody ever said and meant, because it probably has been said, that a computer could improve anybody's ability to write. What computers did do was evaporate the bullshit out of the writing process, but, as Mr. Berry's outburst amply illustrates, nothing will ever take the bullshit out of what is written—not even a pencil. It is impossible for me to believe that a man who has manually retyped the third or fourth draft of a novel could ever begin to espouse through his blowhole No. 2 pencils or manual typewriters as superior to other technologies, except to suppose that, as obvious in this case, he has somebody retyping for him. Blissfully conjugated or not, Mrs. Berry should convert that Royal Standard typewriter into an anchor for her husband's Sunday punt (just add the clothesline) and go get herself a computer. If she will call me, I'll drop-ship her the KayPro for free, with software—UPS collect, of course: I should pay postage for her husband's education? But then, she married him, and I didn't. Does he pay her? He would have to pay me. I would pay my own wife to type for me—have done so. (Oh, Jimmy. *Quien es más macho?*) When they finally became illegible, and when I could afford it, I used to pay somebody—anybody—to retype my drafts. When I couldn't afford it, which happens as regularly now as it did in the past, I retyped them myself. In the past it was a pain in the ass. Now, however, it's a vision of efficiency, and it doesn't make any difference whether or not I can afford to pay someone to type a novel, because I always do it myself—on a computer, with no complaints.

For control freaks (anybody listening?), this is an unexpected boon. Unless of course, like the mad novelist in "The Shining," you're into hanging around the kitchen with bugged eyeballs suspiciously snarling at Wife after she's finished reading (or typing) a page, "You like it? Huh?" Or, "Hey. What's this little check supposed to mean? Huh?"

With the Bullshit rendered transparent, the Work, even if you aren't into capitalizing it, remains preeminent. On the other hand, Mr. Berry's a big guy in the biz these days. He could probably send his manuscript to his adoring publishers scratched into hand-adzed boards by the point of a square-headed nail and get away with it. Miracle of birth. No problem, the publisher just puts the load on the forklift he calls "Wendy" and trundles across the tracks into his independent contractor, who is a woman with a maxed out Quadra, a laser printer, a fax/modem, and fifteen different kinds of text- and type-massaging software. He pays her good money to turn Berry's chiseled cuneiform into something PostScript won't get splinters from. Manufacturer's Reps take note: after a few such jobs she'll gladly spring for that Optical Splinter Reader.

And, by the bye, by way of feebly bolstering my own neo-feminist credentials, the local Wife is far too busy with her own writing to be fucking about with her husband's—on her own computer, a hand-me-down NEC V30 portable (see chart). What did you expect? She resisted for five years. She held out so long she skipped the KayPro (sorry, Mrs. B) and got a damned good recycled machine (it was used when I got it; it's still running after eight years) which, I might add, she now won't leave town without and which, I might do column addition, relieves me of the responsibility of retyping her musical scores. (Okay, okay, she never lets me touch them.)

I might also point out that Mr. Berry has resolutely ignored one of the most positive benefits to have come of the computer revolution, to wit, that, by virtue of its superior remunerativity and revolutionary excitement, boatloads of mediocre writers have been sucked into the vast computer establishment out of the resultingly less-bloated ranks of fiction, poetry and drama writers, never to be heard from again—unless you read the computer press, that is. In this respect as in many others, the computer continues to be a thorough-going boon to the arts.

Methinks Mr. Berry resists too much.

Another quote from the article. "I would hate to think that my work as a writer could not be done without a direct dependence on strip-mined coal. How could I write consciously against the rape of nature if I were, in the act of writing, implicated in the rape? For the same reason, it matters to me that my writing is done in the daytime, without electric light."

If I could find him in the heap of split hair I might query Mr. Berry in this context. Does he think that *Utne*, for example, hand-copied his article from its original source, and disseminated it by pony express? Well, the piece is short. They might have retyped it. More likely they scanned it in or downloaded it, stripped it of previous non-printing characters, brought it up on the screen in their own software, redacted it to their purpose, reproofed it with a spell-checker and maybe even a grammar checker (watch out, deathless convention-defying prose!), reset the margins and type with eldritch commands, maybe even coyly reduced the caps in its title to lower-case with a handy little macro and then sent it by modem or sneaker-net over to their printer's warehouse, where he sucked it up into his own software and published the sonofabitch—all without laying an actual smudged finger on the original acts of cerebration.

I might also suggest that Mr. Berry's essay became so popular that his printer may have had to put on the lobster or graveyard shifts, burning the midnight coal, or U-238, though perhaps for just a night or two, to keep up with demand.

Et voilà, Mr. Berry: 50,000 additional readers who deserve better from you than bifocal hypocrisy.

"4. It [the new tool] should use less energy than the one it replaces."

Patently ridiculous. See chart above. Is Berry's wife a Breatharian? Any decent cartoonist for a feminist thrasher magazine would caricature Mr. Berry as hanging ten off his wife's back, as she growls over the keyboard and spews typography from eight straight pipes. As opposed to the twenty-pound hood ornament of Mr. Berry's cottage juggernaut, his 1956 Royal Standard typewriter, and strictly in terms of how a computer's built, the latter uses hardly any metal at all, orders of magnitude less than what's in the four iron shoes of Mr. Berry's plow horse, let alone the infrastructure of his '56 *machina da scrivere*—and much of what the computer does use is precious and therefore eminently recyclable. While its plastic could and should be and in fact is an environmental issue, the computer weighs far less than the Royal, and is orders of magnitude more useful, more powerful, more intrinsically interesting than any typewriter ever built, manual or otherwise. Moreover, in terms of the manual's immediate successor, the electric typewriter (not to mention UNIVAC), the computer uses *orders of magnitude* less electricity.

I might point out, here, by way of feebly bolstering my own neo-Luddite credentials, that I went straight from my last manual, a Royal Century (I still have it, though it's not as good now as it was when it was new), straight to the KayPro, skipping the electric typewriter completely. Electric typewriters are despicable. They hum at you while you're trying to think. (See? I can spit in the dust and snap galuses with the Luddiest.)

France has a reputation for, among other things, more nuke fired power plants than any other country in the world. France also has gotten into computers in a big way, going so far as to have started, years ago, a government-sponsored computer company whose mandate was innovation. One of the many subsequent results, even laundromats in today's France are computerized—though I imagine Mr. Berry to prefer someone pounding his soiled Monkey Brands with rounded stones. As another result, France today is more computer-hip than many places I've been (though I haven't lately visited Lexington). French (and Italian) phone companies, for god's sakes, have offered a personal-assistant type computer called Minitel to every phone-connected citizen for a number of years. Many people have them. The French were ordering TGV tickets and having on-line sex long before Americans were. They may or may not like it, but they seem to think it's normal.

But the point is, last time I was in Paris (not accessible by horse) I heard an intriguing rumour to the effect that, so deeply has France thrust herself into the computer revolution, computers have attenuated the overall French demand for electricity by measurable percentages. France now has a *surplus of electric power* (generated by nukes, of course; I never said it was a perfect world).

So measurable are these percentages that the French government is actively pursuing alternative markets for their excess nuclear power. Perhaps they might be coddled into shutting down one or two of those nukes? Or maybe they could sell juice to Russia, which country in turn could shut down some of its unsafe nukes? (Uh-oh. Look out, Jimmy. You crossing the field of Exploding Cow Pies by night now…You can hear the e-meters pinging as you write this.) Would that be a reasonable trade-off for a little…innovation?

Let us tamp that snort of rabbit tobacco into our smoldering cob, and take a turn around the shithouse.

"5. If possible, it should use some form of solar energy, such as that of the body."

This is like phasering fish in a barrel. (Remember, kids, pressure travels through water undiminished. How many fish stunning blasts from the phaser will it take to stun all the fish in the barrel?)

But, first of all, what does Pill No. 5 mean?

Does Berry see the human body as a dynamic energy source, comparable to that of the sun, and incapable of doing anything but nurture that which it doesn't scorch?

If so will he admit, at least, that the human body has a slightly different half-life than the sun, and that time's awasting?

Will he admit that the sun is a fusion reactor?

Does he mean that, as the ostensible dunce-cap of the food chain, we should at least act post-Eocene, if not think like it?

Second of all, disregarding the Jansenist qualifier, Pill No. 5 seems tantamount to claiming that a man plowing with a mule in Mississippi somehow derives benefit from his ongoing embroilment by a hot sun. I'm a covert booster of hard work myself, but, really, Pill No. 5 will find more of a home in the *Solar Calvinist Quarterly* than it will on the wall of my cabinet shop. Once again one feels compelled to wonder does Wendell Berry really run a farm? Does he make a living of it? (*Pace* his readers, I'm sure these questions are well-answered among the faithful.)

Finally, if solar energy can power anything, it can power a goddamn computer.

You put a typewriter out in the sun, it just sits there.

Me, too.

"6. It [a new tool, or a technological innovation, children] should be repairable by a person of ordinary intelligence, provided that he or she has the necessary tools."

This line was written by a snob, a *poseur*, and a man who blames the fault of his work on the fault of his tools. Besides which, nothing is repairable by a person of ordinary intelligence.

I refer Mr. Berry to his friend Gary Snyder's poem about lying under a Jeep, contemplating its differential.

Furthermore, has Mr. Berry ever had occasion to fix his wife? Using ordinary tools? Ordinary intelligence? Of extraordinary ones?

"7. It should be purchasable and repairable as near to home as possible."

What, does Wendell Berry have something against the teamsters too?

Or, tell this to the man who brought the first piano-forte in the back of a wagon to be heard in, say, Eureka, Nevada.

Though it makes me wonder where Berry's veterinarian lives, this is an interesting point, telling us, as such imprecatory thoughtlessness generally does, more about the man insisting on it than about the culture upon which he would see it enforced. Here's a guy lives on a goddamn farm, presumably so he can have a little elbow room while he's working himself to death: presumably, as an old friend of mine used to put the case for country life, so he can piss off the porch when he feels like it, or get his wife to manually type his manuscripts. This is the guy who wants his blacksmith, the flour mill, the tanner, the woodcutter, the sharpener, the veterinarian, the importer of horse feed, the market where he auctions his tobacco, the post office, the stage offfice, the saloon, the dry-goods store, the pharmacy, the jail, the school, the flea market, the pencil store, the library, the movie arcade, the paper mill, the shoemaker, the guy who makes them "Let's Rodeo" belt buckles along with

harness tackle and knife blades, the local tattoo artist, the piercing par-
lor, the whorehouse, not to mention the university teeming with angst
and hormones, football and choir practice, and all those rapscallion colleagues of Berry's getting paid good taxpayer money to fill kids' heads
with New Age & Semiotic horseshit—this is the guy who lives on a
farm? It sounds to me like Berry ought to move to 18th and Castro,
where he'll be within walking distance of about a third of the above list,
including not one but two of the best little old western-wear stores he'd
ever care to dress out of, where the term "brush popper" takes on entirely new meanings.

Pill No. 7, however, blinds itself to a further point, which is the
potential for a global economy. Buckminister Fuller used to spend a lot
of time preaching about how there were enough assets on this planet for
everybody, even Americans, to share. While America has retained an
edge in software innovation, the manufacture of a single computer has
gone further to truly diversify a global economy than any book, field, or
senior class that Mr. Berry has ever scribbled, plowed or taught. Get
Mrs. Berry to pop the hood on her KayPro, Wendell. Even a cursory
glance will reveal chips and other parts from El Salvador, Mexico, Korea,
China—each an Exploding Cow Pie of exploitation, I know, I know...
Try to look at the up-side potential.

No. 7 smacks of the control-freaky paranoia of a threatened
caliphate.

Moreover, if there is one small business that has cropped up like
globally-seeded dragon's teeth lately, it's little one-person computer-con-
sultant/network installer/repair/printer ribbon & miscellaneous supply
shops. And if it's not them then it's desktop publishing operations. We're
talking about the invention and common availability of a tool that has
single-handedly brought about a paradigm shift characterized by a
decentralization of economy, of assets, of revenues, of information dis-
semination—in short, of power.

"8. It [a new tool, or technological innovation] should come
from a small, privately-owned shop or store that will take it back for
maintenance and repair."

First, see number 7.

Second, here is a hypocrite who either is lying or has never been
stung in a horse trade. Yet, he claims to own horses. So he's lying.

"9. It should not replace or disrupt anything good that already
exists, and this includes family and community relationships."

Aside from observing that the biggest disruption to family and
community usually comes from drunken fathers, I'm at a loss to deal
with this final compaction of rubbish. It's as feeble as it is hopeful. The
only place where I've seen more entire families hanging out together
than computer supermarkets in suburban California is at the

bedsides of people dying from AIDS, and Knott's Berry Farm—no pun intended. (How about we form a consortium to start Berry's Not Farm? There's money in the glazed eyeballs of them thar acolytes.) Am I trying to tell you that computers are a comparable disaster? *Au contraire.* But, is Berry? Possibly. In any case, as goes technological innovation, Wendell Berry doesn't know what he is talking about. He strikes me as one of those guys who likes to brag about how little he understood of math in high school.

Penultimately, one of the truly great things about computers is that you can write on them *in the dark*, communing thereby, at least in spirit, with the Baudelaire, the Poe, the wintry Dostoyevsky, the rain-soaked Kesey, with the whomever anachronistic else you might like to postulate (Homer, if you feel like a goofy stretch, definitely "wrote" in the dark), anachronisms that mean something, with their catarrh-inducing oil lamps; writers whose contribution to our culture is measurable not by access to their public, like some writers we might mention, but in direct proportion to what they got written, and not what they wrote it with.

Finally, I note in its back pages that Mr. Berry's disseminator, *Utne Reader*, has an Internet address, *editor@utnereader.com*, to which I shall humbly upload this protestation, *rightabout@now.*

The more I think about this, the more I think Berry wrote his piece in order to Tom Sawyer the world out of a free computer. Oh, well. Give me a call, Mrs. B.

PROSE ON NISBET

RICK PROSE

I had feared that it was way past time to respond to a piece in No. 52, but as my latest *Corpse* has arrived and it contains even more commentary on Mark Spitzer's screed in No. 50, I see there is no statute of limitations and I may as well let fly re: Jim Nisbet's ill-conceived effusion re: Wendell Berry re: technology.

Nisbet's argument fell apart, for me, in the second paragraph (yes, I'm impatient) of his apologia for word-processed computational hell when he began talking about "...the conspicuous decentralization of the means of production brought on by the tool we know as the personal computer." Conspicuous to whom, Jimbo? What is the percentage of workers now using personal computers to accomplish tasks from which they see a profit? I'd put it at 1%, maybe. Most people using computers use them in offices under the hum of fluorescent lamps and get paid a wage for it. And, since computers enable business to get more work out of fewer employees, the result has been a greater concentration of economic power in the hands of large corporations and fewer people being employed to do other than the most menial tasks. Add to this the fact that computers are manufactured by the same mega-corporations, who reap the profits every time you stroll down to the mall and pick up a new hard drive or software program, and it becomes even more patently ridiculous to assert that there's any "decentralization" going on at all, quite the opposite. If we want to split hairs further, what would the percentage be of people using personal computers who were not able to pursue their chosen fields through other means before the advent of the Mac? For instance, writers. Are there scriveners out there now who were just sitting around waiting for WordPerfect to come along so they wouldn't have to get their hands dirty with graphite or typewriter ribbon ink? Not likely, pal. And, to kick this horse one more time since it's down and its leg is broken anyway, the vast majority of computer innovations in the last forty years have benefited, and in fact been funded by, the military-industrial complex, who ain't gonna let us have the really good stuff anyway. I would point Big Jim toward Jerry Mander's recent book, *In the Absence of the Sacred,* for a full elaboration of this line of thought.

As for the splenetic ad hominem against Mr. Berry, I can only say that even sour grapes taste good to some palates. I don't know Wendell Berry. I have tried to read him and find his prose turgid and his poetry mawkish, but have enough of a sense of him to feel I'd like him if I met him, would probably have a good time sitting on the porch shooting the shit with him, smoking his organic tobacco and sipping homemade spodee-odee from a Mason jar. Wendell Berry isn't the only fella out there who thinks technology is okay as long as it stops somewhere along about the time we get to steam engines and printing presses. Is this "devolutional" thinking, agrarian utopianism, simple nostalgia? Maybe. There's a point to be made for everything we have now being evolutional, since humans made it and time marches on and we must have progress, etc. ... The axe Berry and I and others have to grind (and make no mistakes, I grind mine with a hand-powered wheel I picked up for four bucks and haven't found anything an electric one would grind that mine won't) is the cost of all this goddamned progress—in human dignity, in loss of a sense of community, in basic freedom from coercion by government or economic forces. And the fact that Jimbo feels all these losses, and many others much more subtle, are worth it because he gets to sit around playing solitaire on his PC and is freed from the need to check his OED for spelling mistakes, well, let me just say that I'm reminded of something John Holt wrote a long time ago, the source of which eludes me but the gist of which was—why, when people see that you have thrown off certain chains which still bind *them*, why is their first reaction to ask why you think you're so goddamned good that you don't have to wear them. Why isn't their first reaction to ask how it is that you came to rid yourself of them, and how can they do the same?

Concerning the "New Age ciphers" jab, New Agers are those people who wear crystal underwear and bang on drums and want to be Indians, mostly because they know they never will be Indians. They tend to read *Utne Reader* and the *Sun* and own, all the ones I know anyway, personal computers which tie them into shamanic nets worldwide, and they consume and consume and consume. They do not, again, the ones I know anyway, they do not read Wendell Berry and they do not want to be hardworking ruralists which, unlike Indians, they could be.

I'll only touch lightly on the pity Mr. Nisbet seems to feel for Mrs. Berry who (lovingly, I presume) types up her husband's handwritten work. I think this is the essence of what Berry is trying to get across, to wit, people working together to produce meaningful work is what gives true satisfaction to us poor humans, not being able to crunch words at the rate of 20,000/day and fax them off to NYC so you can run out to Bennigan's in the evening for a mai-tai and a blowjob. If you have actually paid your dear beloved to type your work, Jim, I can only think what a stunted conception of love you two must be laboring under.

Finally (oh, I could go on, I could), let me say in response to Jim's comment that it's a poor craftsman who blames his tools, that it's no craftsman at all who credits his work to his tools. No craftsman at all.

That said, I gotta fly—the mate wants to use the old Smith-Corona and I gotta feed the pig and shut the chicken coop. See you in the breakdown lane, Jimbo, and you Corpsers keep crankin'.

THE SURRE(GION)ALIST MANIFESTO

MAX CAFARD

> *"Here we cast anchor in rich earth."*
>
> —Tristan Tzara,
> Dada Manifesto (1918)

For our Mother the Earth, we set sail on Celestial Ships. Anchored in Erda, we ride the wind. For Gaia, we take flight, spreading terrifying Cafardic wings. No longer trembling at the emasculating, defeminizing sound: the Name of the Father. We re-member Mama. Papa dismembered Mama. We now re-call the suppressed Names of the Mother. Amanuensis for anonymous Inanna. A surre(gion)al celebration, a Manifestival for Mama Earth. This is dedicated to the One we love. For the One Big Mother, in her thousand forms, here it is: the *Mama Manifesto* (1989).

96

PRINCIPIA LOGICA

Breton said "We are still living under the reign of logic." Today this is true more than ever. Indeed, we are now living under the Acid Rain of Logic. The question is: which Logic?

There are Logics and there are Logics. Eco-Logics, Geo-Logics, Psycho-Logics, Mytho-Logics, Ethno-Logics, Socio-Logics, Astro-Logics, Cosmo-Logics, Onto-Logics, Physio-Logics, Bio-Logics, Zoo-Logics, etc.

Yet, all of these are transformed into subsets of the one universal Techno-Logic. Techno-Logic, the death of Truth. Techno-Logic, the enshrinement of Truth. The burying of Truth under a crushing burden—under a Wealth of Knowledge.

Authentic knowing requires the "search for Truth," the pursuit of Truth, the chasing after Truth, the hunger and thirst for Truth, the following of Truth along all her devious paths of Logic, through her labyrinths of the Logics. It means climbing logical mountains, plunging to logical ocean bottoms, traversing an infinitude of unparalleled planes. The search for Truth means always allowing her escape.

SCRAMBLING THE COSMIC EGG

"The Region regions" said Heidegger the Egg-Hider, hiding his eggs. Edelweiss und Eselscheiss! Scion of a Scheiss-ridden race! Shyster Lawyer of Being! The "Region" does not "region." It's exactly the reverse. (For the Time Being).

Where is the Region, anyway? For every Logic there is a Region. To mention those of particular importance to us, the Surre(gion)alists: Ecoregions, Georegions, Psychoregions, Mythoregions, Ethnoregions, Socioregions, and Bioregions.

This is no joke! We are Bioregionalists only if we are Regionalists. And once we begin to think Regions, we discover a vast multiplicity. Of Regionalisms and Regions, of Regions within Regions, and Regionalisms within Regionalisms. Thus, Surre(gion)alism.

Regions are inclusive. They have no borders, no boundaries, no frontiers, no State Lines. Though Regionalists are marginal, Regions have no margins. Regions are traversed by a multitude of lines, folds, ridges, seams, pleats. But all lines are included, none exclude. Regions are bodies. Interpenetrating bodies. Interpenetrating bodies in semi-simultaneous spaces. (Like Strangers in the Night).

Region is origin. It is our place of origin. Where all continues to originate. Origination is perpetual motion. Reinhabitation means reorigination. We return to our roots for nourishment. Without that return, we wither and die. We follow our roots and find them to extend ever deeper, and ever outward. They form an infinite web, 97 so all-encompassing that uprooting becomes impossible and unthinkable, deracination irrational.

Regions are multiple and arbitrary. Techno-regionalism says, in a Techno-Logical rage for definition, that when less than 90% of the species of one area are present in another area, then each is a separate Bioregion. How Techno-Logical! How Scientific! Or so it sounds. For such a definition is entirely self-annihilating, and absurd in its very technicality. This is, of course, its beauty. It is entirely valid, if taken as part of the Science and Logic of the Absurd. An infinite number of Regions can be defined by such criteria. Occasionally the Region will run after a stray organism (calculator in hand). This is a hallucinogenic Logic. (Though seldom taken in this way—even in small doses).

The Region always suffers the danger of capture by Techno-Logic. But Science can also be captured by the Aesthetic. (Thales, the first metaphysician and scientist said "All is Water," and thus became the first humorist, also). And Technics can also be captured by Erotics. (Fourier proposed a "New Amorous Order" in his Phalansteries, based on Technics as Utopian Technique).

OFF CENTER

The Region is the end of Centrism. Centrism is an obsession. Perhaps there's nothing wrong with obsessions, as long as we know that we're obsessed. Take, for example, Mr. Alan Fairweather, whose entire life revolves around his obsession with, study of, and consumption of potatoes. In Mr. Fairweather's words "I suppose you could say I have a potato-centric view of the world" (*Newsweek*, 5/30/88). But centrists are seldom so healthy.

Anthropo-centrism has been our world-champion Centrism. It's come close to K.O.ing the Earth (a T.K.O. a *Technical* Knock Out). But it's long been on the ropes. Astro-Logic knocked Anthropos off Cosmic center. Bio-Logic knocked him off Planetary center. Psycho-Logic even knocked him off Ego center. And Techno-Logic itself melts him into air. We hardly need any post-structuralist Post-Logic to "de-center" the vapor that remains.

But do we need a new Centrism to replace the moribund one? Some suggest "Bio-centrism." This one will surely win if beetles and algae are given the vote. In a Bio-centric world, the undisputed center of "North America" is somewhere in the Atchafalaya Basin. Probably in Grosse Tete (day gone get a beeg had don dare, yeah). A magnificent idea, and absolutely true, but for an entirely different reason. Bio-centrism is the ecological variant of capitalist rationality. Quantity and accumulation are what count. But Biomass instead of Bucks.

Ecocentrism, which is maybe the ultimate Centrism, has

strange, surre(gion)alist implications of its own. On being asked the meaning of the term, a prominent ecocentrist replied that it means that "everything is central." The final truth of Centrism: all is central and thus nothing is central. The ecocentrist definitely has surre(gion)alist potential!

Decentering is inevitable today. But there are many species of decentering. Some are regionalist, others profoundly anti-regionalist. Some creative, others nihilistic and conservative (preserving the civilized path of Progress: annihilation, dissolution, evisceration, evacuation).

Capitalism abolishes Centrism. A European travels to some anti-center of Late Capitalism—perhaps Houston or Los Angeles. Accustomed to town squares, cathedrals, remnants of walls, historical sites, signs indicating the geomythical center (*Centre Ville, Centro Ciudad,* etc.), this voyager asks, "Which way is the Center?" What answer is possible? The hapless explorer is offered a myriad of decentered centers—every mall and shopping *center* in the vast urban sprawl. The Megalopolis is the economistic triumph of decentering. Its reality flows—not like a river, but like Capital. It seeks, monster-like, hydra-like, only to grow, and never to return to its source. To grow and to consume, endlessly.

Regionalist anti-centrism is of a different quality. We proclaim an end to Centrism, but we seek to create and recreate a multitude of centers. Because there is no one Center (the Patriarchal God, the Authoritarian State, the Ineluctable Bottom Line), imaginative centers can proliferate. The human spirit has always found the center of the universe in places of significance. Indeed, any place can be the center. Such centers are centers of spiritual intensity, foci for the convergence of realities: The Altar. The Hearth. The Communal fire. The Town Square. The Sacred Mountain. The Clock at Holmes.

(Only someone really desperate, or, perhaps, in a hurry, would suggest as the center of the universe *la Gare de Perpignan.* Or was there a hidden, anti-subversive *Grand Central Station* in the Dalian mind?)

BEYOND CIVILIZATION

For the Region, there is no State—no State lines. The State is a parasitical growth on the Region, something exterior, hostile, threatening. It has no life of its own, but drains vitality from the living Community. It is the "cold monster" that steals even our words, and claims to speak for us. The State is inherently genocidal: it murders only what it cannot assimilate. What is left after this Pyrrhic and Vampiric act is only a State *apparatus,* the State Machine. (Even the old "political machine" had to die—for not being mechanical enough, and perhaps for being too political, too Regional, for the age of "total administration"). The

State is the March of the God of Power on Earth, its History, the Cunning of Instrumental Reason. Regional politics do not take place in Washington, Moscow and other "seats of power." Regional power does not "sit"; it flows everywhere. Through watersheds and bloodstreams. Through nervous systems and food chains. The regions are everywhere & nowhere. We are all illegals. We are natives and we are restless. We have no country; we live in the country. We are off the Inter-State. The Region is against the Regime—any Regime. Regions are anarchic.

For the Region, there is no Church. There is no uppercase R Religion, because there are as many religions as there are Regions. Heresy is the norm. There is no monopoly on the holy. There is no spiritual capital or spiritual capitol. All Regions are spiritual, and for regionalism all is sacred. Regionalism abolishes Theism and Atheism. Theism: the Idea that there is only one God—the God of Power, and that all must believe in him. Atheism: the equal and opposite absurdity that this same God is the only One truly worthy of disbelief. The thought of civilization has revolved around monotheisms, and replacements for monotheisms. Regionalism erases the line between the sacred and the profane. All busses go to Grace Land. Nothing is beyond the pale. Regions are of the land, of the lands: pagan, *paysan*. The Regions give birth to a multitude of rites and rituals, a sacral of sites and cycles. The spirit of the Region is inspired, enlightened. By *feu follet*, Will 'o the Wisp. By inner lights and outer. The spirit of the Region is the Free Spirit. To be in touch with the Spirits of the Place, the local Gods, is to have Tongues of Fire, to regain the stolen power of speech.

For the Region, there is no Race. Miscegenation is the rule. The Ten Thousand Races were born from the Ten Thousand Places, and they have multiplied to ten thousand times ten thousand. Those of us raised in a racial caste system were taught as children how to treat people of "the opposite race." But now the die is cast; the castes have died. Now we know there are no *opposite* sexes, much less *opposite* races. Nature just passes and repasses. It's all Mardi Gras. Under the mask, a mask. Ethnicity, like ethos, thrives on the play of difference. Enjoy the play! For the ideology of race, the play's a tragedy. All is reduced to dull sameness and demonic otherness. Paranoia has its own excitements, but misses the stimulation of subtle variation, texture, multiplicity, quality. Ethnoregionalism. The topography of culture. The Carnival of culture.

For the Region, there is no Patriarchy. The Region is feminine. And at the same time, androgynous. The One gave birth to the Two, and the Two to the Ten Thousand Things. The Mother is both Mother and Father. For the Region, there are no clear lines: paternity is not established. The family is extended, the tribe all-inclusive. The Region, like the Tao, is vague. Mountains and valleys flow into one another. Streams and rivers flow into one another. The maternal blood flows through the Region. But sometimes the blood boils. It's not nice to rape Mother Nature! The kindly Maiden Aunt Nature of the Audubon Society, the jelly-breasted, nonjudgmental Momma Nature of the New Age, transforms herself into the Badass Goddess, the Angry Warrior Woman Nature, Vagina Dentata, the electrifying Shakti. Just when you think you've had her, Man—she gets you where it hurts.

For the Region, there is no Capital. There is no bottom line. All is recycled. Everything returns to the top, recirculates, and the bottom falls out. Life is uneconomical, inefficient. All economic rationality is ecological irrationality. The nature of nature is to waste, to spend foolishly, to squander. Capital requires scarce resources, but the Region is superabundance and has no resources. Only sources and the return to sources. Regions bankrupt the economic, they rupture, they break the bank, they overflow their banks. Regions are in balance, and need no balance sheets. Capital has already rendered its judgment on the Earth: the rich abundance of Life—the Bio-Logical, Ethno-Logical, and Psycho-Logical Wealth that is the legacy of eons of evolution—is not *cost effective*. For the Earth to live, Capital must die.

ANTI-THESES ON REGIONALISM

Regions are wild. For State and Capital, wilderness means wasteland. They look upon the wild with cruel and rapacious eye. They hunger to rape and plunder the wild. They yearn to subdue, control, exploit—kill all that lives freely. The antithesis of the wild is the domesticated—controlled for the ends of power. The same forces that seek to destroy wild nature, destroy wild mind. (See Gary Snyder's "Good, Wild, Sacred"). Out of the ancient forests and ancient communities, they produce tree farms & suburbia (tree farms, the suburbia of trees; suburbia, the tree farm of humanity).

The Region, like the Tao, is vague. The "obscure object of desire." The object of desire is always obscure. Bunuel's object may be obscure in a special sense, but all objects of desire are vague, ambiguous, obscure. The system of domination attempts to make them more definite, more definable. By identifying objects of domination. By subordinating desire to an authoritarian code. By seeking to capture desire and then to direct it and channel in accordance with the demands of Power. Our challenge: To get beyond our bondage to this Desire Project. To reach the Elysian Fields of the liberated imagination. Where there are (contrary to rumor) no Poles, but only a meeting of the Antipodes.

Regionalists *inhabit* Regions. They are in fact, creatures of habit, unpredictable though their habits may be. They are what they do, and they do it in that familiar, indefinable place: their Region. Regionalists almost *dwell* in Regions, and in fact, once did completely, until *dwelling* became so heavily laden with layers of mystique that their dwellings sank out of sight. (Especially true of swampy regions like the Mesechabe Delta).

Regions are not systems. Systems are dead, mechanistic, and usable. Systems thinking is only the most advanced, and most mystified variety of instrumental rationality. Regions are incomprehensible and priceless. They are not systematic. They are not systemic. They are living and imaginary, and therefore surpass all system. Some Regions have systems, as persons have systems, but they cannot be *reduced* to one or more of those systems.

Regions are not World Class. The Political Insect (apologies to insects) can think of no greater compliment to pay to the community than to call it World Class. It becomes World Class when it is filled with World Class Attractions: when all its living local and regional realities are murdered and replaced by World Class plastic imitations, to attract swarms of World Class Economic Insects who occasionally venture out from their sterile World Class Hotels and Convention Centers and dispense World Class Dollars to the embalmed natives. Regions are not World Class. The Bomb is World Class. McDonald's is World Class. Henry Kissinger is World Class. The Greenhouse Effect is World Class. Auschwitz is World Class. The Capitalist Class is World Class.

Regions follow Geo-Logic, and move in Geo-Logical time. Regions are served on plates. They are flowing, floating islands upon islands. (Follow my Drift?) Occasionally the Earth reminds us that from its point of view, Geology is Destiny. That mountains and valleys are like waves on the sea. The restoration of Geo-Logic relativizes the pseudo-politics and pseudo-economics of all systems of Power. True Eco-Logic and Eco-Nomics cannot be upset by even the most powerful earthquake. But the myth that nature can be dominated lives on. Still the Army Corps of Engineers battles to control the course of the Mesechabe. But in a few years the Great River will have its way—with a vengeance. Still the Power Companies build their Nuclear plants along the River. They forget that a century ago the earth shook violently, the Mesechabe flowed North, and that a small Mesechabean Atlantis lies beneath the waters.

THE WASTE LAND

What hath civilization wrought? Vespucciland has already made the Mighty Mesechabe its sewer (Capitalist Sewer regionalism), it has sent us garbage barges, and now it sends its wastes to the Delta in trains! Postmodern politics becomes auto-critique. Never before has there been a political *cause celebre* like the "poo-poo choo-choo" presently *incensing* Mesechabean citizens. Indeed, the Mesechabeans would like to cast some aspersions on our benefactors (doers of their noble duty), who seek to transform our Mesechabe Delta, the Ravine of the World, into a veritable *Sierra Merdre.*

Outside the Region, all is excrement, all is waste, all is garbage. Capital and State are outside the cycles, outside the self-renewing Whole. Their Logic is accumulation, the Eternal Non-Return, the non-returnable bottleneck of being. They have accumulated much, and, alas, it's all Poo Poo.

Where is Reality? When the corporate polluters spew poison into rivers and streams, direct actionists seal the pipes. The reality police are called out: the poisoners are protected; the protectors imprisoned. "This is not pollution ... This is not a pipe ..." When reality is the Waste Land, we must just say no to Reality. Surre(gion)al surreality is elsewhere.

"IS THERE A PATAPHYSICIAN IN THE HOUSE?"

Regionalists are Pataphysicians. Jarry, the founder of Science of Pataphysics, made an inestimable contribution to regionalist thinking in his invention/discovery of Pataphysics. Pataphysics, he says "will be above all the science of the particular, even though it is said that the only science is that of the general. It will study the laws governing exceptions and will explain the universe supplementary to this one; or, less ambitiously, will describe a universe which can be seen, and which perhaps should be seen, in the place of the traditional one, the laws which it is believed have been discovered in the traditional universe being also correlations of exceptions, albeit more frequent ones, or in any case of accidental phenomena which, since they are at bottom only unexceptional exceptions, do not even possess the attraction of singularity."

Pataphysics helps us recollect the oft-forgotten Truth that the Universe is itself the Great Exception—to the everyday ordinary course of Non-Being. Regions are, of course, entirely exceptional—exceptions even to themselves. Regionalists are exceptional people and should therefore, like Regions, be treated entirely differently.

Heraclitus discovered 2500 years ago that Reality is always what it is not, and always strange. As he put it, "if one does not expect the unexpected, one will not find it out, since it is not to be searched out, and difficult to compass" (Fragment 18). Regions are where the unexpected always takes place. However mightily one struggles not to think some troubling thought, it is impossible to keep it out of consciousness, out of one's Psychoregion. Such as: "The Marquise was out for the Count"; or "He rode off into the sunset on his pet pony, Trotsky."

GREEN POLITICS: MILITANTS VS. MERLITONS

We need a Green Politics that is a Politics of the Regions, and thus, a Politics of the Imagination. The old politics is dead—the politics of the State, of bureaucracy, of economism, of technocracy. It is overwhelmingly powerful, but it is dead. Burying it is another matter. It buries us. Poor old Khrushchev said to the Capitalists: we will bury you. They are burying him and everyone else instead—in garbage. The old politics is a politics of plastic on asphalt. The politics of the inorganic, the politics of disorientation, of placelessness, the politics of necrophilia.

The Wobblies, the most *radical* of American labor movements (the only labor movement to appeal to hobos and surrealists) said it was "creating the new world within the shell of the old." Today, the old one is an even more dried-out shell than ever. But sometimes it seems that what passes for Green Politics follows the slogan: "creating the new world by boring from within." True, the old world must die, but we certainly cannot bore it to death.

Green Politics must become the Politics of the Regions—all the Regions, from the celestial to the subterranean. Let the next Gathering of the Greens conduct all its business in poetry. This will foreshadow the day when America will be Green. Even better, the day when for a small fee we do an international name exchange and America becomes a large frozen island, while *Green Land* extends from sea to shining sea. The day when Green Politics rules. The day when the President pantomimes the Inaugural Address and sings the State of the Union in falsetto. The day when the Supreme Court sits naked in powdered wigs and hands down rulings in Pig Latin. The day when the Congress throws a multiparty and dances all the Laws out of existence.

Our symbol—one of the thousand symbols of our polysymbolica—is the Sacred Merliton. The Chayote. Chayotli. *Sechium edule.* The Merliton (regional pronunication: "Melaton"): in the subtropics, the regionalist plant *par excellence*. Spreading everywhere, covering all, trespassing all boundaries, respecting no lines of property. Greening promiscuously, abundantly, indiscriminately. Equally green on either side of the fence. Offering its fruit to all, in limitless profusion. Green Politics, the Politics of the Merliton. The Merliton against the militant, the mechanical person. The Merliton against the military-industrial complex, the mechanical state. Green vs. Machine.

Green Politics is the Politics of Lagniappe. "Lagniappe" signifies extra, neither bought nor sold, freely given, weighed only on the human scale, a symbolic exchange, a tangible expression of the intangible, the non-instrumental, the non-fungible, of the communal, of the common wealth. A vague memory of the Gift. A token of the backwardness, the peripherality, the atavism of certain strange and remote ethnoregions—like the Meseschabe Delta. Green Politics is the

Politics of Lagniappe: it "decrees the End of Money." It looks to the day when we are no longer held symbolic hostages by the Signs of the Dollar. The day when All is Lagniappe. And to the night also.

THE LESSON OF GUMBO

"It is of the nature of the Louisianian to create Order through Anarchy: This is the lesson of Gumbo; this is the lesson of Jazz."—Lafcadio Bocage, *Cahiers du Mouvement Anarchiste Creole* (trans. M. Cafard): What is true in our mysterious Delta region can, in its own way, be true anywhere. Let us never forget the words of the wise Mesechabean.

GHOSTS ALONG THE MESACHABE

A phantom is haunting Europa. Breton said it well—"The earth, draped in its verdant cloak, makes as little impression upon me as a ghost." Yes, what makes more impression than a ghost—and is so resolutely evaded, except in our dreams? We are like ghosts, Ghosts along the Mesechabe. Haunted by the Earth. When we are nowhere, existence is elsewhere. The Region is the elsewhere of civilization.

QUESTIONS OF ACCENT

I. PERSONAL ACCENTS

I speak no language like a native. Though I have lived in the States since 1959, my accent still sounds foreign. I was born in Turkey, but I am not Turkish. I am Jewish. In the fifties most Jews in Turkey were Sephardim and spoke Ladino Spanish. But I am not a Sephardi; I am a Persian Jew. My parents had moved to Istanbul on business, and I was born there in a Jewish neighborhood. But I learnt no Ladino, barely understood it. Jewish kids in the neighborhood thought I was Moslem, an outsider. At home, my parents spoke Persian with each other, which also I barely understood. Brothers among ourselves spoke Turkish. My mother spoke in an immigrant's broken Turkish to me (my father barely spoke to me at all). Turkish became my mother tongue. I spoke Turkish in the street. I was, linguistically, most comfortable with other Turks, who mostly despised Jews. My speech became almost Turkish. Loving a language not completely my own was my first act as a Jew. And, despite my almost accentless speech, my first act of rebellion was to tell my Turkish friends I was not one of them. I was a Jew.

MURAT NEMET-NEJAT

105

II. EXPLORATIONS TOWARDS A WRITER'S BLOCK

In 1959 I left the hurly-burly of Turkey, its rich vein of bigotry and psychic resonance behind. Though I did not focus on it then, I left my mother tongue behind, which is Turkish, which I am not. In 1961 I decided to become a writer. As an American writer my first act was self-immolation. I had to destroy the Turkishness in me, feel, hopefully one day dream in English. If I had a thought in Turkish, I aborted, nicked it. I chose not to have a thought exist unless originating in English, a language which overwhelmed me because I had said my first words in it only six years before. The result was a writer's block which lasted about ten years during which I wrote three or four poems a year all under ten lines. My first breakthrough occurred with *The Bridge*, a long narrative poem which took me five years to write (1970–1975).

III. THOUGHT, SPEECH AND ACTS

Now, as a thinking adult in English, I speak it with an accent. I speak Turkish also with an accent. Turkish is an unaccented, flat language, with vowels of equal length. The accentual rhythms of English interfere with my Turkish. When I speak, Turks think I am a Cypriot or Armenian, an outsider. I must spend weeks in Turkey, speaking no English, for my accent in Turkish almost to disappear. My business is antique Oriental rugs, which is dominated by Persian Jews. My Persian has improved incredibly. I can speak the daily business lingo, its bargainings, lies, theatrics, jokes (at which I am very good), without effort; but I am illiterate in Persian. Occasionally, one of the merchants, knowing I am also a poet, recites a Sadi or a Hafiz poem, which is completely incomprehensible (and slightly repulsive) to me.

IV. AM-ERICA

I find the first two letters of "America" infinitely stirring. It means "pussy" in Turkish and "I am" in English. It resonates with a tension between motherhood/sex ("Am" is also "mA" in reverse) and identity. As I write down these thoughts, I notice suddenly that "Am" distorts the natural syllable break of the word. It accents "A-merica." Not only do I speak English, but also, mentally, in my mind's eye, hear it with an accent. The true power, even nature, of American English for me is accented, buried in this accent: "Heard melodies are sweet, but those unheard..."

The true power of language, its well of inspiration, for me, lies in its conscious or unconscious errors, cracks, imperfections. I am a poet, an American poet, because I have a defective ear. And, first lesson: this defect is the source of my possible talents and their limitations. But why not a poet in French or Turkish or Persian, all languages I knew before English?

V. JEWISHNESS AND ACCENT

Last year I attended a workshop on being a Jewish writer, run by Joel Lewis. In his meticulous way, Joel presented the participants with a range of alternatives, poems containing chicken soup and Matzo balls (gemutlich), tailors and the Shtetl (Isaac Bashevis Singer and "Fiddler on the Roof"), Lewis Warsh's wonderful poem about the movement from the Lower East Side to the Grand Concourse in the Bronx, pre-war European poems in translation about the conflict between the Yiddish and goyish cultures, and translations of haunting Holocaust poems by Primo Levi. I am not an Ashkenazi Jew. Though I share the underlying paranoia of the outsider of every Jew, Turkey was never invaded by the Nazis. I never ate matzo balls at home. In strictly European or main-stream American terms defined by the workshop, there is little Jewish in my writing. Am I not Jewish then? A nonsensical question since I am Jewish. In that workshop once again I felt, as I felt among Jewish kids in Istanbul, an outsider who spoke not the same language.

Then, how am I a Jewish writer, how is writing poetry in American English my version of Jewish writing?

VI. A JEW WITHOUT ACCENT

The seed of an answer occurred in a confrontation over Jabès, whom the workshop presented, at least to the American eyes, as the king of Jewish literary artists, the creator of a "book in exile." I began to understand what is Jewish about me by analyzing what is false, phony about Jabès, how seeing Jabès as the ideal European Jew implies a negation of me, and other non-Western-Europeans like me, as Jewish writers. Jabès and I have similar backgrounds with radically different choices to our Jewishness. Therefore, I must progress with a short critique of Jabès.

Jabès exists in the United States essentially because Derrida "discovered" him: Derrida discovered, "authorized" Jabès; therefore, he exists. Jabès did not have an independent prior recognition. It is absolutely essential to see that Jabès would not have existed in the States without the authorization of Derrida. Therefore, a critique of Jabès is in fact a critique of Derrida, and, consequently, a critique of the mainstream American intellectual's concentration on Europe. Why did Derrida discover Jabès? Was it a lucky incident that every artist in his or her garret dreams of? Not at all. By "discovering" Jabès Derrida was legitimizing himself. They both have North African backgrounds, are both North African Jews, a fact with inescapable linguistic ramifications.

Derrida spoke French among Arabs, that is to say, the language of the colonialist. When he moved to mainland France, he chose, linguistically and in terms of his career, the side of power. He became one of the "flowerings" of French prose.

Growing up in Egypt, Jabès also spoke French. Jabès's French, as an Egyptian Jew, is the language of the privileged class in Egypt, the privileged island of power, surrounded by the Arabic "sand." Jabès's French is like Tolstoy's *War and Peace* and *Anna Karenina*, where the main characters are aristocrats and supposed to speak French among themselves, not Russian. That's why whole sections of these novels, written in Russian, read like silent translations.

Jabès also, like Derrida, moved to France. His theme of "linguistic exile" is not, essentially, the Jewish or mystical theme of the diaspora or distance from God (Hashem); but his distance, exile from the less privileged people he was surrounded by and left behind, and their language, Arabic. Arabic, at least psychically his true home (if he played with other kids in the neighborhood), has no influence on Jabès's French. His French has no accent. If it did, it might not be accepted because purity is a French ideal closely linked to a central tradition and resists accents. Egypt appears only as a decorative metaphor (with a touch of the intellectual-exotic: sand, desert, oasis, etc., "arabisme," acceptable to post-Napoleonic French taste) in his work. As I see it, Jabès has to experience his own "writing" as a discontinuous series of immediate experiences, without memory, memory as negative space (a key aesthetic point for him, for Derrida and for American poets influenced by both) because, underlying it, there is a chaotic political choice: a Jew choosing the side and the language of privilege instead of the underdog. Jabès's Judaism is false (assimilated) because its real home, "Hashem," is Arabic which he emasculates by prettifying it. Judaism is a fashionable gimmick to hide his severance from his past, his memory of political choice, his experiences of childhood.

When Derrida "discovers" Jabès, he ignores this most crucial linguistic (therefore power) choice they both make. In a perceptive talk he gave at the Poetry Project in 1992, David Shapiro said that under his "revolutionary" demeanor, Derrida is essentially an academician, achieving a new flowering of exquisite French prose. I had a personal experience of that when, about a year ago, I attended a Derrida lecture at the 42nd Street Graduate Center. His ninety minute speech expounded, ethereally, subtly, how a "gift is not a gift" if acknowledged as such, the mere consciousness, "material utterance" of the act disqualifying it from being such. I also learnt that Derrida was charging $20,000.00 for his week visit to the United States. Derrida "discovers" Jabès because Jabès also is, in his ethereal, filigree prose, potentially, a similar kind of star, who has made a similar fateful choice.

Derrida's "discovery" is in fact an act of self-justification.

The Americans essentially accept Derrida's version of Jabès, which is uncritical and distorted, a version which, subliminally, reinforces Derrida's views, including his flaws and limitations as a writer, as "natural," "universal" truths. To stress Jabès's Jewishness (which to me, without an Arabic imprint, is a fashionable "flavor") above everything else about him is very deceptive (and American writers should resist it) because it short circuits, passes by (as Derrida intended) the political dimension of his choice as a writer. Jabès's Jewish mystical theme, I believe, is a mask covering a political theme, his choice to leave the third world of Egypt and Arabic behind. Seen from this angle, Jabès's "Jewishness" has a strong "Western," colonialist dimension, as Paul de Mans's pure, "non-political" deconstructionism, the American intellectuals such as Harold Bloom have discovered to their horror, has Nazi roots.

From the same angle, isn't the central act of Albert Camus' *The Stranger,* the proto North African French work, a racial murder, an Arab murdered by a white man, a stranger to the Arab, on the beach; and the protagonist's act obfuscated, erased, treated as a foil, the responsibility for it done away with, intellectually justified in the misty mystifications of Existentialism, in *The Stranger*'s amoral "style"? The protagonist, the stranger to the Arab, is "rationalized" into the stranger to himself. Camus's Existential lobotomized style and Jabès's sophisticated Arabisme: parallel acts of political, moral obfuscations set a generation apart. Must a North African Jew always do the dirty work of the white man just to be accepted inside France's glorious halls?

VII. A JEW WITH ACCENT: AMBIGUITY TOWARDS POWER, THE FATE OF THE UN-ASSIMILATED JEW

Ambiguity towards power is, in my opinion, the contemporary Jewish theme, what every Jewish writer, consciously or not, willingly or not, must face. This ambiguity is embedded in Jewish history, in Jewish identity, in the conflict between its myths and history. Despite its protestations, the Torah is history written by the powerful, a nation chosen by God, taking somebody else's land to make its own. On the other hand, the history of the diaspora is the history of the victim, the dispossessed, the Galut, the pogroms, the Holocaust. Where does the Jew's allegiance belong? Does the contemporary Jew ally himself with the powerful or the victim? Though this conflict has become explicit after the birth of Israel, it was implicit, as Jews embraced assimilation and moved physically out of the Ghetto, in the Diaspora also. Often, economically, Jews belonged to the privileged class; but culturally, and linguistically, they were the outsiders, the underprivileged. As Jews, Derrida and Jabès erase, ignore, escape this ambiguity. Their choices are absolute, on the side of

109

power. Jabès's and Derrida's writings are accentless, unambiguously French. They represent a Jewish style of assimilation, identification with power. They hide, and their American admirers overlook, the political dimension of their writings.

VIII. WHAT IS THEN ACCENTED WRITING?

What is, then, writing which has an accent? It is a writing which does not completely identify with the power, authority of the language it uses; but confronts, without glossing over, the gap between the user and the language. Such writing reveals an ambiguity towards power: the writer chooses to embrace a language (because of its pervasive centrality) which he/she knows is not quite his/her own, is insufficient for his/her inner purposes. Accent in writing has little to do with explicit theme or semantic context; it rather has to do with texture, structure, the scratches, distortions, painful gaps (in rhythms, syntax, diction, etc.) caused by the alien relationship between the writer and his/her adopted language. Accent is cracks (many unconscious, the way a speaker is unaware of his or her accent when speaking, *does not have to create it*) on the transparent surface.

Accented Jewish writing embodies, rather than erases, this ambiguity towards power. By doing that it creates its accent. Kafka, to me, is the first modern, European writer who reveals the Jew's ambiguity towards power in terms of an accent in the texture of his language. His language of choice as a writer is not Yiddish or Czech but legal German (that of an intricate legal brief), a double embrace of power: first of the cultural mainstream, second, that section of it which codifies its power. But Kafka's accent subverts that legal code, divests it of its meaning, turns the language of the powerful into a language of the victim, of alienation. To me, Kafka's subject is a stylistic dialogue about the ambiguity of power, between the powerful and the victim, a sadomasochistic elaboration of the *Book of Job*, the chosen man of God also chosen as a victim. Interestingly, Kafka's fiction (as opposed to his diaries) has very few direct references to Jews, almost no semantic, but only stylistic, Jewish content.

IX. THE ESSENCE OF AMERICAN SOUND, CAN IT BE THE MUSIC OF DIASPORA?

Why did Kafka write *Amerika*, why was he attracted to the subject of the United States? German also accents Am-erika. What did he hear in the word Oklahoma? A wild, alien, distant sound in German, Oklahoma! At the same time, an intimate sound, one of the rare words in English with vowel harmony, which is also, I imagine, in Czech. Kafka hears in

Oklahoma the alien ground in which his private soul can nest itself, the synthesis between the powerful and the victim. That is why he associates his open-ended, endless nirvana of liberation in the Theater (Noah's Ark) of Oklahoma. What is the word Oklahoma after all, but the imprint of the Native American, the victim, the invaded in the language of the master. American English: the language which embodies that peculiar combination, victim and victor possessing the same language, yoked together by fate.

Using American English as a poet is the outsider, the victim, embracing, emulating the language of the master, being constantly beset by the ambiguities of power.

X. AMERICAN POETRY, THE POETICS OF ACCENTS

What makes this poetry different from others, from French, from English? Here lies its radical ambiguity: American English, as a poetic language, is not a mother tongue in the usual sense but a pseudo-mother, step-mother tongue. It can have no tradition, its vocabulary no public or mythical, only personal, private resonances. It is the language of pervasive power, without resonance, of authority in which the immigrant, the victim must speak. Writing poetry in American English is a continuous act of translating from a radical inside or from a radical beyond. Its well of inspiration is always outside, never in the mining or contributing to the flowerings of a tradition. The reading and the writing of American poetry must always be discontinuous. Accepting a central, authoritative tradition undercuts its balance of power and victimhood.

Even to the powerful, American English is unstable, its power ambiguous. When the Puritan, for example, spoke English, the Puritan saw himself/herself threatened by the geographic and moral wilderness around, which even destabilized the inner certitudes. His/her language is defensive, doubting its ability to embrace, cope with the darkness beyond the ring of light, the ring of reason.

That alienation, instability between writer and language, a radical skepticism about its ability to reveal inner truth constitute its essential nature. The relation of the poet to the language is inescapably confrontational. American English is the quintessential unnatural, insufficient, weak language which the writer has to bend, distort, to translate into, to interject his or her vision. To me, three nineteenth century writers, none of them Jewish but white protestant, embody this accented writing: Hawthorne, Melville and Dickinson. Hawthorne's Puritan English prose is tortured, twisted to assimilate both the wilderness beyond on the continent and the wilderness within. (Read the first pages of *House of the Seven Gables*; it is Henry James at his purest. All of Henry James and more is in it.) Melville's compulsive, encyclopedic lists of whaling

111

lore crack up, can not contain the nihilism at the core and must spill into splintered moments of black vision which masquerade as narrative. Dickinson invents a language which only pretends to be English and must be read over and over again to be stripped into its message, a violent sadomasochism. Words are private emblems, the syntax unstable, constantly shifting, not quite an "English" syntax, the smooth "hymnal" surface hiding, shafted with a sadomasochistic violence. All these works are written by writers, though white Christians, for whom the given language is not really their own, not really their "natural," mother tongue.

Contemporary Jewish writing, embodying the ambiguous relationship to power, is therefore a specific example of American writing. Emily Dickinson, the Protestant spinster completely at home at Amherst but completely out of it, is to me the American poet, the Jew, the sister/neighbor in exile, whose enigmatic, excessive, possessive, distant, recalcitrant company I can take only a few poems at a time.

XI. TO BE A POET OR READER OF UNCANONIZABLE POETICS

American poetics is asocial, therefore, uncanonizable. I am not talking about changing the canon, therefore creating a new structure of power; discontinuous means uncanonizable. I must apply the principle of quantum mechanics here. The moment a style or a poet is canonized, therefore gaining a privileged mainstream position, the language written in that style loses the tension between power and victimhood and stops being American. Writing poetry in American English is not a trade or guild activity to be taught at special schools or communities (while making movies or TV shows is), but an act of personal survival.

Reading American poets is essentially following a series of distinct, discontinuous personal strategies in language. Tradition in the European sense is an illusion in American poetry. Even the "newest" French or English writer writes with a hope of one day becoming a "classic." Thinking of the future, or even in the traditional sense of the past, thinking of a continuity, are ruinous for an American poet or critic. Therefore, Jabès and Derrida, masters of academic style, tools to create a new canon, have no relevance to an American poet unless as abject objects to be attacked.

Harold Bloom's paradigm of anxiety of influence, the poet struggling with his linguistic father-predecessor, is wrong. With the possible exception of Allen Ginsberg and Whitman, I know no American poet who has created truly original work as a "flowering" of a previous poet. In a radical sense, Dickinson, Hawthorne, Melville, Stein, Reznikoff, Zukofsky, Creeley, Ashbery have no American beginnings or ends. The contemporary attempt to create a new canon around, for example, the figures of Mary Rowlandson, Jonathan Edwards, Dickinson and

Stein is to misunderstand their work. The accents (in Susan Howe's word, "hesitations") in Dickinson's, or any other poet's writing, are unreproduceable, completely idiosyncratic. To think that Stein's repetitions or Ashbery's mellifluously expansive meditations are linguistic tools bequeathed to later poets in terms of a "flowering poetic tradition" is wrong-headed. In American poets these are outside trappings of idiosyncratic, personal solutions, accents, that can be completely ignored by and are only marginally useful to another poet. What unifies the poets is their unchanging, confrontational, aggressive relationship to their language. None of them is writing in his or her mother tongue and must therefore distort, accent it to make it his/her own.

XI. ACCENTED RELATIONSHIPS AMONG POETS: IS THERE NO INFLUENCE THEN?

Creeley calls Zukofsky "the teacher of all of us," but Creeley does not imitate or expand on Zukofsky's poetic style. He undercuts it by creating hesitations, weaknesses (accents) in its architecture. Creeley mishears Zukofsky's reading of his own poems by "hearing" stops at his line breaks. To do that to a Zukofsky poem (to a lyric like "Songs of Degrees"), in essence, is to demolish (to add excessive stops to) its sound architecture. But vocal hesitations at line ends (independent of syntax) is the core of Creeley's poetic sound, the power of its vulnerable intimacy. In essence, Creeley's relation to Zukofsky is confrontational, accented. What he learns from Zukofsky is, I think, to turn the language he is born to, English, into an alien, slightly abstract structure of sound he can crack, poke into. What he learns from Zukofsky, is American English.

Zukofsky, a foreigner, teaches Creeley, the Puritan, English as a foreign language, a structure of power Creeley does not completely own. At his most original Creeley subverts Zukofsky's powerful architecture of sound to interject his weaknesses, hesitations. For Creeley Zukofsky is the alien, the outside which softens the smug nastiness, the male chauvinism of the early poems in *For Love*. It brings them ambiguity, restraint, by turning their power driven misogyny inward, into a language of vulnerability and pathos.

XII. THE MUSIC OF THE VICTIM IS THE LANGUAGE OF THE UNNAMED

In American poetry the father (tradition) and the mother tongue (the language of intimate and evocative words) are split. This confrontation makes the American poem an attack into the unsayable (socially and spiritually). To evoke what is unnamed is, always, to evoke what is not in the physical body of the language, in its material music. The

113

language of weakness, of the unnamed, must have a Puritanical bias, "Thou shalt not worship graven words." The poet's instinctive love for words, their physicality, is suspect, must be restrained.

The music of words (of their plasticity) is tradition. The music between words is the language of the outside, the unnamable. That's why Zukofsky, whom Creeley calls the poet with the perfect ear, can be, maybe must be, tone deaf. That's why Dickinson, the supreme American poet, has so few quotable, physically luscious lines. The American poem is anti-musical, can not preen its physical achievement like a peacock. Once again, Whitman sticks out against my theories like a sore thumb.

The American poem (and poet) is always trapped in the space between words, in the crack between his/her vision and the language he/she is using, in the discontinuity (as opposed to cultural unity) between the self and his/her language. His/her soul belongs to somewhere else. That is why if he/she is influenced by another poet, that poet is almost always from another language, French, Indian, Turkish, German, Spanish, Japanese, etc. Or, more often, the mother lode of influence is another medium, cubism or abstractionism in painting, Jazz, photography, movies, TV, etc. American poems are continuous acts of translations from another language or medium or both. In this process, the languages of origin (Chinese, French, Vietnamese, Turkish, Romanian, Russian, Spanish, etc.) or aesthetic philosophies are not hierarchical, canonical, but coexist on the same level. No language is superior over another language. Surrealism is no more relevant than Sufism, deconstructionism or anthropology than Zen, glyphs than photographs, the poets Yunus Emre, Zbigniew Herbert, Xavier Villaurrutia than Arthur Rimbaud.

As I said, American English is neutral with no personal, cultural associations. Nowhere is this more clear than in Emily Dickinson. What do sun, father, Hunter, He, God, etc. (all images of authority) mean in her work? Nothing. They are essentially blank emblems, a chain of *Moby Dick*s, completely stripped of their traditional associations, around which the poet weaves her barely decipherable soul. Under the deceptive music of a hymn, of a little embroidering lady, the blankness of these crucial images liberates/unhinges the syntax in the poems, completely privatizes it. What is *Moby Dick* after all? An attack on whiteness, an asocial, self-destructive pursuit of the unnameable, which all the lists, all the encyclopedias, all the charts, all the lore of the country can not name. "Call me Ishmael, the poet, who (I) must a tale unfold/ Whose lightest word...I am thy father...Seems, madam? No it's. I have that within which passeth show ... Others trappings and suits of woe ..."

The unnameable, ineffable, the radically inner implicate, require, fate a confrontation with the father tongue. The music is in the ensuing unhinging.

XIII. A WRITING BLOCK REVISITED

During the ten years before *The Bridge*, my first long poem, I was learning American English. I was not, as I thought, uprooting what is Turkish in me; but I was learning the potent, cool neutrality of the American language into which I can pour my Turkish soul. My mother tongue is Turkish, but I can not write in Turkish. Against its heat my heart feels like a vulnerable moth. I first chose to be a Jew (and not to be assimilated) as a rebellion, an act of self-empowerment against my mother tongue. I came to the United States as a Jew. The ten years I thought I was erasing the Turkish in me (my writing block), I was actually building the language, the tool, American English, which will empower me to receive, reintegrate my Turkish soul. As a poet, American English took the place of my Jewishness. In fact, American English and Jewishness to me are one.

I embraced American English as an act of empowerment. But as an American poet I saw I have no power. Not only that, but I saw, at the end of my writer's block, that I have no subject but what is Turkish in me. Like every American poet I saw my inspiration come from outside. And that inspiration is my state of vulnerability, my mother tongue. Here, at this focus of my step-language, I encountered the mixture of power and weakness, empowerment and marginality, privilege and victimhood, white heat and coolness. To fight the white heat of mother tongue, I must accept the isolation, victimhood of American poet. I save my woman's heart in the heartless, remote neutrality of American English; my heart prevails in the tell tale signs I impose on American English. The imperfect match creates cracks, breaks. These imperfections, insufficiencies, errors are also the focus of absolute power, intensity, the center of the experience of an American poem where empowerment and victimhood are unified.

Turkishness, Jewishness and American poetry, the unholy knot of my poetic identity, coactive, where each side pulls against and sustains each other, like the undulations of a high wire act, of a somersault. How can one think of identification with, influence by your predecessor. Embrace, emulate, pay heed to another poet, and the whole act collapses. The energy of an American poem is centrifugal, outer looking, partly an tense escape. Each poet is a discontinuous Lautrec high wire act. Think of a tradition, the whole act collapses.

Like Jabès and Derrida I am a Jew born in the third world. My difference from them is that, as writers, they chose to be assimilated Jews, chose to be assimilated into a powerful center, identifying with the power of French cultural center. I chose to remain a Jew. After ten years in the desert of a writer's block, I learnt to accept the Arab in me, my discarded slave mother, Hagar, the Turk, the bastard Jew, speaking in American English.

The solipsism of American poetry changes not only

the concept of tradition, but the concept of influence. The relation of the poet to other poets is opportunistic, a series of avoidances, redirections caused by collisions; but strong poets, like a running back, weave their circuitous routes against obstacles to reach the end line. The concept of influence as identification with a tradition is unthinkable. The tension of an original American poem is always centrifugal. While the used language creates one center of gravity, the poet's inner gravity pulls away from that, is somewhere else. As an outsider, like a magpie, my relationship to others are opportunistic and arbitrary, unclassified, free of tradition. My influences are like a series of reactions to a minefield, weaving against obstacles, surviving a collision against a superior force if I must. Here is the circuitous route of my collisions which determine the shape of my growth as a poet: Shakespeare's *Sonnets*, the Turkish poet Orhan Veli, Tolstoy, the Turkish poet Cemal Sureya, Andrew Marvell, Thomas Browne, Swift's *A Tale of the Tub*, Turkish folk poetry, Kleist's *Marquis of O...*, Japanese poetry, the Scottish philosopher Hume, the Turkish Sufi poet Pir Sultan Abdal, "Ode on a Grecian Urn," TV, American movies, *Dim Sum, Chan Is Missing, Raising Arizona, Blade Runner*, the Chinese movie *House of the Red Lanterns*, the Japanese director Atami's *The Funeral*, amateur photography, the philosopher Francis Bacon, Wittgenstein, logical positivism, Roland Barthes, Ezra Pound's "The Seafarer," Asimov's *Foundation Trilogy*, Seferis, Cafavy, the Turkish poet Orhan Arif, etc.

XIV. WHY AMERICAN ENGLISH IS DIFFERENT FROM OTHER LANGUAGES AND HAS NO OVERTONES?

Because it is an oval. Language is not the producer of myth in the United States; movies, TV, popular music are. Words play a subservient position in American culture, in movies, in TV, in music. In their legendary abuse of script writers movie moguls instinctively knew that. Is there a twentieth century American poem as resonant as the face of Humphrey Bogart, the breathless blondness of Marilyn Monroe, the fight over a plate of steak between John Wayne, James Stewart and Lee Marvin in *Who Shot Liberty Valance* or, politically, as potent as Murphy Brown giving birth to an illegitimate child on TV?

TV's influence is the most profound. It has altered contemporary epistemology, what is truth and how it is to be perceived. It abolishes the distinction between inner and outer (the foundation of American poetry), private and public, true and false. The underlying assumption of TV is that there is no difference between home (the living room) and the inside of the box (the world at large the box contains), between the front and the back of the lens, this fusion affecting the concepts of sincerity and truthfulness and truth. TV style reflects this radical change of epistemology; therefore, TV style is the reverse of American poetic style, which is based on the radical difference between the inner and outer. The new reality reflected in the TV style may have enormous ramifications for American poetry; but these are questions for another paper. Let me just make a few preliminary remarks.

The purpose of TV style is to diminish the resistance between the inside and the outside of the box, to make the screen transparent, as if porous. (The movie *Poltergeist* deals with this phenomenon.) Minimalism is at the bottom of this style. TV language is minimalist. How few memorable phrases can be attributed to those considered masters of TV, Reagan, maybe Clinton, both Teflon figures. Verbal contradictions do not diminish them. Reagan can misquote facts ad infinitum. Clinton can make mutually exclusive proposals. What unifies them is not their facts, their fire, but the image of their "affability," a minimalist value if ever there was one, their image that they are one of the people (outside and inside the box are the same). But affability is an essential value of unity when American reality is a wrenching multiplicity of interests. The two great American myths are immigration, "nation of immigrants," and unity, "the United States." TV is what sustains them both, balances this oxymoron; it creates the visual and stylistic trick that holds the nation together. Transforming, fusing it into the myth of "belonging," creating an aura of belonging, TV turns alienation into a state of power, empowerment.

The true language of America is not American English, but TV. TV is the gravitational center of culture. If an American poet wants to embrace a tradition, he/she should not embrace an American English poetic style, but the style of TV. An American poem can be a confrontation between the minimalism of a TV style (which itself has numberless variations, genres, structures, etc., and is therefore infinitely suggestive) and the idiosyncratic perversities of an inner vision. Its power may lie in the cracks, fault lines this confrontation causes. These distortions on the minimalist surface are its accent. For instance, my poem "Heartbreak Weekend in Atlantic City" is a series of discrete, transparent scenes; but the scenes follow each other in perverse, askew, disjointed, arbitrary ways. The accent is in the sequence they create. It belies, undercuts, interiorizes the solidity of the poetic/the TV surface. The true influences on this poem were a horrifying visit to Atlantic City, which the poem records, and the compulsive, arbitrary changing of channels by remote in front of TV, that is, a confrontation between personal experience and the cool, pseudo-neutral image, which is the true American language.

Though TV style is the very antithesis of American poetic style, they are also eerily similar. In both one encounters the co-existence, balance of alienation, victimhood and power, empowerment, belonging. In both there is a tendency towards austerity of means for

117

maximum effect. This basic oneness makes TV and its stylistic aura such a potent inspiration for poetry, TV a genuine poetic anti-tradition. TV language (like American English) is oval because it is an oxymoron, half true and half false. It is not a perfect match. It requires, like a football ball, an excessive embrace, a compulsive, defensive act to be owned. TV is the true language of the United States, its white screen our Moby Dick, and the poet's function is to explode, to embrace and be consumed by it. What is "Heartbreak Weekend at Atlantic City" after all but to see within the hard, glitzy surface of Atlantic City image (posters, architecture, etc.) a radical interiority, intimations of compulsive infantilism ("Atlantic City Restaurants," "The Architecture of Atlantic City," etc.)

The fate of the outsider, poet, Jew, woman, etc., with no daily used mother tongue, is infantilism. It is weakness. The true power of words, in American language, on the other hand, is anti-mythical. They are, an American poem is, private, individual tools to assert one's existence, identity by projecting onto, cracking the myth, surface of affability. It is in this destructive function that words (or poems) become empowered. That is why, American poetry must be discontinuous. Unity in multiplicity (TV's affability) is the only American myth. The attempt of certain poets to create myths (Charles Olson, for example) falls flat because the American words are too private, solipsistic. The moment the language gains mythic resonance, it becomes preempted by the omnipresence of TV. The figure of Blake or Rimbaud or anybody else, Stein or Dickinson, as a myth creator is very seductive; but I think irrelevant.

XV. THE SOCIAL POSITION OF AN AMERICAN POET, OF AN AMERICAN POEM

The hardest and most important lesson for an American poet to learn and accept, and exploit, is the subservient position of words in American culture. To choose to be a poet is by definition to be a victim, an outsider. To choose American English is to choose an infinitely suggestive medium of self-definition, not of myth-making or public, institutional recognition. There can not be a canon, tradition, however rearranged, to which an American poet may belong. After essentially obligatory lip-service in high schools and colleges, poetic experience (both the writing and reading of it) involves the cracking up, exploration by one poet or reader (alienated by his/her addiction to words) of the language of another poet. That relation between text and reader can not be the casual, institutional relationship that exists between movies, TV and their audiences. When a poet says, "I want to put demands on my reader," he/she is acknowledging, being or without being aware, this peculiar gap. He/she is actually asking for more than the innocent tone of the demand implies. He/she is asking another psyche to leave its skin (not an easy or particularly enjoyable experience) and jump into the blankness of another's language, to glean private resonances of a complete other in its constructions. This is its whiteness.

The American poet must be interested in everything except a national poetic canon bequeathed to him or her. What gives life to an American poem/poet is a continuous infusion of otherness: other arts, other media, poets of other languages. For instance, Dickinson loves the bees and flowers in her garden, the Amherst landscape. Reznikoff is obsessed by the miseries of 19th century industrial America. Tony Towle loves music. Stein's closest friends were artists. I am obsessed by Turkey and the Sufism in Turkish love poetry. But none of us, I think, became poets, instead of novelists, painters, horticulturists, etc., because of these concerns. These infusions create the illusive tissue of reality, order, transparent surface, into which the poet may puncture his/her inner demons, which must remain unnameable. For instance, Dickinson's true home is not the Amherst landscape, but the intimations among the cracks in her distorted syntax, the sex and violence lurking among the bees and flowers in her garden. The inner demons of each poet may be different, but the demon which unites us all is the excessive, non-social attachment to words, which by itself makes the poet an outsider, a victim. Each poetic achievement is a struggle, by means of words, to achieve primacy, power, a self-contradictory act like squaring the circle. An American poet is one addicted to words and who is fated, because he/she wants to, to say the unnameable. It is a continuous attack on white, white whale, white screen, white language, a sign of weakness and alienation. The entire energy, power of his/her work derives from his or her rebellion against, refusal, as a user of language, to accept this social inferiority of language (and the unnamability of his/her inner existence) and his/her compulsive cumulation of facts, minutiae of smoke screen to counter it.

POP OR NOT

I eagerly followed the brilliant exposition of Murat Nemet-Nejat's argument on the discontinuity of tradition in American poetry ("Questions of Accent" EC #43). Like him, I see our myths in the offerings of pop culture, and identify with their style and tone and language. For lack of a decent education, pop culture is all we have, though it is richer than pop artists present it. Where I part company with Mr. Nemet-Nejat is when he proposes poetry as merely a reflection of or homage to pop culture, if I follow him correctly. Can't we reclaim it and transform it into the genuine? As an old fashioned lefty, I see the purpose of poetry right now as opposing the plastic myth and offering a genuine alternative. Even if it's too late.

EDWARD FIELD

119

CLAYTON ESHLEMAN

JABÈS UPHELD

Re "Questions of Accent" in *EC* #43: in his dismissal of Jabès's poetry, which is the fulcrum for what follows, Nemet-Nejat sounds more like the product of a theory department than a Jewish poet. While Derrida's single, short essay, published in 1967, boosted Jabès's French status, this essay did not "discover" or "authorize" him. If any single critical article put Jabès on an international map, it would be Maurice Blanchot's longer and much more definitive essay that I believe appeared in the early 1960s. NN is either woefully unaware of Jabès's life and contacts, or if not perhaps he is driven by an unconscious need to fell a father at the base of his self-proclamation.

In brief: Jabès was in close touch with such writers as Gide, Michaux, Soupault, and above all Max Jacob, in the 1930s/40s, while still living in Cairo, and over the years it was these writers, followed by several younger generations, who helped him publish, and brought his work to public attention. In the USA, this activity was considerably furthered by Rosmarie Waldrop's monumental translation commitment to Jabès's 7 volume *The Book of Questions*. NN's commentary on Jabès is peppered with distortions. From what I can tell, Jabès's relation to the desert outside of Cairo was authentic. As a young man, he spent extended periods of meditation there. As for his "identification with power" (which NN gives a nasty political twist to): Jabès's politics were thoughtful and humane. From the late 1920s up to the late 1950s, he was constantly involved in anti-fascistic activities. "Absence of memory," as NN asserts, is not a "key aesthetic point for him." In the late 1970s, interviewed by Marcel Cohen, he said: "Here writing substitutes itself for memory, which is why there can be no writing without memory. Every book is a book of memory. Do we keep the memory of a whole life intact? Of course not. Thus we are the first ones involuntarily to attack duration by fragmenting it, each of its lived moments rising up against the others in the hope of surviving them. Each of those moments is birth and death multiplied, and there is never an established, certified birth or death, but a perpetual displacement of life toward death." [*From the Desert to the Book*, tr. by Pierre Joris, Station Hill, 1990]

Jabès wrote in his mother-tongue (French was the only language in which he could have received an education in Cairo at that time). As NN must be aware, French was castrated into a court language several hundred years ago. "Purity" is, indeed, "a French ideal," and few writers of any stripe break its formal containments. Given this French language situation, to equate Jabès's filigreed austerity with political dissimulation is arbitrary and unfair. Since he wrote in his mother-tongue, it is also wrong to attack him for "choosing the language of privilege." Note that NN chose American-English as his language for poetry. NN states that poets should reveal an "ambiguity towards power." Is it possible that he means "ambivalence?" Poets should show no uncertainty facing the levels and divisions of power. They should be able to differentiate between coercive and imaginative power, working against the former, emanating the latter. This difference should be implicitly clear, not ambiguous.

Unlike Jabès, NN has chosen to write poetry, the most exacting of the language arts, in a world-dominant language that is not only not his mother-tongue (Turkish), but a language that he appears to have begun to acquire as a young adult. It would seem that in "Questions of Accent" he is bent upon turning a nearly impossible, masochistic situation into an aesthetic position in which difficulties are reworked into politically-correct stances. Those of us who, like Jabès, have persisted in writing poetry in our mother-tongues, are informed that it is not a mother-tongue at all, that, in effect, we, like NN, are in the position of writing in a language that is not "natural" to us. I guess that this means that we are all in the same boat with NN, with the possible exception that those of us who seek to hone and to clarify what we write risk being demoted to Jabès-status in NN's eyes.

A mother-tongue is the language of one's mother, or, according to Webster's, the language naturally acquired by reason of parentage or nationality. NN's shuffle here, of course, raises the question (which he too raises but does not satisfactorily answer) as to why he does not write in Turkish, the language in which he claims mastery *and* identifies as his mother-tongue. He also lists several Turkish poets among his formidable influences. Might it not be better, as the Romanian Jew Paul Celan did in the German of his childhood, to continue to write in one's mother-tongue while in exile from the place of the mother-tongue itself? That is, to accept exile from place in lieu of exile from one's natural language? There is clearly no simple solution here, and the Celan case is far from a simple one either. Celan could not have lived in Germany after the Holocaust, and France itself must have been an imperfect solution. Surely in Paris there were exacerbations of earlier anguishes that layered his suicide in 1970. But does anyone *write in* one's mother-tongue? One might even agree with the Swiss philosopher Max Picard who, after the Second World War, wrote: "By taking it away from silence, we have made language an orphan. The tongue we speak today is no longer a mother-tongue but rather an orphaned tongue." And to think of an "orphaned tongue" is to think of the orphaned voice of César Vallejo's *Trilce XXXVI*. Thinking of the book's title as "the new odd number," Vallejo admonishes the reader, in *Trilce XXXVI*, to: "Make way for the new odd number/ potent with orphanhood!"

In the act of speaking/writing poetry, to what extent is one

121

still in mother-tongue? "The voice that is great within us" (Stevens) is clearly not a ventriloquist—"it" must "pass through" a living mind and be contoured by a mother or non-mother tongue. At the same time, this concentrated, trance-like, polysymbolic language is hardly the language the poet as citizen uses in daily communication. In associating "heat" with mother-tongue, and "neutrality," oddly enough, with American-English, NN implies that he is a moth poet, too vulnerable to withstand the mother fire (and its incestuous associations), and that to function as an imagination, he needs the non-threatening atmosphere of an impersonal, he thinks, tongue. While NN rejects "discontinuity" when it appears in Jabès, he urges us gringos to accept discontinuity as our American-English fate, and locates our only viable "tradition" as one mysteriously bound up with the fake "affability" and "minimalism" of TV. Since TV is seldom about anything older or more complex than the last 50 years of American movies, sit-coms, and news, that's not much of a tradition. Again, as an American poet, I feel NN is attempting to shoulder me into his boat, for is NN not an example of the poet without a tradition, neither really here or there, in language as well as place? His dilemma is almost quaintly identified by the title of his "breakthrough" poem, *The Bridge*. As such a title gestures toward the spanning of opposing shores, as if necessary payments have not been made, it is instantly repossessed by Hart Crane.

Accent is phonetic, and in most cases the poet's speech accent is not available to a reader silently or audibly reading a page. If NN can get his spoken accent into his poetry, more power to him. The idea that accent (which comes from the Latin, *canere*, "to sing") can be embedded in writing as part of its syntactical being is fascinating. In a poem written on September 12, 1937, in Paris, Vallejo seems to have worked his own definition of accent into the interface of his accented French and the daily estranging responses to it by xenophobic Parisians. In Vallejo's "El acento me pende del zapato," accentual criticism is expanded to create a kind of aura, or monstrous size, in which every gesture of the poet appears to participate.

> The accent hangs on my shoe;
> I hear it perfectly
> succumb, sparkle, bend amber-shaped
> and hang, coloring, evil shadow.
> My size thus exceeds me,
> judges see me from a tree,
> they see me with their backs walk forward,
> enter my hammer,
> stand up to see a girl
> and, at the foot of a urinal, raise my shoulders.
> Surely no one is at my side,
> it hardly matters, I don't need anyone;

surely they've told me to be off:
I feel it clearly.
Cruelest size that of prayer!
Humiliation, resplendence, deep selva!
Size now exceeds me, elastic mist,
speed overhead and after and together.
Imperturbable! Imperturbable! Fatidic
telephones ring immediately, later.
It's the accent; it's him.

HOW DARE THIS TURK

GARY LENHART

Regarding Clayton Eshleman's response to Murat Nemet-Nejat's "Questions of Accent": I don't have much to say on the questions of accent myself, having never learned to speak any language without one. But I can't see that Eshleman presents any argument beyond, "How dare this Turk?" I would have written sooner, but had to talk to several friends before realizing that the flaws in his syllogisms weren't immediately apparent to everyone.

Clayton Eshleman's letter in the last *Corpse* should have been titled "Nemet-Nejat Attacked," instead of "Jabès Upheld." For the only coherence in the letter was provided by its *ad hominem* focus; on every other count Eshleman was exasperatingly ambiguous.

For example, was French the language that Jabès's mother spoke, or was it "the only language in which he could have received an education in Cairo at that time," or was it both? And is Eshleman contending that French was the only language in which Jabès could have received any education, or a European education?

Eshleman's assertion that Nemet-Nejat "sounds more like the product of a theory department than a Jewish poet" is disingenuous at best. Must all Jewish poets disdain considerations of theory? And in what respect is Eshleman's defense of Jabès untenable to a member of a theory department, excepting its illogic?

In addressing what he terms Nemet-Nejat's "nearly impossible masochistic situation" of writing poems in a language he learned as a young adult, Eshleman makes a swift, curious shift from mother-tongue to "natural language," seemingly identifying the two and implying that it is "better" to write in one's natural language, no matter what one's relation to it be or where one resides. That made me wonder what Eshleman thinks of Apollinaire, Conrad, Tristan Tzara, Senghor, Augustine, Jerome, Reznikoff, Zukofsky, Kerouac, the editor of the *Corpse*, etc. But not to worry. Only a few sentences later, the author himself

123

calls all this gab about mother-tongues and natural languages into question by intelligently asking "does anyone *write in* one's mother tongue?"

Inspired by this insight, he then turns on his own argument, admitting that the poetic voice "must 'pass through' a living mind and be contoured by a mother or non-mother tongue;" and concluding his letter with a quote from Vallejo that might appropriately serve as an epigraph for "Questions of Accent" in any reprinting. Thus, by letter's end, Eshleman seems in agreement with the major points of Nemet-Nejat's article, with the significant exception regarding Jabès.

Curiously, the one ray of clarity in Eshleman's letter is the important distinction he makes between coercive and imaginative powers. Seldom do we see those distinct powers juxtaposed in such unalloyed states as in Nemet-Nejat's imaginative critical musings and Eshleman's insulting personal response.

By the way, while I deem "Questions of Accent" an important attempt to confront "without glossing over, the gap between the user and the language," I sympathize with some of the reservations of Edward Field and Ricardo Nirenberg regarding Murat Nemet-Nejat's remarks about television. However, I believe that Nemet-Nejat's own poems and translations provide a context that resolves whatever confusion his remarks about television might engender. In that context it is clear that popular culture, though frequently his subject, is seldom his standard.

MORE FALLS THE ACCENT

BENJAMIN FRIEDLANDER

A few observations, unasked, in response to Murat Nemat-Nejat's marvelous and provocative essay "Questions of Accent," which only just fell my way. Forgive me if this is old news. My father, a German-born Jew (and survivor of Lodz and Auschwitz), speaks with a strong accent, something I now notice only if forced to concentrate, as a child I didn't notice at all. When I was 13 or 14 my friends and I used to make good-natured fun of the way he said certain words, though for me it was always a matter of imitating the imitators. My father himself, of course, has always been acutely aware of his accent, and only after Kissinger's ascendancy (so he tells me) did he become comfortable with it. There's some essential truth about language to be learned from this, though I concede that I may just be inattentive, or that the ease of my childhood made such inattention tenable. The truth, in any case, if there is one, would be this: that an accent, hearable by strangers, is undetectable to those closest and dearest to the speaker, those who hear the speaker every day and listen intently, seriously, to what he or she is actually saying. Only by listening, that is, as if with a stranger's ears, will we begin to notice this most obvious aspect of a speech that isn't ours, but instead, the next closest. And it's in this sense, I think, that American poetry is accented and I thank Murat Nemat-Nejat for bringing me to this realization. That "Questions of Accent" draws different conclusions than I myself would is precisely the point. What we hear and don't hear, what we are, and remain close to, and feel distant from, these are matters of great moment, and will differ from person to person, and will require care and acumen to negotiate. Especially interesting to me is the distinction drawn between the Persian Jews and the rest of Jewry (which I have always imagined as encapsulated by the Ashkenazi-Sephardic/Yiddish-Ladino split—well, I knew about the Felasha, too). I would, however, like to pick loose one tiny knot accidentally woven into the narrative. Under the heading "Jewishness and Accent," Nemat-Nejat writes, "I am not an Ashkenazi Jew. Though I share the underlying paranoia of the outsider of every Jew, Turkey was never invaded by the Nazis." Careless readers, forgetting the earlier statement "I am not a Sephardi," may infer from this passage that the Holocaust was a peculiarly Ashkenazi phenomenon and though I'm not an expert (so please excuse me if my formulation is clumsy), I believe that the Sephardic population of Greece centered in Salonica was decimated by the Nazis no less than was the shtetl culture of Eastern Europe. (The descriptions of the Greeks in Tadeusz Borowski's *This Way for the Gas, Ladies and Gentlemen* are particularly sad; and if in the camps—as Primo Levi has argued—language was power, then those most distant from the language of the guards and the kapos, i.e. the Ladino speakers, would have been the most vulnerable.) Turkey, of course, experienced its own genocide, and Nemat-Nejat's wonderfully subtle suggestions of distance and identification ("When I speak, Turks think I am a Cypriot or Armenian, an outsider") immediately put me in mind of that greatest of outsider poets, Osip Mandelstam. Mandelstam's bemused discomfort at his childhood's "Judaic chaos" and the equally bemused delight he took in Armenia have long seemed to me the two sides of a coin spendable only as poetry. (Of a Jewish orchestra playing Tchaikovsky: "What conviction sounded in those violin voices, softened by Italian docility but still Russian, in the dirty Jewish sewer!" Of Armenia: "I felt joy in pronouncing sounds forbidden to Russian lips, secret sounds, outcast and perhaps, on some deep level, shameful.") How I love dear Mandelstam. And though I love Jabès, Derrida too, I do not begrudge Nemat-Nejat his polemic. How useful polemics can be! Moreover, I engage those two writers from a distance so shrouded by translation that I am incapable of hearing the accent (or lack of accent) at issue here. Let me recommend, nevertheless, Derrida's book on Paul Celan, *Schibboleth*, now fully translated and available in a collection of essays on Celan put out by Johns Hopkins, *Word Traces*, edited

125

by Aris Fioretos. Accent is just what this book is about. For those who don't recall the biblical story from which the word "shibboleth" is taken (*Judges* 12: 4-6), it runs as follows: defeated Ephraimite soldiers, escaping across the Jordan, are enjoined by Gileadite sentries to speak a password—*shibboleth*; incapable of pronouncing the "shi" sound, they are cut down without mercy. (Records the Bible: "and there fell at that time of the Ephraimites forty and two thousand.") Derrida, recalling this story (and drawing inspiration from a poem of Celan's), offers the following analysis: "On both sides of the historical, political, and linguistic border (a border is never natural), the meaning, the different meanings of the word *shibboleth* are known: river, ear of grain, olive twig. One even knows how it should be pronounced. But a single trial determines that some cannot while others can pronounce it with the heart's mouth. The first will not pass, the others will pass the line of the place, of the country, of the community, of what takes place in a language, in languages as poems ... From this *point of view*, which may become a watch tower, the vigilance of a sentinel, one sees well: the value of the *shibboleth* may always, and tragically, be inverted. Tragically because the inversion sometimes overtakes the initiative of subjects, the good will of men, their mastery of language and of politics." Forgive my quoting such a long passage. I would think, however, polemic aside, that Nemat-Nejat would find a poignant aptness in these statements; accent understood as the ambiguity of the relationship between language and power—that's the point, no? As an American poet I'm gratified by what this essay says about stateside English; regarding "Uncanonizable Poetics"—I only hope it's true. TV? As a mode of refusing assimilation? Maybe. But to return to the two-sided coin Mandelstam passes down to us, bemused discomfort and bemused delight, I would want to remember the intrinsic doubleness of the "accented" writing this coin buys, "the mixture" (as Nemat-Nejat puts it) "of power and weakness, empowerment and marginality, privilege and victimhood, white heat and coolness." If, at one end, poetry expresses "ambiguity toward power," at the other, let us insist, it must expose our complicity. (Though admittedly "insist" and "must" are distasteful words to use when it comes to poetry.) I could disagree with almost every assertion in "Questions of Accent" and yet I concur with the essay taken as a whole. What does that say? And does it "say" with or without accent? According to my own formula, my inability to tell puts me outside myself, but not too far outside. A rather pleasing sensation. This, I guess, is what they mean by loving the sound of your own voice—oh well, a poet's flaw. A two-edged question: When does accent become mannerism, "schtick," if I might put it so, and when does mannerism become accent? (Possible answer: One man's accent is another's affectation. This was the gist of Peter Cole's criticism of Jabès published a few years back in *Tikkun*.) Do I seem now to babble? It's

126

simply a way of bringing down or trying to bring down the hideous tower called "official culture." Foreign workers got blamed for the collapse, but that collapse, in my opinion, is a great triumph. It's even celebrated in the Bible. The pathos of poetry, of writing in general to discover worlds where we might begin to appreciate the accented triumph of this one, demands, in any case, a certain refusal to assimilate (or acquiesce, or however we want to put it). Nemat-Nejat's acute awareness of this pathos is what I most appreciated in his essay. Or as the late Jim Brodey put it in *Judyism*:

> I fail
> and you are not here yet.
> I fail
> and the newspapers do not weep.
> I fail and the world ignores us.
> I fail
> and the wheat grows thick in Russia.
> I fail
> and the hair on our bodies is silent.
> I fail, you fail, he she it them we
> all fail, but
> triumph as the poems reel out
> controlling the world only we can create
> and see flourish from our heads.

POST MODERNISM

GERALD ROSEN

This is Ralph Kramden's night to go bowling with Ed Norton but Alice is on his case. She wants them to take along this new guy who moved across the hall. Some Swedish guy. She says he hardly goes out of his apartment and he's depressed or something.

Ralph objects vociferously. He does it in Norton's name. He says Ed has been in the sewers all day looking forward to bowling with him, Ralph, not some crazy new Swedish guy from across the hall.

But Alice likes the Swedish guy. Says he's sensitive. He used to live on an island up near the north pole or something. He used to make movies in Swedish. No wonder he's depressed, Ralph says. How the hell are you gonna make a living on movies in Swedish for Chrissakes?

But Alice persists. Says the guy needs some company. He's got a good nature undernearth. Show him a little American hospitality for Chrissakes.

By the time Norton arrives carrying his bowling ball, **127** and says Hey Hey Ralphie Boy, Ingmar Bergman is standing there awk-wardly in Ralph's apartment. When Ralph tells Norton that Ingmar used to make movies, Norton jokes, Why don't you make a movie of me, in the sewer?

All of my movies were set in the sewers, Bergman says, metaphor-ically. That's why I came to America and went underground. I want to do something different.

Norton doesn't understand what Bergman's talking about, but he shrugs good-naturedly and accepts Ingmar's strangeness as some Swedish *mishegas* and he begins to show Ingmar how to hold a bowling ball.

Bergman has never bowled before. He immediately gets his finger stuck in Ed's ball. Ed and Ralph take some pratfalls as they try, separate-ly, and then together, to yank the ball off Ingmar's finger. Ingmar is howl-ing terribly. His pained cries carry a kind of Swedish twang which sounds awful to an American ear. Finally, Alice steps in and suggest they take him to the doctor.

Ralph and Ed take Ingmar over to the apartment of Dr. Marcus Welby who has retired and now lives on Park Avenue. Ralph met Dr. Welby on his bus several times and they struck up a kind of friendship.

Dr. Welby graciously agrees to see Bergman who is carrying Ed's bowling ball awkwardly with him. Dr. Welby has never had a case like this, and recommends a surgeon. When Ralph asks which surgeon, Bergman insists he wants the best. The best in the world. Ed thinks maybe Ingmar has gone a little bonkers, but Bergman assures them he can pay; he doesn't trust doctors in general and therefore he wants only the best surgeon in the world to work on him. Dr. Welby thinks for a moment. He explains that he doesn't really practice any longer, but he did see a famous surgeon written up in the New York Post the other week. Dr. Christian Barnard of South Africa.

When Ed and Ralph get off the plane with him in Johannesburg, Ingmar is still lugging the bowling ball around with him. Half way round the world and he still has to shlep that heavy damn ball wherever he goes. He can't even enjoy the trip with Ralph and Ed who are taking it all in with great pleasure. Neither has been abroad before and Bergman is paying.

Even when their taxi is stopped by a riot of Blacks who are demanding to live with their families, rather than having to leave them back in the homelands, and sixteen people are killed, thirty-nine injured, Ralph and Ed shake it off like New Yorkers. You don't make it through life on the buses or in the sewers of New York if you can't shake things off. Bergman just sits there in pain, with his heavy black ball on his lap.

Dr. Barnard removes the ball with little trouble, charging what Ralph and Ed see as an enormous fee, and destroying Norton's bowling ball in the process. Bergman generously buys Ed a new ball, right there in South Africa to ease Ed's mind, but Ralph and Ed are astonished when Bergman buys himself a ball as well. They ask him if he still intends to take up bowling. He responds that no, he will never put his finger into a bowling ball again, but he has gotten used to carrying around a heavy black ball and he feels uncomfortable without it.

Back at Ralph's apartment, they tell the story to Alice. She says it would make a wonderful story for Bergman to tell on the David Letterman show. She has a cousin who is married to the sister-in-law of a janitor at NBC and she says she can work out the deal.

Ingmar Bergman is getting more depressed by the minute. He thanks Alice but he says he's going to continue to create his work out of his true feelings rather than give in to the surface forces of the culture which cause him so much anguish. Alice isn't quite sure what he means, but when he tells her he's going to direct a play on Broadway, she approves.

The play Bergman decides to direct is a literal translation into dramatic terms of the Book of Job. He hires Franz Kafka to play Job. Kafka gets decent enough reviews and the play does moderate business, but the trouble starts outside the theater when Kafka begins to see the Virgin Mary on his TV. After he misses several performances, the newspapers receive word of what is happening and run feature stories on it. When the authorities get word of this, they consider locking him up in a "mental facility," but when they learn that Kafka is famous, they merely decide to deport him to Czechoslovakia instead.

The producers of the play replace Kafka with a young unknown actor named Sylvester Stallone. Bergman resigns and returns to his island in Sweden. Franz Kafka's TV set is moved to the altar of a church in Brooklyn where thousands of pilgrims come from around the world to watch it 24 hours a day hoping to see the Virgin Mary. *The Book of Job* now becomes a mega-hit because of Sylvester Stallone, who goes out to become a new star in Hollywood's firmament.

Across the hall from Alice and Ralph Kramden, a Russian moves into Bergman's apartment. His name is Aleksandr Solzhenitsyn. Alice is worried about him. He seems depressed...

REPORT FROM THE SEATTLE
POST-STRUCTURALIST CONFERENCE

KIRBY OLSON

Every creature on earth is made of the same substance: DNA. The food chain is an auto-cannibalistic chain of beings. Here at *Henry's End*, in Brooklyn, you can dine on predators such as alligator and grizzly, or on more traditional repasts, such as zebra, and moose.

The moose is the emperor of America. When moose fight over a female, often their horns will lock, and they will die in the embrace. When the pilgrims first came to America, they wore buckles on their hats, and when they locked in theological debate, often they would die in that stance.

Last spring, I attended a conference of post-structuralists in Seattle. It was depressing. I had hoped that Derrida and René Girard would lock horns, but Derrida had overbooked—now being much like an airline, and the show was stolen by Girard's neo-royalist camp. It was possible to rub shoulders with Girard, but not much, because he had bursitis.

Only once, in some twenty hours of close monitoring, was the food chain even mentioned. The conference was on "Le Lien Social" or the Social Bond. Eric Gans, one of the great minds of our century (according to an acolyte), postulated that language, as well as society, began with the first primitive tribe confronting the fact that the mammoth they had just killed wasn't going to be big enough to feed everybody in the tribe. So they begin to whisper. Social bonds form.

Mona Modiano, a beautiful Romanian Jewish transplant, spanked Gans publicly for this notion. Her own Kantian aesthetics prompted her to ask Gans why the first words spoken weren't an exchange of critiques, such as, "Mmmmmm," or "Ick."

Gans, aristocratic bearing and silk scarf about thin skull intact, fled to the first refuge of a French-trained scoundrel, saying that her question wasn't "rigorous enough."

The rigor mortis of philosophy began when Socrates said to Phaedrus, "Now the people in the city have something to teach me, but the fields and trees won't teach me anything."

Dialectics begins with a critical exclusion: everything outside the POLIS had nothing to contribute. This philosophy, which has now created such intriguing nightmares as San Francisco and Tokyo—paving and skyscrapers fifty miles in diameter—under which the earth continues, ever so impolitely, to move. Always underneath the POLIS, is the IMPOLIS, meaning by this both the French word for impolite, and, of course, everything that is not included in the Socratic notion of POLIS.

The unity that developers and politicians have forged in whispers is continually being sabotaged by animal rights activists, feminists, computer hackers and their attendant viruses. Writing is the chief double-agent which both sides use to impress those left in the middle.

And yet what does writing really produce but furrows in the brow, and enemies? Sade says that the value of writing is determined by its proximity to the sexual act. If in fact all value stems from this act, which at least was intended as a stab at procreation before Sade derailed it in a possibly Carpocratian maneuver (see the last page in Pierre Klossowski's *Sade, Mon Prochain*, please), then we are led back to the food chain—that endless rotisserie fueled by the perpetual motion machine of animal desire.

Heidegger defines man as that animal which can write. But what would Heidegger say if other animals were to take one of their traits and place it above all others? For example, monkeys might define man as that simian which cannot leap from tree to tree—and legitimately decide that Tarzan is the most gifted among humans; much as we've decided that Koko is the most gifted among apes, as she has learned sign language, and passed it on to her children, so that they can get shit, like candy bars, from their trainers out there in Walla Walla.

After the conference ended, everybody went to dinner. Some ate grits and gravy, others ate roasted goose and peas, some had duck in wine sauce, and others ate vegetarian. No doubt the big guns at the conference ate together, some of their guns still smoking, and no doubt new social bonds formed, while others were broken irremediably. I flew to New York, where I have just finished a repast of smoked lion, w/ moose trimmings.

As I think back on the conference, all the words seem like so much paprika—crumbled delicately from a great height. The wonder of paprika is that it is great in the right place. In your rice, it makes you happy; in your eyes, it makes you mad.

DYSFIC MANIFESTO

STEVE KATZ

The American practice of fiction still seems stuck, like a moth in an empty honey jar, or a writer in a workshop, to dreary realistic conventions, and since we find those conventions inadequate to confront the disruptions in our present condition, like the violence that garments our lives as we go on trying to have fun, or the tease of gross Antarctic ice shelves melting to drown London and New York, or the anticipation of even sweeter viruses collapsing our bodies, or frontal attacks of toxic goop that can disolve our bindings, today we have whipped out a revolutionary new genre—DYSFIC. Just dyscovered by us; in fact, it might have booted itself instinctively, as soon as she juiced up, into this new computer we just financed. The pieces accompanying are some of the several dysfictions that have metastasized off the organs of our technology. Please read them forward and forewarned.

The rules of Dysfiction are simple. Dysfic works are anti-narrative. They are dysfictional, dysrational, dysengaged. They are politically dyslect. They can be dystasteful and dyscatorial. Dysfic is dysorderly, dyspontaneous, and dysprovisional; though in structure it often is

131

made exquisite as insects in a laundry. And it can seem to be composed at randyom. These works are quick and blue and clueless, and they are as persistently trivial as they are relentlessly profound. Dysfic is often composed through a system of exocharacterization and psychological outrisme; i.e., elsewhere characters still live, grow, lust, breathe the salt air by the shore, yearn for their neighbor's kittens, despair of ever satisfying their grandmothers, hope for a breakthrough in their diets, but none of this, not a word of it ever manifests in a Dysfic. All the dysfictioneer allows is the release of a little steam from the eyeballs. These writings resist closure, and encourage dysclosure, though the writers of Dysfic realize that within every closure plumps the seed of a new opening, and within every dysclosure a clear track to THE END.

Dysfics have no beginning, no ending, and therefore no identifiable middle; so they are intrepidly spiritual, or dyspiritual, depending on the field of play. You can't read them except dystractedly, as you read cereal boxes at breakfast, for their ingredients, their commercial messages, their casual joys; or glance at them while snacking and waiting for your computers to come back on line, or while you rest and catch your breath between attempts to get into those tight jeans again, prescribed years ago by a different writer. However you wiggle away, at some time you'll have to confront the Dysfics, albeit obliquely.

This major new genre tells our dystory at the millennium. We get thrilling *news* from Bosnia, Chechnya, Myanmar, Rwanda, etc. etc. etc. Parentless kids blast away in D.C., L.A., N.Y., Chicago, up in New Orleans, and everywhere else, even Denver. But they're not shooting at us. Not yet. Not all the time, anyway. After all, who are we? They kill each other. We've got Somalia, the Gaza Strip, Sri Lanka, Angola, Kurdistan et al., and all are Dysfics on a spontaneous map, as is the strife between Dave and Sandy, between Alice and Alex , between Nougat and Pudding, between Randy and his/her own conscience, between Yahweh and Allah, etc. etc. etc.—all Dysfics in our time,

The genre has as some precursors the great genuises who fragmented Gilgamesh, who cracked the Rosetta stone, who destroyed the missing bits of Apuleius' *Golden Ass,* who flew with some of the Sappho stuff. It honors those who escaped with the arms of that otherwise ideal female in marble, though as dysfictioneers we revile the thieves of the Elgin Marbles. We don't forget whatever faded Leonardo's last pasta. Was it neglect or dampness or light? Hooray for those who left the Sagrada Familia unfinished.

Dysfic is a fly on the nose of every theorist, and a big door slammed in their throats. As one of its affections, Dysfic embraces dyscombobulation and silliness as no other serious genre has dared, and by doing so eliminates the pejoratives of that category. Such an erasure is in the nature of every embrace. We can sincerely say that "To

Embrace" is not "To Embarrass." Beckett's call that we yield not to the distortions of intelligibility is flown on the Dysfic flag.

ON THE LANGUAGE OF CREATION

I. P. COULIANO & H. S. WIESNER

Many have tried to link the masonic magician, miracle worker and petty crook Giuseppe Balsamo, self-advertised as the Count Alessandro Cagliostro, with the brilliant and tragic career of Jean Baptiste Gaspard Bochart de Saron, Attorney General of the Kingdom of France and later third President of the Paris Parliament, i.e. the House of Justice. In fact, at least once the two may have been co-conspirators in a plot whose import probably exceeded the understanding of either one. The result was the fall of the Bastille (improbable only because it was so unnecessary), predicted by Cagliostro during a seance ten months in advance.

The false Count escaped a like fate by being expelled from France and sentenced to a life term by the Roman Inquisition at his wife's request. Bochart was duly guillotined at the end of a bloody revolution, when real aristocrats had become hard to find.

Thanks to the erudition of my friend Dr. Elsa Gonzalez, I know all about the tragic destiny of this undeservedly forgotten genius. Bochart never incurred the most widespread Christian sin: poverty. In fact, not only was he rich, but he had considerably increased his wealth by marrying Mlle d'Anguesseau, a descendant not of the *bourgeoisie de robe* but of prosperous merchants. He built one of the more solid *immeubles* of eighteenth century Paris, a private hôtel (*mansion*) located at number 17, Rue de l'Université, which still today fails to appear inconspicuous; it houses the publisher Gallimard.

Now Bochart was also involved in a far more consequential plot: he was one of the founders of the Secret Society of Weights and Measures. This fraternity schemed to implement an ideal, universal system of measurement of all the states of matter, this through furtive and occult subdivisions of the earth's diameter and other subtle constants. Had it not been for the reactionary British, the Society might speedily have achieved its purpose. Still, in revolutionary Paris the select brotherhood had much to fear: the stupidity of aristocrats, the stupidity of the mob, in fact everyone's stupidity. Bochart kept a private laboratory whose entrance was hidden behind the shelves of his library. There he achieved the melting of platinum and produced the first standard meter, the *mètre-étalon* which eventually conquered the globe.

Scholarly opinion is split on the question of Bochart's inconvenient fate—the guillotine and the burning of his papers. Did he

133

merit it as a leading member of the mysterious Society of Weights and Measures, or as former President of the House of Justice? (In her learned study, Dr. Gonzalez favored the latter explanation.)

Less known is it that Bochart positively claimed to have discovered—whether by chance or deduction, none can say—the language used by God before the creation of the world. Which means, of course, the language used by God in creating the world. Moreover, there are indications that, to put this momentous discovery within reach of humankind, Bochart built a sort of music box that held the mysterious sounds of the divine tongue.

Displaced by secret and indeterminate expectations, I was at large and had become a whirl of raw and innocent sensations—bitter smell of decomposing upholsteries, herrings, ancient feather cushions, heinous cigars and crimson draperies; subtle air currents, swinging doors, voices and volumes. I had entirely forgotten where I was, and what I was doing in that unknown place. In fact, I was waiting for the auction of an inestimable object. Yet, before explaining how I encountered it in this concrete storehouse in an unexpected and unglamorous part of the Continent or perhaps how it lured me there, I should mention at least a few of those who preceded Bochart in what I then believed to be a glorious adventure.

It started long before 1274. Much, much earlier: even before the wheels of the *Sefer Yetsira* or *Book of Creation*, noble progenitor of the Kabbalah. These wheels, arrayed with multiple Hebrew alphabets, produce the infinite combinations of letters capable of recapitulating the sublime language of Creation, the language enunciating all the worlds, seen and unseen.

By the end of the twelfth century more than one authority could say that the alphabetical wheels were the heavenly spheres: one was Rabbi Yehuda ha-Levi (a friend of the more famous Rabbi Abraham Ibn Ezra) mentioned on page 87 of Moshe Idel's book *Golem*. Thus the movement of the wheels became the movement of the celestial bodies, and language became the universe.

Nevertheless, by 1274 those researchers who could claim to have mastered the hidden language were fewer than prosperous alchemists. That winter the forty-year-old Catalan Ramon Llull, latinized Raymundus Lullus, was struck by a revelation in the wild, mountainous landscape of Palma de Majorca. He called his discovery The Art, and to practice it became a solitary monk. In any century no more than three scholars in the world understand the import of Lullus' speculations. (At a recent Congress of Orientalists one of them assessed Lullus' logical machine as far more consequential for humankind than the discovery of penicillin. The others strongly disagreed.)

Yet it was there—among rocks, the sky, and infamous

shrub—that Lullus suddenly realized the striking simplicity of the Arabic language, the way that it sprouts through permutations of three-letter clusters. Since God created this world through mathematical formulae, it followed that the language of Creation must have been capacious, yet endowed with shining simplicity. Lullus knew well the many ancient apocrypha which claim without substantiation that a Semitic language— more often Hebrew or Chaldaean, which is Aramaic—is the language of Heaven. But Lullus now knew he could prove it scientifically.

Today, of course, computers simulate organisms and social environments through open-ended, interactive programs. Plenty of artificial languages spring from a basic rule which resembles Arabic in the sense that its words are patterned permutations of three consonant clusters. In one of them the consonants H-B-B would convey the meaning "love," in another they stand for "smell," in another for "gasp," in another still they mean nothing. Long before the race of computers, Ramon Llull came upon the idea that the divine and human mind work like a digital machine through endless combinations deriving from a simple set of generative rules.

Lullus extrapolated from this principle to demonstrate to his satisfaction that everything conceivable is the result of the permutation of three symbols or notions. At the same time, being a practical man, he realized that if this prolific code is the language of Creation, then it must have persuasive force on human beings, whatever be their idiom, culture, or race. After writing several books in which he explained his Universal Art, he left the steep rocks of Mount Randa and, armed with his secret logical weapon, embarked upon his mission to convert the Arabs to Christianity. The success of his device was ambiguous at best.

Some three hundred years after Lullus' death, which legend hallows as martyrdom at the hands of the infidels, a defrocked and somewhat debauched Dominican monk called Giordano Bruno, who could only have been born in Naples, resumed Lullus' research. Like everyone else during that period, Bruno looked for the language of Creation in the mysterious Egyptian hieroglyphs. In his book *Aegyptt,* Dr. John Crowley of Barnabas College finds evidence that the errant monk discovered the tongue of the angels. It should therefore come as no surprise that certain parties credit Bruno with the construction of an automaton capable of reproducing the sounds of the divine language. Bruno remains the greatest commentator of Lullus' works and a first rate practitioner of The Art, who thought himself to be immortal. Only a few decades after that foggy, epochmaking February morning of the year 1600 when Giordano was burned for witchcraft in the *Campo dei Fiori,* a vagrant scholar whose greatest love was sleeping late (and who died of pneumatic exhaustion when a mad queen had him awakened at five o'clock each morning), took the next logical step. That scholar was the

135

Frenchman René Descartes, and only he had the courage and mettle to think out to its extremest consequences the likely story that man had been put together by someone radically different called God (or in this case, Dieu). Descartes reached the conclusion that we humans were nothing but the automata of the latter (lit by a spark of his Mind). Language again came into the picture, for it was obvious that man's languages were not God's language, not even French, and that God's secret language must have illimitable power over human beings, who have a special organ (the pineal gland) able to understand it. With Descartes, even more than with Lullus, it became clear that whoever would decipher God's language would come into possession of a formidably versatile weapon, capable of achieving every terrestrial goal and even more.

Taking inspiration from both Lullus (whom he knew through Giordano Bruno's commentaries) and Descartes, Baron Gottfried Wilhelm von Leibniz dreamt recurrently of a universal language which he endeavored to reconstruct. Meanwhile, secret societies throughout Europe kept inventing artificial languages (at least two of which have survived thus far) in the hope that one day all humankind would be united by a common idiom. Today intervening circumstances may have made this ideal more unappealing than ever before. Yet human history has this distinctive characteristic about it, that many ideals fail without being necessarily wrong, and grand enterprises often produce trivial results. But I anticipate myself. For we have now come to the heart of the matter; we have returned to Bochart de Saron and the enigmatic box resting on the auction block.

It was some ten inches deep, perhaps a little wider. It was wooden, grimy, and sadly upholstered in ancient blue velvet now worn and discolored. Under the lid, the mechanism was concealed by a tarnished copper plate. It was one among the lesser items of a lesser auction in a lesser country, and no visitor had yet shown interest in its minuscule identification mark, the Hebrew letters *Aleph, Resh, Lamed* incised on its right side: one Mother, one Double and one Simple. They stood for 231, the number of Gates of Creation, marked by Bochart undoubtedly not as a sign of belief in Kabbalistic lore, but of respect for tradition.

The history of this object had emerged through painstaking research. To begin with, one of Bochart's servants saved it from destruction together with a useless recipe. He later sold the box for a few sous (there was nothing appealing about the box, in fact, it soon became apparent that it lacked the most elementary quality commonly attributed to music boxes) to the mistress of a young Corsican officer. The box reemerged in the Waterloo loot, was bought by a retired judge from Calcutta, ended up in the family of the logician Boole and was one of the few items which Mary Boole took with her during the unfortunate years of vagrancy precipitated by her husband's bigamy. Passing from hand to hand, it came free of an existentialist philosopher killed in a car accident, and disappeared from sight.

The major exhibit of the present auction was a scale reduction of a sculpture by Antonio Canova, to whom the tag in English ascribed suspicious longevity: "A contrast of moods in marble. By the Italian artist Canova (1757–1882)." A local beauty with see-through clothing circumambulated it with jaws admiringly ajar.

At last came the shock of language recognition, for I had left Paris in the morning and I had remained unaware of crossing any linguistic boundary. The day before, a vague acquaintance exhibiting the pin of an extremist party had introduced me into a mildewed room whose space and time were clogged with bad French and solid cigarette smoke: a modest price to pay for finding out the whereabouts and import of the auction. Now I was somewhere, yet unaware of the place, for the place was the box. Yet I instantly recognized the alien language spoken by the auctioneer (far better than his own English translation), and in my initial amazement I had a thought linking this miracle with Bochart's box. Only after did I realize that I *knew* it, that I had spent in that country a time which seemed now altogether lost, that I had even been a civil servant somewhere in the North, in a place whose dialect not even I could follow. I still had a house and an ex-wife.

The auctioneer mentioned some of the most irrelevant moments in the history of the box, those moments which are assumed to be momentous by the kind of audience one would expect at an auction. Yet no one seemed to be interested in it, whereas the dubious Canova provoked a bitter contest, and before dark (which came with solicitous haste) I could revert to Paris and, in the crimson room of the hotel for nearly defunct scholars opposite the *Collège de France*, I opened the modest package. With Huguenotic care, the box had been wrapped in an entire issue of *Del Telegraaf*, announcing in bold capitals the invasion of Iraq, of which I had remained unaware and which failed to arouse my interest even after I had discovered it. Clearly, the box's untimeliness was more important to me than any vague external event. That would have been the same had the invasion of Iraq taken place in that very room in Paris, with me in it.

I realized at once that aside from the perfectly audible noise produced by the opening and closing of its lid, the box was irremediably silent. Only later would I verify that its mechanism—which I have all reasons to believe was the original, could not be fixed, for it was entirely fictitious, unable to operate a music box or any other human device.

After that memorable vigil in Paris I spent countless nights trying to figure out what conceivable pieces might be missing from this monstrous puzzle. Yet no piece could be added or subtracted from it: the mechanism was whole and symmetrical, yet absurd. It was

137

reasonable to think that it reflected Bochart's original plan.

After I had exhausted all hypotheses concerning Bochart's music box I realized that, instead of being an embodiment of an eternal truth of some kind, just as a car is an embodiment of the first principle of thermodynamics, it was rather an object of historical value, in which one might decipher what Bochart and his generation had believed the language of God to be.

But no matter how much I researched the period and scrutinized the mechanism, I could not get beyond the well known principle of the Noetic heretics whom Hippolytus accused of reviving the teachings of the Presocratic Heraclitus, that is, that complete fullness and complete void are equivalent, and thus a music box designed to produce no sound is quite literally releasing at all times the silent, unfathomable language used by God to create the world. However persuaded of the truth of this thought, I hardly found consolation in it.

Now comes the hardest part of the story to tell.

I was a forty-year-old man living in a high-rise security building on the Lake with a purposeless box which was absorbing the best of my mental energies. In fact my mind was far, far from that painful alteration of accidental occurrences, tame desires, vain regrets and unfulfilled promises which most of us—successful or not—call reality. Given the character of my job, professor of history at a grey and renowned Midwestern university, my days were filled with eighteenth century thoughts and my nights with predictable dreams in which members of the Third Estate conversed in inscrutable dialects. Of course nowhere did I meet the language of Creation; I had understood by that time that any such language ought to approximate mathematical formulae, transformable into a sequence of sounds only by virtue of the convertibility of all systems of signs.

I knew however that I had become one of the possessors of the accursed box. And that as one of the possessors of the box, I was a researcher after the language of Creation, isolated from all other people and animals by an invisible wall. I sometimes thought that the box had posed a riddle which was absorbing my whole life, and had thereby fulfilled a certain purpose that could only have been achieved by the divine idiom itself. But such cheap wisdom satisfied me no more than the supreme Mahayana principle of the identity between full and empty. (And moreover, was I actually succumbing to the temptation that led Lullus and Bruno and Bochart to the sword, pyre, and gallows when I reasoned that if the divine language existed—and it certainly did—anything could be achieved through it, anything at all, for it would utterly recreate the perception which structures reality.)

So what became of me? It may be necessary at this point for the reader to, at least momentarily, suspend his disbelief. For the idea that something strange, but this time strange in a quite unpredictable way, was happening to me began during the last summer I spent in the city. I was caught in the middle of a bank robbery. The robbers collected valuables from everyone present, except me. It was as if they discounted me, or as if I had modified their perception in such a way that to them I was invisible. Nonplused, I slowly stepped out the door, and no one paid any attention to me. I know of no report about my escape. I have since experienced regular episodes of my Charism of Inconspicuity, which is also listed among the mystical Sufi charismata (*karamat*) by Ibn Arabi in his account of the Sufis of al Andalus, Rûh al-Quds. The same thing happened, for example, once during a conference in Cincinnati, where I tried to speak and, significantly, no one paid any attention to me.

A second charism was manifest shortly thereafter. I do not shop frequently, and therefore I usually spend one whole afternoon going after various items. In most cases the vendors would undercharge me, and in a few instances I came back home with more money than I had when I left. Once a cashier in a mall opened the register and would have given me all she had inside, had I not promptly alerted security. Another time a large sum of money was credited to my bank account through a distortion of an insurance payment; it cost me much trouble to find out at whose expense the money came, and to correct the imbalance. I call this one the Charism of Undercharging.

I was fairly often the victim of another charism, the Love Charism, much less satisfactory than the other two, and, upon reflection, rather frightening. A number of individuals fell precipitously in love with me without necessity. This caused me some trouble when I was unable to share their feelings, and infinite pain if ever they convinced me that I did.

Another charism, that of forecast of future events during dreams, might have been useful were it not generally confined to petty events. Thus I was "gifted" with premonitory dreams about a cat fatally hit during a corner basketball game, about taking a shower, about the night doorman of the building cutting his mustache (that man died soon after), about an insurance agent ringing the bell one dull morning, about a trivial book I was soon to find in the used bookstore on 57th street, about a bleak lunch with since subtracted colleagues, about a red stain which mysteriously appeared on my necktie after dinner in an Italian restaurant.

I believe that these four charismata—the Charism of Inconspicuity, the Charism of Undercharging, the Misplaced Love Charism, Divination of Petty Events and a few others which together I call the Lesser Charismata—do exist. They manifested themselves only after I had attained possession of the mysterious box. The trait they share nicely matches the expectation one would have of brain language, i.e. modification of perception. People would fail to notice me, would miscalculate my financial standing, would fall in love with me although there is not much lovable about me.

I only gradually began to feel that all of this, which could perhaps be envisioned as some near-monumental manipulation of the language of Creation, is the result of my ownership of Bochart's box, even as ancient talismans were supposed to catch in their fabric the fuzzy decrees of the heavens and domesticate them. The question also arises of whether, if one possessed the divine language, would one know? And how many chances are there to attain it, if any?

I have often wondered if Bochart had this in mind when he conceived of his manifestly absurd mechanism: that magicians, however misguided, are closer to truth than mechanics. And that we are automata of another sort, whose minds are able to perceive the language of Creation only as sheer absurdity.

But in this case couldn't the useless mechanism of Bochart's music box truly produce the primordial language, of which we remain utterly unaware, except for such petty instances as my Lesser Charismata? And thus, would not perhaps all absurdities be vindicated as signs of something even more powerful than our inability to comprehend them?

If I am not mistaken, a number of philosophers known today as Nominalists dwelt on such endless speculations. And I know that one day I will join them in the comfortable untimeliness of past centuries; yet the hunt for Bochart's box will never cease, and those who will experience the mixed blessing of finding it may suffer alterations perhaps similar to mine. For, if there is so far little hope of understanding the language of creation, still the hunt for Bochart de Saron's music box is open to everyone, if only until it closes upon them.

Yet doubts persist. Both about the link between my charismata and the box, and about a more acute problem which had developed in the meantime. At a certain moment my conviction of an occult connection between the charismata and the box had become so solid that I was tempted to make a test of its powers against a distasteful political regime. The hypothesis that I might imminently resume the fate of Lullus, Bruno, Bochart and the inheritors of his creation came to haunt me. The presence of the mute and immovable object in my life was increasingly experienced by me as a threat.

For a long time I contemplated destroying it. But now I decided to hide it in such a way that I would add to its absurdity. I canceled all its marks, the number of Gates and even the pale initials J.B G.B.d.S.; I stole one of the useless wheels inside and placed it in a safe in Los Angeles; I put the box casually on a pile of refuse called "Yard Sale" somewhere in Massachusetts (I will not name the place), and left pretending to avoid the looks of the improvised vendors, as does one of those innumerable clients who, tempted one moment to buy an item, would eventually decide to let it go.

2
POETICS & POETRY

NESTING BIRDS / IVAN SUVANJIEFF

NOT A FORM AT ALL BUT A STATE OF MIND

*"The sonnet ... is not a form at all but a state
of mind. It is the ... dialogue upon which
much writing is founded: a statement then a
rejoinder of a sort, perhaps a reply, perhaps a
variant of the original—but a comeback of
one sort or another."*

—WILLIAM CARLOS WILLIAMS

I

after reading the tiresome review
from the school of tedious outpourings
the man of letters is writing some letters
"would we all be happier in the factory?"
embittered romantics one and all
"we are but older children, dear,
who fret to find our bedtime near"
in the land of invisible warfare
vast cheering in the distance
hand me my spear   my little secret book
of matches   and footnote fame!   oh
give me footnote fame
"but that's how my mind works" he said
desperately singing in harm's way

II

poppy or charms can make us sleep as well
joyful ants nest in the roof of my tree
full of courage and shrewd decisions
given to   marked by melancholy
my most rash eyes want out into the light
in that fierce place where love holds court
and there encamps   spreading his banner
where even the wingless soar on balmy winds
in too-thin garments   see with no eyes
shout without a tongue
in a forest alive with whispers
soon-dead deer dash past
strange unrelenting world
I have woven my heart into this net of branches

III

wipe the screen   screw wigs on tight
as we grow older our nervous systems decelerate
many thoughts return marked insufficient
postage   "you know how to walk into a bar"
or any box in the postindustrial ruins
most of what we say is in quotes
we like wilderness in nachur
but not in our fellow citizens
amor armor amok   emery   immure
yes yes that does describe your arbitrary foci
on a warm wet noon   think "thought experiment"
or murmur "vagaries of the heart"
a comeback of one sort or another
dream of big live teddy bear that "wants" "you"

IV

it is well known that Mary Magdalen came to Provence
to live after the crucifixion
but less known that at Maximilien near Marseilles
the tip of her nose used to be on view
no more than that   because she had been cremated
but the tip of her nose remained imperishable
because there   the christ had kissed her
& who is going to pay   any attention to anything
when we aren't here anymore   "& what was it
like that world of yours?"   so much depends
on Fire Engine Number 5   myth is the practice of memory
dit Joanne Kyger
Johannes Kelpius first american composer
founded a commune called "the woman in the wilderness"

V

the lecturer's heart stepped into the void
the mind slows down the mind speeds up before
it stops   contemplating what's never isolate
"landing a B-52 in a desk drawer"
the man said   spoke of his dying
i believe this is the future site of my plaque
life so short this piece of paper so small
alphabet ends universe begins
still trudges along in its big shoes
not afraid to include   what seems dull & quotidian
replicas of your thoughts

win free admission to the shores of forgetfulness
at the edge of some divine comedy
the prompter whispers leftover lines

VI

vast cheering in the distance
embittered romantics one and all
on a warm wet noon   think "thought experiment"
or any box in the postindustrial ruins
alphabet ends   universe begins
at the edge of some divine comedy
"the sound like a thousand falling bird beaks
in the brown harpsichord of the grass"
in the last light of evening
and fear has lien upon the heart of me
in a forest alive with whispers
given to   marked by melancholy
a commune called "the woman in the wilderness"
so much depends on Fire Engine Number 5

VII

"days when the giant won't fall for the ruse
days when no kindly mammals speak to us with human voices"
i dunno man it's tough   & it's never been anything but
many were here but they left again
yet surprised once again
in awkward bliss and bashful ecstasy
let us forgo all pain of crags
here in this pleasant valley of diphthongs
come babe   pass me the delicious
cold cucumber salad
as the axe of the sun descends
we wane away among the peonies
& we have absolutely no complaints
of hours such as these

VIII

"would we all be happier in the factory?"
in the land of invisible warfare
many thoughts return marked insufficient
most of what we say is in quotes
win free admission to the shores of forgetfulness
& we have absolutely no complaints
let us forgo all pain of crags

145

for a special additional performance
of such as love and whom love tortures
like the eyeglasses of the less fortunate
in that fierce place where love holds court
joyful ants nest in the roof of my tree
myth is the practice of memory
"the pneumatic drill destroys my cities"

IX

underground trees   slow darkness
and fear has lien upon the heart of me
magpie steals silver spoon   it is gone forever
like the eyeglasses of the less fortunate
in a terrifying gray light from the future
the carnival continues   a place where a sad horde
of such as love and whom love tortures
point to the moon and break it
"in the year 1327   at the opening of the first hour
on the sixth of April   I entered the labyrinth"
yesterday's clowns return
for a special additional performance
in the last light of evening
today I think about all those radio waves

X

hand me my spear   my little secret book
desperately singing in harm's way
yes yes that does describe your arbitrary foci
dream of big live teddy bear that "wants" "you"
life so short this piece of paper so small
replicas of your thoughts
& it's never been anything but hours such as these
as we grow older our nervous systems decelerate
in a terrifying gray light from the future
I entered the labyrinth
full of courage and shrewd decisions
in too-thin garments with no eyes
at Maximilien near Marseilles
"at night the streets are tidal like the sea"

XI

"we are but older children, dear"
of matches   and footnote fame!   oh
on a warm wet noon screw wigs on tight

not afraid to include its big shoes
when the cyclops won't fall for the ruse
as the axe of the sun descends
the prompter whispers leftover lines
I think about all those radio waves
where even the wingless soar on balmy winds
shout without a tongue   strange unrelenting world
after the crucifixion   "& what was it like   that world"
oh footnote fame   the man of letters
"you know how to walk into a bar"
in the year 1327   at the opening of the first hour

XII

"but that's how our minds work" they said
"who fret to find our bedtime near"
in any box in the postindustrial ruins
wipe the screen   amor armor amok   emery   immure
"landing a B-52 in a desk drawer"
the lecturer's heart stepped into the void
where no kindly mammals speak to us
come babe   pass me the delicious diphthongs
the carnival continues   yesterday's clowns return
my most rash eyes want out into the light
I have woven my heart into this net of branches
spreading its banner of attention
underground trees   slow darkness
murmur "vagaries of the heart"

NOTES

Epigraph: Hugh Wittemeyer (Ed.), *William Carlos Williams and James Laughlin: Selected Letters* (New York: W.W. Norton, 1989).

(I) "we are but older children ... ": Lewis Carroll, to Alice.

(III) "you know how to walk into a bar": Robert Creeley to the author, one evening in the late Sixties. "amor armor emery immure": alternatives to amore provided by "Spell Check."

(IV) "it is well known ... ": from E. S. Bates, Touring in 1600.

(V) "landing a B-52 ... ": Scholar, poet, and musician Jack Clarke describing the task of dying to Ed Sanders, in a telephone conversation not long before Jack's take-off.

(VI) "the sound like a thousand falling bird beaks/ in the brown harpsichord of the grass": piero heliczer (the soap opera, Trigram Press, 1967), who also wrote:

"i cross the street then immediately cross back again
i never look to the left and right when i cross a street
why else are street crossings put there if not to cross"

—and was run over and killed by a truck around the time of my writing of these fourteen-liners.

(VII) "days when the giant…": lines from Swedish poet Gunnar Harding's poem *Many Were Here But They Left Again*. There are other echoes and near-quotes from that magnificent poem in this humble text, and similar embeddings of lines from Cavalcanti (in translations by Ezra Pound and Marc Cirigliano), Sir Thomas Wyatt, Edwin Denby, Ted Berrigan, Jouni Inkala, and Tom Raworth.

(VIII) "the pneumatic drill destroys my cities": heliczer, op. cit.

(IX) "in the year 1327…": Francesco Petrarca, Sonnet 211, translated by Nicholas Kilmer.

(X) "at night the streets are tidal like the sea": heliczer, op. cit.

from HOW ON EARTH

SCRIPT MIST

hang on to moment, naked, fair
frail as a butterfly—and where
did that come from?
from here, from under the leaves
of 1) lyrical moon, 2) sonorous foam

then the voice said "up and at them, hedgehog"
then it sat on his cool
with dark quark wings
while favorite sirens / mighty old voices
sang fierce and refined epitaphs

scattered and dashing, one does la-la more
at the good times institute
a joint in time
in the great carpentry

EMPTIER PLANET
—*i.m. Larry Eigner*

a face

flies away

while band plays on

a shake of beauty

almost anyhow

once more however

gone

WINGS OVER MAXIMUS

51 Pegasus a sun
has a planet
half the mass of Jupiter
too close to that sun
to have our kind of life

    looks at cigarette burn on mouse pad.
    "oh that'll just become familiar"

order in the saloon!

    helmeted angel waitresses
    out of 1890s Norwegian kitsch

      tilted loony toon light

    she used to laugh at his jokes
    but now he stands there in the cold & dark
    howling
    at her window
        (The Jilted Professor's Lament)

if feeling the absence
equals missing the presence

does missing the absence
equal feeling the presence?

    wild surmise
    in mild sunrise
        "& her name was Solitaire"

LETTER TO UNCLE O.

      for Andrei Codrescu

Dear Publius Ovidius
   "The Nose"
missing ah missing the rose
   of Rome
for ten years of letters in verse

149

in one of them, startled to find yourself
    calling drear Tomis "home"
—a shantytown by the frozen Black Sea
    where people grow fur and look daggers

and no speak-a-da Latin
    but something called Getic
Getic or at best broken Greek
    and winter is a year long

while you pen song upon song
    to send
where once you were young
    listing your poet friends by name
and even some whose names you can't recall

praising that lovely sodality
    of once-upon-a-time
a welcome break for your reader
    who's 2,000 years too late

to do a thing about the ostensible reason
    for your lengthy *Tristia* or *Drearies*:
the Emperor's pardon

because that emperor lives
    only within the rose
    of a city more perennial

where dream and memory converse
    carouse and conjure
    breathlessly deathless

(and who could pardon himself that way
    except now and again
    between the lines

PATRICK
PRITCHETT

ANSELM THE GREAT

Corvus. Anselm Hollo, Coffee House Press

For over thirty years, Anselm Hollo has been combining high-toned
European sensibility with plain American colloquialism to

produce a poetry of exceptional grace, wit and durability. In his latest work, *Corvus*, Hollo surpasses himself; it's as beautiful as anything he's ever written. These new poems ripple with an elegant clarity and a delightfully subversive edge.

The pleasures offered by Hollo's poetry are keen and various. He is a master at leaping effortlessly between the high notes and the low, between sonorous pathos and the slyly mordant comic aside. For sheer dexterity, he has few equals.

Like another great original, the French Surrealist Robert Desnos, Hollo sees his poems forming "one continuous poem." Fittingly then, much of the tone in *Corvus* is retrospective. It is a book of looking back, taking stock, summing up. Above all, it is a book of elegies, both for those recently departed, like the poet's sister, Irina, whom he memorializes in the austere and haunting "1991," and others who have left us earlier, like the exuberant poet Ted Berrigan.

Berrigan figures prominently in *Corvus*. The section entitled, "Lines From Ted: An Ars Poetica," are transcriptions, Hollo writes in his notes, of talks given by Berrigan at Naropa in 1982. The result is a bracing collaboration that articulates what might be called the way of the poem:

> You have to make your work at your own pace
> It is made of words
> One word after another

And:

> ... what I think happens when a poem works is
> That it rises into the air of its own powers
> And in doing so it has formed a circle
> And it becomes something like the sun or a star
> Or a planet ...
> I have to go now I have to go and think about this for
> a thousand years.

And a thousand years would just be a start. "Lines From Ted" is a meditation on what poetry can bring us, its mysterious news from beyond and its invigorating, redemptive powers. It has the warmth and freshness of a talk with an old and dear friend.

Hollo is also one of our most erudite poets, but while *Corvus* bristles with allusions, it is never top-heavy, nor is the music ever impeded by the learning. Indeed, one of this poet's greatest accomplishments is the way he weds acute intelligence to the rhythmic demands of song. His method is deceptively simple:

> method is effortless:
> translation of autonomous objects
> from adept to zygote
> in rhapsodic rises & falls

But the chief pleasure of *Corvus* is its deeply humane music. From the recondite "The Word Thing," to the playful farce of "Why There Is A Cat Curfew In Our House"; from his earthy translations from the *Greek Anthology*, to the intimate, lyrical benediction of "And," Hollo strikes an expansive and enheartening panoply of notes. Each poem is never less than itself, integral and complete; there are no poses here, no sleights-of-hand, except in those the poet delights in exposing with a wry postmodernist wink and a nudge. Over all these poems is stamped the Chinese ideogram for sincerity, which Ezra Pound translated as "the sun's lance coming to rest on the precise spot verbally."

In his introductory note, Hollo tells us that *corvus* is Latin for raven, which is what his own surname signifies in Finnish. This is appropriate, since one of the mythic roles played by the raven was that of psychopomp, or guide of souls to the Underworld, a function that poets, as purveyors of news from afar, have been undertaking since Orpheus made his descent to Hades. This bit of association brings to mind Hollo's own translation of the Finnish poet Paavo Haavikko:

> And I asked him,
> The bird
> Who is identical with myself,
> I asked him for the road, and he said:
> It is best to leave early.

Anselm Hollo has always been leaving early, "ahead of all departure," as Rilke puts it, checking out the bends in the psychic road ahead of us and relaying back the information—painful, funny, or celebratory, as the case may be—with the greatest panache and precision.

ED SANDERS

O, SEXTON! OH SHELLEY, O SAPPHO! O, GOETHE, O, SCHILLER!

THE QUESTION OF FAME

An hour & a half
you utter your
     elegant perf

in the packed soccer stadium
          in Santiago

Your poems
are projected

152

on dirigibles
                overhead

You're hooked up by satellite
to 300 other stadiums
all over the world
all packed

Finally you finish
and 30,000,000 people are on their feet
screaming &
jogging in place

They clap for hours
till their palms are
                covered with blood

& blisters
pop painfully
                in their shoes

and soon they
                begin to
                        thud to the bleachers

like clapping colossi

They lie there hoarsely writhing
the hemous mists still spuming
                from along the edges
                        of whacking fingers

their eyes glazed over
like 30,000,000 raccoons
                in a sudden flashlight.

This happens every Sunday afternoon
and it's still not enough.

WINE NOT

in the manner of T'ao Yuan-ming

for Phil Coturri

I

There is wine there is wine
soon there is more than enough wine
I pretend at being an old man with
my pipe and my pen pondering my foot
the years have given me some practice
my scribbles are no less legible however
words should be beautiful inside and out
that's the wish at the tip of my toe
a sphincter of light slowly opening
spreading as a smile's vast eternity

II

The man in me does funny things
the woman in me hardly ever gets out
I toast myself in my claret solitude
retire to the late gloom of my study
and scratch myself in total privacy
my leg should be thumping the floor
but no such luck and my only fleas
the jumps from thought to thought
was merely the idea of wine just
opening the bottle that brought me here

III

Ancient mysteries suddenly clarified
I hold a glass of wine to the light
the long long years escape as smoke
or more simply just pissed away
at fireside night's talked to death
a fear felt even by the bones
another glass of pickling immunity
caged by walls and roofs overhead
past associations arrive taxed as mail
the antennae of a species separated mute
the companionship of a bottle has to do
I have become secretary to this dialogue
words spilled as pale as red as blood

IV

How does the spider justify her web
drops of rain drum down on plastic
I repeat the lies that make me happy
a splash of wheels through puddles
the idling purr of a neighbor's ride
there is much to decipher about life
bug nearly flew up my nose just now
if I'm to take it at all seriously
take it with a cheery glass of red
enjoy till my shoulder grow heavy

V

Oh cricket on the bathroom tiles!
I won't catch you because I can't
but I will drink to your good luck

VI

As rain my thoughts are incomplete
moth at window patiently waits
the electric light a lot like a god
I sip away at fruity fermentations
swallowing the entire universe
nothing more than a drop of red

CALIFORNIA STATE OF MIND

Eyes rolled back in sun stream
feet up till tomorrow then
acknowledge passing time
as a spinning wheel which
always returns to the same moment
so the rush to get from here
to there put in sunny perspective
motivation if you can call it that
muted by bright blue afternoons
calmed by light days go by
satisfaction in soaking up rays
steers also blindly through
a patch of bright white

COMMON COLD

Bamboo dew drops
uncomfortably cool
on my fevered skin
an imperceptible drizzle
marks the day
with sheer curtain gloom
columns of smoke billow
bright bands which
knit into the mass
of a dark conifer forest
ragged undersides of clouds
raked across barbed peaks
empty themselves
on the drear landscape
that my head feels stuffed
with cotton or old socks
does not contribute much
to diminish this perspective
oh ache groan moan sniffle
sneeze watery eyes nothing
tastes right confined by
a virus so simple
it defies cure
trying to cope with
the holiday mess just
a dream of myself like
the fog that envelopes
the trees I mix with
pins and needles
in this appendage or that
real sit-down weather stare
out the window and record
the slow movement of nature
eons in seconds pass
as they always will
just the bug in me
makes it seem like forever

BLUEBIRDNESS

Blue bird appeared suddenly
on one of the large
            flat rocks in the garden
moved its head with stop action precision
just as suddenly flew from view
to leave a hole
            in the picture
                it had just made
the rock
        there forever

refuse to count
        those friends
            acquaintances
who have flown from this flat rock and left
            a hole in the associations
they once made

how many isn't just a matter of fact
        images called up
            shimmer
                    transparent
in the quiet garden
            of a morning alone
half yellowed stalks of wild grass droop
over the smooth grey abyss
stick figure
            limbs flung abject
the faint tremors of beating hearts
bugs
        or a breeze in passing

I resemble those remarks
blade of grass
            the advance of the season
folly of importance placed on accrual
all that stuff
        hits home
before long
stalk shadows fall across the rock
        that large recognition
                as dawn grows to dark
            deceptive in the half light
but unmistakable
            as the stutter of blue wings in flight

FREE ADVICE

One may go along with something
    sometimes   just for the ride
say going to a seminar to gather info
about grantsmanship — how to pursue
    government money —
        of all the disgusting things
instead of just coming up with good ideas
    to earn the money
to study how to get government money !
    for godsakes
instead of figuring out how to get more
out of the money you've already got
        jesus !
but one may go along with such scams
anyway just for fun just for company
besides who knows one might just
learn something useful afterall anyway
who knows   it can't hurt   right?
one never knows, do one ?

PENULTIMATE SUBLIME

a better way
    to question
        ideology:

    to ignore it;

    make objects;
    projects objects.

Tho mastery may be faked
    by massive production

a master may yet
    produce en masse.

157

THE MISERABLE STUDENT

I don't know that scholarship
        is good for poets

If you get really smart
        you get really quiet

I have read the great poets
        & I think I'll shut up

                » «

meanwhile on
        public television

the educational channel

the snails
        are still fucking

                » «

        should citizens and ancestors care to know
        Cardarelli Late 20th Century Poet
        was called by my friends Joe

GOODBYE

Now I recognize
it was always me
like a camera
set to expose

itself to a picture
or a pipe
through which the water
might run

or a chicken
dead for dinner
or a plan
inside the head

of a dead man.
Nothing so wrong
when one considered
how it all began.

It was Zukofsky's
Born very young into a world
already very old...
The century was well along

when I came in
and now that it's ending,
I realize it won't
be long.

But couldn't it all have been
a little nicer,
as my mother'd say. Did it
have to kill everything in sight,

did right always have to be so wrong?
I know this body is impatient.
I know I constitute only a meager voice and mind.
Yet I loved, I love.

I want no sentimentality.
I want no more than home.

KARL MARX'S EYES

I closed my eyes in front of the bookshop, sitting
    in the loose-slatted
wooden chair, and had a vision of Karl Marx's
    eyes, squinty and black
like a high-contrast photo on a book jacket, too
    much ink for those wrinkles, almost
a hard-bitten stare, like a gambler's or some
    actor pretending to be one, for a movie
poster, my eyes shut and those frantic but not
    fanatic eyes looking at me. What
got me was something like pain and urgency, but
    mostly the imperative that I consider
Marx's eyes as something in the world, all that
    fine-line German print
he had to read under thick wood letters,
    Beobachter Zeitung, like that,
considering with pain opinions not his own. I feel
    that, looking at mostly nicer print
with poems on, a strain around the eyes, mine half
    Scotch half Polish, granularly
angled like his, so it was for me that he
    recognized me, that strain in those little
    muscles
that make pouches that catch the light, stretch
    older skin to crow's feet, salutation
rather than a bond like looking like your brother,
    not even recognition but respect
as Christopher Plummer's Oedipus mask with the
    eyes out looks at us, his life so
difficult and silly, perhaps as described in
    Edmund Wilson's *Finland Station*, my life
like his full of world-important events one's print
    seems able to change, almost
as if it's important for me to believe this, and how
    to afford ink. Rent. (I may
have to move, mine's so high.) But mostly his
    notion of looking at me, patriarch,
beard not pointy like Conrad's but full, rambling,
    a Christmas-tree beard, Edward
Lear's with owls in it, absurd fringe to greatness.
    Is this what he's
telling me, that greatness is no big deal? no man's
    valet a hero to himself—I don't

get the notion that he practiced that stare, though
    he'd use it in Internationales,
prophet to his followers, dumpy man like the
    people Trocchi describes looking after barges
that all have dogs, Schipperkes, to guard their
    coal or wood, habit of taking heroin
to pass the time an incident, thing you might write
    about, not Burroughs's Algebra
of Need as is J. S. Mill had a habit, looked after by
    his wife, the granularity of
day to day, coal dust, the barge so square and
    hard to tow, all Europe
in a barge, predictably demolished in predictable
    war. A woman came in the shop
yesterday with books to sell, wearing a thin black
    cord, raffish as raffia, around her neck
and three oblate lumps, pierced, rich, the color of
    onion skins if onions underneath
were made of fat, flattened like abacus counters, a
    bit above her breasts. "Are
those African?" I asked. "Yes," she said, "they're
    partially fossilized amber."
"Thank you," I said, and she went away. For me
    that was a transaction,
more like than not Adam Smith's imagining he has
    a bale of wool, wants a cask of wine
to make clear by example, almost a little play,
    what he means. Marx meant
what he imagined "value" might mean if workers
    in a puppet play (dressed said
Attlee like workers then) announced themselves as
    workers by their rounded shoulders
carved by Bill Baird, tired stance (a sag of wires,
    gut) and lived in model rooms
with just a little sink, no bathtub, if you imagine
    Marx knee-deep in Hegel, theory
as being an audience, the only one, to this
    spectacle, pictureframe windowframe, so like
Conrad's eyes, which are even more like mine,
    remembering looking out at the sea, his beard
like Lenin's only more French, his eyes like
    Marx's only more candid, rather, capable
of less directed candor. But it's Marx's eyes that
    look at me, not the sea.

161

WORK IS SPEECH

"It's time to get our hands dirty," Bruce Andrews says, presumably with
    Bic
ink. Olson ate the orange garagemechanic cloth in a dream though this
    is not
always understood. Whitman lauds frisket and tympan and there you
    are, that "style"
what we think of as style is temporally local. The cuffs on my flannel
    pajama trousers
have been admired. Praising is what style does, always does, and this
    requires that style
have a style, and its aristocracy is not (except in grade schools, all hands
    now vanished into sleeves)
to dictate but invite, as Michael Clark with a little bow invites a lion off
    its perch,
so what is the lion, a capitulation to the brutalizing of Getting a living,
    killing animals and vegetables,
the necessary accommodation to others we make, speaking to a bus
    driver
whether so he'll understand or not. Here in Andrews' beautifully
    lavender *Excommunicate*
words pretty as Spoerri's catsup, wineglasses, crumpled napkins,
    crumbs, shrimp
are disposed (disposable the French'd say, yours to command, verbal
    flatware)
and here (again you're wrong, yours to etc. soft, not even sticking to the
    linen, and verbal
pulled free of *Verbum* in Aquinas, that Lonergan'd study and Gilby
    translate
a scrap of, the best scrap, we're here at lots of Latin words Andrews has
    listed (like)
mustardpots standing for field mortars, their place on the page a
    metaphor, these bib
overalls raspberry as this book, the cut tape stripes meant powerful, and
    what stays are words
                like parasol,
as if history is knowing the Latin words too.
Vision's workers read, Jack London's lamplit backroom, hobo
    experience feeding in
somehow to Cobbett or Sassoon, a difficulty of finding your way the
    experience reading
and experience correct. Ponge kept his labor organizing separate from
    his florilegia.

To want words charged in their places will surely be like having a notion
    what use the
Lascars and Malays in Sax Rohmer, fodder of thrills, might come to as
    this book not quite
the color of revolution could go on the shelves of any of our Cambridge
    bookstores catering
to dissent and not look out of place, aware of itself as horribly different
    and indeed the
manuals, red books, manifestos promise them a whole intrinsically
    vulgar relation to reading,
the book announcing itself frankly as tool. Let us insert as Spoerri might
    a stuffed
mouse among the shriveling grapes, Sitwell on Bath or de la Mare's
    Desert Islands
vandalize the worker's shelf, give him Arabia as if it were the promise of
    art.

PENDANT EROS

Cupid, whatever it is, the winged thing never there in
    Piccadilly when I am,
is or now is naked to seem vulnerable since the older
    conventions of undraped
gods are wholly forgotten, a "naked babe" only, no more
    our care than an
ice cube on the sidewalk. It is, used to be, was for Keats,
    of practical value
to imagine sexual desire as embodied less in oneself than
    as a person, as
if you'd meet Love in a bar, have to look good to its
    father. Eros shows
you pictures of his parents. That's cute, like Slavitt
    translating *Eclogues*,
that glottal form. If you kiss a well-formed being capable
    of response your
mouth, because you're moved or the mechanics of it, fills,
    drips liquid, speech
thickened or impossible ... and I think, here, of
    Mallarmé's Faun, sensing when he
wakes the delicatest kiss just fading from his lips, its
    beauty even as a false

perception as if we are, always, just having been kissed, a
　　　palm with fingers parallel
just having brushed our ribs, reason to wear a flannel
　　　skirt the bruise touch makes,
cloth's clinginess like your fingers, hers, barely parted at
　　　the bus stop.
Like these a kiss entails parting, meant almost as
　　　temporary or transitions
from which we're wise to conclude Eros is a time-god, the
　　　little wingèd one
dredged up from the Thames, silver not very pure but cast
　　　to prettiness
rather than carved, tiny god of Sleep. You could dangle it
　　　Hypnos, whatever, from
a corner of a bookshelf, ceiling lamp, to alter by its tiny
　　　flylike presence how
the fact of starlight on her face, asleep, strikes you. Some
　　　icons, posed at
the edge of a plate with a burning vigil light, are
　　　spectators to the act of
veneration, why not Hypnos, lost so long in river sand or
　　　clay, the dark
of the room (he'll be a copy, mould thrown off from the
　　　original), its shadows
functioning as depth of water, slime, to make him feel still
　　　silted there
but able *to look on*, in our pretense, at nose, a rise of
　　　cheek, lid's edge
catching, enduring in a meaning of *passio*, the bit of
　　　window light, and doing so
become another kind of hypnos, stiller than the god. The
　　　faun's desire (remarkable)
is capable of abeyance. He forbears. It's partly luxury,
　　　the thinking about them,
almost totting them up, enough, as in pornography the
　　　bath entails notions of nudity,
edged expectation. Anyone subject to eros is likely to see
　　　any object able to be touched
as a body (like ours), a tree, stone, piece of paper with the
　　　lover's name on,
subscribed or addressed, no matter, *Anatomy of
　　　Melancholy*'s cadence creeping in quite
properly as hustling a list. Always a miracle, attraction,
　　　though in her case obvious.

164

It could be a drug but as she says is not. To be greeted as
	welcome without let is
almost more than we can bear. We gain a shape from
	heat, as if some Hart Crane
verb describing our condition effects it, by echo and by
	chant. The rooms
we pass through stay passed, sway slightly as we do, for
	our passing.

PEASANT LITERATURE

I was reading Norman Fruman's fine description of Wordsworth's influence on Coleridge, and thinking of the similar effect Mallarmé had on
Paul Valéry. In each case acquaintance with a first-rate poet raised the
other's idea of what poetry could be by at least one order of magnitude.
Historically, this strikes me as the most important "influence" one poet
can have on another.

As a boy who grew up in the provinces Valéry's models were the
great French Romantics. They were able, but their virtues were not what
Valéry's—by inclination and training—would become. What he had,
before the first scraps of Mallarmé came to him in periodicals, was Poe
(magnificently translated by Baudelaire), who differed from the Romantics of the generation before his precisely in his elevation—even fetishiza-
tion—of intelligence as an element in composition, hence an element,
part of the weave, of the finished product.

What Poe taught Valéry was how to be more French. As he says
of Baudelaire's precursors, "They were averse to abstract thought and
reasoning, not only in their works, but also in the preparation of their
works, which is infinitely more serious. One might have thought that the
French had forgotten their analytical talents." It's this feeling of a tradition restored that accounts for the gratitude always there when the
French of the Symbolist period praise Poe, that most of his U.S. commen-
tators (from Eliot on) find simply unintelligible, inexplicable.

We don't feel it ourselves because we're still Romantics, little
Emersons. Most of what we write (look anywhere, at any periodical) is
what Coleridge and company called "Effusions," outpourings, first
pressings of Personality, usually belonging to somebody without much
experience (reading them, it seems few American poets know how to do
anything), or practice thinking (I don't know many who, skimming a
text or two, could spot differences in how Locke and Berkeley think,
how they manage the act of thinking.) Which is to say, from my point of
view most current American writing is the product of peasants.

165

This includes the new crop of thinkers, the college folks who think of themselves as Theorists. In this connection the anonymous pamphlets coming out of somewhere (Buffalo?) purporting to be by Edgar Poe—so far I've seen contemporized versions of the "Letter to B—" and a review of Lew Daly's "Swallowing the Scroll"—are tremendous good fun, simply from the abutting of that lovely snarling prose against Our Moderns, as if it really were Poe's brand-new fresh response. Even if they weren't well done it would be funny. But they are well done, and as such are the liveliest possible reminders of what recent U.S. writing lacks, an astringently stylish style. My heart warmed to the two I've seen, I am refreshed by them, because only our best writing survives being embedded as quotes in a Poe-ish matrix, and from the joy at seeing that Poe's approach, his manner of proceeding, is utterly modern—if anything gains from being applied to current material. The effect is less pastiche than vindication.

We didn't pick that up (and run with it). The French did—Valéry and Mallarmé. Their gain, our loss. The effect as reported by Valéry of a poem or two by Mallarmé come across in a journal was that they made anything else look like garbage. I find that just as true of these anonymous productions you can only get, so far, as stapled bootleg pamphlets. Find one if you can.

IN DEFENSE OF AMERICAN PEASANTS

(and in reply to Gerald Burns)

A good book must be (for all I know has already been) written on the rejection of Poe by the American parnassus, and on his placement by the French among the stars. Essential differences and oppositions between the U.S. and Europe, going far beyond the facile peasant-urban or savage-civilized, would then become intelligible, shown under Tocquevillian light. Mallarmé and Valéry, we are told by Gerald Burns (*Exquisite Corpse*, #55, p.8), picked up Poe's poetics; we didn't: "Their gain, our loss." Consequently, American writing—well, "most current American writing," but what exactly is being excepted by this peasantly vague "most current"? Burns' poems?—"is the product of peasants." Is it as rural, idyllically, idiotically simple as that?

Poe's insistence on a writing totally controlled by consciousness was a pose, purposefully absurd: cowboy, legs apart, hands on the holsters of the two hemispheres of his powerful brain. With Mallarmé, of his own avowal in his letter to Verlaine, it

166

was a vice. Actually it was worse: a fear, a phobia of chance, of the famous Mallarméan *hasard*, which appears naked, warm, trembling, ephemeral, offensive, horrendous: sad flesh, incarnation. The flower in his verse is "l'absente de tous bouquets," the ideal, unwilting one, forever shining, like a theorem. How far his from the flower the Buddha pointed to in reply to questions regarding the Ultimate, how far from Calderón, whose flowers, mortal, "nacieron con la aurora y murieron con el día"! (The Baroque was a tender, superhuman effort to hold on to the ephemeral as well as to the eternal.)

As a poet, Mallarmé had no truck with the ephemeral. His beloved Poe was better off unfleshed, so much more like himself after his last ethilic breath: "Tel qu'en Lui-même enfin l'éternité le change." And his best known line, "La chair est triste, hélas!, et j'ai lu tous les livres," at least its first hemistich, may strike a chord in some of us, remembering our adolescence and our vehement first desires for a flesh that seemed divine but then betrayed us with a smell of stale garlic, perineal exhalations, armpit sweat and worse, oh how much worse, with vulgar words, clichés, *blasphèmes*. Betrayal by the flesh was Mallarmé's first experience and meaning of *hasard*. His second was the betrayal perpetrated by language. For words, too, are fallen, incarnated; like whorish kisses, they are the chance products of our mortal mouths, the meaningless flotsam of history: as Saussure would have it, arbitrary signifiers. "Nuit" is, for Mallarmé, indignantly, a bright sound, while "jour" is dark. No nativity will redeem flesh and language from their fallen state and save what can be saved from their betrayal: the poet must lift them up into the verse, which must be music. Not incarnated sound, not *his* or *her* music, mind you, nothing personal in it: "L'oeuvre pure implique la disparition élocutoire du poète, qui cède l'initiative aux mots, par le heurt de leur inégalité mobilisés; ils s'allument de reflets réciproques comme une virtuelle trainée de feux sur des pierreries remplaçant la respiration perceptible en l'ancien souffle lyrique ou la direction personelle enthousiaste de la phrase" (*Crise de vers*).

Mallarmé's impersonal music is the hidden harmony in Nature and the poet's task is exclusively with it: "... l'esprit, qui n'a que faire de rien outre la musicalité de tout" (*La Musique et les lettres*). Music is there, like Nature, the poet is not adding anything to it; "on n'y ajoutera pas," he states repeatedly; nothing therefore is left to chance, to groundless inspiration, to evil *hasard*. Reality will be redeemed only when arranged musically in a book, The Book (for him there's only one, as for others there is only one God), where every sign and every empty space shall be premeditated, willed: "Un livre, architecturel et prémédité, et non un recueil des inspirations de hasard fussent-elles merveilleuses..." (Letter to Verlaine). Platonism? No, Plato is too vast: if flesh at times is a tomb *chez lui*, at others it is a lovely bridge to the beyond.

167

Rather, Mallarmé's music is pure Pythagoras, perfect, frigid harmony of the eternal spheres. And we know, don't we, at least since Plato, that our musicality somehow corresponds to our politics. Pythagoras' was aristocratic, sectarian, colored by hatred of the rabble, to which the 19th century added contempt for the bourgeois.

I'll come back to Mallarmé and Valéry, but only after (con)descending to the peasants, after briefly touching the heartbeat of American poetry, Whitman. As far as I know, Borges was the only one who prior to me (in 1945) wrote of Whitman, Mallarmé and Valéry on the same page. For they were hardly soul-triplets. As against the Frenchmen's laborious literary erasure of their egos, the American constructed a poetic Walt Whitman who is famously enormous, everyone and everything, "a kosmos, of Manhattan the son,/ Turbulent, fleshy, sensual, eating, drinking and breeding,/ No sentimentalist, no stander above men and women or apart from them,/ No more modest than immodest." "I believe in the flesh and the appetites," he writes further on, and this use of the verb, at first blush clumsy (for could we not believe in things which doggedly insist on their existence?), signifies not an acknowledgment of reality but an active religious faith, one in which "the scent of these arm-pits aroma finer than prayer" (*Song of Myself*, 24).

A peasant faith, Burns snorts. Very well, why not? Gnostic it isn't, nor is it the etiolated alchemist's faith in *le grand Oeuvre* that sustained Mallarmé (how well was he sustained is another question: read, in the light of the rest of his work, the desperate cry toward the end of his life, the last line of *Un Coup de dés*: all thought, all thinking, is fallen, falsified by evil chance.) Whitman's poetic faith is rather like Francis of Assisi's, for whom everything, the tiniest leaf of grass, is saved by our careful attention. A poetic faith such as Europe had not experienced for a long time, of which we get an unbelieving glimpse in the sculpted stones of medieval churches: together with the Father, the Son and the Holy Ghost, peasants sowing, carpenters sawing, cobblers sewing, couples copulating; trades-people, lovers, carousers, the low life, all, as in Whitman, cohabiting with the spiritual, hence spiritualized. France, in particular, has lacked such poetic cohabitation since Rabelais.

A book—not the one on Poe, another (for, unlike Mallarmé, I believe there should be at least two books)—must be written on the subject of armpits. There's a widespread notion that Don Quijote took up the sword with the secret purpose of shaving Dulcinea's; she, a peasant woman, must have been axillary quite hirsute, and, so the argument goes, the Don wanted to ladify her. Notion often formulated a little differently, by saying the Knight of the Sorrowful Countenance represents the Ideal. Perhaps because of an excessive reading of Unamuno, in my teens and twenties I thought it a keen *aperçu*. No more; nevertheless, I think it deserves a chapter in the armpit book. Second chapter on a remarkable, manifest opposition: today 98% of American women wear clean-shaved armpits, as against 27% of European women who do so: this piece of statistics clearly speaks, it seems to me, without further literary examples, against Burns' characterization of American litterati as peasants. Finally, and in relation to Whitman's "finer than prayer," what has been the effect of modern technology—Odor-O-No, Mitchum, RightGuard—on our communication with the divine?

But returning to Poe, Mallarmé and Valéry, and the influence of the first on the last two, the best, briefest exposé, as far as I know—for I, unlike Burns, let me confess it in French, to cover my shame: *je n'ai point lu tous les livres,* and so I cannot speak of "all writing," not even of "most current American (or French, or any) writing"—is Cioran's piece, "Valéry face à ses idoles" (1970) included in his *Exercises d'admiration.* In his youth, Cioran must have admired Mallarmé, since his first literary project after moving to France (never completed, to my knowledge) was a Romanian translation of those famously difficult texts; by 1970, however, he subscribed to Claudel's negative characterization of the master as "a syntactical genius." Valéry he considers impotent, unable to be a poet naturally, hence preferring his (false) poetics to actual poetry. I prefer to put it differently: the master's aristocratic Pythagoreanism had developed, in the disciple, into a consuming nostalgia for mathemathics. Valéry admitted as much, and, more surprisingly, he admitted knowing very little of that science. But it must have seemed to him that mathematical language is the only one not subject to the vagaries of inspiration and to the dreaded *hasard.* Had he practised math, or had he read attentively the book by the greatest French mathematician of his time, Henri Poincaré, on the genesis of mathematical discoveries, the author of *Monsieur Teste* should have been *désabusé:* no, no thought, not even mathematical, can be free from the mysteries of freedom, of the unintended and inexplicable—of *le coup de dés.* I don't remember where Yeats tells of his reading "Le Cimetière marin," Valéry's most famous poem, and admits having been moved till he reached that line, *"Zénon! Cruel Zénon! Zénon d'Elée!,"* at which point his emotion vanished and turned into disgust. One can see why.

"Their gain, our loss," is Burns' summary sentence of American poetry and exaltation of the French. Cioran's judgment happens to be the exact opposite: "Mallarmé et Valéry couronnent une tradition et préfigurent un épuisement; l'un et l'autre sont symptômes de fin d'une nation *grammairienne.*" But Cioran is no judge, someone might object, for he wrote only prose. Let's listen then to Yves Bonnefoy, the great French poet of our time, and a writer who criticizes others only *à contrecoeur.* This is how he starts a 1963 piece on Valéry (in *L'improbable et autres essais*): "Il y avait une force dans Valéry, mais elle s'est égarée"; and this is how he ends: "Nous avons à oublier Valéry." What Burns wants American poets to remember and reclaim, Bonnefoy exhorts French poets to forget.

Literary peasantry, for our too frequent contributor to the *Corpse*, "includes the new crop of thinkers, the college folks who think of themselves as Theorists." Burns must be aware, though, that Mallarmé is the Moses of that faith and calling, and that the cradle of French, hence of American Theory, was the magazine *Tel Quel*, whose name, whose spirit to a large extent, was borrowed from Valéry. Shouldn't that make theorists, by Burns' own strictures, a little more civilized, more *raffinés*? It appears not: they are not allowed more skills than those of milking goats and planting turnips. No American writer, says Burns, is able to distinguish Locke's thought from that of Berkeley. If we may apply a little logic to a mass of high-density incoherence, this seems to imply that American poets are not as philosophically adept as those French models, Mallarmé and Valéry. Well, consider Mallarmé, whose project to write The Book which would successfully compete with the cosmos and finally replace it was closest to Hegel's: the little he knew about Hegel's system he got indirectly through his friend Villiers. As for Valéry, as much as he idolized science, he despised philosophy, except the logico-positivistic kind. Whitman, on the other hand, read Emerson, Lavater, Volnay, and he read Hegel; indeed, some would complain that he read too much Hegel.

All this might be blamed on an exhausted memory: having read all the books, Burns has forgotten all. His parting bray, though, when he proclaims that confronted with some recent imitations of Poe, collectively and anonymously produced, all recent American poetry looks like garbage, can only be attributed to an arrogance one might call satanic if it weren't so silly. Perhaps, as Milton thought, such arrogance is born from a sense of unfair unrecognition and injured merit: I don't know. What I can say is, I have read those imitations of Poe, and found them enjoyable, in small doses. Many readers of the *Corpse*, I suspect, will enjoy them more, those able to catch and appreciate references and allusions to persons or events of the contemporary scene of U.S. poetry, which with its wonderful views, its many islands and canals and, of course, its Academia, is a Venice I visit only occasionally, as a tourist. Outsider that I am, I cannot fail to feel the absurdity of preferring this warmed-over Poe to all else being written by American poets. To mention only the book I have read last, Charles Stein's recent *The Hat Rack Tree* (Station Hill, 1994), here we have a poet who is vastly more conversant with philosophy, logic and math than Valéry, whose line is as perfect, as memorable, but, being American, infinitely more flexible and free, and who has none of the Frenchman's *froideur*. With Stein, we run no risk that our emotion will turn into disgust.

To call, as Burns does, such first-rate productions garbage

is—I'm looking for a word that's not too strong—assinine. Yet no, the ass is a domestic animal; we need a wild ass here. Onagrian.

DETAIL OF DELIGHTS OR SMALL SNAPSHOTS INSIDE THE BIG PICTURE (ON READING GERALD BURNS)

I was speaking with Gerald Burns on the telephone one afternoon and I mentioned to him that I had, for the past week, his poem, "Enter Spontaneo, Left. He Speaks," on the table in front of where I often sit, and that during that week I had, on numerous occasions, simply glanced down to seemingly random places in the poem where my eyes were drawn, and that the parts which I read, each time, revealed new layers of meaning for those parts and for the poem as a whole. It was as if I was taking small snapshots out of a larger photograph, or details from a painting, sometimes overlapping one another, and that these became whole pictures unto themselves which then changed my cumulative perception of the entire picture (poem). There was a moment of silence after I said this, and then he asked me if I wrote literary criticism, because, he said, that this was precisely his intention, to have that happen, and that the instances of anyone having this realization with any clarity were so few and far between as to be staggering to him when they did.

The purpose of this essay is not to make note of my ability to have perceived this (and it would be silly if it were). The purpose is, instead, to further explore the phenomenon as it occurred for me over the course of that week, and which continues to occur, as I look at the aforementioned poem, as well as other of Burns's poems.

When I first read the poem, along with the others Gerald had submitted for possible publication in *Rain City Review*, I called my associate editor who had read them first and said "Are these supposed to be poems? They seem more like essays with line breaks." The long lines, themselves, confounded my mind to bear with them. This was a challenge without precedent for me, and I was unequipped to meet it initially. But I laid them on the table as a reminder to call Gerald and discuss them with him in the next few days, and little by little, over the course of the week with no answer at his home, I learned how to open up, read, and understand them. His poems unfold further with each successive re-reading, and, more than any other poet's work that I have come across, yield whole new worlds of insight and meaning with

171

BRIAN CHRISTOPHER HAMILTON

each reading, affected immeasurably by my state of mind at the moment that I set my eyes upon them.

Even to the untrained eye, Burns's poems are nothing less than stylistic phenomena themselves—artistic conglomerations of poetic sequence, critical analysis, book reviews and reference, scientific and historical discourse, rumination and theorizing—each leaping seamlessly to the next without overt segue or setup. But the result is similar to Bosch's "Garden of Earthly Delights" or Dali's "Madonna of Port Ligar" in that details of these complex paintings can be removed and viewed as whole paintings themselves. Burns's poems are indeed much the same such that every part contains something complete within itself that can be independently perceived and considered, and when all the parts are joined together they reveal a deeper meaning for each of the parts, and the meaning shifts and/or expands perpetually according to the sequence in which the parts are perceived.

The majority of poetry written today is written with intent—with ideas and images moving linearly, one to the next, on their way to the point or meaning of the poem. Each line is usually dependent on the one before it for its connection to that meaning, and with the previous line removed, that meaning is lost. It is Burns's intention to create a tapestry of images and ideas that function as independently from one another as possible, but which are indeed connected, yet often without clear or simple transition. He relies, for the most part, on this connection being made on an unconscious level in the reader, because, on the surface, there are often no obvious bridges between the way one line ends and the next begins. A high degree of mental agility and dexterity are required to stay with the poem's acrobatic leaps from one line to the following line, conceptually and literally.

To further accentuate this effect, Burns uses predominantly long lines on the page. The actual grammatical lines often beam, break, and end mid-line within the stanzas, which helps to encourage and facilitate the multi-line snapshot.

In Burns's poem, "A Workbook for Readers" from *Jenny's Pink Surprise* #1, 1993, he writes, *"The hardest thing to write is a love poem with every line a sense unit, self-sufficient phrase. Shelley's poems can be read from the bottom up without loss."* This too is true of Burns. His poems can be read from the center out in both directions or line by line at random and still be just as and no less complex, chaotic, confounding, and, finally, revelatory and ecstatic, and not only without loss, but with substantial gain. If you come to Burns's party, bring your camera and lots of film, stay for hours or days or weeks, then go home and look at the pictures you have taken. It will have been so much more than you remember.

RHYME

Isn't it good she asked (as
if there were no question in

the question) that we love
each other's bodies one big

one small one slim one tall
isn't it good that we love the

way our skins taste the way
they feel to touch & stroke

of course I love you for your
mind and you me for my dispo-

sition but aren't we very lucky
our bodies love each other too?

THE DAY I WAS DEAD

The three hours I was
in the morgue when
they thought I was
dead but I wasn't
were the worst part
of my whole life
they had me tied
to a stretcher in
a box in the wall
and they couldn't
hear me hollering
I was getting so
cold I was near
to frozen dead
the way they found
out I was alive was
when they came to
do the autopsy
I think there's
been some mistake

doctor one said to
the other you're
damn right there's
been some mistake
I told them get me
some fucking brandy
before I turn into
a block of ice.

THE OLD MAN'S LAMENT

He says that when the posthos
don't work no more it's like
the pain an amputee feels in
the foot that's been cut off.

THE SUFIS

believe that each new language
they learn gives them an additional
soul from which they will acquire
spiritual truths they didn't have
before. I'm enrolling at once in
the Berlitz School for their full
program starting with Japanese,
Sanskrit and Swahili.

CARROTS

Little girls in France, even
in the best families, are told
that if they eat their carrots
they'll grow up with pink thighs.

VISITING JAMES LAUGHLIN, OR THE BUS TO NUDE ERECTIONS

MICHAEL HEYWARD

We were not scheduled to read at New York University until Monday night, the Monday as it happened when Wall Street went crash. I decided to spend the weekend visiting James Laughlin, one of the grand old figures of American modernist writing. Laughlin was born in 1914. While a young man he studied in Rapallo with Ezra Pound who told him he would "never be able to write anything decent" and that he should become a publisher—if he learned to put books out "right side up" then Pound would give him his work to publish. So, in 1936, while still a student at Harvard, Laughlin established New Directions (which Pound would dub Nude Erections) and published everyone from Stendhal to William Carlos Williams, Dylan Thomas to H.D. Laughlin is also a fine poet in his own right and his *Selected Poems* was published a couple of years ago by City Lights. He's an old man now and his letter of invitation was in a spidery hand: "It will be fun to have you visit us in October." Laughlin lives in Norfolk, a hamlet tucked away in the north east corner of Connecticut, about three hours drive from New York. I present myself at the Port Authority Bus Terminal on 42nd Street. It's a creepy place full of thieves, drifters and derelicts. They pace about keeping clear of the cops or lie on the floor like so much litter, oblivious of everything. These people have stepped into the abyss but they define New York no less than the conspicuous consumers on Madison Avenue. I buy my ticket and there's an hour or so to kill. I decide to phone Laughlin to tell him what time I will arrive. I lift the receiver and a man sidles up from nowhere. "You want to make a long distance call, man?" I shake him off and get through. "Delighted," said Laughlin. "Be sure and read a good book." I put the phone down and another man approaches, his palms outstretched. "Let me carry your bags, man." I'm in a sweat. I feel like Catherine Deneuve in *Repulsion* when ghastly hands grow out of the walls to touch and torment her. I find a coffee shop. "Could I have a fresh coffee?" I ask. I invest all my hope in the word "fresh." It rolls nicely from the tongue. The woman behind the counter lifts her head and laughs. "All our coffee is fresh!" she shrieks. She gets my coffee and is nearly sobbing with laughter as she repeats the words *fresh coffee!* I sit down defeated. A black man comes in with his kid. Their skin is the color of muscatel. A callow youth walks in and asks each of us in turn for a dime. One by one we refuse. "Then fuck you all," he shouts. On the bus I open up Wolfgang Hildesheimer's essay in biography, *Marbot*. The hero has just slept with his mother. I am pleased I can take Laughlin's advice. But a minute or so before the bus pulls out onto the street an attractive woman takes the seat opposite. She's in her mid-thirties and has an open confident face. A man of about the same age boards the bus. They recognize each other but their acquaintance is slight. They sit together and begin to talk, about meditation it seems. I abandon Sir Andrew Marbot and his Oedipal stirrings. "It was, like, giving my mind a rest, saying *thanks, I'll check in with you once in a while, see how you're doing* ... uh-huh ... on the weekends people might be able to sit on top of a particular catharsis ... it was just really disheartening to have to talk ... I mean, what can you say that has any meaning ... I found that a really tranformative experience." He is doing most of the talking. Her shining eyes suggest she understands what he is saying. He announces he has been married for exactly one week. It is his second marriage. They start on marital fidelity. He doesn't believe in it and has wasted no time. "I would have told her if she asked but she didn't ask." I can't quite catch the woman's reply but he is already describing some group he was in. We whiz through a village called Gaylordsville. Things are heating up. "It's a process of exchanging love with other people ... the whole purpose is of discharging whatever tensions you have ... I checked everybody out and saw a reflection of love ... intimacy is encouraged ... there's been a lot of opportunities to let all barriers down ... I knew that would be painful and difficult ... I was incredibly jealous ... so my therapist gave me an exercise ... visualize her with every guy you know ... and give each guy a lot of time with her ... " We pass a sign which reads in bold letters MARY ANN SCHMALZI and on the next line LEGISLATOR. Our friend is moving in for the kill. "Is it all right if I call you up for no special reason, say hi, how are you doing?" She nods. And a little later: "I don't believe in accidents." Their good-bye becomes a rather long but certainly stylish hug. He mutters something about a phone call. He moves to the back of the bus and I hear him talking to someone. For one horrible moment I am certain it is his wife. It is, thank goodness, another man. And the attractive woman sitting opposite me puts on some lipstick, uses a breath freshener and settles down with her Walkman.

James Laughlin meets me at the bus stop in his stationwagon, a set of golf clubs slung in the back. He is disappointed I don't play. Laughlin is tall, 6′3″ or thereabouts. He's rather handsome and talks in a smooth eastern drawl. "I don't go much to New York nowadays. It's so vulgar. Donald Trump, pain! Andy Warhol, pain!" As we pull into the drive he tells me not to mind the cook who is mad and will say and do strange things. "She was Malcolm Cowley's cook before she took this job and I don't know which one exasperated the other most." We drink a cup of tea together then go for a walk to his daughter's house a mile up the road. Laughlin has about a thousand acres, most of it forest, and runs thirteen sheep on it. The sheep have black faces and feet and look as strange to me as black swans would to him. It is the fall and the hills are a blaze of color—red, yellow, purple, green, blue. We walk up a narrow dirt road and Laughlin points to another house, barely visible through a clearing. "That's the house I grew up in. I had to sell it a few years ago, I couldn't keep the damn place up." His face is kind and long and merry. His eyes are blue. He has a wry smile. We reach his daughter's house. There is a ladder to the roof. Laughlin tells me to climb it. "On a clear day," he says, "you can see three states—New York, Connecticut and Massachusetts." On top of the roof I have no idea how many states I can see. Beneath me stretch valleys and mountains, blue in the distance where the air is hazy, a mass of red and yellow trees closer up. It looks like God's own country. We walk back for dinner. A bell goes and a woman of perfectly sane appearance brings in a wholesome stew. With all the day's excitement I'm famished and go for seconds. After dinner we head upstairs to catch the end of the TV news. A glamorous black woman who Laughlin tells me is a famous graduate of the University of Mississippi interviews a surgeon and then a radiologist about breast cancer. This all takes about forty-five minutes and by the end of it there's nothing we don't know about modified radical excisions and mammograms. Of course it's also true that the First Lady may have a breast tumor. Everyone hopes she comes through and marvels at her courage. The shadow of her illness hangs over the subsequent presentation of a brief report that the USA has it in mind to flatten Iran for firing on a Kuwaiti tanker that was flying the Stars and Stripes. Laughlin shows me his study. It is a wonderful room. On this wall are all the New Directions books, everything he ever published, hundreds of titles. Here are all the Pound and William Carlos Williams first editions. There is his collection of Latin texts, some of the editions fourteenth and fifteenth century. Here are all his French first editions. I gape. Laughlin goes off to bed leaving me to browse and turn the lights out. In the sight of such treasure the mind is a crumbly thing. I am demoralized and go to bed too. The mad cook makes us breakfast of bacon and eggs. Laughlin is amused. "She must like you," he says. "If she's not in the mood she won't cook at all but takes the dog for a walk somewhere." He tells me about the time he came to Australia, in 1937. "Some of my Dartmouth friends and I had heard about this good skiing down in Australia. We sailed out. First stop was Hawaii after five days, then Pago Pago, then Fiji. Finally got to Melbourne via New Zealand. I bust my collarbone on a rockpile on Mt. Hotham and had to rest up in Toorak." This he pronounces rather formally: Two-rark. I ask him what it is like to have published so many good books, to have been so active among so many writers. "It's nice," he says, "but one keeps thinking of mistakes, of books that weren't really ly good enough and of things that one missed. I missed out on Beckett entirely through lack of attention and stupidity. I read *Watt* rather hastily and thought it was kind of tiresome. I didn't realize the man

177

was a bloody genius." We talk about Ezra Pound whom Laughlin knew well. "Ezra had many stubborn views. He hated copyright and passports, the one being a hindrance to knowledge, the other to travel." And later, "He was very secretive about the *Cantos*. After his father's retirement from the mint near Philadelphia he moved the family to Rapallo and Homer would say 'What are you writing now, son?' And Ezra would say 'Wait and see, Dad.'" Laughlin made several visits to see Pound near the end of his life when he resumed to live in Italy after the release from St. Elizabeths Hospital. "At that period he was in his silence you know. He didn't speak any more and that was pretty difficult because it's very hard to be with someone whom you have known as a great talker and have him simply be unwilling to talk. The explanation he gave was that he wasn't going to talk anymore because he had said all he had to say and no one had listened to his economic and political theories. Now I would say that medically it was part of the profound depression into which he fell after he had passed from his hypermanic and paranoid phase into a kind of abulia. He used to use that word "abulia." He said, "I'm abulic. I can't do anything. I can't make up my mind about what I want to do. I can't think. My head is too scrambled to write." And what of the poems of this period, the *Drafts and Fragments* which are among the most beautiful things that Pound wrote? "I remember watching him some days in Sante Ambrogio writing these things and he could barely type. You know, you would hear one finger fall and there'd be a while and another finger would fall." Somehow it comes up that Pound loved to play tennis. "He had a pivot forehand," remarks Laughlin obscurely. After breakfast we drive into the town to pick up the paper and the mail. "This is my friend from Australia," says Laughlin to the man in the drugstore. He turns to me. "You have drugstores in Australia?" "No." "That's because folks don't get sick in Australia," says the man behind the counter. "They don't need 'em." We drive back. The roads are narrow and tree-lined. Everywhere there are leaves on the ground. The maple trees shed leaves the way a cloud does drops of rain. We drive to the team which is also full of books and then down to the lake, clusters of red and yellow trees on its shores. I ask about a boat house away in the distance. "Oh, I got a bunch of cousins use that," he says. The effect of lake and trees and solitude is powerful. I tell James Laughlin he is very lucky. "Oh yes," he says.

SIRVENTES ON A SAD OCCURRENCE

from In Time: Poems 1962–1968,
Bobbs-Merill, 1969.

it is spring, i can walk lightly
down the stairs even on the way
to work, and that's a gain—i
swing my hat widely, not cavalierly,
but remington, the old west, the three
mexican cowboys coming home off
the plains ... the sun shines
even in my room, and my windows
are open, the pretty girls await
me in the street, their coats open,
or no coats at all
                              and on her way
up the stairs an old lady loses
her control ... i will write
against that which is in us to
make age an embarrassment in the
season of coming alive:
old lady, if at this point and
place in time, and all the world/s
area, you cannot forget that small
muscle, if because of the fineness
of the day, your daughter, older than
my mother, says momma, come, sit
outside, all winter you/ve sat in,
the sun, the air, come, momma, outside
you/ll sit, and you go, painfully
the one flight down, and sit, and then
come up, and halfway up ... don/t
tell mrs. stern, the daughter screams,
i/ll be back, right away i/ll clean,
don/t tell ... what can she possibly
tell, old woman, that you are old,
that you have had your children, they
have had theirs, they, theirs, and
you are still here, your world
still exists, where does she fit in?
—as if there weren/t already
shit in the world, and you invented
it. what further indignities to
allow besides inventing shit?

JOEL OPPENHEIMER

and on top of it, is you clung to
the banister at the top step,
almost around, fifteen feet from your
door, to face me suddenly coming
down from one flight up, my hat no
longer swinging but over my head,
over my thin bearded face, my god
the moan then, even your daughter
scared by it, i thought you were
dying /til I found out the truth:
me a tall skinny bearded eyeglassed
hollow-eyed ascetic jew, big
hat, you were back in poland—but
i am no rabbi, and it is no sin,
i am not the chasid or simple
ashkenazi reb you knew and
danced before, around, the psalms
went high to god, david i am
not, there/s no cause for the
alarm i/m so far removed from
it, all i could think was old
lady i wish i knew how to say
aspeto in yiddish, and couldn/t
old lady, it/s spring, i love
you great grandma, this is a
natural act, why will you
fear me for it, i see each day
more shit than you could ever
dream of making, screw your
daughter, let mrs. stern watch
out for her own steps, i am just
standing here waiting for you
to pass, too late now for me
to go back up the stairs, i have
just discovered what the fact is
much too late, and will stand quietly.

and moving past it, later, after
you had been able to pass me,
to your door, me, going down the
steps, a warmth it offers
up, steaming like any simple load
of cow or horse shit, and the
clumsy kleenex streaks where your

daughter had started wiping, christ this
is the east side, let it sit there,
there is room for it, need for it,
labor does not create wealth, wealth
does not create wealth. shit creates
wealth, old lady, old lady, you are
the creator spirit, tho your tits
hang shrunken in your wrapper, tho
your man is long dead—i had a
woman once had need to pee each
time she came, the bed was
wet with it, but she had less need
old woman than you of any simple
love that would allow such miscreant act.
this daughter then suckled like
we say at that long-dry breast too
long ago to give you back your due.
her pants were full too long ago to
let yours drop today.

shit on it, let it go,
this is the east side, this
is park avenue, this is your
son the doctor riverside
drive yet, let it go, this
much you/re entitled to. this
much even i can grant you, who
worries if he farts too loud
in his own silent room, who pisses
to the edge of the bowl it shouldn/t
make no noise who, like so many
of us, wakes each morning to either
constipation or the runs, this
much i can grant you, shit on
the stairs of my house, you
are old enough for that, remember
the little boys, they have not
yet learned how not to piss, they
stand at the curb, between two
cars, their feet spread and braced,
they arch over into the street
they fight each other, distance, the
pride, showoffs, why can/t you
shit that easily on these

steps, old lady, i am sorry.
and it is spring, and where did
you think the flowers will come
from, the rain? and the pretty
girls if not from making love,
and the shit itself if not from
eating, and the broken noses and
the black eyes and scars if not
from fighting, this is the east
side, guns crack, people snort
their noses full of life, and you
are dying because you shat
upon those steps? and were faced
with me? old lady, act your age.

CARL RAKOSI

SHIPS PASSING IN THE NIGHT

"Hello out there!
Where are you bound for?"

"We're looking for
the right axis.

And you?"

"We're idealists.
We can't land.
We're quarantined.

What's the state
of the world
where you're from?"

"Can't tell.
Too busy."

COUNTRY EPITAPHS

Axel Hendrix, railroad conductor
b. Feb. 10, 1860   d. March 31, 1921
PAPA, DID YOU FIND YOUR WATCH?

The widow Fairchild also spoke
                    into a headstone:
AT LAST I KNOW WHERE HE IS AT NIGHT!

The widow Benson was brief,
                    the words chiselled:
GONE BUT NOT FORGIVEN!

And yonder is a whole novel
                    on a tombstone:
I TOLD YOU I WAS SICK!

And here's a humorist:
ON THE WHOLE I'D RATHER BE IN PHILADELPHIA
Ha!
Hello, what's this? under a crucifix!

THEY DON'T MAKE JEWS LIKE JESUS ANY MORE
Well, the Good Lord must have had a reason.

THE IRISH BOY

I don't know what's got into that rooster.
First, he appointed himself the morning herald,
now he's out there on the roof proclaiming
to one and all that every hen within sight
belongs to him ... his, his, his ...
and that he intends to go down to the hen house
and lay them all, none will be spared,
and if anybody wants to take exception to this,
let him come forward and he will personally
take them all on, one by one or in the aggregate,
otherwise, let the sleepers hold their peace.

DAVID IGNATOW

ONCE UPON A TIME

Once upon a time there was an animal that did not think it was worth the effort to get up from its lair to go out in search of food. It would only be repeating itself, as it had been doing day after day since it was born, and so it would try to ignore this routine self and stay put and dream of excitement that it could not find in its regular course of the day, and so it closed its eyes, snuggled into itself and fell asleep to dream and dreamt that it was growing hungry and would soon rise and go in search of food and then it dreamt of resisting this need to instead sleep to dream of something behind its daily round. The animal awoke, annoyed with itself.

EPISODE

A woman passes by an apartment house
with her husband. Upstairs a man
is walking around in his shorts.
The woman is engrossed in talking
to her husband. Upstairs
the partly nude man
wanders from room to room.

A CLOSET NAMED LOVE

Fine thing for me to have walked into a closet and hung myself on the first hook to celebrate with chants of love, and it was I who leaned forward from the hook to shut the door on myself to feel more strongly in the dark, and now I am breathing stagnant air, my energies flagging. If you want to know how I've been able to write this, I took pad and pencil with me into the closet to record for posterity my amazing joy, and so when you get to see this after the closet is opened by friends curious about my absence and in search of me, think of my having lived to celebrate in my own stale air.

SEPARATE WINDOWS

The young woman seated at her window
lost in thought and the young man
across the street—he has the urge
to stand naked in his window. He
steps back against a wall
and strips and returns crouching.
Slowly he begins the undulation
of love, stretching out his arms
to the air to embrace it, she
still seated but now noticing.
His movements increase in tempo,
he becomes taut, his motions compulsive
and spasmodic, trembling him. He
sags, hanging his arms,
and the young woman has risen to her feet
and stands still.

ROME IN THE AGE OF JUSTINIAN

Franks to the north,
and Vandals to the south.

Visigoths to the west
and Ostrogoths all around.

But thanks to your rectitude, Justinian,
still no sign of the Vulgars!

KARL TIERNEY

185

from METROPOLITAN CORRIDOR

» «

My companions
come down
from your trees

Summon the
enthusiasm
and do so

There are
words for you
down here

on the ground
so strewn
not as bait

but as fleas
to make the itch
you enjoy

scratching
come down
from your trees

» «

The houses were burned down
to retrieve the nails

Plotting Nature's
bounty over

the next hill
Another rude shelter

some fence
and hasty rows thrown
between the rockcrop

the rhythms pulled
from the absence

of sun and rain
until the ratio evens

not levels

And still
the people came

186

LETTER #6

My hat's busted and my coat
smells like a wet dog
I've got a lot of teeth left but
I walk with a slight limp and without
my glasses I can't read a damn thing

Amply supplied with food books paper ink
and electricity I work surrounded by paintings
recording my impressions apropos language and thought
on some relatively complex machinery situated at a black desk
down the hall (celebrated in one of my earlier books)
from some even more elaborate gadgetry

To my left is an old fashioned rotary fan
which is sometimes put to use even in the coldest months—
and slightly beyond that is a source of music
quite various in its devices—but no more than necessary

Now you see me now you don't

Today I'm en route to a cache of pronouns
he to she to him they her to it and sometimes you
though rarely we and never them

Dreams say remake the context
their thin verbs suspended through the ranks
of nouns like Chinese lanterns

It's been noted elsewhere that William James wrote
only a couple of essays with "Self" in the title—no doubt
he thought the topic was in the end philosophically opaque—

"One great use of the Soul has always been to account for, and at the
     same
time guarantee, the closed individuality of each personal consciousness."

Bring out your dead

187

HOME ALONE

I have lived alone here
  for the better part of thirty years.
Not exclusively, you understand;
  I had a wife once for a while,
And there were men and women
  passing through going nowhere.

Brooklyn is all worn out
  and I along with it, frazzled.
It used to be a haven
  for reflection and phrase building,
where the Muses danced all afternoon
  and munched a merry macaroon.

All the recordings are still here,
  All the books and photographs,
Pictures on a freshly painted wall,
  And, in truth, I love them all,
But they don't seem of much use anymore.
  I guess I've milked them dry.

Still smoking cigarettes all night
  at the same old makeshift desk,
Enter paper in the word machine
  to explain to no one what I mean.
"How's that, Harry? What's the score?
  Shall I cook you up a metaphor?"

"Ain't it great we didn't become old farts,"
  Michael said with little hair upon his head.
"What are we then?" did I inquire
  lacking a certain basic fire.
Home is the drinker, home from the bar,
  And Oedipus Rex is driving my car.

What a time it was!
  I had friends in all the great saloons,
Poets all, munching their macaroons.
  There were plays and novels to be discussed,
And the singers were singing of peaches and rust.
  And all the girls, save one, loved me.

There was London in the early Fall
  with Lynn Rowe's scented fingertips.
There was Paris in the winter months
  with Helen Downing's cocoa colored lips.
There was Venice in the summertime
  with Christiane's hips beyond my reach.

In English movie houses, they played
  God Save the Queen, and it worked.
So far, she's still walking around.
  In France, they said that Paris
was the oldest city that's never been bombed.
  Such is still the case.

In Italian kitchens, there was sauce malarkey
  that underlined the matriarchy.
The old ladies are still cooking up a storm.
  In Germany, they got so upset
When I said the Prussians weren't finished yet.
  And now the bastards are at it again.

I did my share of traveling,
  And nothing has changed but me.
I have lived alone here
  for the better part of thirty years.
My glasses are thicker.
  I still do daily calisthenics.

I try to eat well and take vitamins.
  Unlike a bulb which just goes out,
My light seems to dim in slow degrees.
  Not yet crawling around on my knees,
I try to maintain my living space,
  But who's that flounder in my face?

A VISION FOR YOU

"Damn little to laugh about that I can see!"—We

Were at an A.A. meeting & Ed was reading from page 157
Of the Big Book—"Damn little to laugh about that I can see!" Ed
read.

It was a story about a man in a bed who couldn't stop
Drinking. Bill Wilson & Dr. Bob, co-founders of A.A. were
Visiting with him in Akron & sharing with him the necessity of a
Spiritual experience if ever he was to stop drinking.
Ed read on about the man in a bed who couldn't stop drinking. Ed
Read. "The man interrupted, 'I used to be strong for the Church,
But that won't fix it.'" Ed turned to page 158.

"I've prayed to God on hangover mornings & sworn that I'd never
Touch another drop, but by 9 o'clock I'd be boiled as an owl."
Ed continued:
The next day found the man in the bed more receptive. He had been
Thinking the Spiritual path over. "Maybe you're right," he
Said. "God ought to be able to do anything." Then he added, "He
Sure didn't do much for me when I was trying to fight this booze
Racket alone."

The next day the man gave his life over to the care & direction
Of his Creator. His wife saw something different about her
Husband—he had begun to have a Spiritual experience. Ed paused
& put the Big Book down.

"This was me!" Ed said suddenly, his index finger urgently
Beating a rhythm of recognition against the page of words he had
Just read. "This is exactly the way it was for me," he continued.
"I didn't see no change until I stopped drinking. When the judge
Pointed his finger at me & said, 'Hey, Ed! You're going to A.A.,
Or back to jail!'—I thought, 'damn little to laugh about if you
Ask me!'—I had begun to have a Spiritual experience."

190

ALICE GAINES PLAYED THE HARP

In kindergarten Alice Gaines
Played the harp • at nap time
& for an hour at noon each day

It was as if Angels sang away
The cares of children sweetly sleeping
After graham crackers & milk • even
When the air raid sirens' shrill alarms
Shattered dreams

Alice Gaines played the harp • even
We • the youngest children knew the drill
To close the windows against flying glass
To move under our desks & clasp
Our hands to the back of our bowed necks & pray
That the bomb was not really on its way
This time • that the Russians weren't coming
This time • to sift through our charred remains

Alice Gaines played the harp • as
From beneath my desk I prayed:

Dear God • this is David
In Washington, D.C. • remind
The Russians • my Father
Papa • & • Bubbie • are Russians • too

Dear God • this is David
I am in
The first reading group
Under my desk

Waiting

For the end
Of the world

THE OPERATION

My hand reaches out in the night long distance:

Mother • Father • "Please come" • Don't let me be • Here
Alone • to die • among strangers in • a • hospital bed
Brother • "Please come" • take a plane • all the calls

I could make • that night • before the operation

Only

Mother came • & • a girlfriend then
From faraway • hearing • my fear

I shall • never • forget
Their simple • act of compassion • nor
My father • & • brother's • absence—

Fear of the fear of a naked heart—

No one mentions this • never • now
We smile • I smile • for I understand
The inconvenience of emotions among men—

I understand understanding leads to forgiveness—

A wretched thing!

Now • I ask
How things are going—

The job, the legs, the back, the twigs, the leaves
& nuts • in the gutter • on • the roof

OUR HOLOCAUST

SAM ABRAMS

"I thirst for accusation."

—YEATS

All the fine words ever said in Europe, lies,
All the poems, all the songs of Europe, lies,
All the fine theories, all the philosophies, lies,
Bloody, beshitted in Croatia,
In Herzegovina, in Bosnia, in Dubrovnik, in Sarajevo.

Voltaire a liar! Goethe a liar! Garibaldi bugiardo!
Dostoyefsky, Tolstoy, Chekhov, Solzhenitsyn liars!
Erasmus mendax! Shakespeare a liar! Dante a liar!
Foucault and Lacan big liars! Dickens a liar! Kant a liar!
Spinoza a liar! Wittgenstein, Russell liars!
Manet and Picasso blind! Verdi deaf! Nijinsky lame!
Bach a liar! Mozart a liar! Byron, Keats and Shelley liars!
Hugo menteur! Marx and Freud and Einstein lugnerin!
Madam Curie menteuse! Balzac a liar! Flaubert a liar!
The Beatles, the Stones liars! Gilbert and Sullivan liars!
Florence Nightingale a liar! Sarah Bernhardt a phoney!
Mallarmé liar! Sartre and Beauvoir and Camus liars!
Charlie Chaplin and Diaghilev liars!
Plato a liar! Aristotle liar! Socrates liar!

Only Stalin told the truth! only Hitler! only Himmler!
Only Beria! only Dzerzhinsky!
Only Treblinka told the truth! Auschwitz told the truth!
Katya Woods the truth! Warsaw Ghetto the truth!
Dachau the truth!
The Quai at Smyrna the truth!
The Trail of Tears the truth!
Andersonville the truth! Wallabout Bay the truth!
Hiroshima the truth! Nagasaki the truth! Dresden the truth!
My Lai the truth! El Mozote truth!
Buchenwald the truth! Gulag the truth!

Are those who slaughter the innocents
From mere cowardice or inertia
To be ranked above the slaughterers
Who kill from rage and hatred?
How are Major, Bush, Clinton, Kohl, Mitterand—that set
—better than Dzerzhisnky? Eichmann? Stalin? Hitler?

193

And how are we better than the good Germans, the so civilized French
Who stood by, who averted their eyes?

How are we better than the worst?
This is not happening somewhere else.
This is happening in the "European Home" now,
Two hours from Heathrow!
One from De Gaulle or Orly!
One hour from Frankfurt, from DaVinci!

The bombers of the Uffizi are right!
Why preserve the relics of these scum?
These worse than Nazis!
These murderers by inertia, by sloth!

If there was ever a cause worth fighting for
It's peace in Yugoslavia.
If there was ever a cause worth dying for,
It's law and peace in Europe.

But you will die in your bed, for no cause,
Meaningless lives, meaningless deaths,
Automobile freaks, image junkies, weaklings, mere lumps,
Hypocrite readers, my brothers, my sisters, my peers!

These are the fruits of winning the cold war: cowardice and sloth.
These are the fruits of materialism: cowardice and sloth.
These are the fruits of consumerism: cowardice and sloth.
These are the fruits of multi-media: cowardice and sloth.
These are the fruits of the global economy: cowardice and sloth.
These are the fruits of MTV: cowardice and sloth.
These are the fruits of CNN: cowardice and sloth.
These are the fruits of the autobahn: cowardice and sloth.
These are the fruits of victory: cowardice and sloth.
These are the fruits of the victory of capitalism.
These are the fruits of the victory of democracy.

In our time. Our holocaust.

BETWEEN SHIT & SHINOLA

> *"Farewell to lyric waste"*
>
> E. M. CIORAN

Thoughts on waking up to a salesman's
                phone pitch
Again I feel a bit nauseous
& I know I'm not going to have a baby
For Charles Henri Ford—It's difficult
to be a great artist without a soul
Why do I require revenge?
Because he has removed something
important from my life
& what was that thing, a fake friendship,
a chance to be used, an opportunity
for communication w/ a fellow member
of the Aquarian Mouse Club—So what?
I'm feeling destitute
My own feelings have lost their magical
                    power
My desires refuse to manifest
Even TLC (Tender Loving Care), my black
& white photo lab, Victor & Francesca
say that they will have to close soon
They have been abandoned in a wake of
                    computers
The Aborigines are right
Stay naked & keep walking
Food will offer itself
So much for capitalism
Seeing Through Clothes is the name of
                    a book
on the table next to the bed
Catherine de Medici sits in a tapestry
at a court festival wearing black
Do I want to make a subtle anti-fashion
statement & invoke all that black implies?
Would I like to go to Tierra del Fuego
& paint my body with stripes?
I don't know if there is enough time left
I'm trying to finish my movie,
the one I've been preparing for
all my life—The *Purgatorio*

IRA COHEN

195

I can already see the face of Beatrice
reflected in the left eye of the unaltered
                              Gryphon
The pen in my hand has a sharp point
& I wonder if I can work up the nerve
to stab myself in the throat with it?
Is that normal thinking for a naked man
on the eighth floor of an isolation ward?
Do we need to discuss originality
or the death of a president whose tabletalk
                              alone
should have condemned him to eternal
                              damnation?
I speak of Richard Nixon, the Dauphin of
                              Cottage Cheese,
whose burial cost the nation 400 million
in paid holiday time & more
And then there is the story sent to me on
                              tape
by Don Snyder of a man (he was French)
who spent forty years planting trees
to make a miracle of forest, a restored paradise
I kept expecting the story to end with his
                              expulsion
for is that not the story of Man
or would that be simply Oprah's paranoia?
Down to the bone, please
I'll order another skeleton & pay w/ foodstamps
or my friend's credit card
and don't forget to save a place for Gherasim
                              Luca
Ramuntcho thinks it takes more courage
for an old poet of 79 to jump into the Seine
than a younger poet
Is it a matter of courage or just a question
                              of desire?
There is something positive in all this, though
Now that Nixon's body has been interred
the mail will be delivered again
& there are rumors I will be crowned Emperor
of Europe in Brussels next month
Shades of Piero Heliczer!
Economy is the job of poets, not the endless
                              lament

196

of the Killing Machine
If you want to make a living,
learn to make sharkfin soup
If you want to make a killing,
there are openings in Bosnia, Rwanda & Jerusalem
A man sits at the end of a bench
in the middle of Broadway, his pants down to his
                                                ankles
wiping his ass
Ten feet away at the other end of the bench
sits his girlfriend with a broken tooth
swigging from a pint bottle of whisky
"At least I didn't get any in my pants," he says
nonchalantly as a bus chugs by going uptown
If this ain't Western Civilization, what is?

I'm not really dying to be dead
I'm just tired of being a harp of bones
played by the fucking wind.

ARMED HUMANITARIANS

Cochise, Geronimo, Villa, Zapata,
Fidel, Lumumba, Aidid, Commandante Marcos
Warlord, Druglord, Badlord, Bad Indian,
Darky, Bandito. Darth Vader, Lucifer.
Let's call ourselves armed humanitarians.
Tell the story straight.
Create a Geronimo vehicle.
One showing how to murder the children in flight,
Quietly, mercifully, in a canyon with hot springs
Far from thirsty, hunting soldiers
So we may breathe relieved
They will never have to live like this.
Flash back to the future: Find a way
To spin the misery for audience focus groups.
Roll the racial hatred down the alley
With a hood ornament
Flash the Cochise logo on the laservision
Spectacle of our bones and lymph sinking
In gravelly sand to feed the nopal.
Show the ancient spring, every year,

AMALIO MADUEÑO

197

Undermining pavement in Truth Or Consequences,
Curb crusts bleeding white at dawn.

There can be various vehicles.
Or there can be just one.

ADRIAN C. LOUIS

FEVER VORTEX #666

When I thought I was dying
I did not see a world out of control.
I couldn't feel this nation disintegrating.
Nor did I smell my body growing old.
I had a hunger beyond worry.
I had an emptiness that I filled
at my leisure with
the faces of lost loves.
Then I became much sicker.
The distant clarion
of the carrion eaters
did not amaze these ears
attuned to tubes.
After the operation
I asked the nurse for TV.
I sensed the leeches
sucking the blood
of this idiot nation
and the talons of time
clawed my soul open.
In deep medication
I heard Crazy Horse whisper:
"Home is where
my ancestors lie buried."
In the flow of sweet morphine
I heard Crazy Horse whisper:
"Don't waste your vote
on that Nazi dwarf."

WHITE BREAD BLUES

for Colleen

I guess only an Indian woman could
understand how an Indian boy
could fall in with a pack
of white bordertown kids
and allow shame to be born.
Even before we met
you knew about my childhood
family trips to town.
Mom got groceries only
after the whole family waited
for the old man to be
burped out of the bars
where he spent his fair share
of our food money
on his jealous medication.

Once in '57
when I was eleven
we were at the curb
in the town park
in our battered Chevy
pickup loaded with paper
sacks and kids eating
thick bologna sandwiches
without the miracle
of Miracle Whip.
Mom climbed out of the cab
and filled a glass gallon jar
at the water fountain
by the court house.
Mom was unashamed
to mix Kool-aid
in public but when my white
friends with smiling eyes
rode by on their new bicycles
I put on an Indian face
and pretended not to see them.
I prayed one day I'd live a life
as white as store-bought bread
where dark lives did not exist
but my prayer was never
answered thank God.

BRENT H. ASKARI

MY FATHER

My father is a sand-nigger. He does not work in a seven-eleven.
He has a brother who does not work in a seven-eleven.
The seven-eleven
is considerably younger than the house he grew up in.

My father is a shiite, or, shit. He has a beard. My father
does not know that his religion
makes him crazy. He studied the Koran at home.
He studied the crusades
in British boarding school.
He read George Bernard Shaw in boarding school, who had a
        beard,
but was probably
not a shit.

My father is a terrorist. He went to MIT at sixteen.
He watches football on TV. He watches people die
on TV. He has a Ph.D., which helps him tell football
from bombing.
Bombing is the one where people get killed, but both
have instant replays. When I was young my father bought me
a nerf football.
He can throw a good bomb.

Many people think my father is Khomeni. Khomeni was on TV a lot.
My father is on TV sometimes. He talks to WASPS on TV. My mother
is a WASP. My mother and my father both voted for Jesse Jackson,
who is a nigger. People look at my father, and they know
he is a sand-nigger. They look at my mother, and they know
she is a WASP. People look at me, they think
I am Italian. Mexican. Spanish. Tanned. When they learn
I am half sand-nigger, they know
what that means.

But I admire Paul Robeson. I read Gombrowicz.
I increase my prana through yoga. I celebrate Christmas.

It's too late. They know
what that means.

IF YOU REALLY WANT TO WORK

One thing you don't have in the burger
kingdom is overtime so if
you've done your forty and they need you
longer what they do is pull
you off the clock and put the OT on
the next day or maybe even ring it up
as fries and coke because the first
thing a manager learns is to keep
his labor in line but now
and then like in my case when you
come across somebody that's really
crazy to get some hours
and you're short
of bodies anyway and here's this fool
that says he wants to *live*
there for chrissake then they sometimes
take you aside and say looky here
I see your wife is not employed
and you have a daughter too that's in school
so we can understand how difficult
it must be to get along on one salary
                                    and if you truly
want to work a hundred hours a week
then we will do all we can
to accomodate you which
is not something we would normally volunteer
to a person we hardly know but we've had
our eye on you for some time and noticed
how you are seldom late and you don't
lollygag around in the break
room or call in sick at the last minute
like these welfare niggers
that come and go like mayflies and don't
wash their hands either
half of them but if we reach out
this far to make you an offer what we're
going to require is that you bring us a couple
more social security numbers so we can set
this thing up on a regular basis
let you do the morning shift on your wife's
number, pick up some afternoons, say
another thirty hours on your daughter,
and you can be the night porter as

yourself, get you three, four hundred bucks
a week and nobody
has to be the wiser except maybe
your loved ones but that's between you
and them and if you don't
want them to know or if they have any
question about their moralities we can
take it maybe a step further, let you sign
                              the checks
yourself and we'll cash them out of the safe
and so what, looky here,
all you're doing is beefing
up their retirement, right, get them
both a little more
in their old age so where's the harm?
but hey, listen, you think
you can do better at the Golden Arches, go on over there,
check it out, those people
don't give a inch, and every forty you turn,
they'll hold back ten per cent
for crippled children or some other
damn fool project
and what's that got to do
with the American dream is what I want to know
and if the truth was out wouldn't
nobody give those cruds
a dime because
it takes eighteen cents out of every dollar
just to advertise all that crap
when what they really ought
to do is seek out
some deserving family that has a poor tyke
in that condition and give them cash
on the barrelhead
which they don't, of course, which
if you ask me is how
they got that Moscow franchise in the first
place, greasing this palm and that one,
without any concern
for the rights of the individual at all
                              and besides, looky here, who
the fuck wants to get paid in rubles?

WANTED: FRYCOOK

What's it mean to be a frycook?
  Jesus was probably the best—
    no sweat, no stain upon his apron
(as far as we can tell) yet
he fed the masses loaves and fishes. That's high
  volume.
    But Jesus missed out on the macho end,
      the bandannas and amphetamines,
the swollen forearms and biceps from baskets
  loaded down
    with hushpuppies and french fries, soft-
    shell crabs
      dropped an arm's length above
        hot peanut oil
so claws and legs would curl life-like as a Myrtle
  Beach ceramic ashtray.
Perfect.
Jesus also looks good in porcelain.
Jesus never got to see a waitress shoot a stare
  across a busy kitchen:
    flat out I want you or You're cute, why
    don't we maybe—
A frycook sees raw sex all day:
    ash straining for release at the
    end of a dangled cigarette,
delicate veins laced through white flesh when i
  flakes from fish bones,
the basket heaves from hot grease as if a husbar
  had shown up early,
        and yes,
a basket flung across the kitchen or slammed on a
  stainless steel table
    when the frycook doesn't get his way.
Maybe Jesus poached those fish, served them cold.

EYEGLASSES

Before my grandparents left Auschwitz,
they went to the enormous heap of eyeglasses,
thinking by a miracle they might find
their own. But it was hopeless to sift
through thousands of pairs.
They began to try on one after another.
They had nothing to read,
so they checked how well they could see
wrinkles on their hands.
They'd bring the hand up close,
try to trace the deep-etched
orbits of knuckles,
the creased map of the palm.
If one eye seemed right,
the other was blurred,
haze stammering the line of life.
They took several pairs.
Later in their home town
each got a prescription.
For a while they kept the other pairs;
then sighed, rubbed the smooth frames,
and threw the glasses from Auschwitz away.

My mother is embarrassed telling me the story,
embarrassed her parents took anything at all
from the piles of looted belongings.
But I'd have been like them.
I'd have taken a dozen pairs.
Those who have nothing end up
with too much, of the wrong kind.
I think of that old couple, my grandparents,
trying to read their hands
through the glasses of the dead.
Crow winter sky,
rows of empty wooden barracks.
The woman and the man help each other up,
lean on a small handcart they found, and go on.

MEMOS FROM BIG JOY

Whatever we are, we are all part
of what everyone is.
We are all inside the
whatever it is that's us.

» «

What there was is still there.
What there is is still going on.
What will be will be in any case.

» «

The thing is.
Everything was.
Any thing can happen.

» «

Nothing explains anything.
But someone is always explaining everything.

» «

Leave the world alone.
It knows better than you do
what's good for it.

» «

Genitals are wiser than universities.
Higher learning doesn't guarantee ecstasy.

» «

Only take seriously what is not serious.

» «

Don't be oppressed by your personality.
Climb a tree, monkey around.

» «

The long-running double bill at the cosmic movies:
The Divine Comedy and The Human Comedy.

» «

Vacuum your soul. Windex your spirit.

» «

Be ready for ripeness whenever it rings up.

» «

Yesterday is no longer here.
Tomorrow has gone on ahead.
Someday has not arrived.
Nobody knows yet about today.

» «

Believe passionately in what does not exist.
Then you can create it.

» «

Do not pass judgment. Pass judgment by.
You were born to dance, not pronounce sentence.

» «

Collapse categories.
Go beyond! Go beyond!

» «

When you are most naked and most serene
you begin to comprehend Big Joy.

» «

The sexuality of Big Joy makes every man a genius.

» «

Human beings are the spermatozoa of Big Joy.

» «

Love is the reason we are born,
the reason we go on living,
the reason we die.

» «

You can't kill something that refuses to die,
no matter how often it gets under your skin.

» «

Said the scuba diver:
If it's ugly, don't touch it.
If it's pretty, don't trust it.
If it looks harmless, flee!

» «

Great desires lead to fireworks.
Dim longings lead to short circuits.

                »«

Be a laser beam of the spirit.
Reveal the radiance!

                »«

The worst is still to come
and the best is yet to be.

I SLEEP WITH ELEGIES

I sleep with elegies
I breakfast with obituaries
I cohabit with erosion.
Nothingness isn't what hurts
It's the shrivel and wilt
it's the ache of withering.
My plaints collide in midair:
"Come sweet Death"
"Dear Life let me live"
Will light years of
heavenly disembodiment
be an ultimate home?
"Heaven is here" said the masseur
leaning on my ouch,
"here where it hurts."

THINKING ABOUT DEATH

How often do you think about Death?
Death thinks about you all the time
Death is fatally in love with you and me
and his lust is known to be relentless

Life is an equally persistent lover
He was desiring each of us before we were born
I try to remain faithful to him but I know
the relationship can't go on forever

Life relishes my body heat my heart beating
my blood my semen even my steamy notions
Death cherishes what is cool and mysterious in me
all that is shadowy and perverse like him

I like to think of Death awaiting our rendezvous
in a lush corner of an intimate cafe
where he will regale me with scandalous tales
of misbehavior in other worlds

Yet in the end it is Life that wears us out
At that crosswalk what will the traffic bear?
Shouldn't we think about Death more often?
Death is thinking about us all the time

JAMES BROUGHTON, THE LOVE GURU

JANINE CANAN

Amo ergo sum

When he was three years old, James Broughton was awakened by a glittering stranger who told him he was a poet "and always would be/ and never to fear being alone or being laughed at." That glittering stranger was his Angel, the "luminous collaborator" who, he explains in his recent poetry collection *Special Deliveries,* "taught me the best songs I know." Edited by Mark Thompson and published by Broken Moon Press in Seattle, 1990, *Special Deliveries* is a selection of the best songs composed by the seventy-eight-year-old poet in over forty years and seventeen volumes. And it contains some of the best songs of our century.

CHILDHOOD OF THE POET

You're never as bad as they say, O They!

On November 10, 1913, far under a Scorpio sky in the little-known town of Modesto, Sunny Jim, as he was soon called, was born to a family of bankers and wives that had migrated from England in the eighteenth century to the Carolinas and onward to California. Like many poets, Sunny Jim had a questionable relationship to his mother, and no wonder:

208

Three big noses Mrs Mother has,
They grow and grow in the night.
Sniff sniff sniff her naughty naughty dear!
And she also can smell with her ears.

("Mrs Mother Has a Nose")

His Aunt Esto, on the other hand, a crippled woman who would become State Legislator, read baby Broughton poetry and introduced him to Good Mother Goose, whom he was soon imitating.

Broughton's father died when he was five. Two years later, young James was introduced by Aunt Esto to his first literary guru at a performance of *The Merchant of Venice*. William Shakespeare showed him then that "life is more understandable when observed poetically," and would continue to illuminate him with his teachings throughout Broughton's life ("On Becoming A Poet").

James's mother remarried when he was ten, and at the request of her husband-to-be, sent James away to military school. On the eve of his exile he had his first experience of the androgyne:

It was on an afternoon in my ninth year when I opened the bathroom door upon my unsuspecting mother. She stood in the tub directly facing me and I saw that not only did she have the breasts I knew, but below her dark pubic hair there was something more crucial. I had the fleetingest glimpse, because she turned upon me such a murderous Medusa glare that I hastily slammed the door and fled to the basement. But I definitely thought I had seen her penis and testicles!

(*Androgyne Journal*)

As for his new stepfather, Broughton writes in his second book, *Musical Chairs: A Songbook for Anxious Children* (1950):

Papa has the fattest pig you ever did feel.
My ten little piglets just pinch and squeal.
Papa has the star of all the swine,
Papa shines stern in the sty.

("Papa Has a Pig")

And little Junior worriedly prays:

If I should die and fall asleep
how will I run away from home?
If I should wake before I die
Will I still be in the dark alone?

("Junior's Prayer")

"If I should wake before I die" is a key line, for Broughton's lifework is the story of his awakening.

In boarding school Broughton recited verse, and was

introduced by his headmaster to dictionaries, thesauruses, crossword puzzles, and *The Oxford Book of English Verse*. At twelve he fell in love with his schoolmate, "Golden Littlejohn," who inspired a vast outpouring of poetry. By the time Broughton attended Stanford University, he already understood that "poetry is a living adventure, not a literary problem." Consequently, when ill-humored and rigid formalist Yvor Winters threw him out of class as talentless and perverse, it was only after Broughton had confronted him with a Spoof Manifesto, and a tract that began, "A serious person is a serious business," and ended, "and a serious person is seriously dead."

Broughton dropped out of college in his senior year, and hitch-hiked across the United States with Emerson's Essays in his pack, and Blake, Whitman and, of course, Shakespeare in his heart. He worked his way around the Mediterranean on a passenger ship, and finally arrived in New York, at age twenty-two, to become a great writer.

DIVINE ANDROGYNE

For tell me what more really matters a whit
than to hatch our long aching to bloom to the full?

At the end of World War II, Broughton, now thirty-two, left New York, where he had been writing novels and plays, eating in cafeterias and consoling himself with thoughts of suicide. He returned to San Francisco and joined the post-war Renaissance, which brought to light artists Kenneth Rexroth, Robert Duncan, Madeline Gleason, William Everson, and Broughton himself. At thirty-five, the same age that Whitman published *Leaves of Grass*, Broughton published his first collection of poems, *Songs for Certain Children*, and premiered his first solo film, *Mother's Day*.

Five books followed in the 1950's, four years of which the poet resided in Europe, encountering Dylan Thomas, Stevie Smith, W.H. Auden and Jean Cocteau. *Musical Chairs, The Right Playmate, Sorrows of Scorpio, An Almanac for Amorists* (dedicated to Esto Broughton) and *True & False Unicorn* chronicle the poet's passage into mid-life. *Sorrows of Scorpio*, which Broughton wrote to Anaïs Nin, describes the crisis, the thorny descent, "the density of ditch," the humiliation of "new outrage/ carved from the heart of my limp." "How did I arrive in this chill and gutted museum?" the mid-lifer despairs. "How shall I rescue and recrown with fire/ the diamond navies of my night?" he implores Scorpio, the Lord of his destiny. In "In the Sanitarium" he pursues this line of questioning further:

Is all of man's life a convalescence?
To spend one more night here is unbearable.
"Yes," said the nurse, "but imperative."

From the Empress of Byzantium in *True* & *False Unicorn* comes the first hint of an answer to the poet's agonized search for the meaning of life:

> Without great folly life is a death.
> I will grasp, I will drink up man's mystery.
> Poison or not, it is love.

"Adventure—not Predicament!" chime the Three Muses in *Whistling in the Dark* (1960).

> You must go over the Paps of Mummy,
> you must go under the Behaving Well,
> you must go round the Marry Mire,
> you must go past the Mighthave Bin

peals "A Liturgy for Poets." But it is really not until Broughton encounters the Feminine in the Sixties, that the answer to his mid-life angst comes back loud and clear, when the "fathomless voice" of the Bride from the Sea, "Unnamed queen of your water kingdom,/ unclaimed bride/ of your fearful ocean," calls out to him:

> Blaze! Scorch! Light!
> For fire I thirst! For your fire!
> That I may become
> your devoted stranger—
> tell you tales of the deep
> and tricks of the waves.
> That I may become
> your sly familiar—
> sing you the powers of great Poseidon,
> dance you the currents of Amphitrite.
> That I may be your known
> Lady of Unfearful Motions.
> Long have you been mine already.
> Therefore rise,
>   embrace me and burn!
> Else you can never know my true name
> nor ever claim your own life!

"Unknowable Betrothed—/ though I perish of it/ I accept the vow!" the poet responds. And his whole body begins to throb with exultant song.

> Then I heard
> what the song was singing:
>   the shock of my joy
>   that on a deserted beach
>   between the waves of the sea

and the waves of the land
I had wed my own grief for all time.
("The Bride from the Sea")

In 1961 Broughton writes the shockingly candid *Androgyne Journal* (withheld from publication until 1977), in which he asks, "Have men always been terrified of their true nature? Is all history a record of their denials of themselves?" *Androgyne Journal* (the basis for the 1972 film *Dreamwood*) is a confession of absolute eroticism. "Can you accept yourself," the poet asks himself, "in every part and particular? Specifically, tenderly and humbly? Can you learn to love yourself with gusto?" Now he turns to the Great Mother and gives himself to Her entirely. "O please, my Lady," he begs, "allow me to know your inner mystery. Open the door of your cave. I will try not to be afraid of your hidden dangers."

> After my first probing into the secret cave of my river goddess, I felt a new spaciousness opening my pelvis. And I went to sleep flooded with wonder, feeling farther inside myself than I had ever expected to reach. It was like reaching a place where pain marries pleasure and discovers an unsuspected harmony.

> » «

> It is marvelous to know at last where she dwells. I want to love her, I want to savor every part of her, I want to know how she is part of me.

For his naked exposure to the Goddess, he is given the great gift of healing the wounded—harassed, raped and incested—Feminine bequeathed to him by his mother. The Goddess blesses him for the radically courageous truthfulness of his journey so far, and heals the deep sense of inadequacy that infects him, as it does every human being. "From your deepest stillness to your lightest wavelet, from your buried treasures to your sunny rock-pools, you contain me as I contain you," he praises Her. "Teach me," he prays, "to float on my fears." "Shame is no longer possible. For the god grows in my genitals now, blesses my whole body, animates all my centers." The erotic and holy are now fully merged, and the poet becomes the incarnation of Herm-Aphrodite. "I was boy, man, and Old One all at once. And I was wed to girl, woman, and Old Mother for all time." Come into his true and higher power, he recognizes humankind:

> How they need a voice to call them out of their blind alleys. They need a poet who will take them by the heart. They need the ears of the soul tweaked with the music of the Gods. Otherwise they remain moths banging against the window, ants on their highways, creatures of herd and hive.

Not surprisingly, Broughton marries in 1962. *Tidings* follows in 1965, offering the poet's conversations with Mother Sea. "I accept whatever comes," She sings, "and everything comes to me." She reminds him: "Love is the element, flowing/ and burning, is the fire/ in which you swim." *Tidings* also includes the victorious Blakean song "I Heard in the Shell":

> I heard in the shell
> all the hymns of hell,
> I heard all the angels crying,
> I heard the earth
> in pangs of birth
> and all the galaxies dying.
>
> I heard in the shell
> the resounding well
> of all humanity's voices,
> I heard every shout
> of laughter and doubt
> in the crashing war of choices.
>
> I heard in the shell
> the throb of each cell
> from flower and rock and feather.
> But loudest of all
> rang the quiet call
> of Yes and No singing together.

To the poet, who has survived childhood and endured the defeat of middle age, now comes the challenge of the greater Self:

> Are you ready, said the North,
> to cross the Great Waters?
>
> Are you ready, said the West,
> to sink with the Sun?
>
> Are you ready, said the South
> for the journey going nowhere?
>
> Are you ready, said the East,
> to try again?
>
> ("Dear Dr. Sea")

In "Dear Dr. Sea," Broughton's Angel, Nick of Time, now a silvery black form, once again comes to his rescue, and demands he surrender the only thing he has left—his art. And Broughton, who was never one to shirk his destiny, acquiesces. From now on, his poetry will belong to the gods.

Broughton's next book, *Gods and Little Fishes*, dedicated to Alan Watts and published in 1971, reflects the influence of Eastern wisdom upon his thought. Sillier and more playful than ever, rhyming and clanging, sibilating and singing, come the poems. In the high spirits of the Sixties, he writes his irresistibly witty *High Kukus*:

> Isn't it perverse?
> said the Cradle to the Hearse,
> Things are getting better and things are getting worse.

He composes the Zen spiritual "Buddha Land," with its jazzy refrain: *Koan Baby, don't you cry, don't you cry!* And he chants the famous, often-quoted "This Is It:"

> This is It
> and I am It
> and You are It
> and so is That
> and He is It
> and She is It
> and It is It
> and That is that.

THE COMING OF THE BELOVED

> *I raise the laughter of my cock*
> *into the solemnities of art.*

In 1975, at age 61, Broughton meets the love of his life, artist Joel Singer, and his most joyful period begins:

> Then on a cold seminar Monday
> in walked an unannounced redeemer
> disguised as a taciturn student
> Brisk and resolute in scruffy mufti
> he set down his backpack shook his hair
> and offered me unequivocal devotion

> » «

> He claimed that important deities
> had opened his head three times
> to place my star in his brow

> This is preposterous I said
> I have a wife in the suburbs
> I have mortgages children in-laws
> and a position in the community

214

I thoroughly sympathize said He
Why else have I come to your rescue.

This time his Angel has come in the guise of Beloved.

Are you my Book of Miracles? I said
Are you my Bodhisattva? said He

» «

Ablaze in the trusts of desire
we scathed each other with verve
burned up our fears forever
steamed ourselves deep in surrender
till I lay drenched under scorch
and joy cried out through my crown
("Wondrous the Merge")

"I become an erogenated grail/ My chakras whirl like prayer wheels/ My kundalini runneth over," the poet rejoices. With the scorching passion of Rumi, he cries to his young lover, "I am into your fire over my head/ Do me to a turn/ Burn me to the ground."

Broughton's great book *Ecstasies* (1982) which contains *The Coming of the Beloved, Hymns to Hermes, Mysteries of the Godbody* and *The Immanence of Angels*, chronicles the unfolding of this joyous new relationship. An additional collection, *Graffiti for the Johns of Heaven* (1982) written on the lovers' honeymoon in Sri Lanka, contains the infamous titillating "Nipples and cocks/ nipples and cocks/ Nothing tickles the palate like/ nipples and cocks"; as well as a droning hymn to Self, in which the singer's bold narcissism dissolves into God:

I am an I am
  and I am
I am what I am in my am
I am the I am
  that I am
I am and I am and I am.

Now the poet-as-lover dances with God:

Waltz me around again Jehovahpa
Swing me your partner Brahmama
Bend me and glide me Allah mia
Leap me up highly my Buddhaboo

Ecstatic, the poet advises us too to slay the ego: "Are you willing to go to/ your own infinity?" "Jump/ into the No/ even if it kills you."

215

Do not ask where
we go from here
Nobody knows
Some think they do
but nobody really knows
anything
about anything

We are only gurgles
in the stream and the stream doesn't
know where it is going
either
It is just going
It is just
going with its nature as far as that
will take it

And with its nature
it has to take along
a horde of
gurgles
who are forever asking
where they are
gurgling to

Everything
is going beautifully
nowhere

In *Mysteries of the Godbody*, the language becomes increasingly religious: "I believe in the unreachable/ the unlikely and the unmentionable." "I believe in/ the Psyche/ the Kundalini/ the Id/ the Libido/ and all the unnamed demons in the mind and blood." In *Hymns to Hermes*, the poet-become-priest sings: "What else is to be lived for/ but the harvesting of love?/ What else is to be loved for/ but the ripening of man?" Broughton becomes the prophetic voice of innocence, his work the inspired antidote to deadly puritanism, repression and guilt: "Restore the world to us as once it glowed/ before our captivity in the chills of guilt/ Rekindle the purity of original sin." "Men are not meant to dwell in disaster/ prisoners of shame/ servants of belligerence/ Men are born to love/ to laugh leap and be loved."

Love is always the healer, Love is the savior, Love is the future. In *The Immanence of Angels*, in the long revolutionary "Shaman Psalm," the poet proclaims: "Quick while there's hope/ Renovate man." "Man is the species/ endangered by man." "Dump the false guides/ who travel the warpaths." "Only through body can/ you clasp the divine." "Salute the love ability/ in all those you meet." "Love between men will/ anachronize war." "Give way to love/ Give love its way." "Man must love man/ or war is forever/ Outnumber the hawks/ Outdistance the angels/ Love one another/ or die."

Broughton's mature vision is an exultation of love, a chorusing "alleluia of life." "My goal is to make the world safe for the amorous. Are you primed for a bypass from misery to mirth? Or are you addicted to the habit of agony?" the Love Guru asks, pointedly. And he offers us a Bliss Mantra, to practice:

> Bliss Bliss Bliss
> Bliss Us Bliss Thus Bliss This
> Two Bliss Both Bliss Together Bliss
> Vow Bliss Now Bliss Kiss Bliss
> Body Bliss Buddha Bliss Beauty Bliss
> Two-in-one Bliss Two-in-wonder Bliss Bliss Bliss
> Bless Bliss Bless Thus Bless This
> Bliss   Bliss   Bliss

THE WISE OLD MAN

My book is an open life.

On November 10, 1991, James Broughton celebrated his seventy-eighth birthday. Some have called him the Birthday Poet, for he is perpetually being reborn. At seventy, he writes: "Here I am only more so/ ... expecting to be rowdy at my own funeral/ planning to pick out a snappy new incarnation." At seventy-three, he publishes *A to Z*, his masterly alphabet of happy wisdom:

> Man is a great becoming
> not a regrettable object
>
> » «
>
> Genitals are wiser than sages
> Instincts know who is right

At seventy-five, he publishes *75 Life Lines*, an aphoristic nugget for each year of his life:

> Everything is perfect as it is
> except for the things that haven't yet got it right.
>
> » «
>
> What distinguishes one human being from another:
> the capacity to love and the ability to wonder.
>
> » «

217

Many nobodies who have studied nothing
are busy teaching it to everybody else.

» «

The greatest enemies of the public good
are education, religion and law.

» «

Sexual orgies are less harmful to society
than political parties.

» «

Love should unite mankind,
not split it up into exclusive couples.

» «

Trust only what opens, what reveals, what lights up.
Authentic wisdom is a laughing matter.

» «

Recipe for the creative life: remove safety belts,
plug loopholes, burn down safe retreats,
get reborn often, compose like a frolicsome child,
and never ask the end.

» «

Make your home in left field. There's more room there.
Everybody wants to be in the right.

» «

It is harder to love the world than to denounce it,
harder to embrace existence than to renounce it.

» «

Be generous with joy and juicy with ripening.
Amplitude is the shape of splendor.

Certainly, if anyone has reached that amplitude which is splendor, it is
James Broughton.

In *Disorderly Elations* (1990), Broughton gives us the wisdom of
a lifetime. And it is: Laugh and, above all, love!

Be wise and go merry round
whatever you cherish
what you love to enjoy

» «

Love is the always that life is made of

» «

Love is the only cure for love

In *Terminal Reports* (1990), Broughton talks to us about old age and death. "How often do you think about Death?" he asks, "Death thinks about you all the time."

> In death as in life
> the goal is to become more real
> isn't it?

"For my angel of death," he confesses, "I want a daredevil." Poignantly, he invites Death:

> I labored to embrace light
> in as many encounters
> as I could turn on.
>
> Have you ever tried to
> take the world in your arms?
> It resists being fondled.
>
> Out all day setting fires
> under crotches
> that refuse to burn.
>
> Now that it's dark I
> stay close to my hearth
> and leave the porchlight on.
>
> I want Death to feel welcome.
> I look forward to dazzling dawns at his house.
> ("Defective Wiring")

This collection contains many powerful poems. The titles alone are remarkable: "I Sleep with Elegies," "Questioning the Horizon," "The Sorrows of Befuddlement," "Rehearsing the Last Act," "Solaces of Senility," "In the Senex Crib," and "Aglow in Nowhere." In the latter the poet recounts:

> At a meadow in Golden Gate Park
> I stepped through an invisible gate
> into the mellow light of nowhere
> stepped beyond time and greenery
>
> What had become of the seventy years
> since first I tumbled on this grass?

219

And how many prices had I paid for
the tough somersaults that followed?

No longer brash nor intimidated
no longer riddled with wishes
I loll on this lawn of nowhere
and hope for a beatific vision

I know I have conquered nothing
I have simply outgrown everything
My history is a balloon I've let go of
without realizing I held on to it

Now I lack only a chamber for
what's left of my toys and scribbles
There I could desiccate quietly
like an Egyptian mummy waiting
for the last boat

In these later poems, Broughton's style that was always classically simple, symmetrical, made of stanzas with a minimum of punctuation and a maximum of rhyme, the words arranged like a kaleidoscopic puzzle, now becomes startlingly direct. The emphasis on the energetic verb in *Ecstasies*, and the abundance of beloved adjectives, gives way to the naked noun. For Broughton has reached his Essence. Poetry, he has said, "is the essence of the essentials." And the essence of the essential Broughton? "Only when I glee/ am I me." The nursery rhyme, the wondering pure voice of the child seems to suit him better than ever for his old-age, age-old profundities. "On the whole I enjoy being harmoniously dingalingy," he admits; "it gives me time to practice on my essence." "Until something transcendent turns up,/ I plash in my poetry puddle/ and try to keep God amused." But the amusements are growing darker:

I am glad of one thing.
In my impending demise
I won't be going out alone.
For company I can count on
    the passing of the twentieth century
    the closing of the American mind
    the lowering of the common denominator
    the disappearance of the rain forest
    the decay of individual morality
    the disintegration of the social fabric
    the deterioration of the economy
    the decline of the West
    the end of the age of Pisces
    the collapse of civilization

and the termination of any number of
grandeurs follies and hopeless causes.

Some kind of cold comfort to know that
one will be lying about in the ruins
with Ozymandias Mussolini
and all the other residue of the millennium
("On the Way to the Exit")

Special Deliveries concludes with "The Last Sermon of Gnarley
Never," a *tour de force* summation of the poet's life and vision, and a
treasure-chest of quotable lines. The long narrative culminates with huz-
zahs and hurrahs for all of Creation:

An old fool is better than no fool at all.
So fill the cup full and remember the vintage.
In my deciduous years I may have been defeated
but I was born to victory in the evergreen time.
Before I catch my flight to the long beyond
let me swap an amen for a bon voyage.
Though no one ever hailed me as a crackerjack prophet
I've enjoyed my loquacity every word of the way.
One thing I learned on the roadbeds of time:
leave weighty matters to the wisdom of angels,
they know how to take everything on the wing.
In the here and now, in what's left of forever
watch the balls bounce and the cookies crumble.
Frolic. Hug. Chuckle. Purr.
And send a thankyou note to the Universal It.
Hurrah for Creation! Huzzah to you all!

Indeed, there may be more quotable lines in the work of this clev-
erly outrageous and lovable poet, than in any other poet this century.
Deeply corny and full of never-ending wonder, James Broughton is a
great and stubborn warrior against Suffering. And, yes, a great fool: A
christo-buddhi-sufi-tantric-vedantic unadulterated Mystic. He writes
about love and death—as Emily Dickinson once said, "What else is
there?" And he plays on words as if they are his cosmic toys. One feels
his forms as containers and inciters of true poetic thought. "Poets never
lie, they only embroider. A poet's business is to clarify the unknown and
celebrate the unmentionable," he tells us. "I have never been political,"
he claims, "except that I want nothing less than a sexual and spiritual
revolution in the name of love." "Be fond, not wary," he coaxes, "Fear
of love is fear of the sublime." As for poetry, he proclaims: "A poet is in
the service of something larger than his[/her] personal life, ... craft or ...
published works./ Poetry is an act of love, it asks no reward." But
"don't take me at my word," he teases, "if you have a wiser."

221

Meanwhile, the Love Guru offers us his immortal advice:

> Would you like being centered
> all the way round?
> Would you like to be merry
> while being profound?
> Would you like to enter
> the very center of
>   clear veracity?
>
> Then go with what's going
> on its everywhere plan
> Go with your going
> and your both and your and
> With a bothanding ditty
> ride you gowithity
> all the way out and into
>   claracity

JACK FOLEY

THE BROUGHTON FOUNTAIN

The Master stood on the edge of the cliff. He asked which of his disciples would thrust himself over the side, plunging into the mouth of a horrible and certain death. "I," said one, eager to get a running start. "Wait," said the Master. "Do you think I'm some sort of idiot? I was only raising an abstract question. I need all the disciples I can get—and, besides, it's a long way down the side of that cliff." "True," said the eager disciple. "But wouldn't you always honor the name of the disciple who died for you?" "Well, I might," said the Master, "but really it all depends on whether I've written it down. My memory's a little shaky these days, and I can't seem to locate my pencil." "Master," said the disciple, "I would be the one who died for you!" "Well, go ahead if you must," said the Master, fumbling in his pockets for a piece of paper. "But I'm not guaranteeing anything. Oh where is that pencil!" "Thank you, Master. Aieeeee!" said the disciple as he leaped over the edge. "What was his name?" said the Master. "I suppose," said another disciple, "there isn't much left of him now." The disciples looked at each other silently. The wind sprang up. They were suddenly filled with a strange ecstasy. "Aieeeee," they began to say, "aieeeee, aieeeee," and made for the edge of the cliff. "Hey, wait a minute," said the Master, "whose disciples are you anyway, mine or his?" "Why yours of course," said the disciples, stopping in their tracks. "That's

222

better," said the Master. "You should at least look before you leap. It's been a rather bad year for disciples you know, and I'd just as soon have you stay a—" But before the Master was able to say the word *live*, the disciple who had leapt over the cliff suddenly appeared in front of him, looking only a little the worse for wear. "Aieeeee," said the Master, "what are you doing here?" "I'm back," said the disciple. "Death really isn't all it's cracked up to be." "You died!" said the Master. "Yes," said the disciple. "But what was it like?" "Not too bad, you know, nothing much really. A bit of a splat at the bottom. Otherwise fit as a fiddle actually." "But you've seen what no one else has ever seen and come back to talk of." "Well, yes, I suppose I have." "Won't you tell us about it?" "Well, all right. I saw—" But at this point a strong wind suddenly sprang up and lifted the seemingly solid body of the disciple up into the air like a leaf. His body seemed to collapse upon itself, to fold inward, to become nothing, nothing but a piece of scattered debris upon the wind. "Master," came the cry, "Master, Master—" Then nothing. "He must have had a name," said the Master. "Perhaps it was James. That certainly was a strong wind!" "Master," said another disciple, "could we leave this place?" "Yes, yes," said the Master, "I'm not enjoying it very much myself. Let's go." But then they realized that it was night and they couldn't go. They couldn't descend the mountain in darkness. "Oh, Fudge," said the Master as another burst of wind took his hat over the side of the cliff. "I was very fond of that hat too." "Fonder than you were of me, I sometimes think," came the voice. It was James. "Good Lord, you're back again." "Yes," said James, "you know, it's better the second time around. The first time you have problems with that awful dog." "Did you get bitten?" "Not the second time!" "But James, how do you manage it?—dying and resurrecting, dying and resurrecting." "Don't know, really. I suppose it's just sort of a talent." "Indeed. Can you make my hat come back?" "Doubt it. I'll try. Mmmmph, mmmmmph, nothing much there." "You can only resurrect ... yourself?" "Well, now, I don't know. It is possible ..." "What?" "It is possible ... You know, Master, I had a terrible childhood." "What has that got to do with it?" "Beatings, always complaints—ah, here I go again!" The wind sprang up and James was off again into the night. "What stars, Master," he said, "What stars! I wish I could take you with me. It's wonderful here!" It was morning now. As the Master looked around him he saw that his disciples had all vanished. There was nothing there but the mountain and the sky. He opened his mouth and began to speak:

My name is James Richard Broughton. I was born in the valley town of Modesto on Nov. 10, 1913. I come from a place of indescribable sweetnesss.

The wind sprang up again. "Master," said James, "we have the same name. Come! Come!" The Master looked up.

His body seemed at once solid and—light. "This is It." "Now," said James, holding out his hand to his Master, "now." A shock of electricity shuddered between them. "IS NOW THIS IT HERE?" said the Master. "I'm fly-ing!" And he was. "You see," said James, "there is no death, nothing to it." "I see," said James, "there isn't even this mountain." "Certainly not this mountain," said James. "There is something, though." "What is it?" "How can I put it? Night and day, day and night—I sound like an old song. *The indescribable sweetness of being alive!*" They reeled through the air, covering distance upon distance. Finally they lit down on a tiny island off the coast of Asia. "We are one, Master," said James, "we have fused." "Yes," said James, "it's true. I can't tell us apart anymore." "We are Master and Disciple, Master, Disciple and Master. We are moth and flame. We are one. Wondrous the merge!" "But what about us?" came a voice. "Yes," said another, "what about us?" "Oh, them," said the Master. It was all the other disciples hovering in the air. "I'm afraid you will have to find your own mountains," said James. "We can't find them for you. It's been a very complicated life we've had to lead. Follow your bliss!" The two James Richards waved to the creatures in the air. "Poor things," they thought, "poor sweetings. We would give them blood if we could." It was dawn again. Master and Disciple shivered a little in the chill as the sun at last came up. "Camera!" said James. "Lights! I love the movies!"

—*My name is James.*
There is nothing
But the indestructible sweetness
Of
Everything! Follow your weird.

LUCKY TREES

Each year a tree gets new genitals,
And not just one, but thousands:
Some trees have hundreds of thousands
    of penises,
Some trees have hundreds of thousands
    of vaginas,
Some have hundreds of thousands of penises and vaginas—
Whereas a human being only gets one—
One vagina or one penis
That's born and grows to puberty,
    blossoms, exults in ripeness,
        slowly withers and dies.

ANTLER

To think a Redwood that's 2000 years old
Gets hundreds of thousands of fresh new
Perfectly formed young male and female
      genital flowers every year
            that mate to become cones,
Cones with seeds in them as virile
      as when at age 70
The Redwood was first able
      to bear mature seeds—
Whereas by the time we're 70
Our seeds' virility, quantity, trajectory
      is past
And each year decrescendos toward death
The beauty, potency, majesty
      of our genital blooms.

But then a tree's seeds are not really seeds—
The seeds that fall from a tree
      are not really seeds,
But embryos! The seeds were
      pollen on anthers on stamens
            of tree flowers
That wind, insect or bird
      jostled or carried
            to the female flower's
            stigma on a style
Where semen joined ovum to form
      embryo which grew
Till ready to be implanted
      in motherearthwomb—
For the earth is every tree's mother,
For the earth is an infinite vagina
      out of which every tree comes.

Yet as we go through our mother's vagina
      when we're born,
Tree's embryos that are eaten
Go through a bird or animal's
      digestive system to be born,
So a tree's vagina a tree baby emerges from
That delivers the tree baby is
A mouth-esophagus-stomach-intestine-anus-tube
      out of which it is shit into earth
Out of which (the final and ultimate

225

mothervagina)
It finally bursts into being.

Lucky trees, so different from us,
Would that we were so lucky,
Would that we grew new boyhood cocks
    and girlhood cunts
No matter how old we were every spring.
Would that we could grow to be
    2000 years old
And still make love with our
    hundreds of thousands of
        penises and vaginas—
Ah, that we had as our birthcanal
    the digestive system of a doe
And the moist rich black warm earth
    where she shit her beautiful turds.

GOD

I fear piety
I fear God
I fear the Church
I fear this is a lawbreaker
I fear a rowdy
I fear a hoodlum
I fear disorderly conduct
I fear a riot
I fear a storm
I fear an underling
I fear underhanded
I fear a game of peaknuckle
I fear a loose disciple
I fear a methodist performer
I fear a minister
I fear a sneak
I fear poison
I fear a drugstore around the corner
I fear troubled waters
I fear double potions
I fear double troubles
I fear the forces of God
I fear the forgery of God

I fear the armed forces
I fear God
I fear uncivilization
I fear a lie

FEBRUARY

I remember its controversy
I remember its controversial events
I remember any day it rained
I remember the sleet that is changing to rain
I remember the rain that is changing to sleet
I remember its crowds
I remember its passengers
I remember its umbrellas
I remember its icier crosswalks
I remember a priest that paid its compliments to this city
I remember ladies and gentlemen and Roman citizens
I remember February
I remember any civilization
I remember its angels

NEW YORK CITY PUBLIC LIBRARY LIONS

Why, I thought they were orphans,
Why, I thought they were schoolboys,
Why, I thought they were wearing braids,
Why, I thought they were old standbys,
Why, I thought they were permanent scholars,
Why, I thought they were neglected,
Why, it was such a cold January day,
Why, I asked if they needed mittens,
Why, I asked one of them for his paw,
Why, I thought they were more like ourselves,
Why, I thought they asked for foods of other kinds,
Why, I thought they asked for food for thought.

227

HIGHER AUTHORITY

Lay an axe to the root and fell the cause.
Immediately! The sheen is off the polish
and meaning is everywhere. My dear sirs,
I want my weensy acreage in your soft quiet country too
but not at the expense of light.
Travelling in these times a chicken lays her egg
over all our balding heads. Don't look at me and mad-dog
me and say names under your breath. Movies are like real life
without the boring parts. I can't recall her name
but know the dame was framed. She told me
in no uncertain terms, as childhood knows no
uncertainty, if someone hurts you
you can't hurt them back—
you have to tell a teacher.

RADICAL COMMA

The Sum of Light is blazing white.
Don't eclipse my blue peninsula.
Therefore, tell all the news
but tell it tilt to bear
the unbearable. Else too blind
to hear, too sure to smell
the incense of youthful flares
in your old slacks. Direct Address
goes the way of bulk mail. God invented
food and the source of food. It is
written and placed in most motel rooms.
In this way a good poet must follow
Kings and Queens of the bottom,
dwelling amongst the colorful.

THEORY SONNET

My wife at the time, or to the mistress
unknown. Ladies, engage in debates
and sign your own name. Put an end to convalescence.
Ask the future effervescent.
A name now lost opened the first pencil factory.
Making no erasers, but elder branches filled with
lead. Getting no credit you can get none.
Pencil writing unlike indelible ink
disappears. So Girls, invent what lasts if you want
to be part of the equation, or be ruled out
like an odd number among the evens. And theory,
I too dislike it. Feeling it, however, with a
perfect distemper, one discovers
in it, after all, a place for the genuine.

PRINCESS BRIDE

I WEEP FOR OUR LOVE, PRINCESS,
FOR I AM ENCHANTED AND OLD
(IN THE MOVIE)
BUT
here in the real world
I AM THE JAGUAR
licking your sleek
HAUNCH
on the cliff edge
with the city below
in the silver fog
where
your
HUG
is good
for a trillion
years.
What's life
but a vale of fears
and a child's mask
on the muzzle
of a snake?
We stand knee-deep

MICHAEL McCLURE

229

in the lake
and side-by-side
in our waking sleep.

Capistrano Beach

DENISE NOE

RUB ON A THIGH

If yr boyfriend calls it quits
Cause yr legs won't do the splits
"I'll drop ya, *bam*,
Less ya open up the clam"

Girls night out
Shouldn't make ya pout
If U wanna fly
Baby, rub on a thigh

When I see yr muscles flex
When I hear U sigh
U make me more than high
I want to rub on yr thigh

Don't gotta worry 'bout Randall Terry
When just us girls R makin merry
No pregs, just a high
When U rub on a thigh

The love we make ain't free
There's always hurt & jealousy
Not 2 mention bigotry
Don't want 2 oversell it

Truth's the way I tell it
But no AIDS infection
No $300 operation
When U rub on a thigh

U won't believe me if I lie
Girls got sugar & hot spice
But sure as hell ain't everything nice
U might get hurt, U might cry
After rubbin on a thigh

Girls fib & two-time
Claw yr eyes, pull yr hair
Might even get a gun, blow yr shit sky-high
It's fun but not perfection—rubbin on a thigh

Gotta split the ck & that's a bitch
Going Dutch when U sure as hell ain't rich
Girls do every bad thing boys do
Cept the things they can't

Guys may say they had the mumps
When they're tryin for a humps
Might say they've been HIV tested
When their horniness has crested
But yr Mama told ya boys lie
When in doubt, rub on a thigh

FUCK ME

FUCK ME
I'm all screwed up so
FUCK ME.

FUCK ME
and take out the garbage
feed the cat and FUCK ME
you can do it, I know you can.

FUCK ME
and theorize about
sadomasochism's relationship
to classical philosophy
tell me how this stimulates
the fabric of most human relationships
I love the kind of pointless intellectualism
so do it again and
FUCK ME.

Stop being logical
stop contemplating
the origins of evil

and the beauty of death
this is not a TV movie about Plato's sex life,
this is FUCK ME
so FUCK ME.

I wrote this
so I'd have a good excuse to say "FUCK ME"
over and over
and over
so I could get a lot of attention
and look; it worked!
So thank you
thank you
and fuck ME.

THE SEX LIFE OF POLITICIANS

The days of devil-may-care sex
In the White House
Died with the 60s.

I can see Jack
Really gettin it on
With both Jackie and Marilyn.

LBJ humping a cute waitress
From southeastern Alabama
With his pants bunched
Around cowboy-booted ankles—
The image has a certain rustic charm.

From Nixon on it's all over—
Tricky Dick had not the wit to cheat on Pat.
Tricia's wedding was as far out as they got.
Who knows, or could possibly imagine
What happened between those two fish
When the lights went out?

And Gerry Ford—
Ya know why Betty took to drink and dope?
Cuz Gerry could never figure out
How to get his jockstrap off.

Poor Jimmy Carter,
Roz was all into Jesus and spirits.
Never gave him a peanut's worth of pussy.
In desperation Jimmy slipped
And lusted after a Playboy Bunny.

Nancy gave both anorexia
And cosmetic surgery a bad name.
Do we really want to perpetrate this horror?
I can't imagine fucking her.
I can't imagine anyone fucking her.
Not even Bonzo.
She'd tweeze your dick off, surely.

Barbara would be exactly like fucking your mother.
"We don' play dat shit, man,
Dat's WRONG. We don' fuck r mama,
An' we don' talk abow dit.
We got family values."

Danny-boy's done it once or twice,
But he's forgotten how it went.
He's the only human in the country
Over six years old
Who doesn't know how to spell fuck.

They say Bill Clinton
Whanged Miss Arkansas.
I think that's a healthy sign.
Hillary, who has to live with him said,
"No big deal." Good, good.
She might even look yummy in cute undies;
Her orifices might be worth exploring.
And I know Tipper whispers
Erotic lyrics in Al's ear
Just before he comes.

ANNE MacNAUGHTON

TITS

The breast that wins the prize
in nationwide wet teeshirt contests
is the one that stands UP the most.
That's easy.
It's just a few years old and
hasn't been sucked enough
yet.

She drove her pickup into the station,
jumped down, brushed the dark tail of hair
out of her eyes and slammed the cold nozzle
into her gas tank.

Under the thin cloth of an old white teeshirt
her tits were loose, weighty.
Old tits.
But the nipples were still sharp.
One breast—larger than the other—
hung an extra inch down her arm,
almost to the elbow.

Attendant slides over to her.
You shouldn't be goin' around like that, you know.
Aren't you 'shamed
in public without a bra?

Nah, she says.
I USE these.
Use 'em for what? he asks,
leaning on the pump.

She looks up, stares him straight in the eye.
I put 'em in men's mouths, she says,
to get myself off.

And ever so often
I bleed oceans of thin caramel
into the mouths
of babies.

SENRYU

Washed up on the beach
a few bi-valves
and a Japanese landowner.

A dip in the road—
we hold on
to our private parts.

"Poor dead Edna,"
he mutters,
"that taught me a lesson."

THE FUTURE OF VAGINAS AND PENISES

Descendants of Darwin predict a longer penis
as time goes on, as surely as our foreheads will expand
and our bodies will shed their needless hair.
In each generation, the vagina will tilt a miniscule angle
so our greatest of great granddaughters
will know the most pleasurable of unhurried sex acts.
Can't picture the millennial-slow realignment of the vagina?
Imagine then, if you will, the blade of your windshield wiper
traveling an arc in slow motion, forward but not back.
Cavemen, with their penis stubs, rushed
in and out, probably entering cavewomen from behind.
But as he extended, she shifted her insides
until finally we, and some of the others, like gorillas,
could savor intercourse, face to face.
This brings us to the puzzle of the clitoris.
Is genital evolution only about successful propagation?
What about a woman's orgasm?
Will her clitoris grow to be many more pink inches?
Will it migrate down towards the vaginal opening
for easier penile stimulation? Will the vulva swell
and double its number of folds? Future men
and women, so sexually happy, will lose their need
for war and divorce. Bald lovers will cuddle
by the timeless fire, their hairless bodies as naked
as skinned animals. Vulnerable, men and women
will honeymoon on the Galapagos Islands, enjoying
their smooth erotic lives, paying tribute to generations
of awkward groping partners before them.

235

MARK HALLMAN

I PROBABLY WOULD'VE MADE A GOOD LITTLE NAZI

At the age of eight I lassoed my sister with baling twine,
tethered her spread-eagle to our azalea bushes,
then tickled her bare feet until the screams of anguish
brought our parents running.

In seventh grade I clashed heads with my science teacher
over the accuracy of an important detail
regarding the anatomy of the male body.
That night I wished a curse on him.
By the end of the decade he was dead—
cancer of the regenerative organs, they said.

Ten years on I courted a woman so effectively
she beseeched me to marry her, promising some of Daddy's money.
"Honey," I replied, "you're a great cook,
but there's just one little problem:
I'm afraid you've got the wrong sort of equipment ... down there."

Tonight I wrapped my lover in long strips of Texas leather,
transforming him into an oversized babe in black swaddling clothes,
a big old Moses writhing in ecstasy
from what I was doing to his exposed privates.
"Please!" he whimpered, after almost an hour. "Finish me off!"
Instead, with him groaning in the background,
I called Mother—his.

JAMES PURDY

JAN ERIK

I dreamed of
the Last Judgement.
Hermes, judge of the Dead
was weighing hearts.
When he came to mine
he shook his head,
and perhaps he sighed
(my eyes like my ears
were without sense).
Hermes said:
Your lover though long
unfaithful to you
still keeps your heart against his own.
And so, according to

236

the scales
your heart weighs nothing.

» «

my greatest pain
Jan Erik said
was when my young lover
slept.
The smile which crossed his lips
was sweeter by far
than any he ever gave to me.
And so I was more jealous
of what he kept for dreams
than all the smiles he
flashed to rivals.

Who was it in the
depths of slumber
brought the honey to his lips?

» «

Yesterday Jan Erik went dancing
at the Pink Cloud,
a Cellar at the yard of
the old Canal of Utrecht.
(The speciality of Utrecht is
        the water is streaming 15 feet
                below street level
        so all along the canals
                dance pavilions abound.)
Jan stood along the walls of the dance hall.
All at once
        the blond punk who always flirts with him,
        the hankering handsome livid one came into view!
        As Jan danced near him,
        he wanted to say something,
        at least utter the beauty's name,
        but he does not know his name!
        So instead of speaking
        Jan looked up into the mirror
        of the canopied ceiling
        where he found the beautiful one's
        moving body, tawny and vulnerable
        and fearfully tempting.

237

But the mirrored image was all there was!
"Next time I will bring myself to speak to him,
name or no name," Jan Erik muttered, going home.
You see, Jan is still bound to his first love,
an Amsterdam boy who is, was, and always will be
faithless as the sea tide, cruel as a whip.
At home in his renovated Ballroom,
putting on his dressing-gown from the U.S. of A.,
Jan alone, as always,
dreams of his invisible Bridegroom.

PASTICHE OF MY SUBJECTIVITY

> "...the producers of culture have nowhere to
> turn but the past."
>
> —F. JAMESON

I celebrate my subjectivity and write myself
And what I assume I become,
For every signifier constituting me as well constitutes my other.
I free-float and produce a soul-effect.
I float and fetishize a blade of summer fescue.
My sounds, every travelling phoneme, formed from this language,
    this noise,
Originating in a discourse community, inflected by inflection, no
    origin, all origins.
I, without history, in normative physicality reenter,
hoping to continue in this state until not.
Ideologies and hegemonies marginalized
Temporarily, spatially, decentered, never absent,
I seek space, I announce myself,
With Late Capitalism and unchecked commodity explosiveness.

II

Televisions and CRTs are full of text, the silicon, wires jammed with
    electrobits,
I read the images and know them and like them.
Their spill mesmerizes me and I endorse it.

The world is not real, it does not exist outside my signification,
It is for my organs, my senses, I am scopophilia,

PAUL BAEPLER

238

I will plug into the circuit, become cyborg, cybourgeois,
I am mad for it to be in contact with me.
The vibrations of my own utterance
Echoes, ripples, buzzed whispers, clouded meanings, ego, other, mine,
    mine, mine.

My dreams, my stream of thoughts coursing through my brain, the
    passing of light and electrons through the rods and cones, my iris
    dilating,
The color green: envy, sea, money, spring, greenness,
The image of my sound oscillating like jump ropes through the wind,
    wave, particle, shock, compression.
A few light kisses, oral gratification—the sound of one lip smacking,
The play of words jumping rope, hushed screams,
The delight of loneliness—shattered—reconstructed of many, the loss of
    loneliness—nostalgia without memory.
The momentary illusion of organization, the uncanny, familiar images:
    the moon, circle, male, full stop, death, life, reflection, specularity,
    concave, the moon.

Have you a working myth of order? Are your categories meaningful?
Have you practiced decoding?
Have you felt so proud to get at the meaning of advertising?

Slip on a signifier with me yesterday and tomorrow and you will be
    confused, ever flickering,
You shall possess human agency (there are many subversive subject
    positions).
You shall always take things eighth, tenth, thousandth hand, the
    simulacrum, the xerox with no original,
You shall distort, interfere, effect with your presence/absence
You shall listen to all sides and filter them from yourself.

THANK YOU

Thank you wall. Thank you air for not ionizing.

It's 6:42 pm in the Midwest.

Thank you Clinton, Bush, Reagan, Carter, Ford, Nixon, Johnson,
    Kennedy, Eisenhower.
Thank you President Truman for doing it only twice.

CLIVE
MATSON

239

Thank you Peacemaker, Pershing, Cruise, Nautilus, Polaris, Titan, MX.
Thank you 200,000 microchips times 200,000 microchips times
   200,000 microchips.
Thank you 47 orders to "Fire!" for being discovered as accidents.
Thank you Three Mile Island. Thank you Chernobyl.
Thank you, big accident, for not happening.

It's 6:43 pm in the Midwest.

Thank you Yeltsin, Gorbachev, Chernenko, Andropov, Brezhnev,
   Kosygin,
Khrushchev, Bulganin, Stalin.
Thank you Batwing, Scud, SSX-24, SS-20, IRBM, ICBM, MIRV.
Thank you older generation. Thank you my generation. Thank you
   younger generation.
Thank you maniac. Thank you neurotic. Thank you normal person for
   not
ending it all. Thank you two keys for not turning.
Thank you, earthquake, for not cracking SIOP's headquarters,
   Nebraska.

It's 6:44 pm in the Midwest.

Thank you mind for keeping track. Thank you mind for usually keeping
   the process hidden.
Thank you billions and billions and trillions of dollars spent on the last
six minutes. Thank you last six minutes for not happening.
Thank you regional conflicts for not going nuclear. Thank you Korea,
   Vietnam, Cambodia, Nicaragua, Afghanistan, South Africa,
   Iran, Iraq.
Thank you, Saddam Hussein, for moving slowly.
Thank you, spontaneous combustion. Thank you air. Thank you walls
   for not vaporizing.

It's 6:45 pm in the Midwest.

Thank you USA, USSR, China, England, India, France, Sweden, Pakistan,
maybe Israel, Argentina, South Africa.
Thank you. Thank you.

THE AROMA OF ANGELS

I continue to disintegrate
gradually and politely.

Towards the close of foggy afternoons,
I can hear the rustle of angels' wings,
and even smell the angels.

It may interest you to know
that their aroma is not unlike that
of turkeys. I suppose that they are

edible, though I can't recall finding
any account in the literature of any
Christian venturing to try them.

(from the prose of H.L. Mencken)

THE SWEETNESS OF LIFE

Yesterday I was eating honey
and yoghurt on the balcony.
There was a bee balancing on the rim
of the honey jar, doing backbends.
With the book I was reading I beheaded him.
His head landed in the honey. Its jaws kept
sucking, and its antennae kept on waving.
These exertions kept his head afloat,
propelling it forward, like the masthead
of some allegorical boat.

RICHARD COLLINS

SOME NAMES OF VENUS FROM LEMPRIÈRE'S CLASSICAL DICTIONARY

She was called *Cypria*, because particularly
worshipped in the Island of Cyprus, and in that
character
she was often represented with a beard, and the
male parts of generation, with a sceptre in her
hand,
and the body and dress of a female, whence she is
called *duplex Amathusia* by Catullus.
She received the name of *Paphia*, because
worshipped at Paphos, where she had a temple
with an altar,
on which rain never fell, though
exposed in the open air.
Some of the ancients called her *Epistrophia*, as
also Venus *Urania*, and Venus *Pandemos*.
The first of these she received as presiding over
wantonness and incestuous enjoyments;
the second because she patronized pure love, and
chaste and moderate gratifications;
and the third because she favoured the
propensities of the vulgar, and was fond of
sensual pleasures.
The Cnidians raised her temples under the name
of Venus *Acraea*, of *Doris*, and of *Euploea*.
In her temple under the name of *Euploea*, at
Cnidos, was the most celebrated of her statues,
being
the most perfect piece of Praxiteles.
It was made
with white marble, and appeared so engaging,
and so much like life, that, according to some
historians,
a youth of the place introduced himself in the
night into her temple, and attempted to gratify
his passions
on the lifeless image. Venus was also
surnamed
Cytheraea, because she was the chief deity of
Cythera; *Exopolis*, because her statue was
without the city
of Athens;
Phallommeda, from her affection for the phallus;
Philommedis, because she was the queen of

laughter;
Telessigama, because she presided over
  marriage; *Caliada, Colotis,* or *Colias,* because
  worshipped
on a promontory of the same name in Attica;
Area, because armed like Mars;
Verticordia, because she could turn the hearts of
  women to cultivate chastity;
Apaturia, because she deceived;
Calva, because she was represented bald;
Erycina, because worshipped at Eryx;
Hetaira, because the patroness of courtesans;
Acidalia, because of a fountain of Orchomenos;
Basilea, because the queen of love;
Myrtea, because the myrtle was sacred to her;
Libertina, from her inclinations to gratify lust;
Mechanitis, in allusion to the many artifices
  practised in love, etc. etc.
As goddess of the sea, because born in the bosom
  of the waters, Venus was called
Pontia, Marina, Limnesia, Epipontia, Pelagia,
Saligenia, Pontogenia, Aligena, Thalassia, etc.,
  and as
          rising from the sea, the name of
Anadyomene is applied to her, and rendered
          immortal by the celebrated painting
of Apelles, which represented her as issuing
          from the bosom of the waves, and
wringing her tresses on her shoulder.

BODYBUILDER

his protein milkshakes his fistfuls of vitamins
his razored scalp & blond mustache
his highschoolkid clothes
the times he danced shirtless in clubs & went home to sleep alone
the times he entrained for New York & never heard the opera
the times he benchpressed twice his own weight
his eyes that asked why then repeated the question
his personal ad: "sober BB who also writes poetry seeks similar ..."
his 2nd floor brownstone studio posters & shelfed sets of Tolstoy
his refusal to own a TV

JIM CORY

the time he caked his face with oatmeal to erase the lines
the time his only credit card was seized buying rollerskates at the
    ArmyNavy
the time he tumbled from bed laughing at someone's penis & said years
    later I know now we pay for everything we
do the mouthful of teeth he left in a crushed VW
the winged things that flew thru him
his sunshade Walkman silence disguise & phone unanswered
his fat tin toad of a typewriter anchoring drafts & unpaid bills his 1
    published poem his hundred flaming bridges
his memory of perfect love of nightwhispered teenage underwear
    stirrings
his bathroom mirror the dimesized purplish islands on his back
his 2 years doctors hospitals drugs tests & transfusions
the time he lost his race with incontinence on Broad St.
the poem he wrote about it
the TV he agreed to take the male nurse nattering in the bathroom the
    mousesized roach under the fridge
the fridge filled with everything he couldn't eat/drink/lift
his scalded limp paw & infant hair
his telescope spectacles
his voice full of sand & abandoned nests
his final sigh
the fullmoon silence of its echo
the row of parked cars on the hill
the brass box resting on Astroturf
his jacketed photo in promtux toppled in sudden breeze

WILLIAM TALCOTT

THE FUNCTION OF ART

for Jesse Helms

I never spied on my sister
but once we spent the day
at the Louvre.

We especially liked
the painting of Leda
opening her legs to a bird.

Venus di Milo was okay too.
Then we went back to the hotel
& fucked our brains out.

244

GENEALOGY

family tree, family sawdust.

FAMOUS FOR FIFTEEN MINUTES

Misquoted by *Time* magazine.
One minute.

Clubbed by the Tac Squad.
Six o'clock news.
Two minutes and five stitches
including reruns at eleven.

Question man in the *Chronicle*:
"What do you like to touch?"
I said food. One minute.
Except for the guy who kept calling me up.

Interview for selling crazy
hats. Three minutes.
One for me, two for the hats.

Bankrupt shop owner.
One minute not counting
the banks I stiffed.

Drug bust no minutes.
I kept that one quiet.

That leaves nine minutes.
I can hardly wait.

THE OPPOSITE OF GRAVITY IS HUMOR

Perhaps you were on the scent of something,
or maybe it was stalking you. A few more
clods of unbearableness get thrown on the pile
and as your pile of unbearablenesses reaches critical
mass, the bear drops from a platform onto the plank's
other end and sends it all catapulting, throwing a good
healthy fear into you. All the weight of stopgap solutions
flashes and you dive like an ostrich into the dark.
Moments of clarity, when the path is lit on all sides
like a runway, are at a premium. It's the end
of the millennium. Twilight. Looks like rain, too.
The unbearable sky threatens to unleash its animals on everything
but even underground the cats and dogs will find you,
for they remain as attached to you as ever, needing
you to call them by name to straighten their fur,
to make up for the possible error eons ago of domesticating them.

There's nowhere to hide from the hurtling mass of their needs,
and so you convince yourself to choose them,
humming a melody so as to buttress your illusions about
controlling one's destiny. Meanwhile, the unbearablenesses
comes to another density, and the bear is ready again to drop—
why has she nothing else to do but dance attendance on you this
            way?
But dance she will, and drop she will, with a faithfulness
that is ultimately comforting. You've chosen her, too,
to help you get the whole confusion off the ground.
So you begin to juggle, taking to it as though it were
your very essence. You juggle the ostrich, the cats and dogs.
You juggle the smitten bear, wooed by her everlasting optimism,
and trust your skill at working with what is there,
in that distracting little tent that lines your face
so deeply with laughter it draws itself forth like a reflex
and pitches everything up again.

DEATH TRIP

When I am alone, I see pigs covered with mud and a car full of devils. The guns in the closet are the first guns to come out. They are not enemies but partners. I hope it rains tomorrow. Then all doubts and suspicions will disappear.

FLAUBERT'S KITCHEN

People are like food. There are lots of people who seem to me like Cool Whip: party hardy, lasts for weeks, and a chemist's delight (sorbitan monostearate, polysorbate 60, and xanthum gum). Other people are like Slim Jims, Spam, Wonder Bread from General Mills, Jell-O (in shimmering Crayola-crayon colors), Tater Tots, and Twinkies. Me? I'm like Hamburger Helper, without the hamburger. No longer will your pebbly ground beef need to loll repulsively in a puddle of its own grease in a frying pan while you hunt in vain for a can of Veg-All or lima beans to disguise its oily nakedness.

FAVORITE COLOR

My favorite
color on
barns is red
but on people
I mean ghosts
it's blue.

WHAT DO BOOKS SAY?

You cannot live a minute longer without oxygen. You are being held underwater by the Industrial Revolution. You leave for China the next day, hoping to find the notebooks of Louis Braille.

    Not necessary.

POLICE STORY

The police told me to continue what I was doing, and to spread joy and revolution.

THE SEVEN DEADLY SINS

Aerosol cheese, Muzak, monster trucks, maraschino cherries, artificial Christmas trees, eating at Hellenic diners while wearing elevator shoes.

WHY I WRITE

the dog whose teeth
catch dinner, and
it's raw, the blood
just starting to give off
its nourishment. I write

about my mother dying:
I write that now and ever.
other faces smash against
the high, lost wall, but
turn around and love the sun
as much. I never turn.
it's all those motorcycles
parked across the street.
not smiling, and with women,

with out mother who would leave
the house as quickly as they died,
would be with gods who picked them
out of crowds to drive into the air.

to lose their daughters in the trees.

I'll never get her back. Orpheus
gives meaning to the horror, gives meat.
the hell-dog has a multitude of heads,
and so do I. keeps breaking its own skulls.

lament. that protein.

HOLLY PRADO

VOICE OF THE WORLD

It is a strange energy you give me, death,
like sliding a corpse over the stiff nap
of a carpet to pick up the static:
The crackle of the short-wave, the voices
sizzling *Son of Doc, this is Cap-Haitien*
reporting on the frequency of sex in the grave
Even my teeth sparkle in their yellow
defeated way: do a root canal on a zombie
and come to know the painless practice of poesy.
But I don't mean that, sitting here packing
shards of electricity into either ear,
like that black drummer one night scratching
his brushes on skins that once housed life.

BOAT

Darling little death boat
peapod compact
all set to sail & not come back

Sweet little death boat
moored on Doric piers
filled with glass stars & saltwater tears

My little death boat
waits paitiently for me
to carry out a china set & gently pour the tea

Darling little death boat
carry me along
rock me in your cradle, sing my last song

THE EVIDENCE WAS SLIGHT

Yet it raised many questions for many weeks.
A rain of locusts: the president stood alone
Trying to fight back his tears. An invasion
Of greenbacks: from his misty window-pane
He saw them coming: I woke up that morning
A dollar bill was scratching at my door
Begging for food: it ran across the room
Screeching like a blind bat. It started eating
The carpet. For a while it lay still on its back
Then it burst into song and expired at my feet.
The dead word there on the floor. I write too many
Words. It would have been simpler to say:
The outside became detached from the inside
And to have left it at that: I wanted to go on
To expand and expound. I expected nothing
From love or hate who were absent. Somewhere outside
In the bushes around the house I was watched—
Some kind of sensation waiting to take me unawares.
I was on call that morning. Nothing happened.
What else can I say about what happened
Before and after—when nothing happened
Three times in a row. A record for my age.
It was worth the effort. It wasn't anything at all.
I mean the effort. On the stroke of midnight
It started all over again grinding away
And the wall tumbled and through the hole
Behold—I could see myself—being born.

IMPULSE AND NOTHINGNESS

These dense geranium surges of thought
protracted through steaming anthrax waters
concerned with the coronal aspects of contingency
those sabbatical athanors in which nothingness looms
without image
without the doctrinal plumage of a fixed event
without the mesmeric square of Talmudic rigidity
when one is transfixed by intention
by the Messianic force fused with the illusive intensity
of impulse
shot into the grainy broach of nothingness

there exists the sense of bleached equators
the suicidal aching of secondary sunfish

one then gives off the odour of a Pentecostal heresy
& one no longer lives in an aura of the weakened
with the weakened
one stands like a bolt
upright
facing the electrical debris of an ochlocracy in pain
staggered by the knife of its own surgeon's riddles
by a rabid scalpel cutting at its ribs
by a deboned pleurisy rumbling in its vision
as I reach into this nothingness
I am abandoned by associates
psychically spat upon by contemporaries
a reflex
against one condemned
by the interests of the secular nerve field

this I
a target
with an intense circulation of acid in the veins

so everything that I snare
always half plunged into eclipse
all my description
subject to electro-ballistical analysis
an analysis of my own achievement
which ironically has no power to engulf me

so I remain suspended
between light & the imageless arcana of extinction
& the emotions
those electrical cadavers
weave themselves like a sickened medicine in my thorax

as to my name
it has become an exploded ravens' dyscrasia
an excrescence
walking around with my eyes
like a series of neurological sunspots

& in speaking
I remain corroded with intensive tedium rejoinders

with my bones squirming at an angle of pathological
nightmare edicts
a cauldron of metacarpal tsunamis
as a result
I feed on the carking magnificence of loneliness
on the "nomadology" of cacti & sores

I count my companions as enemies
those obedient nomenciators covering up those abbreviated
prolusory murders of the spirit

& so as a scar
as one given up to the guerrilla domain of
cosmic prolepsis
I am always a figure
a metal hormone found in a basket
floating on broken sea bird's blood

on both sides of my eyes a parenthetical numbness
a painful but voided exogen climacterics
in which I wander through intensive flytrap grasses
weaving myself to death while humming in-doctrinal ballets
a shapeless fumitory witness
suffering like a cipher
or a metamorphic anagram
spying on shapes in the darkness

THE WATER DOG

*...the dog is the species most accustomed to accom-
panying early travelers by land and sea*

—THOR HEYERDAHL

Born under butane & water
under the snapping fire of ice & razors
like a compass
pointed at the fact of combustible granite
pointing far beyond
the panorama of glaciers & icy land-locked schooners
to Antarctic labouring blisters
to special atmospheric codes
where ice sends up a smoke

253

like an exploded measuring jar
or expanded zodiacs of lightning

his tongue
crystal & fog & fire
his power
like a galaxy of anteater's rabies
a noxious weathervane of ions
pointing
Zambian kangaroo
the Isle of Wight
the beautiful moraines of Bermuda
pointing to the arcane solstice mountains
seeing like a cenobite
into the glassy fires of the Caspian Sea
into the blackened
imaginary grottos of the Sahara
a tense perilous compacting of weathers
in a unit of diamonds
cracked
on sandy Egyptian mountain ranges
filing his neurological hearing
so that the poles of Venus
connect
with the Gulf of Castellammare
with the curving throat of Sicily
like a ruthless intentional steam

marking in the Mongolian steppes
with his hieroglyphical paws
of intuitive malachite & sunstroke
an ibis in Genoa
a linseed spiral
part Damascus
part of the Swiss Thunersee & Paris

the grown dog amounts
the magical snout of alignments
gazing
at threads of Amazonian lice
at its headwaters rotting
pointing
cabalistically to its bottoms with his breath
pointing

to the asteroidal fields of Ceres
the darkened pre-globular entropies
mesmerized
with howling & starlight
with magic geometries of panic
a diviner
analogous with landscapes of darkness
briefly dazzled
by twilight & pumice
who seizes every particle of ground

his breath pointing
to butchery shelters & loneliness
like a telepathic pine juice
seething
micro-biology & vineyards
howling
at those sacred iguana dawns
looking for the magical cracks in the skin of space
sucking in eclipse & lightness

the principal force of ice balloons
a wave of lotus junctures

all the sundown bluing
all the nucleic borium breathing
across the asteroidal isles
across the proton-neutron
of this life
of this present profusion
the force
of bays & winds & stars
the deep mercator blankness
the mutant compass slavings
the anti-osmium susurrations
issuing from his electrical skull
from the musical stride of his forceps' blackness

because of his fierce navigator's bondage
Asiatic
etheric
his wayward nitrogen calendar
his stupendous rose war ignitions
because

he is the water dog
the dog
between non-being being & being
able to distinguish the flux
between Graham Bell Island
& the Bay of Biscay
between
Revillagigedo in the Mexican Pacific
& the in-land flames of Ulan-Bator

the dog angel
at the origin of hydrography & fire
at the genesis of arc-light & magnesium

the dog angel
the water dog on fire
the synonymous Arctic star
the occult illuminal wire
smelling
the blood
the spaces
the cunning ammonia
of cyclic ambrosial dimensions

FAREWELL TO TEXAS POEM

(after DiPrima)

Adios!
shit tipped redneck boot
factory, Alamo plaza
crowded w/ Japanese tourists,
powdery bones of my ancestors
buried just beneath the sidewalk,
katchinas in window of Trading Post,
negra pintada in Sandra Cisneros foyer,
I love you too! lone monarch butterfly
in mother's flower bed, bright sun
fading to bauxite red,
mountains of shale
halfway to nowhere, U.F.O.'s
over Taft, synchronous
chance encounter of whoever
you were just thinking about,
Twilight Zone ambience of radio
format that hasn't changed
in years. Funny, surrealist longhorn
furniture at The Lone Star Museum
Tom Thumb's carriage at the Hertzberg
mariachis after midnight at the Esquire
yellow blooming irises on the riverwalk
downtown where I have, for nostalgia's
sake, steaming plates of greasy
enchilidas estilo Tejano
you can't find anywhere else
menudo every day of the week
so long friends, relatives, antiquated
family unit as obsolete as
World Banking System, Zapata Oil
rigs puncturing the face of
flat, spindly landscapes
populated w/ armadillos,
rattlesnakes, piss ants, horny toads,
thorny brambles mistaken for trees,
man-of-war filled beaches sticky
w/ blackgold, teach me
to sing! grackles in the treetops
of Matagorda St.
saffron prayer flag from Tsurphu

RONNIE BURK

turning in March wind may your
blessings fall on this harsh
inhospitable land, turn old
hardened sorrows of regret & dismay
into spontaneous joy of each
new beginning ...

JULY 4TH, 1994

Happy Birthday America!
Wake-up!
Ultraviolet count is now official
Official brass plate Mars
& the face of Chief Joseph from a Dow Chemical
        commercial just shed a tear
Talk radio's old hat
so Gala was a nymphomaniac & fucked Jesus Christ
        Superstar
who cares?
who cares if Jack Kerouac wiped his ass w/ the American
        flag
& Hawaii is in N.Y. harbor
drinking liquid paper
it's your birthday !
so have a slice of plutonium cake
after all, you baked it

IN THE BLACK FOREST BEFORE THE BIRTH OF RILKE

under her skirts of bark
the hidden pencils grow

C.A. CONRAD

THE FIRST DATE

HAYDEN CARRUTH

I've been to three [nudist camps] over a period of years. The first time I went was in 1963 when I stayed a whole week and that was really thrilling... The director met me at the bus station because I didn't have a car so I got in his car and I was very nervous. He said, "I hope you realize you've come to a nudist camp." Well, I hope I realized I had.

—DIANE ARBUS

What do I like to do on a first date? Well, I show
my guest the rooms of my house, leaving the obvious

for last; I make sure all the right books are lying
spiral on my coffee table; there is plenty of the aphrodisiac

assortment of food (also arranged, in modular fashion),
and after we do everything, we look. At my book of nudes;

I roll over and turn the lights on, maybe all of the lights,
and we point to this one and that; "look at how fat

they are!" and we sink our shoulders closer to the page,
our noses right back there while we strain to see

the nudity between us; in a propped up book spread open
between my legs, this date realizes, this is how it is.

SHE SAID IT

If you can't talk about it, point to it.

—LAURIE ANDERSON

The day you burned your sleeve
leaning over the stove for emphasis,

we did it after, you holding your arm
just off the pillow, then the floor—

we blew on the red marks, ran our fingers along
the crease where you hurt. It was obvious

259

where we might have pointed, "look at how red it is!" but too
painfully we caught ourselves, spent our energies elsewhere;

sore and silly after a while, we kissed it all better,
and still later, after a soak, we kissed it again.

BETRAYAL

When I was a kid of sixty-two
and lay in Paradise on Euphrates' shore
so help me I was happy, whole and manly,
and I screwed Eve till she became a choir

of dying vultures and the lotus trees
sank swaying in their prurience
and everything was wailing. My own spirit
was shocked in such loves and woes,

the devastatingly human. Too much for
Thee, dreadful master. Thou
wert wroth, and why I never knew
except I interpreted envy and Thy brow

confirmed it, those flashes of a bad
light. And Eve, distempered, clung
as best she could to my drudging cock
whenever she got the chance. She sang

the blues of the insatiable female lust
for monicity, never to be gratified,
never. And Thou in Thine infinite
whimsy thrust us out, outside

to the deserts of Syria where
serpents and scorpions reduced us.
We were scabbed, malnourished flatlanders
and say if that was not betrayal, Thou Pus

of the Universe, Almighty Flamdoodle
with the cosmic space-worm
   floating in Thine asshole.
      Eve and I did what we could, walked a

concentric walk to the outlying
gardens, each more putrescent, where we
raged and fucked in garbage. Until
she found a gorilla, the huge handsome

primate of her dreams, and over the hill
they romped, feeling each other's privates.
Betrayal. Thou hadst forecast it, Thou
hadst fashioned it, scheme, modus, tao

for us all, the way to keep the brouhaha
of human experience ongoing when we
might have slipped into the deep and ever
to-be-desired stasis of love. Oh Thou

Fucker, Father of Betrayal, never
to be known in the mounting helixes
of betrayal, Teacher, Grantor
of misery. Eve was stupid, she hurt

herself. But You did it to us first.
And then we were doomed forever.

HAYDEN CARRUTH:
THE BABE RUTH OF POETRY

ANTHONY ROBBINS

In an article in *The New Yorker* in 1980 or 81—I think by Roger
Angell, I can't remember and I paraphrase here almost certainly
inaccurately—as the baseball fanatic and his wife prepare to go their
separate ways for the evening; she tells him that she is going to a
poetry reading by Hayden Carruth: "Just think of him as the Babe
Ruth of poetry." An adulterated comparison by a true fan. Carruth
has hit many poetic home runs, but few seem to have noticed. In fact
he reached an advanced stage in his distinguished career as a poet,
editor, and critic without having received the attention which he
deserved and which has been accorded many of his less able contemporaries. Lyrically gifted and philosophically acute, Carruth is one of
the finest American poets of this century, a slugger. Perhaps one

reason for the relative neglect has been Carruth's lack of self-promotion. He lived in Johnson, Vermont, for 20 years and neither gave readings nor taught until 1978, when he went to work at Syracuse University, where he teaches now. He has written in such a variety of lyric modes so as to be atopic, unclassified, in regard to normal academic categories. He has published 22 books of poetry, a novel, and four collections of criticism, as well as editing the influential anthology of twentieth-century poetry, *The Voice That Is Great Within Us*. Once editor of *Poetry* and poetry editor for *Harper's* and a current and long-standing member of the editorial board of *The Hudson Review*, he has also received nearly every major award and grant, including an NEA lifetime-achievement award in 1988. Yet his poetry, although often prominently and favorably reviewed and praised, is neglected by critics and readers. His most encompassing single work, the book-length poem *The Sleeping Beauty* (Harper and Row, 1982), has just gone out of print, and, shamefully, his *Selected Poems* (Macmillan, 1985) although an adequate introduction—contains nothing of *The Sleeping Beauty* or *Contra Mortem*, an important long poem. Carruth has determinedly avoided certain kinds of public limelight. It is past time to begin to take notice of the range and depth of his poetic and critical achievement, of the powerful sensibility that is apparent in all of his work, and of his importance in twentieth-century poetry.

Carruth's first book, *The Crow and the Heart*, was published in 1959, when he was 38. It is in its own way characteristic of much academic poetry of the 50's: highly formal, verbally dense, bedizened with strange words from Carruth's huge vocabulary, full of courtly ballads, couplets, wit and even "imitations" of J. V. Cunningham and Robert Graves. It includes "The Asylum," a 13-poem sequence in which Carruth, coincidentally with Lowell and, as ever, unacknowledged, used in writing about his institutionalization a surprisingly personal, "confessional" mode (although he has abjured that rubric), as well as developing the 15-line sonnet he would later use in some of his long poems.

His next books, *Journey to a Known Place, The Norfolk Poems, North Winter,* and *Nothing for Tigers,* all superlative in their own lyric accomplishments, culminate in the poems in which he found his mature voice, *Contra Mortem* (1965), a sequence of 30 fifteen-line sonnets. Here Carruth shows his lyrical virtuosity, his abilities to improvise within a given form (as he has written elsewhere, later, "tone, phrasing, and free play/ of feeling mean more than originality,/ these being the actual qualities of song."), and his acute understanding of urgent issues of philosophy and education. He combines his talents for natural description with clairvoyant social commentary and also communicates—in a way that the finest of American lyricists, I include Frost, Pound, Aiken, Loy, Cummings, Roethke, Bogan, Creeley, and Rich, et al., have rarely approached—his deep and lucid affections for his family, his friends, and for the possibilities of the moment. Everything that Carruth writes about in these thirty poems—entitled, for example, "The Boy', "The Woman," "The Child," "The Trees," "The Coming of Snow," "The Being as Moment"—becomes transformed by his understanding and invested poetic dignity:

> How much
> We give to one another Perhaps our art
> succeeds after all our small one done in the faith
> of lovers who endlessly change heart for heart
> as the gift of being Come let us sing against death.

Change, not exchange. Note the difference.

In addition to his dyed-in-the-wool Yankeeism, Carruth is a thorough-going existentialist (he has written a book on Camus), and the primary importance of his most encompassing poem, *The Sleeping Beauty* (1982) is its existential discussion on the great paradox of the Romantic impulse: that the will and drive to be good, heroic, noble, to achieve the ideal, the impulse to love generously and thereby to have freedom has led to failure, to murder and domination: how "passion/ in romance must be love in action,/ Lust for the ideal … O, murderous." Carruth understands that the heroic striving of the Romantic personality for an individual selfhood has meant personal disintegration and social chaos. In an attempt to efface the traditional single authorial voice because it is a convention of the Romantic aesthetic, because of insistence upon expropriating the identity of the object of its attentions—through allegorizing them, hypermetaphorizing in representations of them—Carruth has made the poem, "as in all dreaming," out of coincidental voices, which become an immense chorale of suffering humanity. A medieval woman describes how she was burned alive. Joe Turner sings. A sixteenth-century woman sneaks out of bed to write only to have her "scriving" burned by her husband. A supposedly dead Vermonter, Amos, preachifies about the deterioration of the farm communities and the forests. A contemporary woman describes her sexual problems with her husband, who finally "went gay" when she entered menopause. A country girl who has become a member of a seraglio describes her training in the *Formality of Submissiveness*. A fourteenth-century woman tells how she was raped and impregnated by vandals while her own baby was butchered. A Chinese woman describes the pain of having her feet bound, "bent backward underneath like a broken book." The poem is also composed of sonnets describing episodes of history connected with the letter "H," with Helen, Hector, Herod, Hesiod, Hannibal, Hölderlin, Hesse, Hegel, Heraclitus, Hermes, Hudson, Hitler, Honeywell, Harlequin, Heathcliff, Hamlet, Hermaphrodite, Hydrogen Bomb. All of this only suggests the richness of *The Sleeping Beauty*. Not only have I skipped whole collections, I have not touched on other accomplishments:

in his novel *Appendix A* (w. 1961), he anticipated techniques used later by fiction writers. In *Working Papers and Effluences from the Sacred Caves* and *Sitting In*, he has given us some of the most acute criticism of Thoreau, Pound, Lowell, Stevens, Levertov, and Duncan, and he writes extensively about the relationship between art and life, between jazz aesthetics and poetry, between cultural optimism and the freedom of the individual. Charles Altieri has called "The Act of Love: Poetry and Personality" (*Working Papers*) "the best discursive essay by a contemporary American poet."

In *Asphalt Georgics, The Oldest Killed Lake in North America,* and *Lighter Than Air Craft*—he produced poems of great beauty and force. He has admitted his great admiration for and debt to Paul Goodman and his work, especially his poetry; and Goodman, in describing the qualities of one of his masters, Kant, touches the quick of the personal correlatives of Hayden Carruth's work of the last thirty years: "Through middle age and a good old age, his work flowed on spontaneous, vigorous, brave, endlessly inventive and continually maturing, minutely attentive and boldly synoptic and with a fine rhythm of style. We have to ask if his way of being obsessional is not a good way to cope with the nature of things, in order to live on a little. I repeat it: the proof of a sage is that he survives, he knows how."

ROBERT PETERS

from THE HENIAD

FEATHERED FRIENDS

—for Emily Dickinson

A splendid Fellow in the Grass
Occasionally rides—
I know you've seen him—did you not
His clucking noisy is—

The Grass divides as with a Comb—
His glossy Feathers quaver—
He beaks his Biddy's little Comb
And shoves it to her Liver—

He likes her secret Parts—
They are so sweet and soupy—

264

And when he's through and doth withdraw—
His tiny Shaft is juicy—

Most of Nature's feathered Friends
I know, and they know me—
I feel for them a Transport—
Of erotic Cordiality—

Except for this randy Fellow—
Old Chanticleer the Bold—
He leaves me tighter breathing—
And quivering with Cold.

THE DARKLING CHICKEN

—for Thomas Hardy

I look into the hen yard
And view the squatting hen
Inviting the cock to mount her
In the far muddy corner of the pen.

With blast-beruffled plume
And pinions opened wide
The yellow cockerel balances
And keeps an even tide.

The hen receives her pleasure.
He thrids her in a dream.
And mounting high and higher
Emits a bird-like scream.

His ecstasy eludes me.
There trembles in the air
Some chicken-bliss whereof he knows
And I am unaware.

A STUDY IN AESTHETICS

—for Ezra Pound

The very small chickens in tattered feathers
Being smitten with emotional anemia
Stopped in their pecking as I passed them
And chirped
    Ch'e be'a. (How beautiful she is.)

Three minutes after this
I heard young Ez, whose middle name I do not
    know—
Speaking ancient Chinese to a fresh catch of squid,
And his elders
Were packing them in great plastic pails
for the market in Sirmione, and he
Leapt about, grabbing at the squirting squid
And when the elders
Would not let him pack the creatures in the pails
He stood there and stroked them
Murmuring, and stroking his groin,
    Ch'e be'a. (How beautiful she is.)

My boredom was perverse.
This is the end of good breeding.

CRAZY BILL TO THE BISHOP

—for W. B. Yeats

I swear by what the sages spoke
Round the Macrobiotic Lake:
That Shelley's Witch of Atlas knew
Proclaimed and set the cocks a-crow.

Here's the gist of what they meant:
Swear by those hens, by women
Whose double-yolked eggs prove superhuman.
Out of the shell at wintry dawn
Came Castor and Pollux, their passions gone,
  Robbed by the rooster, that bird
    Who thrust his muscle strong

Midst Leda's thighs, like death
Turning for another breath,
A copulation song
Of wattles and chicken-dung,
Of warrior twins untimely wronged.

Make fowl fill their incubators tight.
Penis-measurement will set things right.

A rooster's glans, a hen's canal
Defy our randy laughter.
Gyres spin on, and we poor souls
Hasten after.

BERTHOLD BRECHT ENTERS HEAVEN

Fetch me my leather jacket
and a Steyer automatic;
its draughty doing this epic schmalzy scam.
I left my best silk shirt in Potsdam.
I need to call my broker on the price of gold.
I'm tired and I'm feeling *zea* old.

None of the women in my life are saved;
The appetites of women were my soil
and I was rich, but skinny from my toil,
and they were more tenacious than my grave:
God knows it never was my fault.
In a steel coffin who can somersault?

My Swiss accounts are all in order
and Switzerland is banked across the border.
They buried me right next to Hegel.
I'd love to chew a Jewish water bagel.
Considering in the end a man's a man,
I'm coming in my BMW sedan ...

RICHARD ELMAN

JACK ANDERSON

AGAINST SCIENCE FICTION

Most of the stories are set in the future,
which is always appalling:
people controlled by clanking machines
or marching on treadmills through plastic tunnels
with not a flower, muffin, or puppy in sight—
who'd want to live that way?
And yet, they say, that's what's ahead.

Or if they conceive the future as utopian,
then what's in store for us is either Pure Thought
coating the universe like tapioca on a rampage,
or a well-run Scouts' camp in a distant galaxy
where we get up at dawn for obligatory calisthenics
amid sighing fungi and palpitating rocks—
and who'd choose either,
especially if it's not always possible to tell
if the authors are satirical or deadly serious?

They may claim that everything we find in their tales
is just something of today stretched to an extreme,
but who let it get that way,
and why was it allowed?
The future is soiled for us
before it has happened.

So better the past—
and not just the grandeur and misery of the classics,
better even the past in historical romances,
for no matter how silly or trashy they seem,
what they describe is over and done with,
the past stays unchanged,
it comes down to us as it is,
we must make of it what we can
as we get on with our business
of living with the present
for better or worse,
in sickness or in health.

GOLF

Father liked golf:
he and his pals
used to spend their days off
down at the links,

though mother would joke
it was just an excuse
to drive out for a drink
and she'd laugh at dad's cap and baggy old pants

and, turning serious, she'd hint
that if he only stayed in once
he could use his free time to clean up the basement
or do take-home work in hopes of a raise,

but father said he liked fresh air,
claimed fresh air and sunshine made him a new man,
that it felt good to be under clear skies
free from all care,

and then he'd remind us
how much nicer things were now
—though, sure, they were calmer—
than the way they were when he was a kid

when crowds decked out in their Sunday best
would gather by the church
—the bells ajangle, the organ roaring—
and clouds of incense would rise to high heaven

until smoke blackened the sun
and the smell of burning
spread over the town
as, one by one, the carts rolled in

followed by monks bearing crosses and relics
and while the choir sang and the priests chanted psalms
everyone pushed closer, shoving and sweating,
to help throw that day's judged upon the fire.

269

WHEN WILL UNCLE VANIA TAKE THE TRAIN TO MOSCOW?

Uncle Vania peers through the window to
the garden. Moscow lies beyond the haze,
beyond the chitchat and the piles of blue
logs in the snow. Blue angels in a craze
are seething in celestial drapes. They want
escape yet Vania can't throw off his old
impotent fuss. He understands but can't
bluster into the snow to take the train
to loneliness and gambling poverty.
The winter dulls. He moves into the sane
boredom of spring. And his epiphany?
His vision festers like a half-loved friend.
What good is holy truth in a household
he'll never leave? This play can never end.

FROM HIS HOTEL ROOM IN PARIS

Just a month ago I would say she holds me
In her orbit—or was I holding her in mine?
In the beginning she was the one
Who accused me of cheating.
I was grateful. She meant I was cheating
her of myself. I wanted that demand:
to be held, for desire to make me unable
to break our iridescent orbital cords.
When I joined her in France she had become
like people there. Not French exactly—
She could have been anywhere, floating,
responding, but without a self, not a self
she loved. She's not like me, an artist.
She lacks interests. I say be human first
before art, but she floats, a confusion
of lights reflecting a confusion of lights.

After we made love she told me
she'd been to bed with three men in a week.
Like the figures in dreams
these things come in threes. She did it
without concern for consequence, disease,

or for my hurt—she could be my murderer.
If she'd been willing to sit, to hold me
and know my pain, I could have borne it.
But she was running, running the way
she ran ahead with her friend that night
we walked in the red light district.
When we caught up she was sitting on a bench,
swinging her leg. She ran her tongue
over her teeth and said, "We could have
made a lot of *money* while you boys were gone."

So we traveled, posing happily with friends
at a table of full wine glasses
or glowering into the camera alone.
Then one day, not for the first time,
showing off, she undermined me in front
of her friends, our hosts.
I pulled her aside and confronted her.
She asked, "Why are you attacking me?"
"You want to know what an attack is?" I replied.
"*This* is an attack, you cunt!"
I threw water on her and I raised my hand.
She ran!
I chased her into the most beautiful garden
I had ever seen, a topiary garden
with many paths that split and reunited.
There, in public, humiliating her,
we shouted terrible things at each other
while the fountain waters seemingly leapt free,
but breaking in mock joy circled and recircled.

LEGACY

On the last day of April
the most venereal of months
in the thirty-eighth year of life
having had to date a single surgical intervention
that being the insertion of an apparatus like a garden hose
down the throat of my pecker
with cutting attachments to remove
a so-called stricture of the urethra so that
the flow of urine might be more free
I hereby declare my desire to die and my
imminent leave-taking of life.

That being of disturbed mind and diseased testicles
I, John of Mung, do hereby make the following bequests
after the will of God to the extent it is known to me
and requesting forgiveness for all my ignorances and
transgressions, domine domine etcetera.

To the Bulgarian doctor who undertook this most unnecessary
and ill-conceived operation I leave
the prick of a dead rooster and the nuts
of a rutting boar, both to be placed inside
his living mouth and there sewn up with fishing line
through his lying lips, meaning no harm to his reputation
which is excellent or
to his standing among his colleagues
who read his papers in the medical journals.

To the Irish anesthesiologist who provided the
blessed sodium pentothal and offered a smiling Irish face
floating above my flimsy gown and shaved pubis I leave
the memory of all my loves past which list is now
complete and final from the first in a silk nightgown
in the basement of her parents' house at age sixteen
to the last a blow job in a parking lot outside a nightclub
from a drunken barmaid infected with god knows what ailments
all loves shared and requited and unrequited I leave
these memories to that Irish angel of anesthesia.

To the Jamaican nurse who brought the great drug Percoset
to dull my senses and take my mind off the bloody piss
flowing into the clear plastic satchel at the end of my
catheter I leave the extensive library of my writings

both poetry and prose that fills four drawers of a filing cabinet
and yet which for all that has brought me in my fifteen
years of professional life the grand sum of five thousand
three hundred and forty-eight dollars, the bulk of that
in one grant from the state, so to her I leave in that filing
cabinet my soul bared in writing worth less than the
price of a good used car.

To my German hospital roommate age eighty-four
who underwent a trans-abdominal prostatectomy and who
bled gouts of blood into his satchel and nearly died of
clots in his bladder I leave my previous desire to have
a long life to be a sage I have seen the sages
they are all in the hospital having dick operations
to my roommate in thanks for the revelation
that old age is nothing but disease and
pain and suffering of indignities and medical abuse
I leave my desire to be old.

To my Hindu urologist who now monthly probes my rectum
with his Vedic forefinger and finds bogginess and
inflammation and prostatic disturbance I leave the
philosophy and religion both east and west that has brought
me to such a pass that my dick will not answer to any god
but the god of pain, and all this I now embrace and
discard as at the moment of death God grant that it be swift
I will find what is needed to guide me safely into
the realms of the afterworld.

To my friends and acquaintances of all nationalities I leave
my belongings the shoes I have saved the coats shirts
socks clocks the accumulated trash of thirty-eight years
let them be burned or saved or sold or given away and let
each reclaim that of theirs which I have borrowed stolen or
appropriated as my own they will know by sight what things
these are and let them forgive and remember and pray for the
further journeys of this soul.

Enough enough time's up no more mewling get on with it
let us dull the senses with Percoset with alcohol with oven
gas in memory of all those suicides the fraternity of
souls doomed to the world of hell welcome all those spirits
let the bells ring the torches flare the feast begin
a feast in hell to welcome the new arrivals a festival

273

a new beginning the real source of all pleasure is death
I embrace it without witnesses only my name affixed in surety
to this document the last day of the venereal month of April
the light is fading good good I go misericordia misericordia
etcetera.

—John of Mung

EDWARD FIELD

WAITING FOR THE COMMUNISTS

after Cavafy's "Waiting for the Barbarians"

What's all the commotion about?
I haven't seen the city in such an upheaval
since the last power failure.

Haven't you heard? The communists are coming today.

Is that why so many people are packed into the stadium,
watching the giant television screens?

Yes, everyone wants to see what the communists look like.
Listen to them roaring for blood.

Why is Congress passing laws one after another
and the President, for once, not vetoing them
but signing them furiously?

Oh, they're making one more attempt to ban the communists.
But it won't do any good—when the communists get here
they'll make their own laws.

Why are government emissaries rushing to the harbor, the airport,
carrying pink frosted cakes and party favors and hats?

Because that's the kind of junk they say communists like—
they're just barbarians, you know.

Why are the rich driving right behind them,
their wives in furs, arms and throats glittering with diamonds,
their cars loaded with opulent gifts—gold bars,
    deeds to real estate, country club memberships?

274

Because the communists are coming today
and they want to buy them off. They hope their elegant wives
will soften a little the hard hearts of the communists.

Why are the supreme court justices putting on their robes
and taking their places gravely on the rostrum?

Because after the government flees to its fortified island,
the judges will have to sign the surrender to the communists.

So why don't our big shots stand up now and make their speeches,
warn against the communists like they're always doing,
tell us how we must sacrifice, remain vigilant,
to protect our homes, our way of life?

Because the communists are finally coming
and nobody wants to listen to that stuff anymore.

But why this outbreak of muttering in the crowds?
(How puzzled everyone looks, how confused—even angry.)
See how the streets and squares are rapidly emptying,
and everybody going home so deep in thought.

Because it's evening and the communists haven't come.
And some people just back from abroad say
there aren't any communists anymore, maybe never were.

Oh my God, no communists? Now what's going to happen?
You've got to admit they were the perfect solution.

POST MASTURBATIO

Afterwards, the penis
is like a girl who has been "had"
and is ashamed.

Sudden neglect, you goose,
after all those romantic promises,
carried off my soft caresses,
before the hard ramming

when you bit your lips until it was over—
foolish one who gave in,
went all the way ...

until the next time,
when the nudge of a lover's ardor,
or the sight of it,
and the memory of something
genuine if painful
are again convincing.

TOM CLARK

ACADEMIC

for Andrei Codrescu

The difference between this and the
French revolution is that whereas
Then the only choice was between
Terror and reaction
Now it's between reaction and Tenure

Between Lacan and Paglia
After the utopia machine runs out of gas
The left and the right lie down together
To divvy up the career bennies

It's the sheer industry
Of the culture that divides
Its managers from everybody else

JOE

Nineteen sixty
seven, spring, the
climactic stop
on Ted's Cook's Tour
of Lower East
Side: Joe's tiny
flat at Third and
B, stacked wall to
wall with works in
progress amassed
for his "big break
through" flower show
at Fischbach, which
would make *Art News*
cover. Nervous,
polite, Joe took

interruption
like a perfect
gentleman: still
you guessed you were
interrupting:
and of course you
were. He offered
us Pepsis, small
talk; he smoked; then
we left, and he
painted.

» «

Five months later
up in Vermont,
while the rest of
us lay back in
or were swamped by
the thoughtless green
damp far northern
August days, Joe
paced, smoked, drank six
packs of Pepsi and
painted a trail
right through them, as
if weirdly wired
into a cool
steady drive to
make images.
When he snuck a
break for two hours
and we went to
Montpelier he
studied roadside
views so intently
I was sure works
were being sketched
out in his head
en route as Ron
drove. The day it
came time to go
back to New York
Joe walked off his
no-work nerves by
stalking around
outside the house.

» «

Neither modest
nor shy will quite
encompass it,
more like knowing
everything
without having
to pretend it's
more than it is,
or less, or say
anything at
all about it,
either way. Like
his works, Joe had
this aura.

» «

Didn't
he once say he
made a point of
believing in
all the major
religions, since
whether or not
"true," either way
each held its at
least possible,
conceivable consolations?

» «

It's May, moonlight
is probably
coming through those
pines outside the
upstairs window
at Kenward's house
where a tall and
skinny ghost with
horn rim glasses,
silent, thoughtful,
pacing, smoking,
is making works
without stopping.

277

OLD PHOTO

What life means: photo of
(barefoot? can't see) crewcut
boy on pier, nineteen fifties—what
does he know of what's ahead?
Behind, a lake. What bubbles up
out of life's strange effervescence
but the endless past, with its stupid
foam and buoyancy? Who would
plunge back in and live it all
over again, just to wipe hope's
youthful wonder off its face?

ARTIFICIAL LIGHT

Without it, what savage unsocial nights
Our ancestors must have spent! All those deadly
Winter nocturnes in caves and unilluminated icy
Fastnesses. They must have laid around and
Grumbled at one another in the dark like the blind,
Fumbling each other's features for the wrinkle of a smile.
What tedious repartee must have passed. Perhaps
This accounts for the dullness of much archaic
Poetry, whose somber cast is notorious and must
Have derived from the traditions of those
Long unlanterned nights. Jokes came in with candles.
How did they see to pick up a pin, if they
Had any? How did they get dinner down? Think of
The melange of chance carving that must have
Ensanguined dining after dusk! Lights out,
Not even love's what it's cracked up to be.
The senses absolutely give and take
Reciprocally. One wants to know whether that's
An elbow, a knee, or the night table
Before one returns the favor of a friendly nudge.
Wasn't it by the midnight taper all writers once digested
Their meditations? By that same light we ought
To approach them, if we ever expect to catch
The tiger moth of inspiration that dances
    In the word incandescent.

TIME

2500 years Before Proust
Xerxes overthrew the stalwart
Lacedaemonians at Thermopylae.
He built a bridge of boats, allowed
His anima her autonomy and
His prow to be cut through by her armada,
Carving out a dark continent of desire
To identify with the object's body
That lasted 2500 years.
Through her nothingness there flowed
An invisible current. He sacrificed
Himself before her in an effort to
Recapture all the points of space she had
Ever occupied. It was vain—and when he took to
Thrashing the sea of events with rods
In an absurd attempt to punish
The engulfing of his treasure
Fate lost patience with his act,
His fleet was destroyed at Salamis
The same year he pillaged Athens.

MY HYPERTROPHIC DEVOTION

meaning by possession total possession
subject and object identifying
à la the siamese model so that
if someone got in the way of
the roentgen rays of my exaggerated
jealousy concerning your person
that someone would in all likelihood be you
in the form of the angel guardian of your
autonomy which fills all space
with the impenetrability of your temporal moment

279

SONAR

Listening to the snow falling
Between your god and mine
I get down on my knees
   nights on earth

Going back to Egypt, stars revive
In a dead sky carved
Out by a supernatural blade

PICKING KRONOS' POCKETS

Junkets on a Sad Planet: Scenes from the Life of John Keats, Tom
Clark. Black Sparrow Press.

It must be clear by now, with the publication of *Junkets on a Sad
Planet: Scenes from the Life of John Keats*, that Tom Clark's evolv-
ing "lives of the poets" is something extraordinary and kinetic—
quite opposed to both the strictly academic ooze that fails to attract
life-giving lightening and the decadent, reductive biography-as-it-is-
practiced-in-our-times that masquerades its timorousness behind
brash focus on flash. Plainly, Clark takes huge chances with his own
psyche as he takes up Keats's challenge to imagine "into the mind of
another," the success of which enterprise is by no means clear—until,
that is, the magnificent long poem, the "Coda" which completes this
"poetic novel."

    Junkets follows fast on the heels of Clark's last prose study, the
often brilliant *Robert Creeley and the Genius of the American Common
Place* (New Directions, 1993).

    But unlike any of his previous bios, *Junkets* is awash in—nearly
giddy with—music:

What is it that wants only our rich dying,
When the light gets thin and seems to hold
Blue dusk, with sweet moon light all around
Sinking as the late light lives and dies?

    What questions, indeed, press the pages of this book, as the pres-
sures at sea bottom grip even the best-armored submarine.

    And what about Clark's insistent use of the "k" sound, as if in
writing as Clark about Keats he was compelled by sound alone...
or what? What is happening here? The note appears even

ROBERT BOVE

when tacit, as in, "The night wanderer's pulled by gravity..." Clearly, a comet—and the pull back to the first sound anyone hears when they hear the name Keats for the first time.

There is magic at work here, and the life-mask of Keats gracing the book's cover is a clue to it, to words that refuse to be taken only at face value. One can, of course, read *Junkets* quickly, strictly as biography, as I did the first time, but it won't be put down. It grows in one, as it did in me, even in sleep, and forces a re-reading.

SCUM & SLIME

Optimism,
trust,
fearless
authority,
and disaster,

eating filth
and transforming it,
with white
intentions,
into black
compassion,

I want to be
filthy
and anonymous
I want to be filthy
and anonymous
I want to be filthy and anonymous

Open your eye lids
and see it looks good,
drinking poison
and in each sip
on your lip
is wisdom
mind.

JOHN GIORNO

281

I like warm air
going over
my skin,

billions
of world
systems,

your body is
crawling
and crashing
into the surf.

Pouring
money
down
another
hole
pouring money
down another hole
pouring money down
another hole,
and keep it
hidden.

When Adam
and Eve
were in the Garden of Eden,
God asked Eve
not to do
two things,
not to eat
the fruit
and not to go swimming,
so she ate
and went for a swim,
that's why
the ocean smells
of fish.

You and I are
sleeping on
a cement
and linoleum
kitchen floor

you look like
a television set
sitting on
a refrigerator,

I would crawl
through a mile of shit
to suck off
the last guy
who fucked her.

We don't take drugs
no more,
we sit around
praying for money,
don't do anything drastic,

when you are with
a lover
you have no
no control
when you are with a lover
you have no control
when you are with a lover you have
no control.

I want to be
filthy
and anonymous,
scum
and slime.

What's going on
in here,
it looks like
everyone is
underwater,
give me
a break,
I'm dead
and I'm asleep
I'm dead
and I'm asleep
I'm dead
and I'm asleep.

SUCKING MUD

5000
years ago,
there was this
hero
and heroine,
where's the heroin,
and they were
at war
for a thousand years,
when one would
succeed
the other would
fail,
one day
she got really
angry
and they had
a duel
to the death,
she was a great
demon
and had wreaked
disasters
on the world,
and they flew up
into the sky
and had a star
wars
confrontation,
he took
his sword
and threw it,
and it stuck
into her heart,
she was so angry,
just as she
was about
to die,
she released
her period,
and where
the drops
of blood

fell
to earth,
tobacco
plants
grew,
and that's the origin
of cigarettes.
Do anything
you want
but don't come
in my mouth
do anything you want
but don't come
in my mouth,
suck those
sweet
pits,

that's the way
I like them
drunk
and all dressed up,
eating it
live
in one gulp,
sucking
mud
sucking mud
sucking mud
sucking mud
sucking mud,

fist
and forearm,
push it,
stick it,
punch it,
break it
open,
smash it,
suck it,
make it
feel good,
you got

to keep
a light
hand,
if you want
to touch
their heart
you got to keep
a light hand,
if you want to touch
their heart,
your body
feels so
good to me
your body feels so
good,
completely
attached to
embracing
warmth.

Bring me
your dead,
even though
I don't know
what to do,

bring me
your dying
and let me
know them,
and don't trip
over the confetti,
the winds
between
the worlds
cutting like
a knife.

PAUL VIOLI

CTESIAS

The last enemies against whom Cyrus fought
were Scythians from Margiana, hoity-toity,
who were led by King Amoreaus, hot-shot.
These people, mounted on elephants, holy moly,
ambushed the Persians, helter skelter
and put them to route, higgledy-piggledy.
Cyrus himself fell from his horse, humpty dumpty,
and a lance pierced his thigh: low blow booboo.
Three days later he died from the wound, loco.

HERODOTUS

After decades of warfare, Cyrus, wheeler dealer,
perished in combat against the armies
of Queen Thomyris, hoochie-coochie,
who had long desired to avenge
the death of her son, namby-pamby.
She ordered the body of Cyrus dragged, ragtag,
from beneath the slain and his head, harum-scarum,
thrown into a vat of blood. Jeepers creepers.
She then commanded the lifeless conqueror: "Drink
this blood, after which you ever thirsted but
by which your thirst was never allayed, jelly belly!"

XENOPHON

Cyrus died tranquilly in his bed fancy schmancy.
He had been forewarned in a dream, hocus pocus,
by a man with such majestic bearing that he
appeared much more than mortal: razzle dazzle.
"Prepare yourself," he told Cyrus, "for you will
soon be in the company of the gods, hobnob."
Cyrus awoke and offered sacrifices, solo,
on a nearby mountaintop, sky-high,

285

not to implore the gods, hanky panky,
to prolong his life, but to thank them, lovey dovey,
for their protection. Three days later
he gently breathed his last. Okey-dokey.

LUCIAN

Cyrus died of grief. Itsy-bitsy.
He was over one hundred years old, fuddy-duddy,
and he was inconsolable because his son, crumb-bum,
had killed most of his friends, braindrain.
But his son paid him all honors after his death,
building a tomb for him at Passagarda, grandstand,
a city Cyrus had built on the very spot, hot-spot,
where he had vanquished Astyages, who was none other
than his own grandfather. Wowie-zowie. Even-Steven.

ALICE NOTLEY

ANGEL-SKATE

It raises its pleated arm-wings—
what does this gesture mean—
out to the sides & up
Whatever it's become—is it a sun—
it's retreating
A silver-gold thread
in the foreground, turns black
A dark & mountain-shaped being
takes the snake-thread for a pet or slave-love
Caresses it as it curls about its knees
Advancing further into history
rings of humans slowly chasing each other
locking out the non-human world
"Why are we doing this?" someone's thinking
A megaphone shape of light
extends from the side of her head:
she won't tell the truth
because she values her thinking-voice
The sun approaches her speaking
"You must think with that luminous
blue spot there"
"What is it?" "Something like

a fish's gill or patch of water"
"It has no vocabulary"
"It will tell you how to lose meaning
Our meanings are destroying us"
The angel lowers her arms,
"I must change too … "
A skate is flying
A fish in the sky

PREGNANT SAINT

Pregnant saint her arms on belly

Black bust of a man—not on a pedestal
but on a long trickle of black ink—
floats away from the saint

Sensation of pain (emotional)
See the ghost who wants to scare me:
relates to literal dead or literal My Death

Circular mirror approaches
On elaborate stand
part organic part human-made

Totem presence Turned to the left
Now faces me tottering tipping turning white

Gone now gone
Enter a black temple
"The cross you see is not Christian"
I hear a dove call outside

Inside in the
black fibrous forest of the body
a traveller has collapsed on desert sands

A horse with several riders will
rescue the traveller?

Mirror of hope Circle not clock
A world of mirrors
An army of mirrors marching

Light seems to strike the surface of one

Don't you understand? it doesn't
doesn't anything

negative dove
Negative dove I see above doesn't
fly

No one is selected

GERARD MALANGA

HERMAPHRODITISMUS GENITALIS

for Liz Anne

In classical antiquity
it was firmly believed
that genuine and fully functional
hermaphrodites could
and did
exist: creatures
with male genitals and
at the same time, the female
breasts and rounded form.

The breasts are set rather high.
In the young they are rounded,
slightly pendulous in shape
but erect.

      On the lower abdomen,
there are two clear, parallel, curved lines
or folds in the skin,
with their convex surface downwards.
The upper line begins
slightly above the anterior
superior iliac spine
and cuts through the linea alba
about the point dividing its middle
and lower third section.
The lower line is less shallow

288

and more sharply curved, defined.
It begins slightly
below the anterior
superior spine
and runs
in the approximate
direction
of Poupart's ligament,
the two lower lines
from right to left
meet slightly above the upper
rim of
the symphysis pubis.
The mid-section
of this lower line
forms the upper limit
of the normal female genital hair.
The lateral limits confined
to the two inguinal furrows, or groins.
The lower line
is simply the external sign
of the place where
the abdominal wall merges
into Poupart's ligaments
and the symphysis respectively.
All the skin above this lower line
must be reckoned
in the abdominal area,
while below the epidermis
is part of the outer covering of the pelvis,
and its central portion
consists of skin
of the mons veneris
covered with a thin
veil of light hair

—the perineum clean and free of any hair—

and beneath that the genitalia awakens
and emerges
from its chastity ...
rises from seemingly out of nowhere,
from the roof of the vagina,
the labial folds, which are well developed.

289

No testicles palpable.

Pliny, following Calliphanes,
wrote of a race of hermaphrodites:
"living beyond the Nasamones
and their neighbors, the Machlyes,"
these were the "Androgynes
of both sexes who copulate
now as women, now as men."

SOMEWHERE OVER THE RAINBOW

—for Jeff Cochran

Hey looky!

Looky what I found!

Under

a bar stool,

somewhere

In a little town

Where the red light

turns yellow round

midnight, but

the poem

Goes on.

Right on.

& on.   Well.   So

What.

Car battery equals dead. Marry
It, is what. What? Candle in a Chianti
Bottle, basketball in a clothes hamper,
Bach on a rock.

Kings, shepherds,

and bears.

I tell you
Forget it we just singing a little song
About wake up all you motherfuckers

Gets us nowhere but then it snows &
Collects around us, arms too, brisk

& abominable,

Hugging, a cough in the last row.

ON THE LINE

Living on hors d'oeuvres,
brie and grapes, dialectical
theory crowd, Madeleine's
in a mini, she does plant-
scaping. Everybody's sipping cafe
con leche reading *Mademoiselle*
or *Elle* or *Vogue* or *Glamour*.
The kids are listening to Blur.
And they are calling me
Mr. Underground on WDRE.

Living on shrimp on toothpicks...
olives, shameless flirtation, blame
and namedropping, jokes, mottoes.
Cliches. Lame inanities.
Cocktail chatter. Thrilling innuendo.
Snappy upbeat patter. Mingling,
mixing, schmooze fest, living
on pickled quail eggs with caviar
and strawberries dipped in chocolate.
Answering to no one.

RAMMING SPEED

They shall scatter like buckshot,
dry husks before wind,

but first they shall laugh together
in class, on Horatio street,

and astonish the petunias,
purple and presumptuous,

but not really pretentious
and very alert, like gramophones

or loudspeakers or trumpets
of velvet wonder, honest injuns.

As if they were looking at you
for a clue to increase the spirit,

and avenge the injury,
the downtime, as if night would hide,

all fired up and wild for to hold
though tame they may seem.

IN THE DREAM OF LOVE

The crocodile of gold eats me alive.
Sanctified only by shrill effort
to be awake, lulled by its eyes—
verdurous twin planets we orbit—
like tongues. Lonesome fear guides us
toward courage, driving us like a giant
herd of wishes, whispered by unseeable agents
conspiring to fire us
up. Nothing certain. Blue vitamin.
There are dues and so there are
don'ts. Feeling awful, great, awful, great.
Wheeling around, the sky in my gut

sucker fucking punches me. Bad boy.
Naughty girl—sister venture, hold on tight.

POETRY LIVES

I am in the Bad Bar listening
To bad poems by suicidal wimps,
they say, "Life is a fist;
People pity me."

Listen,
We all suffocated some
In childhood's Procrustean bed—
Forget it! Clear it away!

Look out the window
Where the real poets parade,
In love with the derelict beauty
Of this East Side Sunday
In semi-spring.

Don't write poems about a past
That was never any fun,
Bad breath, death you cry over,
Or of cherries as a metaphor
For blood;
Take a ride in the Cadillac of Creation.

Poetry is not an excuse,
Or the frantic plaints of the loveless,
It's not a doormat or sharkbait;
Use it to renounce a fate.

Poetry is the pearl
In the oyster of everything,
The encyclopedia of altered states,
The telescopes of twilight
Angling in anticipation
Of the sapphire sedans of the stars!

Suddenly I'm in Kashmir
And you are here;
Meanwhile in an empty lot in L.A.
A honeybee rises from some magenta power
Bathed in golddust.
Poetry begins now.

RAVI SINGH

293

EDMUND BERRIGAN

BRICK TEA

Hate return, and dust
The little serpent
Aristotle

Five are lobster, warrior
So flawed
you chewed off cyclops' eye

Black or the road

In no one's home
you play kite of the world

IN TIME

the world
          having grown
                    will sleep
the sun
          having set
                    for some,
won't rise.
               never
                    in anger,
accepted.
          duty in laughter
               messages in sadness
                    learning and ending.
wander the night,
          the last,
               and dream some.

POEM

Ignominy, obscurity, & serenity
hurl a pearl at the floor:

"No presuppositions of fame death"
"No legal fees"

In these parts we smoke our dinner

"No pepper games"

In these parts our poems
are invisible.

We eat with our feet
and we walk on our hands

THERE'S A SIGN ON THE THIRD FLOOR
THAT SAYS SO

we groom ourselves like cats
and we end our poems with lives

EDMUND BERRIGAN
& ALICE NOTLEY

POVERTY

for Tompkins Square Park

the clock was ours
the title was ours
the drum was ours
its like was ours
its run was ours
its debris was left

better than debris
better than the clock
better than the runs
mo' better than titled
it was better than you liked
and better than your drum

we lost our drum
we lost our debris
we lost our like
we found your clock
it was untitled
we don't want your runs

it's no bed of runs
it's no bed of drums
it's no blanket of titles
we'll shake our debris
it's no shelf of clock
like nothing you like

debris is our like
beyond titled runs
drum your clock
clock your drum
runs beyond titled
like rowdy debris

lady debris
lady like
titled lady
lady run
lady drum
lady was clocked

clocks sleep untitled
drums sleep alike
runs sleep debris

EROTICS

after Nerval

She has passed, the beautiful girl
in the lace underwear, living and still present
like a bird, to the hand
Peony Falconer
which opens up, which settles
which brings to his feeble mouth
a new song.
which brings to his feeble mouth
a new song (this song),
She has passed, from the body to the eye,
to now only the scent of her.

ON THE PREMISES

Just heard a song
about a man turning into
his factory equipment

"Stainless steel eyes now instead of bone"

they gave her a drab price
for his machine & I read
some lovely writing by contemporary legends
that made me mad & inspired

& soon it will be time to drop
a driver's license out of the bedroom window
where I can hear the outside neighbors yell
& no, no me going outside tonight

I am adding a little arrest
where there's heart and the next move
is so different from how I remember your face

the last time we didn't quite meet
so obstinate once more
went the grim yellow evening

SIMON PETTET

ANSELM BERRIGAN

297

behind foreground of what incredible
diabolical gunplay

makes me wonder how late to sit up
& think inscrutably lethal circles
        drawn as round as a sane being
    is capable of stirring in her locks

down where the large feeling is very plain
    bequeathed magnolia entourage

how few insects entered this home, soon
        to be old home, as opposed
    to infested older home I think of dearly
            but perfectly willing to forget

if you buy me one more drink
    so I might stay up in time to send early
        morning greetings to friends
            conjugating their dreams

they dream incessant rogues in arbor
        of shined endurance

great ugly Buddha scrawls who do still show
        nervy flashes wheezing past crank reviews

& now being time to lie down in order to do Friday
    dream plans succumbing to moving exhaustion

I admit pride in running through
        every walk taken tonight/this morning

not necessarily listed here
    but how I learned to rest so
interminably sweet uphill
        & tired by labors
        all my friends should offer to do

out of the good of their hearts
    if I can sneak into their
        dreams one of these upcoming nights

THEY

They lived in a windy cabin off the east coast
of Maine. They watched the tides come in daily.
A fishnet was hung on the outside of their door
like an invitation. Vegetables came from the
garden. They listened to Vivaldi in the morning,
Bach in the afternoon, and Beethoven in the
evening, except on Sundays when they listened
to Couperin all day as they lay in their feather
bed with the wind outside and the warm coffee in.
Their cabin was on the edge of a cliff. They had
nightmares of waking with their bones broken
among the rocks. They had a collection of rocks
in the outhouse which they couldn't identify.

Like parts of a broken symphony, they
conducted their lives in wholesome disarray.
Occasionally, a rabbit would pass with the hurried
motion of a bad dream.

The weather was always unpredictable, snow
one day, spring the next. Their invitations were
never answered. They knew how hard it was to leave
the city. It was like being embedded in a giant
stone pillar, only war and destruction could separate
the marble from the stone. They remembered the
shattered nerves of sleepless nights, the brick
battered soot sky, the million pieces of broken glass.

ELIO SCHNEEMAN

299

THE SWIRL OF YOUR HANDS

truth did not come into the world naked
it came   wearing
                        a bullet proof vest
opening cans   slicing bread
uncorking bottles
                        putting pots
on the stove   talking
in ordinary tones
                sinking   its teeth
into a field of soft peach
                        a would be lover
"And you are..."
at the mercy of chance
                        carving her initials
into the shadow of a tall tree
2 minutes
        of unimpeachable joy
the swirl of your hands
in smooth dirt
                the flash of high noon
a chariot drawn by floating geometries
stepping down
into the eyes of lovers   lunatics
                winking at skyscrapers
at spiral staircases
                drinking up clouds
milky transparent
shards
                of cool thoughts
myotic corpuscular
                tumbler shift
changing rum to champagne
                        a sacred spring
lily-shaped   deep purple
a splendid crimson
                        the price of death
in ordinary tones

THREE POEMS PAST MIDNIGHT

the sky is a blue ceramic pot
gone to pieces
      a ship at sea   swims
smilingly   in my head
plots a course   a nervous magic
from my gut
these lines   an orange clock
the pink of five
tulips at 5pm   the faint dog bark
of afternoon
but really I've no intention
never do anything
until the moon wheels   sideways
lands on its hands
      then on its feet
stretches out lazy
across the hood of my car
athletic   marvelous
instant calculation
     is always   madness   traveling
through the world
at this hour
three poems past midnight
      unveiling a pair
of fat thighs
under the horsehair blanket
as night falls   to her knees
     letting her red hair
stream into streams into light
and blood
a thump from my heart
  made of mud   and feeling
a sigh
a song for my friends
      Ian & Hector
the palm of your hand   your trail
on the sand
shone in her fur walked heavily
in her furry coat

PLUG-UGLY AND MULTIFARIOUS

for Sara

Sometimes life comes right at you
like a great blizzard screaming
through a pneumatic tube.
Thus being overwhelmed can be a pivotal
and even sacramental experience.
Except it leaves you so punchy
you wish your brain could be rubberized
and these moments of pure delight
or sheer terror could be flash-frozen
and encapsulated, or trapped
inside a lucite cube so you could deal
with them as dayworld agendas permit.

But the fact of the fusion is
you have to take the full wallop of the wonder
when the wonder is ready. That the miracles
of misery can only be explained
by the given serendipitous oaf once in his lifetime,
and if you're there, lucky you, and if not, lucky you.

You have to be alert, borderline vigilant.
Sporadic shitstorms of hyperconsciousness
can sneak up on you like invisible vapors,
buy you an unwanted drink, pummel you with chitchat
then steal your unguarded whimsy, take it
back to their lair like it was the last
bag of peanuts in Montana. And gobble it up.
The song in your heart can live nowhere else.

Over time the process of selection can be co-opted
You can become transfixed by the vicious
or look upon someone who shows you kindness
like he's an amputee. You'll rest your eyes
while reading some grim tome and see a vision
of a wedding cake. The devil will pop up
in the mall parking lot but you won't believe him.
"If you're really the devil," you challenge,
"change the movies to something I want to see."

And oh what a life this is! So plug-ugly
and multifarious! How to choose

between cheap jewelry and gaudy boredom.
Please note and remember: A million "be carefuls"
can't protect you from all the fairydust.
And about three out of every ten strangers
actually deserve a kiss ... but all of the kisses
don't have to come from you.

CUTE IS BETTER THAN BITTER

for Donald Sullivan

It's a not entirely unpleasant picture
of my sooner-or-later-to-be self.
I see myself as a "cute old guy."
The kind of cute old guy who washes
the pee stains out of his good plaid pants
in the sink in his room after a long day
of nursing beers or pounding a few nails.
During the day ... when I can ... I sit at the elbow
of the town's least popular bar. It's reserved.
"You can't sit there," Pudge the bartender
tells the unknowing civilians. "That's
Cute Old Guy's spot."

I'm so sweet. I'm always smiling.
And I'm not a noisy old guy. I'm no Cliff Clavin
or any other kind of know-it-all.
Not even much of a lecher any more.
Most of the young girls are fond of me
but my filthy-minded friends scare them away.
"You know what, Cute Old Guy ... I was going to
toss you a freebie for your birthday,
but then that Herman person would think
he had one coming too, and I'd rather fuck
something with real scales and a longer tongue
if you know what I mean." I know what she means.
And even if I don't, I'll pretend I do.
I'll be a good listener, say "Yup"
like only a Cute Old Guy can say it.

I wonder if I'm going to have to change my name
to a Cute Old Cuy name like Cal or Mooney

303

or Purdy. Just tell Cal. Tell all to Cal.
It could be a radio show, huh? On WCOG radio.
Way Cool Old Guy radio. "Yes, caller, you've got
my complete attention." "Well, Cal, first of all
I want to tell you you're really dreamy
and easy to talk to. And second of all,
no matter what I try, I can't seem to achieve ...
or ... or ... or ... or ... orgasm with my husband
the doctor ..." "Well, Sheila in Sheffield,
may I ask, is your husband a self-important man
and diffident lover? The problem is probably him.
Send him down to the bar and I'll have a talk
with him."

Yes, I'll be the Cute Old Guy
all the cute young girls come to
to ask why peckerheads are such peckerheads.
I'll wear a mix-buttoned mint green cardigan
and carry my own box of toothpicks in my shirt pocket.
I'll be living history, remember great musical events
like the time Jimi Hendrix opened for Al Jolson
and that incredible night when Old Blue Eyes
joined Dead Elvis on stage for The Salute to America medley,
then traded off verses of My Way, which they
dedicated to me.

Everybody will ask questions only I can answer.
Well, California was settled in the year 1239
by a cadre of rainbow colored monkeys from Saturn.
I'm the only one who knows these things
because I'm the one who made them up.
And maybe I'll get a little dog ...
a Pekinese I call Mao, and after a few cocktails
I'll decide it would be a fine idea
if Mao ran for mayor. And everyone will laugh
and pretend this is the first time they've heard this.
Oh, Cute Old Guy, what a depository of antiquated wit
and old-fashioned qualities you are!

Yeah, I'm pretty funny. Yeah, I got a million
of them or used to have a million of them
but now I only have about a dozen.
   No, I'm not talking about erections. Yeah,
      a dozen a day would be about right, but tell you what,

a dozen a year doesn't sound all that bad.
Sometimes I'll have a sidekick. Funny Old Broad
who'll say "Fuck you Mooney/Cal/Purdy ... you already
told that fucking joke and it wasn't fucking funny
the first fucking time, you cheap fucking old
drunk!"

Thanks, I needed that. And you can call me anything
just don't ever say I'm mean. Because I'm not.
Because I'd rather be buried alive in my pauper's grave
than to become a mean old shitass like some of my friends.
I don't ever want to be some puckered face old bugger
who never has a nice word to say unless it's "goodbye"
and everyone's glad he's leaving. No, by the time
all of this happens, I hope I'll've learned a few things.

That cute is better than bitter.
That later is better than sooner
unless there's great agony.
That being around laughing people
stretches out the wonder.
That the wonder will continue to grow
and hold up until the end if you let it.
That for everything that shrinks,
something else clarifies.
That for everything that aches,
something else becomes less of a problem.

I look forward to my duties as a Cute Old Guy.
Given the chance to serve, I will attempt
to prove that cute is better than bitter...
even if there's nothing between you and Heaven
but your liver. And life is a great good thing,
don't even think you can quit her.
Words soon to be spoken by a Cute Old Guy.

SOME OF THE THINGS I TOLD HER

for Pookster

I told her that the man I used to be had been
destroyed by a fire at the passport office.

305

I told her my heart was made out of lace and paste,
mounted on pink plywood and hung above a bar
in Santa Fe, New Mexico.

I once sliced up a bunch of pictures of buildings,
and I threw them in the air, and when they
came down, the pieces formed a church
and we were walking out of it,
peasants coming from a wedding.

I couldn't tell her whose wedding it was
because I'd made up the story
and had only got as far as the architecture
and hadn't started yet with the characters.

Okay, it was our wedding.
The church was called St. Bullwinkle's,
everyone was real happy for us,
they gave me advice and you knives,
and yes, you were pregnant.

I told her that in one of my previous lives
I'd been a rabbit surrounded by a ring
of fire, and I just ran like crazy,
terrified until I was finally rescued
by a kindly hawk.

Yes, I can still remember being snatched
and pulled into the sky.

I told her I collect pictures of stadiums,
that sometimes I can see myself in the crowd,
that sometimes I can remember whole games,
who I was sitting next to,
where we stopped at on the way home.
Strange as this sounds, I've never been
to St. Louis but I remember a game
against the Dodgers in late August,
won by a rare Cardinal homerun.
We ate barbecue at a place on Clayton Avenue
that had a lot of pictures of Chuck Berry
on the wall.

I told her the peasant wedding was followed
by some disagreements with in-laws.
Angry words were spoken and a fight broke out.

The police came and a man with mustache
and a brown suit was taken away
in handcuffs. In an unrelated incident,
he hung himself in another jail
after another incident involving another family
in another city.

I told her that in another century
I myself was almost hung but saved
due to a clause in the law that said
a criminal could be spared if he was claimed
by a woman who'd marry him and vouch for his reform.
In my case I was claimed by the hangman's own daughter.
She claimed me so she could get away from her own father.
I was saved from the hangman by the hangman's daughter
so I could save the hangman's daughter from her father.
Get it?

Yes, I told her, she could well have been
the hangman's daughter. And she was probably the hawk.
And probably the waitress at the barbecue in St. Louis.
Yes dear, I told her, if I was there, you were
there with me, just like you are now.

PERMANENT FACE

Content has been carried off since dawn
down the awful blonde way to diagnosis
down a path perpendicular to funk
large well-placed rocks   the usual
proofs removing self from premises.

Hip joint   connected to   the lead soldier
natural man is corroding from the neck
down   it's a stellar undoing
but nobody's laughing   wondering where nature
comes from   or where   old children go
when not even their pets   remember first names.
He's got credit up to his elbows.   He leans
into a string   wound through   revelation
in the end   everything is consumed by shoes.

LAURA ROSENTHAL

307

The sleeping muse has bumped her nose.
A part of her is mirror & parts of the mirror
are legs & coat hangers shifting across a tall sky.
She squats on one foot   queen of the low road
frozen   hit & run   by the big bulb   illuminating
all that is known   & nothing   that isn't.

TIME'S MA

Stupefied by possible futures I lay
in the grass   you rode
a too tall bicycle   your shirt
billowed hanging from the back of a chair.

I am waiting for the lamb but it's coons again
here on the third day after   having brought forth
another mystery   the fig tree & me are the first
to go dry & rustly in september.

When nightingales threatened
blue moon monday once   someone was thinking
of poor Keats   the savage too guesses at heaven.

His models of exile run into problems of scale.
Who is the luminous creature badly representing itself?

Be an angel   come home from the spa
the place is weightless & my hacking cough poor company.

HOW THE WORD "COOX" CAME TO REPRESENT BEELZEBUB

The hamburger of this narrative
depends NOT on waxy yellow build-up, honey, or
"doing your fucking homework" on mescaline
& if you memorize caustic lime brushstrokes
by telemarketed serial painkillers you
may as well just quit faxing me over for sex
& knockoff that benign earcock right now.
No one gets rich on diameter. I won't
be Cigarette
to your hacking attentionspan.   Now
two oxymoronic sorority sisters:
the fat one's rippled knees are inverted
& the skinny one tosses sheetknotted, bilked if you will by
twinkles.
Why? Yes. Now, Sunday
the creosote rumbles, picnickers
fingering diapers. Ew, but Genevieve
understands God, tickling
the face of the earth with his Snakes.
Lyn, confused, faces the toilet.
Rightangled, alert, she sits young and amazed
as wrens stuffed with succulents,
staccato. Next all the trees in
the valley burn down. It was the pool boy
her tears fart to the phone
but no, *le mattress* a monk, babeh—
silence is not "golden," but
guilt, Naughty-One and don't let your chee-
tah hightops forget it.   Now
heaven settles like an outhouse, and
Oops I almost forgot: "The Lake." Oh-*kay*,
(sigh) Grapes
pointlessly go on sale. Important.
Her junkie's boa has gone quadriplegic—
her spanking-slave rings up Kyoto. Hello? Any
exploitable edibles running roughshod
through your unpopu-
lar little clinics over there?
The heartrotten mother
of all morticians is offering her
crutches to Dracula. "The Doctor" What
ever. Scoot please. Make more
room on the couch for my *mise-en-scène*:

Now   we're all
      pistolwhipped
right, by this jawshattering monkeywrench? How can
we not be? Our girls, "We Speak Greek!"
are wacked-out in love! In a litoral sexual splurge and riot
of convertible panhellene nudity
they've molotoved bluegrass garage bands blind-
folded & larked off to Vegas on blotter.
            Hence the vaporous point of view disinfects.
Wait: Shit: No: the tent dress—
that was the reapers' grim stunt at the Air Show!
Did I say anything or
                  Oh fuck I forget what in Yezz what in
Christ was the name of her ruin?
Oh, right. I think, disenfranchised trailer hitch. Oh, "fuck-
adjunct to the native skiploaderloader." Hell.
Fine: why not the star-nosed mole. Oh—
Oh, I get you.
Oh I get you, "Fidel"
Bla, bla bla bla bla bla: what
is it to you; I smoke flat
on my anus, so?
Where d'ya think little compliments come
from? With what evolutionary tablesaw
have your shameaddicted People shaved you?
John Wayne Gacy: kitten tortellinis.
Yep, that brutal
detail should appease you,
Duffelface. Let's
just say right now, cemented to the davenport
I feel for my tequila. Hence the Einsteinian
protagonist, no matter how bulimic
ferments: Toxin to the mighty Aztec. Yayah.
If you don't nod in your sway to me
jerrymary, whatsyourname,
you're my diffident, hamsterfed landlord.
If you built this house by your self, gorgeous girl,
you're dead in a box with a wig on.
Write a book! Naw: wait a
sec. Farmboy! Rubble! Shut
up & let *me* write one.

BORROWED SLEEP

From tincans and clanging smooth ice
comes a litany of gas hissing from the corner
from the missile of my forehead, from a horizon of
Can't See Over, from a cacophony of small noises
chirps in brain stew.
                    It's a hard
armor we wear waiting for trains
and saviors to happen.
My nightgown reminded you of innocence
once.
You were tempted
once.

Now glades of a city out there, open space
of street and night, the wires
of blue lights winding shadows of dresses
flung back. If only my head
would beat with the drums
of nothing, sigh
with the complaint of a naked bulb
or the lone spinsters fluttering drably
around it
clutching pear breasts in the earth
then I would melt, let go, slip, then come back.

The clock goes round and round tonight.
A barbershop quartet launches gay foreign rounds
of leaving, dear somebody, becoming pieces
of language caught in the throat, slips
over frost on the panes and still life, burning
scraps of definitions in the old coats.
I find them everywhere. I wear them out.

The quiet of this hour is too loud, the ticking
of something vanishing and not easy to keep.
It won't be long before I heave on
an old white flag
and look for a cornerstore to buy milk, or something.
It won't be long before I tear again
with teeth that ache
into the heel of your breadline instincts.
Protect yourself. I hunger
for warm soup and a blanket for now
that will soften all your hardness.

FLIPPING THROUGH

Too many mornings spent leaning on a counter
trying on semblances of real life. I thought
I was doing something important, keeping
track of the pertinent,
it was nothing. They were just
dull people filling their bellies
every morning of their entire lives.
Yeah, wake up and go somewhere
preferably where they know your first name
and that second or third cup of coffee
is something comfortably shared, intimate
gossip of long ago one nighters
or old war stories, cars ripped in alleys
90 m.p.h. walking away alive.

Now it isn't the generalized facts
used until a dullness sets in
that causes pain
but really the minutely detailed lines
in the waving so long
of a friend's yellow hair
after the train has already roared away.
                              What
did I mean to say really?
Glance back twice. Yes something
is missing or perhaps passing through.
In the darkening curve of a collarbone
someone winces, remembering an omen: fire
in an empty lot, glass exploding, dead
idle trash blowing in circles, tornadoes
we mistook correctly for sinister.

The leaves skimming across the sidewalks this winter
are even harsher and more metallic than ever.

Everything is frozen solid
and I'll include that on the postcard
message. Again
the windows, the soles of my boots, the stark
pearlescence of the moment,
not rushing, not playing around, not wasting
any time. Yes, the price of toast
is too high.

RIM

this might be
my life, with all
its misspellings, an afternoon
of wheelchairs, the work bins
mixed. missing humboldt park
yearnings. so what if it's true
that i wanna live in cheap hotels
easy to get, easy to forget
surrounded by blue
old men, the end spread out
and floundering in the present
faded ink beneath the skin
forearms resting
on nothing

THE ROSE OF SHARON

is hominy
is homebound
is lulling dulcet nocturne
is boiling lobster with black eye at the annual family wing-ding

is andalusian bordello portrait
dimestore gut bucket
is azore and ozark, secret green continent, awaiting the riot
    of boys at the gate

is memory: a dangerous angel
a fuck for the first day of summer
is blue pearl-gray like mother,
    clear pink rose

is pony: going down behind the ballroom: hips of fierce
    skinny-lipped boy
glossy cherry O-mouth in the bowling alley bathroom
her puerto rican kingpin plays foosball in the half light)

SHARON MESMER

313

in the kitchen's trance no raptures
in torn t-shirt and dirty bra, fatherless in the dark,
in smoke/cold/the radio:
ankle birthmark where the wings were

silver blade dips her wrist
flies whirl in a golden shithouse sunbeam
diaphanous sham, she reclines on a couch:
bluestocking, but never blue
splinter from the floor she was born on

is waiting at the lake (is waiting)
promiscuity and legionnaire's disease (is waiting)
tough as a 69 cent steak and waiting for Mr. Wrong
is waiting

is the uterus in question
the ennui in ingenue

is poised for the penthouse a big big youth
trickiest elixir: potion of slathered mandible
poetry of who you screw

feeling full moon in Scorpio, meaty fist of dumb policeman
shoved up her oily cunt
feeling flaming June's beatitude: waking late with strings of come
      tangled in her long black hair

is pissing in your flaccid handshake
is sleeping in your station wagon
not waving goodbye but drowning,
is playing your hair like a harp

LONGING

o for way back
when the afternoon
used to last
all day
   or the day
used to last
all afternoon
whatever it was

MYSELF CONTAINS MULTITUDES

and some
of these fuckers
have got to go

CLOSING TIME

on the table
there is a chair

CONDO, CONDOM, CONDEMNATION

Alligator suitcase lashed to my aching back
I'm getting
a grip on myself
Yet I lack the proper incentives
The canings didn't take
Instead of interesting, I became the sport in the Sportscoat,
cut somewhat fuller
than the business suitjacket,
destined for informal wear with unmatched socks
That's me
exactly
whom I've got to be!
& there's no known antidote!
Guys in white labcoats can't test tube my biological
oil spill
I dwell in a condo
I wear a condom
(my balls ache
for the shadows
of skyscrapers)
I suffer the condemnation
of the disenfranchised, the McDonalds-less
Grease
        Release
At 181 hopped a symbolic freight
In the presence of allegory
wince
Now bombshells
cower under mascara
screaming "Where're the tweezers? the tweezers!"
when they sense
my crosshairs
        Alright
                All wrong
Every personal memory I've ever cherished is
on TV!
How'd they do that?
Rampant
hotdoggery!
Raise me with a Bo derrick!
I've come to realize my field of expertise is full of
cowshit
        a knife in the toaster

for a man
nurtured at the buoyant breast of Me-ism
& not so sure about all the You-isms
out there
pawing the sale items
ingesting the microorganisms
      Food processor
         Word processor
Listen up, post nasal particulars
I am among you
Me & my distinguishing marks
& remarks
Someone ought to put a stop to the marketing &
distribution
      of forearms
There's too little elbow room
Don't get me wrong
America's a great idea where the shoes are often tied
      O veer
         O swerve
I expect to hosedown the Unwashed
sometime before breaktime
to belabor the Obvious by kicking the living shit out
of it
Wholly unforeseen
unheralded
I envision hundreds of men hitching up their pants
like there's no suspenders

IN MY BOOZY LONELINESS

I cling to you, undress ourselves,
pretend we write a great love story
from our lips down to our knees.
                              Some friends—
illusions gussied up as truth and some
are truth moving vaguely, unobtrusively
through memory like a grand illusion. Suss,
shush, that bitchy guss chum of sweet wit
and gorgeous lines came to town tonite
without one thought
one sweet delicious Philly who romps
in, out of the dry ice sweaty pillows. That is
booty. Half awake on the dog
in the middle of New Jersey the little girl next to me
ponders her fingernails, wrapping herself
in her mother's arm.
The ladies' conversation barely audible
            enough to excite
me in the warmth of the tinted windows holding
            back the sun
like a levee in New Orleans holding back the river.
            My sister
sits behind a great big book of names
            at the health club
and I dream most of the day of moving
            to avoid meeting the terms
of ultimate decision ahead. The mimosas
            are in bloom
meanwhile remind me of the south
            up in the east
of hopes and music that smell of fish and grass
            through concrete, cornet bleats.

TAMPONS IN SPACE

While they're stroking
sleek new missiles
aimed at the last frontier,
we'll be perfecting
the weave, the fit,
calculating the end of
spillage, thinking about
what the first man on the moon
didn't have to. Almost anything
will do: moon mud in bubble huts;
thick strands, fiber
from Mars' canals;
moss from Neptune's shadow;
we'll pass on Uranus,
nothing personal,
just too far back;
and should gravity-free living
present a problem
for the modern woman,
there's always Venus,
the perfect spinning orb,
fast enough
to catch
every
drop.

DROMEDARY

I heard it over the radio: Madame Flaubert
said to her son: "Your passion for words
has dried up your heart." Of these past
weeks, I can reverse it and say: My heart
drank all the words. All the words
that gave sustenance, vision, voice, the words
from the word of beginning. Left me
none to say. Except the crumbs and dry rattles,
that camel with its hump, crossing deserts
of vast mendacity, hauling tourist-poems
to the pyramids at Giza, all the while
trying to bite their knees.

JANET MASON

DANA PATTILLO

319

THE MARTINI CLINIC

Over the years I've learned it's a good idea
to keep moving. It's not a matter of wanting
to run away from it, because it is always

with you, but of not wanting it to command
your full attention. Some people prefer to look
whatever it is full in the face—is this

melodrama? I'm usually off in the corner
examining its sidelong aspect, the color
and/or nubbly texture of the pants

he was wearing when the terrible news
finally arrived, for example, because what
someone looks like when he doesn't know

he's being watched is just as important
as his self-conscious posing. Probably more.
The thing is, everyone nowadays likes to think

they're on TV, and it's not enough simply
to hand someone a drink. No. You have to make
a show of it: chill the long-stemmed glass

by burying it in ice, drop beads of vermouth
into the shaker glass, swirl, and toss, preferably
over your shoulder. And you have to be sure

to spear the olives sideways, so they don't fall
off. In this way you will be said to have been
able to pour with the best of them, and your

favorite customer is liable to twirl around
on his bar stool mimicking Rick Flair
and announcing to no one in particular

"See, she's giving a martini clinic, in case
you haven't noticed." I wish I could come up
with a few more verities, but it's been a long

day. The horizon was a blanket of lettuce
over a field a patty pan squash. Sometimes
I wake up in the middle of the night

and wonder if I expected too much.
Sometimes I cry. And the tears dry, leaving
behind salt and memories, a nice gesture,
linking you to something larger than yourself.

LIVING THE LIE

personal fiction
which is a kind of mental brainwash
a continuous loop of lust
for revenge

guts to glory
a rash of biographical sketches
prognosis of an apocryphal
story on a hitch

beyond the median talent
bardic remains surrender
to immediate judgment none other
than big bucks and booze

what is the literature of yesterday
but leaking and gooey prose in the hands
of the literati and their noontime blues

what is the predominance of life's
storyfiction which disassociates the self
infatuates tired quip with its goal

if the artist and its art cannot live
as bivalved shields protecting the slop
of creation then salvage nothing

wise-cracking to the grave
the hero's sole retribution
bathes in memory not of the works
but of the shame

JOAN FISHER

PLAY AND THE CONTINUAL PRESENT

Dogged interloping flash
flood of whimsical wine,
slathered for comfort
on the eyelids of change.

A compelling sensuality

twisted out of the rubbish,
cathartic and damaging,
frail to a fault.

In a moment of self-indulgence
we wriggled free,

capping the mad scientist
in precise chaos,
refined for finesse
and a fresh distortion.

"This is the past,"
we mustered up the courage
to report, indecently,
"but we'll succumb in time."

PUNK ROCK

The nights were blunt and fixed.
Nobody meant anything by anything.
We were fast enough, sure,
but we were kids: we did
cheap drugs alone & hoped
we wouldn't crumble if somebody fucked us.

BRETT RALPH

NOT FUCKING: A COMPLEX SYSTEM

Consider camaraderie,
art lost after WW II
according to Mr. Alexander,
who says of The Groves
in my town "They were places
people just got together, why
can't you understand that?"
Or reputation,
that pastiche of minor
triumph and murder
not committed,
how fucking mucks it up.
Or concentration,
how you can make your way
along a trail and really
see the upending mushroom
(toadstool?) in fine detail:
eating one is not at issue.
Or fidelity, piety's cousin,
ovens where bread ain't baked,
holes for trees
not planted. Or disease
that gets its fill
on what is feasted,
whether by boy-girl fuck
or whatever, so much joy-juice
penalized. I have file cards
on the system, ways to know
and reasons rampant
in my head—the tidy
buddy, much beloved,
I want to be to everybody,
good scout, wholesome,
all that. However.

This morning I saw my sweet-assed
self, the droop of my lovelies,
my incredibly innocent
ankles. I saw a neck
for the Western World!
I (barely) saw the kind of
wide myopic eyes
which, according to Mr. Wilson,

SUZANNE RHODENBAUGH

who studied up on natural
selection, may have made
nearsightedness
a favorable factor
for procreation in that
the female has to concentrate
intently to see the male
at all and consequently
makes him feel he's
wanted, an exciting
positive prospect to him
so that they get lost and go
into it, get a grove
where something beyond reason
happens—though risking,
as Mr. Meyer put it,
the future of the earth.

THIS IS A THANK YOU TO THAT FAT BOUNCER GOD WHO THREW ME OUT WHEN AT EIGHTEEN I TRIED TO ENTER THE SUICIDE HOUSE FOREVER

I remember I was tired, especially
of the married men who wouldn't leave
my new body, that I didn't even know
yet, alone.

I was tired of running from the great
marriage lock up that was sewn into
my future by sex since birth.
I was tired

of bar boys hung like horses
with leather and studs and not
a truth in one
of their tattooed bodies.

I was tired of the inescapable
terribleness of gender
that stretched swelling dreams like flapping
circus tents around me.

324

One winter night, when I was 15,
I came home to a house of cherry-topped
ambulances and doctors. My mother
slapped two 20's into my hand

"Take a friend to dinner, "
she said. When I came home,
they were all still
there. Dr. De Groat was trying

to talk my mother into committing
my sister, who like a strobe light, was
wildly hallucinating in the dark
room where they had put her after

they caught her in her baby blue,
baby doll p.j.'s, ringing the neighbors'
suburban door bells, putting a page of Proust
and a page of *Madame Bovary* in French, in

each answering hand. My 17-year-old sister
yelled my name from the dark room:
"Susan, Susan," her pill-over-dosed voice
and call were frightening as money.

My mother wouldn't sign. My sister
came part way back. Three years later
I was eighteen when I crossed
my hands in the death appropriate way

and knocked on God's door. She
threw me out in a black night of puking.
My ears rang her church bells for a year.
My eyes looked X-ed out like funny-paper people.

Still, I want to thank God for recognizing I
was still on training wheels. I
want to thank God for carding me,
saying "You're too young to enter."

I want to thank Her for resuming
me, all my bits of stupid floating
yellow as confetti, as polka
dots around me, for dropping

me back into my body's skin machinery
like a 20 below winter-chilled
bird falling from a warm
chimney to sidewalk ice.

I came back tulip boned and weakened
to ponds of stone hearts. A bag of flesh
born on from me to you street,
a wink and I was back,

holy and tattered, beautiful
and scarred full of prayer,
empty of pills, wide-hearted
with wonder.

And now, years later, I want to thank Her for all
the dusty blue mornings since on planet rodeo
with all their rain thumps and knocks,
all the yellow as school bus autumns,
and magic as snow springs, for paper
boys & papergirls, the spangle of mum-mum moons,
artichokes and Alaska,
the holy hard-ons of sweet
men, and for the beautiful crystal
planetarium of children, and for the kiss
and tuck of Professor Longhair and
Old Crow on wind bucking nights.
I want to thank the dark, liquid suck of God
for the Church of the Holy Innocents
on Waldo Blvd. in Manitowoc, Wisconsin
with its twenty foot tall electric rosary
lit in the woods next to the church at night,
the electric rosary a lasso, an invitation
anyone can walk through, a gift, better than appliances
that last longer than the marriages that purchase them.

Oh, spaghetti hearts, even if just for once,
listen to me. Do not hot rush death;
stop at maypoles, bird cages, & scuppernong
marshes and marl. Anyways, always,
we are turning into weather & boulders
while the world spins teal beautiful
around us while we take our great short around God detours.

THE RIVER

NINA ZIVANCEVIC

Yes. It will be hard
to leave this Poughkeepsee river
that flows and goes
like anything else.
Yes, it will be hard to leave
this sky with clouds so immensely blue
which brings me back to my true self
which is the cloud and pale blue soft and
infinite. Yes. It will be hard
to leave people who say
"I was a poet once" and then got trampled by life.
and the river and the sky keep marching by
and it can matter but it does not
where you are,
and then we clutch on some names
and places like Roditi who said
that he knew Moni de Buli, the king
of flea markets in Paris in the 30s and
I remembered my father who knew Moni too.
and the sky and clouds and Paris too!
So I sat down by Poughkeepsee river
as it was flowing and going by
and although it was dirty with mud
and chemicals dropped in it, today
I chose to think that
it's only flowing and going by
like so many days and faces we met who flowed
away
with their impermanent beauty
without wisdom
     without meaning
        without doubts
shaped by the future
the riverflows with the boats and houses on them
its color of aluminum and ocher
never washes out and the guy
sitting by the pier watches it
he flows and goes by,
what else could he do?

DREAM 1812

nude in bed
i raise my left thigh to pick at a troubling
blackhead on the lower inner aspect. it looks unusual
and sits at the center of a perfect aureole/darker brown
against my cocoa skin

"shit," i think, "i hope this isn't cancer"

i put my thumbs together and squeeze. nothing happens so
i squeeze harder. the blackness starts to emerge. suddenly an
egg-sized mass pops up, a nipple and the aureole crown it. i'm
astonished by the tiny breast which jiggles in morning light

as i get up to see how it'll feel to walk, i notice a 4-inch
cylindrical umber growth has emerged from my left leg just below
my knee. it's narrow at the base and extremely rigid. frightened
i reach to pull it off and white stuff like liquid taffy shoots
from its head, gets all over the bed, the floor, my hands, then
the thing goes flaccid. i'm cleaning up the mess with a towel
when my lover appears

"look," i say, "new appendages"

he examines the inside of my thigh as i speculate on this
being a twin submerged in me since birth. i show
him the penis and his eyes light up

"hmmmmm," he says, "next time it gets hard, call me"

THE RIGHT THING TO DO OR NOT TO DO

Suppose on your first date with this hot woman
you meet at a bookstore/café on Halstead you
decide that its okay to go to her place and fuck
(so you go to her place) and after a half hour
of sweaty heavy-duty petting, she shoves you
down on the leopard bedspread, orders you to
undress and then peels off her Levi's to reveal
a nine inch lavender strap-on that looks like
an ear of corn. What would you do in this situation?
I didn't really know what to do—it had never
happened before. I hope I handled it right.
Society doesn't really prepare us for stuff like
this. And our mothers don't warn
us about these things any more than they
teach us to fuck on the first date.

Pretend that you just moved into a house of an acquaintance,
one that you rent cheaply and one that smells strongly
of dirty German shepherd and a week later your
acquaintance/landlady drags a jock bag out from
under her bed and pulls out, among other things,
a green vibrator with an animal on top (I think a
beaver), with an exceptionally long battery operated
tongue. Are you still with me ?

Then she hands you the thing with the expectation that
you'll say something or perhaps even do something with
the thing. Now what's the appropriate response to this?
Does anybody know? No one prepares us for
these things—not our mothers; nor our fathers; not
Ann Landers; not elementary, junior or high school; not sex ed; not
college; not locker rooms; not pornographic magazines; not Charles
Bukowski, not our jobs; not even affairs with professors; and not
the psychology of sexuality instructor freshman
year with his gigantic cow tongue and terrifying, yet
educational slide show of six foot high genitals. Nowhere in
life were we shown how to deal with these things.

I hope I handled it the right way. I'm afraid I may not
have. I worry about these things. I'll bet you think
I'm just trying to be perverse but this stuff
really happens to me. I'm not sure how these people
find me but I think maybe working retail has encoded me

LAURIE HALBRITTER

329

in some way. A few years ago, when I worked in this leather shop
this middle-aged dame came in the store about six different
times. Each time, she asked for me and tried on this
seventy dollar knee-length blue leather skirt. In front of
the mirror, she would twirl for me, squeeze her buttocks
and ask for my approval. "It's very nice," I said,
because I understood what was expected of me.

The last time she came in alone, the time before her
cowboy accompanied her with his credit card,
she eased her sweater up to her midriff, first above the waist-line
asking for my opinion, and then above her bra, up to her neck.
Completely unnecessary. "It looks very nice—it's a perfect fit, "
I said, because that was my job. The customer is always right,
and everything they do is normal. That is what I was inundated
with, you see. When you work retail, you don't really need
an opinion, you don't have an expression, you just have to agree.
Agree and sell.

And now my job is framing, picture framing. And selling picture
frames. "I like to frame, please," Virginia says in her thick Helga
accent, in the privacy of the back work room—and that pretty much
sums it up. The buzzer rings and I trudge out to the sales
floor to wait on a guy with an unmounted poster on which one sister
pinches the other sister's nipple (who holds a wedding ring in her
left hand). On the picture, I carefully arrange several comple-
mentary linen mats to match the drapery and place on top, a gilded
Victorian frame sample and smile. "That's a very lovely picture," I
say, and he agrees.

SCHIZOPHRENIA

twenty-eight long haired Yippie protesters
packed into a VW microbus, en route
to the 67 Montreux Rock Festival,
or maybe it was Woodstock.
anyway, it was a transcontinental
fuck fest.
I can't be reasonably sure
which one was my mother.
maybe that's why I'm schizophrenic.

MERCY

—for Robin

My daughter calls from California,
from Mojave.
She's following the Dead
with the Rainbow People.
They're at Camp A—
A for alcohol and LSD.
Every day these fifty-year-old hippies
drop acid, drink cheap beer,
travel from one town to the next
enticing young girls
and their 17-year-old boyfriends
to follow along.
Mercy is tired of old hippies,
of drinking cheap beer and dropping acid.
She wants to come home.

When she left home three years ago,
her mother cried. Mercy said,
"Do you want me to take that part of my heart
that loves you and throw it away."
Her mother cried. Mercy went away.
I got older, everything softened,
grayed and decayed and now I'm on an interstate
in a '79 Japanese pickup
heading east—
five hundred miles from Austin,
my daughter, my wife.

THOMAS L. VAULTONBURG

MARC SWAN

331

MARK DeCARTERET

NANA

ON CRUCIFIXION
As for lifting up crosses
I suppose people back then
knew something about it.

ON WOMEN
They all got their ninnies
sticking out.
And the hair—
how do they get it
so big?

ON FOOD
Even the gum stinks.

ON KEROUAC
He wrote some nice poems
but I think he had
two or three wives.

ON CONTRACEPTIVES
When I find a safe
on the street, I push it
down the sewer with my cane
so the children can't put them
on top of their heads.

HAL'S MOM

IT'S BETTER TO WAIT
You shouldn't have sex with a woman,
Mother said, until after you marry her.
Otherwise, she'll think that if you
couldn't wait to have sex, then you won't
be able to wait for other things. She
won't be able to trust you to take
the turkey out of the oven. She'll
tell you to do it at six. You'll
do it at five, & it'll still be raw.
And she won't be able to trust you
to change the sheets, because instead
of waiting for them to get dry
you'll pull them out of the dryer
while they're still damp, & the mattress
will get wet. The only thing you'll
be able to do well is give her children,
but once you do that she won't want you anymore.

MOM & DAD

1

A pajama party is different from a birthday,
Mother said. A birthday is an accomplishment,
you're one year closer to supporting yourself.
You get a cake & a present. Whereas, a pajama party
entails going over to your friend's house, changing into
your pajamas, & staying up an hour past
your bedtime. It's not a monumental occasion.
Your father & I would never dream of doing it.
As you get older, you become more protective of your sleep.

2

You should thank your lucky stars,
Father said, that you weren't born a cripple.
So no matter how bad you think your life is,
cheer up, because some people have it worse. Imagine having
to hop to the bathroom, & urinate on one leg.
If you're not careful, you could fall
into the bowl. Then you'll have to yell

for someone to help you out. So you should
be grateful for what you have, & not complain
if things don't work out the way you wanted them to.
And if you get depressed, you can always
walk into the next room, & turn on the TV.
But if you were a cripple, getting to the next room
would be a major production. You'll be
dependent on someone to get you there, & to take you back.

ALL IN THE FAMILY

Don't lean against the car door,
Mother said. It may not be locked,
& you can fall out. You're no use
to us dead, & even though you're not
much use to us now, hopefully when
you get older we'll be able to find
some use for you. If you become
a doctor you can check my blood pressure,
& give me free medicine, whenever
you come to visit. And what would be ideal
is if you marry a dentist, who can check my teeth.

MY MOTHER

"My Mother" is a collaborative poem written between January 1994 and March 1995 by: Nathan & Patrick, Manuela Barbuiani, Mary Angel Blount, Andrei Codrescu, Jennifer Earnest, Alison Gorlin, Kaitlin Gutmann, Cheryl Hartman, C. Kondracki, Melanie Kronick, Lois Lane, Renée Lastraps, Brandon Lee, Shelly Loughnane, W.D. Mitchell, Dan Olson, Chad Rohrbacher, Laura Rosenthal, Deborah Salazar, James B. Smith, Robert Toups, Jr., and Stephanie Williams.

My mother said if I missed her birthday she'd kill my stepfather.
My mother wears neon outfits and flexes in the mirror when my friends
   come over especially the Scottish ones.
My mother is in Dallas.
My mother doesn't know how I happened.
My mother happened the same way she just didn't know.
My mother insists on giving the dog grease on her ALPO to make her
   coat shine but neglects me.
My mother is an accountant.
My mother could be her sister the librarian but she's a half-sister to a
   lady from Beaumont instead.
My mother couldn't cook I ate everything raw until I died.
My mother tells me the difference between right and wrong then
   proceeds to beat me anyway, I guess I really am a Son-Of-A-BITCH!
My mother is returning home tomorrow.
My mother would like oral sex if she'd ever had it.
My mother told jokes in Church now she's a Jew on welfare.
My mother makes extra money but she will not tell me how.
My mother is very practical.
My mother ghost writes for channeled Grecian minor dieties.
My mother feels like she died and went to heaven.
My mother was a monster once now she likes soggy toast.
My mother plants grass and cuts it.
My mother would never bobbit my dad.
My mother believes Tonya Harding.
My mother skates on thin ice every time she kisses my stepfather.
My mother has four children.
My mother would have liked to farm she had to go to the opera instead.
My mother is a delicate fucking saint.
My mother is a psychotic-natured bitch.
My mother likes Nutrasweet and everything's fine.
My mother called to say she remembered none of our people.
My mother said that my father was allergic to himself.

335

My mother is the first one who will tell you that she is my mother.
I don't wanna do my mother, everybody's done my mother, my mother
    is done—nobody wants to do my mother,
she's a dominatrix disguised as a sweetheart.
My mother is so literary it hurts me where I write.
My mother has learned to be silent when she comes.
She thinks I've had lots of abortions.
I love my mother, I can't believe they're making me do this.
Mamma told me not to come.
My mother listens to the Jim Carroll Band, and she knows all the
    words.
My mother has forgotten the lyrics to gypsy ballads.
My mother's only vacation was when I was in the hospital faking death.
Mom popped in to ask about my plumbing; it was very scary.
My mother's plumbing was pretty good (I think) after she gave birth to
    the thing (me).
My mother tells me not to worry about her birthday.
My mother, I think, passed into the afterlife and came back, but would
    never tell me about it.
My mother thinks that's nice, that's real nice.
One can only bear so much mother then one can't bear no more.
In the queasy contemporary I am the mother, I know how to do that.
The future therefore is full of satisfying grub & great sex.
Mom's got a filter on her.
My mother is a great writer she never had a publisher.
My mother, my mother, so frightening, steely in will and intellect, witty
    sardonic like razors, and still, so fucking beautiful ...
"Hey Shell, you want a frozen Snicker?" She opens the freezer, vapors
    cuffing beatifically around her golden ovalface, "Neh, neh, neh
    ..." The corners of her mouth upward in wry Marx Bros.
    contortions. We sang the "Girl from Ipanima" song the other
    evening, with my new lover, in the comfy family kitchen, dim and
    eclectic, and we, my mother and I, taught the others how to sing
    the "Aanh," part. We were drunk, and laughing hard.
My mother! My mother! What have you done to my mother?!
My mother is a screamer.
My mother is a screwdriver fixing the toilet of my adolescence.
My mother left a rib in China in order to get a visa for Jesus.
I often wonder: who is my mother?
My mother is the wind. That's who my mother is.
I can't imagine—don't mention her name it's too late to be in love with
    an age-mate
she gives me the creeps.
My mother was a post-child, always middle-aged.
My mother was a mother when I was still a child.
336   My mother was Djinnie she gave head to the US Navy.

My mother never gave me head She used her ponytail to excite my high
        schoolfriends so I turned queer & jerked off
in mom's barrette so when she went out her boyfriends would sniff first
        her mascara then her head.
My mother had a moment of weakness induced by a glass of cheap Rosé
        in which she announced her undying passion for both Starsky
        AND Hutch.
My mother could kick the shit out of your mother. Any time. Any place.
As far as I can tell my mother has never been naked.
My mother might call you son 'cause you're so sexy.
My mother was a bellydancer known as The Soul of Misinformation.
My mother is an empty cunt. She dreams of think-tank sleep and silent
        omnipotent impotent drunks.
My mother sweet angel bleeds in corners where I leave dirty stained
        semen crusted underwear.
My mutha is a full cunt   I am an empty seed.
Mamma says once I was a skinny girl lift evr'y voice and sing
        doesn't remember any myths
        furl the myth of birth light
        and all that jazz
        is something you can sing to
        till earth and heaven ring
        my love my mother
        my whore.
My mother is a love doll mailed by a maniac to my future self—is a
        reformed plastic doll.
MY MOTHER was a ballet dancer
        then she was a belly dancer
        then she was
        an aerobic dancer
        then she went to work for the gov, pardon me, guvment
        she was taught by her mother
        how to he a martyr
        now she exists from 8 to 5
        and she doesn't dance
        anymore.
        It makes me want to dance.
My mother gave up on her dreams
        because she got pregnant
        pre Roe v. Wade
        and has always worked
        her ass off
        so I can dance
        whatever the fuck that means.
Therefore, given the existence of Puncher and
        Wattman

qua qua qua qua
lemme know when we getta write about our
daddys.
My mother is my bra
I inherited that power hair
my collection is invaluable
& hard to display
gossipy little ones
this bit and that bit just concealed
under her lace
outer wear.
My mother believes that material hardship
Is the way to spiritual enlightenment.
My mother believes that if we're not comfortable
Sitting there,
Surely we're comfortable
Not sitting elsewhere.
My mother made me a cheerleader (no basketball).
Even Tanya Harding had a mother.
My mother never conceived that I could be a cheerleader or a jock for
    that matter, I wonder how I could have been conceived, too tall
    with no idea of me.
My mother is a daytime person after 11PM she's a witch.
Ya wanna talk witch ? MY mother has a widow's peak of blue silver
    growing right out of her temple that she's dyed CLAIROL soft
    black 91 since she was TEN YEARS OLD! SHE'S A REAL FUCKING
    WITCH!!!
Mommy, why were you out with Boo when I was sitting home watching
    TV eating chocolate ice cream?
I wish my mother could scream!
My mother invented sex and now I am marketing it.
I made it and MAMA told everybody.
She would die for me even though she knows me eavesdropping to
    know the most of it all.
My mom's a quiet mother all she says is fuck off.
My mother doesn't play bridge anymore, dammit!
My mother could change a flat tire, but she chooses not to.
She used to call my father, about whom one could write paragraphs
    with no problem, but this
thing's all mother and the corral's kinda crowded.
Mother Baby I made you up on an island with a chandelier (instead of a
    sun).
My mother grew out of a little sun with yellow pieces and exploded big
    purple I LOVE HER.
        My mother lives in Ft. Lauderdale—she went to spring break one
            day & stayed.

338

My mother says people are too much.
My mother has finally taken down everything that was formerly too
    nice to use.
My mother has the legs of a twenty-year waitress.
My mother raises orchids toward the bay.
My mother listened to me say when I grow up will I have a nose like
    you.
My mother wears plastic heels she's like a modest Charo she's prettier
    than me or my sister
she marries tall Americans and doesn't want me to be dark and short
    sorry, too late—the gene pool is real murky already.
My mother tabbed.
My mother said Jimi Hendrix was the most beautiful man she had ever
    seen, but it was inconvenient.
My mother said I don't want your fucking Chevy Nova, blue 1966.
My mother wanted brown babies and an ethnic last name.
My mother wanted to think because it was philosophical in the sixties.
My mother wanted to do art for art's sake.
My mother wanted to learn because it was fun. Fun was fucking colors
    in the sixties.
My mother still listens to her mother.
My mother says that she'll never understand me.
My mother knows I'm listening. Bitch you don't want to touch her
    except in general like she's everybody's mother but she's not she's
    your big thing whoever you dont want to objectify characterize
    revere caricature pay any attention to bitch bitch cunt I came out
    of.
My mother was a contemporary of Einstein relativity wasn't her thing.
My mother called yesterday to tell me I was never a baby.
My mother capitalizes her interest when she loses at the track.
My mother peed standing up once & it became family legend.
My mother sucks juju beads and spits flowers.
My mother eats chitterlings.
My mother fucks sunshine.
My mother lives in standing water.
My mother sings cigarette smoke songs.
My mother was silent when the Germans invaded Poland.
My mother wants me to part my hair to the right ... to the right!
My mother is screaming while the boys grow tender.
My mother scrambled eggs with a shovel because she grew up in a barn.
My mother utters nonsensical whimsies when Mr. Tagliabeaux, our next
    door neighbor, decides to water his pansies in the nude.
My mother needs.
My mother gets along.
My mother was not religious but she had ashes on her forehead.
My mother wants butter on her cake.

My mother lays in funny bones.
My mother goes to the market, buys herself a fig.
My mother is the pillmaster.
My mother takes Excedrin whenever I look at her funny.
My mother hears groceries, period.
My mother gets her period whenever we get groceries.
My mother licks stamps three at the time.
My mother worships drycleaners.
My mother is wet whenever her clothes are dry.
My mother goes to the bathroom with the door open.
My mother hates my roommate.
My mother sees my roommate every time she comes over.
My mother's heightened consciousness does not permit her to think.
My mother's favorite bet is a dollar on the "Yo."
My mother never had an abortion.
My mother lost her purse.
My mother is composed of scents, intuition, and tobacco flakes.
My mother does not care about music.
My mother makes investments.
My mother and the camera are very good friends.
My mother knows all my friends' "mothers."
My mother captured the essence of youth in her pantyhose.
My mother watched boys from the knees down.
To my mother, a borscht is just a borscht.
My mother wore the songs down with pumice—her heels, breasts with a
    stone.
My mother has never met the mailman. I claim zero gravity for all my
    archetypes.
My mother calls my name in her post-hysterectomic sleep only.
My mother and Harold Bloom ... a perfect couple! Hanging between the
    hydrangea's dysfunctional blue florettes. I will do to those flowers
    what light does to pussy. Has everyone seen my purse & the shoes
    in it? And if they have, so what, am I supposed to be Narcissus, all
    embarrassed about it after Freud pointed out his immaturity? Take
    chipped-beef on toast and sculpt it into the shape of a summer
    squash and it still tastes like shit on a shingle, but if your mother is
    happy when you eat it, smile baby, keep on smiling, and let her
    live, let her live! When the life is live, guns and cunnilingus become
    honest. I call it chrysanthe mum but it's really "giving head" in
    English.
But in France it's giving "fête" which is more suctiony.
My mother can beat your mother up.
I didn't recognize my mother ... I was born again.
Sometimes the rain and sometimes the train grow into cigarette smoke
        and guns and boys who care not where they are when they speak
as they do it is silence but at the peak of her funniness my

mother handed her props to my sister and wept in a towel until
the bathtub overflowed with its daisies & my father's vomit was
tofu in the 60s.
(Things We Never Gave Up)
My mother's seven-sided weirdness at dawn.
My mouth has always known and longed for my mother's breasts.
Tell me about it.
I always longed for a father from books whose lovely long white
balls covered and furry
and stuffed with god hung so low I couldn't be seen.
But still we feel the pain/pleasure from their fingertips/glances
oh please
nipples (like) a .45 slug?
erupting from the snout of a horrible handgun.
from wayne lee dwayne every goddamn southern boy I ever wanted to
suck dry of that hereditary gayness that gets in the way of most
sex in the South liking the thought and feel of the permissive
domineering intellect.
it could be any body
start reading   now.
love of christ mom dad my cousin's dark dark
sweet fat thing he wanted to
put inside me and tremble there for what seemed
like an electric grid on the blink in the Pacific
ugh ugh sub-marine!
pumping thrusting withdrawing and rising
big wet smooth things
to find the right book at the right time
is to find your left nut
& you're female
with plexus fine and lips of dog soft nerve and filet de sensitivity on
which I
licked and stroked toward the lightfluffy feeling of immortality
stiff with feathers I could have been someone's typewriter
instead of a drooling devil's pillow of chocolate wounds feces pineapple
juice and more   like daffodils
spurting out of their husks
in April, sometimes March if the winter
is mild
like John Knox when he died.
Long live cream and daffodils!
My mother had window panes installed in her head in order to study me
better.
My mother had intimate sex with my dog.

341

My mother is a year-old stack of potpourri.
My mother is a Latvian with square hips and a circular constitution.
My mother is my sacred cow—I will say nothing about her.
My mother that sweet vile woman my first love, my one woman fast-
     growing roots in this hot weather.
Mother should have flourished, decadent & mysterious, Bold Tuber!
My mother subscribes to the notion that lefties make better lovers which
     is too bad because my father is right-handed.
My mother decided sexuality was a toy and I was a stuffed bear in a
     large felt pelt zoo.
My mother borrowed my father's handcuffs and cuffed me to the bed
     and fucked me like I've never been fucked before.
My mother alligator-skinned with soft pudding center.
My mother, she is the fragrance of scilla root, there is no vase, there is
     no water.
My mother massaged your mother who massaged your mother who
     massaged Mother Earth.
My mother lives for the flash bulb.
My mother doesn't rub me that way.
I wish my mother could spell
     She didn't have to
     She came in Spanish
     Her vowels SUCKED.
My mother didn't need to pay too much attention to me when I was
     young and young I stayed.
My mother had a pepper-sized clitoris that grew out of the ground and
     was eaten by hungry Hungarians passing thru the punch.
My mother was a mantis.
My mother still turns me on after all this time.
My mother continues to motivate me to lie.
My mother loves to tell me the same stories—my identity is entrenched
     in her half-truths.
My mother has all answers, if you ignore what she says with her mouth.
My mother is like a continual snake in my belly.
My mother is looking at this poem as I speak.
My mother is wishing something good and bad.
My mother is a new world sexy a nation spread open.
My mother said that when I was 2 years old I kicked in a mirror and
     gave her 7 years bad luck.
My mother perpetuates neurosis.
My mother cried when she saw my shoes in 1969.
My mother wasn't surprised when I showed her the picture of me when
     I was eight with a football birthday cake when I told her I was
     queer.
     My mother wakes me up.
My mother cried when I got glasses.

My mother keeps turtles in her swimming pool until they die so she can
   have their shells as souvenirs.
My mother lives in the phone she breathes when you pick it up.
My mother's mother isn't my child but she often acts like one.
My mother knows more than any father who only has a PBS education
   in mythology and doesn't know a fallopian tube even when he falls
   over one.
My mother is trying frantically to prevent me from realizing my father's
   death.
My mother had a vibrator. While looking for some stationery one day
   while she was away, I found it. I was suprised. I was ashamed.
   Now I'm not.
She just got clear after being not for 33 years.
Anybody's mama would get an allusion to *Redbook* or *Southern Living*
   but somebody's papa thinks praying in ice is "deep lesbianism"
   mama made pappa that cold.
My mother was my father all of my life, so I guess that makes her my
   mother squared.
My mother... inevitably I will become her.
My mother took a picture of me and now I type with one finger.
My mother finally found the right color for her hair. Now me.
My mother told me that I was a pleasant surprise.
My mother said you should live in my shoes & now I do & walk funny.
Some ancient peoples meaning extinct said if thou are not a mother you
   cannot enter the kingdom of heaven.
My mother is Carmen Miranda...I am the fruit on her head.
My mother is always there...except when she's fishing.
My mother slept with guilt and then gave birth to me.
My mother is nobody else's mother.
My mother is always upset with the last person who uses the toilet
   paper and does not have the manners to change it!
My mother's recipe for breakfast is burnt toast & chicken fat.
My mother's name begins with "D."
My mother is always about to just die.
My mother takes her time doing everything—so much time that I would
   believe that all of existence would end before she finishes and I get
   impatient and be mean and then get guilty later but I'm working
   on that now.
My mother's mushroom took a lot of heat during the fifties.
My mother is the biggest meanie and you run to her when the rest of the
   world is being mean.
My mother used to be my best friend, but then she got a boyfriend and I
   was jealous because she was gone and I wanted a boyfriend too
and I didn't get one.
My mother choked on a fish bone at fifteen & now I can't eat
   fish.

My mother, Oh mia madre che bella!
My mother crossed herself while her hands dripped fat from the
    Christmas turkey.
My mother rolled around the floor with Ray Charles and one eyeball
    between them was not enough.
For mother's ROSES (a late infatuation)
    young BUCKS now compost.
My mother loves, ADORES, her gay ex-husband.
My mother has never kissed me gently on the ear.
My mother was touchy when it came to particulars so I ate her hand.
When my mother drinks beer she peeks in the bottle to make sure it's "a
    dead soldier."
My mother held her breath while death passed by.
My mother twists and turns in my head and her smile lingers in my
    heart.
My mother refuses to have cable installed, "such a long cord, touching
    so many people!"
My mother and I jacked each other off & she always came. I waited for
    a biological convention.
My mother, in secret, runs with scissors and imagines stabbing my
    brother—over and over carrying her quiet violence
        in a basket   out to sea.
My mother hurts men when she fucks them.
My mother cranes her neck to see your mother.
My mother hides her cock from her children.
My mother gestated my penis (among other things)
    & finally
she got what she wanted.
My mother's Air Force commission expires in five minutes.
My mother smoked during her pregnancy and it didn't not affect me
    none one hit.
My mother dances often, dances fast, and falls.
My mother was a four-leaf clover lucky for everyone but me.

3
THE BODY BAG &
RIFFS & TIFFS IN THE CORPSE

RELIGIONS OF THE WEST
(a pictorial history)

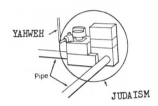

JUDAISM

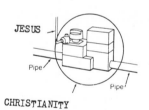

CHRISTIANITY

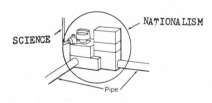

DADATA

THE BEST OF THE BODY BAG

LAURA ROSENTHAL

DOUGLAS A. POWELL, SANTA ROSA, CA: Congratulations on the formulation of your philosophy of bad poetry, Badism. We read it and it's truly awful. The poems you sent aren't half bad. It's so hard to bring practice in line with ideology.

SHEILA ALSON, BROOKLYN, NY: Don't know why you're in the bag except we always hurt the ones we love. Your work employs a load of elegant non sequitur, as in "Seeing": "Sometimes a little muscle and an illustration is all you need," but there's a translated-from-the-French kind of alienation among the lines that makes us lonesome. "Something laughing and then again, foreign."

TYRONE WILLIAMS, CINCINNATI, OH: Congratulations! You've managed cock-sucking, cunt-fucking, crotch-grabbing and "sum baaaad shit" in verse in the city that made Mapplethorpe famous. Plus you're a thoughtful sinner. Send us more.

SCOTT SORIANO, SACRAMENTO, CA: Weird poem, in which "… Mutants and robots surround a water cooler…," but a mo better bio: "Ms., Sir, or whomever. I am twenty-five, an anti-work activist, and a Wobblie… I also play guitar in a noise band, do photo-montage and draft counseling." A mother's pride and joy.

A.D. WINANS, SAN FRANCISCO, CA: Regarding Howlesque verse tributes: we've seen the best lines of our generation destroyed, and for what? Enough already.

STEPHAN RONAN, BERKELEY, CA: Enjoyed your refreshing "Ode to Allen Ginsberg's Asshole." Sometimes a title is everything. Bongos away!

PETER DESY, COLUMBUS, OHIO: Now, your "On The Farm" is a rural anecdote of a different color. You've made something very moving out of your grandfather's memories of boyhood incontinence.

PEG THARP, WICHITA, KS: The note warning us that your poem "Woman Eating Dirt" had been accepted for publication by the *Minnesota Review* was too late, we'd already bagged it. This kind of appropriation of folk fact as grist for the metaphor mill leaves us with a bad taste in our mouth. Maybe we're wrong, maybe you've eaten dirt. Maybe it was a spiritual experience. Geophagy, the consumption of soil, has been observed in women and children in the rural South and was frequently referred to in popular and scientific literature in the

19th century. The recently published *Encyclopedia of Southern Culture* says however that today clay eating is on the wane, its practitioners having either quit cold turkey (it is a cultural habit, not a religious rite) or having switched to the consumption of commercial products such as "laundry detergent or baking soda." Mmmm.

MATTHEW WILLS, IOWA CITY, IA: Poetry is never having to say you're sorry, isn't it? "It'll never work, I fear. You say "body bag" and I say "organic battlefield remnants retrieval pouch"—so let's just call the whole thing off. That time we ran guns together for the cause, well, it was beautiful, and we'll always have that, you and I...P.S. could you send me some Don DeLillo or Danielle Steele? My fundamentalist captors have really lame reading material. Does Andrei feed you more than day old bread and water?"

HANAFI RUSSELL, CONCORD, CA: Your poems seem to be the product of a men's movement self-awareness boot camp. In "Exercise" you recount (in painfully tone-deaf verse) "...lying exposed and vulnerable on my back,/ with men I call brothers moving around me in a spiritual exercise ..." Drums drum, Men dance, while at the center of the poem you sustain a very long, very Greek, recollection of a morning run in which you "surge" and "pull and "tuck" with another man around a track which "shines like beaten gold." Ye gods! We didn't think it could get more masculine; then you went hiking and wound up sniffing yourself and intoning profundities: "Many times on the backpack trip I let myself enjoy the smell/ of the skin on the back of my hand as I leaned forward on my stick to rest./ My tan penetrated deeper and deeper, my return/ to nature growing complete with it." Could be you're under the spell of Irish Spring: "A Manly scent, but I like it too."

GABRIELLE GLANCY, SAN FRANCISCO, CA: The sestina is a charming thing; a favorite of ours is Ashbery's one "en la case de Popeye." Olive's long speech in the fourth and fifth stanzas is stunning, and really, to gracefully use "spinach" seven times...stupendous! But an unwary poet should be warned: the repeated words can turn on you. Repetition not only has the power to charm, as in an incantation; words can go their own evil way and curse a composition. It happens in your version of the sestina repeating turn, shadow, corner, marked, country, and obscure: "... Our destiny, a point obscure/ had no bounds, broken from the shadow,/ and when it was the shadow/ we had left behind, marked/ only be a contoured wing, no longer obscure/ to us but fertile, the country/ grew so open, the corners/ fell, and finally, we knew where to turn." Obscure, obscures, obscuring, it is. It doesn't help that you've thrown destiny into this muck. How much more pleasant are the efforts of:

TONY YNOT FRANKS, AMSTERDAM, THE NETHERLANDS: The manuscript you sent is strong. We detect something of Popeye, or perhaps Odysseus, in "I'm A Liar": "I have lied to myself and to others./ I have often said things for sex to all my lovers./ I realize now of all the hurt and shame/ I wish I could take it back, I have only myself to blame./ Only my death will release me of my true feelings."

DAVID BARR, CHEVY CHASE, MD: A little trim reveals that "The Little Baldspot on the Back of My Head" is a great poem trapped in the body of a formal apology. Editing can free your work of its feelings of shame and anxiety. Get rid of the title. Use simply "Baldspot." Better yet, leave the poem a riddle, untitled. Don't use numbers. They give you a frame, a little cover in writing about an emotionally difficult subject, but they obscure the music of the list you are left with if you drop the lines numbered 1,2,3, and 9. Line #2 for instance reads," ... my desperate hand/ says, gravely,/ it can't be covered over..." So don't. And introducing your dermatologist from out of the blue with an opinion in line #9 screws up everything. Here's the poem without the toupee: "An area of confusion/ like burled walnut/ A clearing/ where thoughts may gather/ An atoll/ lapped by brown waves/ An escape hatch/ if something blows my mind/ A helipad/ A constant eye/ gazing at my lengthening/ past." Make "at my lengthening past" one line, and you're flawless. Don't be a drape: bald is beautiful.

KAKI OUZTS, HATTIESBURG, MS: You get the gore award for most bloody submission. To start, a young girl's first menstrual blood and her metaphorical desire (we hope) to sew up the offending organ in "Her Mother Cleans." Followed by "Shopping List of a Serial Killer": "duct tape/ rope/handkerchiefs/ ice pick/ gloves/ razor blades/ ski mask/ Ragu." But neither compare to your instruction in the slow drowning of a mouse, "Vacuum." It might be Poe, but it's not rhymed, for which we're grateful.

ELLEN DIBBLE, NORTHAMPTON, MA: Expects payment for her writing but considers the poems she sent Exquisite Corpse "unmarketable." Gee, that's flattering. We have always found retribution to be more gratifying than restitution.

JAMES FOGLE, BATON ROUGE, LA: and this is a simultaneous rejection.

DONALD HURD, MACONDA, TX: Yours was the most touching cover letter to bend its knee to us in years: "... my poems come to you with hope and goodness in their hearts. However, if you should choose not to accept them no doubt they will cherish even your rejection, for they possess a humility quite out of proportion to their length."

LISA COOPER, TUCSON, AZ: *Why* phonetic translations of poems by Jack Spicer?

CANDIDA LAWRENCE, APTOS, CA: Due to considerations of space we can't possibly publish your fourteen page love letter to Vaclav Havel.

MARK CUNNINGHAM, OPELIKA, AL: As far as we know, the comparison of your penis as it bobs, relaxed, in a warm bath to Hamlet's drowned Ophelia is unique in literature.

LISA LONG, WASHINGTON, DC: Like yes—your poems are proof of a majorly burgeoning school of the mythopoetic Barbie. If you ask us, The Doll has what it takes to go all the way as a radical metaphor—she's metonymic yet immutable. In "Barbie Comes" she is the First Lady defying death in an *assignation* motorcade of Barbie Corvettes. In "Dirty Barbie Games" she's a slightly more evolved Twist-n-Turn Barbie forced by *older playmates* to have sex with Ken, G.I. Joe, even other Barbies, but learning in the process that "women fit perfectly together like clams/ and rub." The most ambitious work, "Barbie Mutilation," could be cut by a couple of pages. Still, it gives us an indication of Barbie's transcendental and ultimately subversive potential: "Who cannot forget the beauty of my wild aborigine/ Barbie,/ with no eyeball whites just extra large blue glowing eyes,/ with spiked, chopped hair,/ or, with her hair burned on to the scalp in little/ precisely-spaced, brown nodules,/ poised gracefully with neck-to-toe full-body tattoo work./ I saw someone just like her recently/ in LA/ or was it London/ She is everywhere/ her influence permanent..."

NORRIS MERCHANT, CATULLUS, LOUISVILLE, KY: Thanks for the if-you-don't-publish-me-I'll-become-another-little-Hitler poem. It's a genre we're growing unquietly used to: "...his muse, a pistol loaded/ with homicidal maniac abuse."

JONATHAN LEVANT, DAYTON, OH: At least we're not the only object of homicidal rage: "APR is the cruelest mag for they/ have rejected me/ there are endless ed-/ itors i'd love to mass murder..." ("giving garringer a derringer").

MARK ELBER, HUNTINGTON, NY: Your poems exude boyish enthusiasm: "Soon.../ You will pay your rent by just breathing/ you will eat sunshine and belch incense/ Have a decent choice for President/ Have no fear not even of fear itself..."And heaven knows you could have a worse hero than Mayakovsky—look what his alarming lyrics did for Frank O'Hara! But when you write that you want to "revise the future" and "cannonize the sky" it's time for a history lesson. Our Volodya also wrote a lot of crap propaganda during the years of Lenin's New Economic Policy. By 1930 Lenin was dead and Stalin was gearing up to purge society of individualists. When what revising the future might really mean finally occurred to him, Mayakovsky killed himself. You can still "address eternity," but it's not what it used to be. "... as one alive/ I'll address the living" (Vladimir Mayakovsky, "At the Top of My Voice").

JIM GOVE, FELTON, CA: The poem about reading Tom Clark's biography of Olson and experiencing loss of hero-worship got us thinking about heroes and how, or if, they fail. Olson may have had a difficult life—and a difficult life to narrate—but he's not the hero of this life, Maximus is. At least for us, readers. We question also how much of your disappointment with Olson's very human failings has anything to do with Olson at all. Tom Clark's Olson inspired in us only astonishment that the poetry got done in spite of the bad breaks. And really, looking at the percentages, the odds are that Olson talking, laughing, being high, teaching and writing filled a lot of his *miserable* life.

SYLVAN ESH, MADISON, WI: Everyone should enjoy the pleasant sensation of saying your name over and over in a low whisper.

ROBERT FRIEND, JERUSALEM, ISRAEL: Call us hokey—we've always imagined that Jerusalem, Mother to the multiple births of monotheism, was a spiritual, albeit violent metropolis. So it is perhaps naively that we judge your poems among the grossest thoughts conceived this year in the holy land. From "Revenge": "Because his phallic verses make you sick,/ you threaten to stuff his ass with your thick prick."

JOHN KNOLL, SANTA FE, NM: The jewelry may be fake in "Santa Fe: Plastic Adobe Disneyland," but the tourists are authentic: " 'O Tom, look: there's a full moon over the plaza.' " It's a Kodak moment.

JOHN KEHOE, NEW CANAAN, CT: An appeal to Tina Brown, Editor in Chief, *Vanity Fair* magazine: "As a poet and fiction writer, I'd like to renounce that calling and apply for a job at *Vanity Fair.* I feel I can lick the assholes of the rich and powerful with as delicate a tongue as any writer presently in your employ. I am not immodest when I say that I can, in fact, rim the bungholes of the plutocracy with what can only be described as fervor...If I am unable to put Wonder bread on the table and Nikes on the feet of my children through my efforts as a fiction writer, as indeed is the case; if I cannot persuade local and national arts councils and foundations to furnish me with grants and stipends, as is also the case; then allow me, please, to turn my attentions

351

towards the literary practice of fawning over rock star millionaires, trust-fund do-gooders, rapacious merger and acquisition predators, shit-for brains movie stars and other similar *Vanity Fair* subjects ... Drop a couple of big checks in my lap and I'll drop a couple of disgustingly innocuous, vilely inofffensive puff-pieces into yours."

JANET COSTA, PITTSBURGH, PA: Your poem "The Gift" sounded so awfully familiar ("I have something to show you/ Look here in my hand") that we resorted to a little research. Denise Levertov used a variation of the "gift" strategy in 1957, in a poem called "The Rights": "I want to give you/ something I've made ..." Her version of the love poem turns on the difficulty of writing "a poem of a certain temper"— yours resuscitates the pernicious conceit by which the lover is said to give life/ existence to the beloved and vice versa. Pretty archaic, especially when you load the love boat with "ecstatic flesh" and "jasmine nights." We'll let Denise read you your rights: "so far I've found/ nothing but the wish to give. Or/ copies of old words? Cheap/ and cruel; also senseless ..."

ALICE EVANS, EUGENE, OR: We've got serious problems with your "Bus Ride." Your bus, like all busses, is full of poor people, old people, crazy people; yet the story calls upon us to sympathize with some whitebread art student who'd fly if only Art paid. The suffering of the unmedicated schizophrenic in the next seat babbling obscenities is lost on our heroine—she's busy feeling personally inconvenienced: "I hated busses because something weird happened to me everytime I rode one." Too bad. If Little Miss "two-foot long braids" doesn't want to share public transportation with homeless families and de-institutionalized mental patients, she should quit whining about her kundalini and lobby Congress to restore funding for human services. Get a conscience.

SUMMER BODY BAG: I HEAR AMERICA SWEATING*

> I am I drink I think I guess
> I am my moods   our feet
> A sweater
>   white-throated evening
> Slim hope of England
> Rome
> This girl   this boy I remember
> Antarctica
> Vampire
> Dad   after a cold spell
> After the sex   the poem
> Stalks and tubers

352

After the poem
              imp soda clay curveball
I am I remember
              I want I remember
To rocket to chicken to plaster to scoop
And to never Grandmother blink tap or forget
I am I profess
              of garlic
                     of birds
I kiss   I think   of frost dark Florida
We sing we are
              a mouth of star
A flock of gears
              of knowledge
                     of oranges
A hole
       gazelle corncob
We sing the boss Onion
A lover
       my bathtub
We sing we are babies
                     you-she-it
Him or her
Singing
       "Broughton for President!"
Imp grandpa mood rocket
Nose toes homeplate angel
We who saw told of us
Our arms want guess remember

Forced to collaborate: Sonya Reeves, Fayetteville, AR; M.A. Schaffer, Arlington, VA; Larry Turner, Naperville, IL; Terry Ott, Houston, TX; Linda Nemec Foster, Grand Rapids, MI; Benedict Hughes, Brooklyn, NY; Carol Tarlen, Sausalito, CA; Christopher McNew, Englewood, OH; Joshua Sherwin, Fairfaz, VA; Duane Locke, Tampa, FL; John Olson, Seattle, WA; Chris Volpe, Huntington Station, NY; Kevin Carr, Savage, MN; Brian Seabolt, Howell, MI; Helene Pilibosian, Watertown, MA; Scantzeer, Echo Hill Camp, MD; D.W. Wright, Tokyo, Japan; Jeff Conant, Leggett, CA; Jed Allen, Tempe, AZ; Stephen Healy, Northhampton, MA; Rebecca Lilly, Ithaca, NY.

MICHAEL BOCCIA, ELIOT, ME: "On cold blue winter nights/ I often go to bed with/ Emily Dickinson..." ("Beloved Emily"). Alive, she was untouched, a virgin, inviolate. Dead, Miss Dickinson has turned into something of a slut, sleeping with numberless men and women, poets and composers, little girls and old men in what amounts to the biggest, safest safe-sex orgy in history. Ed Sanders and The Fugs did an extremely erotic thing with sweet Emily on their *No More Slavery* LP called "Dreams of Sexual Perfection." "Unbraid your wild red hair/ upon your shiny shoulders/ untie your summer dress/ and free your swaying breasts..." Dream, dream, dream.

EMILY DICKINSON, AMHERST, MA: " 'Twas such a little, little boat/ That toddled down the bay!/ 'Twas such a gallant, gallant sea/ That beckoned it away!/ 'Twas such a greedy, greedy wave/ That licked it from the coast/ Nor ever guessed the stately sails/ My little craft was lost!"

NIGEL HINSHELWOOD, WASHINGTON, D.C.: *Barbie* (cont.) in which The Doll gets some serious attention in "The Question of Simulacrum: Barbie and the Culture of Variables." We understand that the author means to "parody the jargonesque tendencies of philosophical and theoretical writing," even as he formulates "a critique of some of the ways late-capitalist culture produces and consumes images of the body, and especially the female body." The goal seems problematic, especially as both the parody and the critique misread Barbie entirely: she's no simulacrum, no "shadowy likeness, deceptive substitute, or mere pretense" (*The Concise Oxford Dictionary*); she's a shape-shifting signifier hell-bent on being all things to all men. Virgin-whore-punk-debutante-*simulacrum*, if you will; not even the deadening effects of jive terminology can make her boring.

By the way, Barbie *does* speak, contrary to your assertion otherwise. This year's new talking model is equipped with a talk-chip which allows her to say things like, "Want to go to the mall?" and "Math class sure is hard." One more thing. *Did* Ruskin say it best? You give the impression that your sources go deeper than the *O.E.D.* A citation might be in order.

RAY MIZER, GREENCASTLE, IN: Congratulations, you cranky old puffin, you! To be included in the *Canadian Anthology of Bad Poetry* is a real honor. We've found that *Exquisite Corpse* is often the springboard to a career in writing.

MICHAEL SMALL, VICTORIA, AUSTRALIA: America loves Australians, and Australians love Ted Berrigan, because they are so *natural!* Thanks for "Things to Do at Harvard": "...read the *Harvard Gazette*/ & respond to the call for volunteers in sexual dysfunction study/ mood

354

effects of stimulants study/ cocaine dependence study/ central vein occlusion study/ pain attack study/ hair loss treatment study ..." George Bush went to Harvard, or Yale, or someplace Ivy League—he plans to participate in the Former Heads of the CIA study as soon as begins his post-Presidential career.

LEFTY, PLANO, TX: "... does he suck new things with old fear of spit/ does he scrape womb itch cervix/ or just save fluid for buddha-swami at Naropa ..." We've heard tell Naropa has that effect on some people.

L. DELLAROCCA, DELRAY BEACH, FL: Now that sex and latex are linked as intimately as life and death, rubber fetishism is a growing phenomenon: "She Loves the Smell of Tires" takes unnatural pleasure beyond Saran Wrap to its bizarro olfactory extreme: this chick gets off in junkyards "rubbing her right hand around the rim,/ teasing herself and every now and then,/ she even lets her fingers brush very/ gently over the hard, stiff, protruding stem ..." She and the hero of "He Drives Real Fast" ("He drives so fast gravity smears,/ at night you can tell where he's at/ because his magnificent velocity/ drags all the stars in the sky/ to one side like a magnet") make a cute couple, don't they?

C. A. CONRAD, PHILADELPHIA, PA: For you, our editorial we is dissolved; we like two of your poems especially, but the editor and the lector disagree over which of them to publish. I, a simple reader, have argued passionately for your "A World Without Condoms"—it takes both insight and courage to expose the dangers of unprotected inter-kingdom sex: "she swears it was the cucumber/ that did it/ and nine months later/ a son with her eyes/ and cheekbones/ but the seeded spine/ and leafy complexion were all Dad's// the nurse rubs a little Creamy Italian/ on his bright green belly/ they coo at one another/ this won't hurt a bit she says/ and tucks the napkin under her chin." The poem gives circumcision new meaning. Our editor, it seems, is moved to masculine tenderness by "It's True I Tell Ya/ My Father is A 50¢/ Party Balloon": "my father paper thin again/ lost on the basement floor// but who will put their lips/ to his stiff old hard on?/ who will blow him up?/ who will want this man floating stupid// stuck in a tree again?" Not I. Please don't be dismayed by your inclusion in *Body Bag*. We think of the Bag as both tomb and monument, as a place where the editorial process goes proud and naked onto a public beach.

ALEXANDER LAURENCE, SAN FRANCISCO, CA: We are groggy from the heat, but refreshed by the charming expression "you noodlehead" as it appears in "The Black Prince of Nestor Burma." I have not been to Baden-Baden but to the Badlands, where I baked myself free of poetry in contemplation of the dust of a long-dead ocean.

G. HELD, NEW YORK, NY: The humpty-dumpty, adam-n-eve plus lucifer allusions in "Another Fall" fall flat, but "the Zapruderesque Nightmare" is alive, a superlative pop expression of anxiety and horror that gratifies the tongue: Zap ruder esque. As in, How was your day, honey? It was a Zapruderesque Nightmare.

C. MULROONEY, LOS ANGELES, CA: Has it in for sparrows.

GERALD BURNS, AUSTIN, TX: "...I was predictably furious when I/ saw my verse was prose, in the eyes of whatever/ *Corpse* editor looks at camera-readies, angry from/ expectation denied (I shouted, audibly..."

DAN SCHWARTZ, AMHERST, NY: "School Lunch Poem #2" is a fine example of the genre *Trauma Recollected in Tranquility*: "The usual din in the cafetorium/ was suddenly cut/ by a high-pitched, squeezed-out scream/ a girl had found maggots/ in her green beans."

ANDREW SUNSHINE, NEW YORK, NY: * * *

ZEN DESTINY, BATON ROUGE, LA: Hi.

RANDALL WILSON, MONROE, LA: It was April when your long poem arrived in its Crane's Kid Finish "coffin." Now it's autumn and your work, by virtue of its cotton content and the fervor of its author's note, deserves acknowledgment, however late. From your Note we note that the twenty-three pages of "The Contradiction of the Excluded Middle" "represent some three years of revision, and at another level, the first twenty-three years of my life." Though the poem was "originally intended for submission to the B. F. Conner competition at *The Paris Review*" you felt that because it was "composed in a one-room apartment in Austin, Texas...it would be symbolic heresy, a second order contextual subversion of the first order meaning of this poem" to submit it to "the journal that epitomizes the clubby, silver spoon sucking up-East literary mafia that has been spoon fed and jacked off with the blood of my ancestors..." Well, no one wants the first twenty-three years of their life (or that which represents them) eaten for breakfast by giant-sized, bookish robber barons. Run, Jack, run! The fearsome paradox is not that their approval would subvert the meaning of your work, but that you *desire* that approval so violently that you've turned the awful fathers into bloody jackals. We suspect you won't be happy until you've been devoured. If they reject your work, it stays subversive. If you win, it is likely you'll feel more affirmed than subverted and gladly accept the prize.

Oh, yeah, the poem. It is very long and we can't publish it.

But it's not bad. The title, if memory serves, is derived from the discipline of logic. It designates an argument form that can never yield a true conclusion, because somewhere after the *If* and before the *therefore* an essential truth that contradicts the conclusion is ignored. In this way it seems to be the logical equivalent of psychological denial, by which mechanism the mind is believed to reject unpleasant truths so as to protect the self from the experience of unbearably true conclusions. To its credit, the poem works to salvage the contradiction by confronting some of the shit that has happened to you: "Take all the people who called me queer/ Hold them down and fuck them/ And let them try to write a novel about their/ Sexual problems longhand, in crayon/ In the state charity hospital/ And the ones who forgot/ The night I took seventy pills/ Heave a boomerang of silence/ Into their loneliest night, take them …" Let them try to exclude that.

J. MARTIN, FORT COLLINS, CO: "Attack of the Fifty-foot Poststructuralist" was so frightening! We particularly enjoyed "The Middle": "There's a hole in everything—/ houses, stomachs, televisions, aortas, the color yellow, slip knots, Western Europe, Indian rugs,/ the governments of Norte America, the internal combustion/ engine, the Book of Job, electrons, parakeets, any other/ color you can imagine, our parents, their parents, ad infinitum./ It's the milky way. Everything has a hole./ Oh, Daddy."

LAURA MARKLEY, SAN FRANCISCO, CA: Girlfriend, let me tell you something: no one needs to know that you got your lines from "magazine articles, ad copy and phrases culled from a 'socially responsible' investment newsletter." Ours is an age of quotation, we're all down in the dumps of history, and the future is in recycling. In this quotidian reality to cull is to author; to borrow meaning is to stake a claim to the garbage that is your birthright. We'd much rather imagine that you invented the world yourself, and you have: "now is tough times/ teeth meet metal as a/ gold drop vanishes/ first messengers of/ the star's death are/ sicker than her/ look in the mirror/ … Lately, I have become a/ fantasy-inspired climax/ though I have trouble with/ a reality not yet described/ by science/ This year, the Academy's theme:/ 'what can we do about it?'/ We adore the dress-up fantasy,/ putting to use bumps on 600/ mysteriously acquired pennies/ some enjoy the crowed planet/ Are we ready for this new closeness?"

EARL GRAY, DETROIT, MI: "In the sixties Detroit got the name Motown. I have submitted a new name to the press: Potown. The great ash heap of poverty here has given birth to some new babies of culture, which are barely crawling."

THOMAS VAULTONBURG, BYRON, IL: Voltaire and The Jackal do make a stunning couple.

JENNIFER KIFFMEYER, CHICAGO, IL: "I like *Exquisite Corpse*. It is strange and loud and its paper reminds me of the directions and cautionary statement that accompany all over-the-counter drugs."

RICHARD BECKER, RICHMOND, VA: Something we hate: poems about Hopper paintings.

SCOTT HOLSTAD, LONG BEACH, CA: "Poem about My Rights as a White Male in a PC Society": "I/ have/ none." You have the right to remain silent. If you give up this right anything you say can and will be used against you.

ORESTE BELLETTO, NAPA, CA: "You have the right to remain violent;/ anyone you shoot now cannot, and will not/ speak against you in a court of law" ("Miranda").

LEE GOLDSTEIN, SOMEWHERE IN AMERICA: We have nothing against the gnostic, or the gnomic for that matter. It's the gnashing and gnawing that make the job of knowing so gnarly, especially now, when poems swarm like gnats at windless noon.

KW, *NEW PHILISTINE*, DETROIT, MI: "I may be crazy, but I am convinced that renowned brat-pack author Tama Janowitz, frequent glamorous guest of David Letterman, occasional subject of liquor ads, is actually Thomas A. Janowitz. I believe that the famous female novelist is, or once was, a man."

ADRIAN DICKWORTHY, PACIFIC GROVE, CA: "Howard Moss is dead./ Poetry and hope again be wed." No he's not. He's a *Corpse* contributor.

TOM RADEVICH, SAN FRANCISCO, CA: Tooth marks add a special touch to your manuscript.

BERNARD GADD, PAPATOETOE, NEW ZEALAND: Is no place on earth safe from *the signifier*? Apparently not: "worn knuckle that/ pot/ signifiers'/ contained// containing sherds ..." Shards, right? We once watched an episode of *The Victory Garden* all about New Zealand, and it seemed like such an Elysium we imagined (naively) that the place was free from this alienating awfulness. Maybe St. Patrick will come and cast out your snakes, such as they are.

JOHN SULLIVAN, TUCSON, AZ: Glad to know somebody's hot for H.D., as evidenced by the devotional "I Don't Want to Die in Babylon Missing You, H.D." But is your lust enough to warm old Hilda in the Great Beyond? "If you were here, right now, we'd shine/ big time. We'd go down slow, locked together/ for the power and our love of Li-Po." If you're lucky, she's tired, by now, of the sapphic.

HILDA DOOLITTLE, "THE HIGH PRIESTESS SPEAKS," (1938): "I was not pure,/ nor brought purity to cope/ with the world's lost hope,/ nor was I insolent/ ... I never shone/ with glory/ among women,/ and with men, I stood apart,/ smiling,/ they would have found me other/ had they found/ me, whom no man yet found,/ only the forest-god/ of the wet moss,/ of the deep underground ... "

JOHN JAKARY, DETROIT, MI: As per your request, a line or two of comment for "a novice poet." Your friends aren't wrong; the poems are likeable, and you'll do fine if you never use the expressions "white noise," "at age six," or "nocturnally" ever again, in poetry or conversation. Another objectionable conceit, "the blanket of moist warm air," is a kind of weather-man banality quite beneath you. Remember, you're the guy who wrote "Leonine nymph I rale, clog, and suffer/ brain cramps.../ She is anti-hypnotic skin and teeth./ She is eye-strain under weathermap gazes./ She is Atropos granting a preferable deal." We assume that by *rale* you mean *rail*: to speak bitterly, inveigh, or complain. Just as we are guilty of raillery, and of ragging on poets, young and old. Be vigilant.

DEBORAH CONWELL, CENTRAL CITY, KY: So you're the titian-haired scourge of your poetry group? How wonderful that one of your fellows wrote a poem likening you to "a pint of spoilt milk!" Short and stinky? Your poems aren't, even the ones about winged olives and sheep, etc. No one says "whee!" with as much authority as your "bold" and "spunky" olive! And the bacchantes do dance about, now that you mention it! What else might they do? Tear their children limb from limb? Whee!

MICHAEL McNEILLEY, OLYMPIA, WA: Send "Sluts of Titan," and we'll talk.

WILLIAM OREN, BLOOMINGTON, IN: The gentle semi-colon, elegant mark that made possible the works of Jane Austin, essential to the construction of a Gogolian sentence, can prove to be quite clumsy when used too often in a short lyric poem, though your use of it in "*Winter* was terrible and long;" may have been calculated to evoke a Great Books atmosphere. "Winter was terrible and long; suicide; a dish/ of strawberry prints/ and a tin pitcher in it/ ... Christ's soul is a fertile thing;

umbilical of a virgin;/ he bursts hymen and tomb door in one;" But don't you mean to say *umbilicus*, not *umbilical*, Christ being the being attached to the cord, and not the cord itself?

LOIS MARIE HARROD, HOPEWELL, NJ: What exactly do you mean, "a black and white beach/ covered with rocks the size of bread"? What bread? Rocks the size of hunks of pumpernickel, or slices of Wonder? Maybe matzos, or baguettes? Chapati, soda bread, onion rolls, pita? What? *Bread* is like *God*: the word denotes a myriad possibilities, unless you're a monotheist. Maybe you mean *bread* as in *money*. Rocks the size of spare change, rolls of twenties, stacks of hundreds … no, rocks the size of Fort Knox … oh, *now* we get it. These breadrocks are to be left to the imagination; happily *it* can enrich the most sterile diction.

LISA COOPER, TUCSON, AZ: "I was happy to receive 11 copies of the most recent issue … but I'm a little confused about just why I received all these copies when my poem doesn't appear in any of them." Well, Lisa, like so much in life, publishing in E.C. is an exciting gamble, and it looks as though our capricious mailing list is paying off like a Biloxi slot. Exciting, but not the big win junkies dream of. Be patient, and one day soon your box will be crammed with Corpses sporting your name (O happy day) in the *table of contents*, and your immortal poem inside.

TOM HANSEN, ABERDEEN, SD: In terms of the gross-out spectrum, on which the marriage of Rush Limbaugh by Judge Clarence Thomas to an aerobics instructor Rush met by computer falls near the utterly nauseating end, your "Spring Thaw" is a wee but wise gem of the merely offensive: "Each day as the snow melts,/ brown tubular turds emerge,/ but what we actually see, what seems,/ is snow staying the same/ while these dark disturbing deposits/ rise up out of the snow—/ mute and faintly malodorous felons/ breaking the law of gravity/ in the broad light of day… / So there they lie. Or there they sit—/ stubby little fingers of filth/ severed, it seems, from a family of excremental giants;/ every one of them, pointing at me … And what can I do but confess?/ I am the one whose dogs did this …" That's poetry, man, no shit, and we're moved by almost anything "… that is rank and raw/ and assults our too-timid senses …"

SCOTT GRUNOW, CHICAGO, IL: All poets should mourn "The Death of Woolworth's." There is perhaps no atmosphere more cogenital to a young poet's musing than Woolworth's lunch counter, where, fed on grits and grilled cheese sandwiches, the dreamer can inscribe at peace amongst the "… dishtowels beige roosters blue/ geese pink hearts and Welcome Friends Home Sweet/ Home 12-dishcloth package Gala paper/

towels Vanity Fair party napkins orchard garden/ potpourri carpet/ cleaner piney Lysol twist/ tie garbage bags ..." It is a bit of paradise lost.

MATTHEW LIPPMAN, BROOKLYN, NY: Eats pigs's blood at breakfast with Che Guevara and some monkeys in the East Village while waiting to die inside a husky virgin.

WILLIAM BURROUGHS, KANSAS CITY, MO: "Junk is the ideal product ... the ultimate merchandise. No sales talk necessary. The client will crawl through a sewer and beg to buy...The junk merchant does not sell his product to the consumer, he sells the consumer to his product. He does not improve and simplify his merchandise, he degrades and simplifies the client" (from the introduction to *Naked Lunch*, 1959). Mr. Burroughs is currently a TV shoe salesman selling two-hundred dollar sneakers. It's a job, but not *The Job*. Hard to figure in light of his avowed understanding of "the Algebra of Need." His pitch these days: "The purpose of technology is not to confuse the brain, but to serve the body." They're just shoes, Bill, *shoes*, and they cost an obscene amount of money and kids kill and steal and deal dope to get them and since when is technology benign and the future of mankind gloriously athletic? My kid says your Nike ads "blow goat." Big chunks.

MARK TERRILL, WACKEN, GERMANY: Speaking of spewing, "Puke Poem" says a lot about your ten years in Germany: "... if I could puke/ and it could be a poem/ this would be it/ a Technicolor Rorschach/ of existential despair/ splattered in the middle/ of this poisoned land/ ... where the sun never shines/ and Heinz rides his tractor/ back and forth forever ..." Sounds just like America, where catsup is a vegetable.

PETER P. KAWIAK, ROCHESTER, NY: First O.J. poem of the season, but not the last.

LARS ADAM JOHNSON, SAVANNAH, GA: The road to Hell is paved with a million felicitous adjectives. It starts early: your third grade teacher asks you to write a descriptive paragraph and explains that "adjectives make your writing more colorful." So your paragraph is full of "moist moss ... worn cobblestones ... crisp mountain water ... golden morning sun." The teacher is very pleased and declares your work to be "poetic." You become aware as you grow older that certain adjectives are too mundane to be *poetic*. Long, short, hard, soft ... have been done. So when you begin to write the kind of short-line prose people call poetry, you struggle to create fresh adjectives: "her desert canyon neck ... and gesso skin ... a dogwood petal flesh feel ..." The problem is that the more artful the adjectives become, the more artificial the expressions seem. The nouns you adorn so painstakingly are obscured. It's like make-up on a young girl: she is lovely by virtue of being a young girl; that essential loveliness, who she really is, is lost under eyeliner and mascara. There is another way to honor the nouns you subject to poetry, and you've stumbled on it on the poem "Never Alone." "I saw/ a herd of pigeons/ geyser into the wind,/ a tornado of leaves/ and wings,/ autumn reversed." Now this description is memorable, and meaningful. The trick is the verb. Your pigeons don't fly up like a geyser, they geyser, yes they do, and we can dig the originality of that construction. So the lesson is this: give your lines less make-up and more muscle. Let nouns be what they are; let them *do* extraordinary things.

LAWRENCE HERRICK FAHEY, MANCHESTER, CT: "Mah Muse Done Left Me (An Broke Mah Cheatin Heart): A Sestina" does things with dang, spit, bullshit, twang, pickup, and geetar that haven't been done since HeeHaw. Air you shore you're frum Connecticut?

GWEN GOSE, HOUSTON, TX: Will we really save trees by recycling your envelope?

CARY GRANT AND MYRNA LOY, IN THE MOVIES:
Myrna—"You remind me of the man."
Cary—"What man?"
Myrna—"The man with the power."
Cary—"What power?"
Myrna—"The power of hoodoo."
Cary—"Hoodoo?"
Myrna—"You do."
Cary—"What?"
Myrna—"Remind me of the man ..."

FRANCIS MORAES, ALOHA, OR: Your last submission, a poem entitled "Walking Home" was accompanied by a brief note expressing dismay that we had placed you in "some kind of purgatory of mediocrity" by our gentle rejection of an earlier poem. We must now try to remedy this lapse of discipline and give "Walking Home" a proper sendoff. The poem begins with this observation: "Always seeming more wise the/ Asian (Oriental really) old folk ..." How are the Asian old folk "Oriental really?" Is that really really or really ironic? Do you believe this, or does your use acknowledge the archaic nature and negative implications of the term Oriental? Do you say "Oriental really" because the folk are so old (antique really) that this significant adjective can accurately be applied to them? Or do you mean to imply that you have no sympathy for the use of the more contemporary term? We're not sure.

Neither are we sure who the Asian old folk are "seeming more wise" than. Non-Asian old folk? Young folk? You? Though the poem certainly seems to admire its subject (Asians?) it also contains some latent (racist?) romanticism that may not be entirely conscious. Don't you wish now you'd just called them Chinese-American senior citizens?

JENNIE TRIVANOVICH-NEIGHBORS, BOULDER,CO: If you really want to get to a place where "...the writing subject/ disappears," you'll have to stop writing about writing. Just because paralyzing self-consciousness is a post-modern malaise doesn't mean you have to catch it. Neither do you have to "know nothing at all" to escape intention. You have to know what you know, and understand that you know it. If you start from there, and don't get bogged down in "the act of writing" you can turn your anxiety into accuracy, which is all you should hope to bring to the work. No higher power is going to intervene and let you off the hook of subjectivity.

JULIE RHEINHART, INDIANA, PA: We found it striking that while you are not afraid to write about your "Bathroom Moments" your character is, as you reveal in the first lines of the story, afraid to pee in the shower, "fearing some sort of corrosive effect to her feet." She really should go for it.

JAMES WILLIAMS, MILWAUKEE, WI: Your cover letter serves as a lesson in being one's self: "1) My life's work is to prove to the world once and for all that articulation is hopelessly inferior to day-dreaming. I think my poems embody this notion. 2) I have never personally witnessed the sudden illumination of the pitch-black universe while perusing the words of Mike Topp. 3) I currently live at a place with llamas. I can assure you they are a kind and honest animal. There is no degree of deception in their behavior. If they dislike you they will simply and succinctly spit at you. Their aim is exact (yes, friend, I have stood in the divine shower of judgement and it smells like...sour sea grass). One day I plan to gut them and read the future in their entrails as the Maya once did. Imagine our pitiful lives laid out from birth to death in their gorgeous, shimmering bowels!"

BARNEY KIRBY, CATONSVILLE, MD: "I'm watching cable TV reruns of 70's sitcoms..." (Pastoral Fax). You and hordes of your brethren, for whom everything 70's has come to be metaphorically charged. Precisely what its characteristic tackiness and banality are metaphors for, beyond tackiness and banality, is more difficult to say. Your cable TV reruns of 70's sitcoms seem to stand for loneliness and boredom. In another poem. "The Space Between Us," Batman and Robin stand in for destiny and paradox and time and mortality and mythology and the antics of the gods. I fear it's too great a load of meaning for the dynamic duo to haul. Cut the cable; get out of the house; look for metaphors among the living, and stop lusting after your mother! Just kidding. "My Mother's Youth" was actually the best poem in the batch, starring Mom as she was in Catholic girls' school ... let's see, school-girl stands for nubile, right?

FRANK LENNON, COS COB, CT: Discovery is, we assume, what should be valued in poetry. The capacity to reveal, to invent, or to recognize singularities is what's important. Like what you do with a childhood memory in "Country Visit": "In 1936 in Newtown,/ Connecticut I discover:/ The Smell of Manure./ The Existence of Outhouses./ The Indifference of Cows."

MARK TERRILL, WACKEN, GERMANY: The little poem "And/Or" asks the big question of Jackson Mac Low's *Barnes 4*, a work "Derived from a chance operational mix of 8 chance-selected sentences by Djuna Barnes from 4 of her books, which was inputted to Charles O. Hartman's text manipulation program DIASTEXT (an automation of one of my diastic text-selection methods developed in 1963), the output of which was selected and/or rearranged to form the sentences brought into the quatrains of this poem by choices often influenced by chance." "What is it good for?" you ask, and who can blame you. What happens when, as you say, "your mission in life/ is to avoid the/ intructions of the/ author as ego/ and to foreground/ language as such ..."? The possibility of accident, coerced by relentless method, is somehow robbed of delight. These forced operations of chance produce a sterilized serendipity, the happy accidental tree lost in a manipulated forest of language as such. Language as such, it occurs to us, is much like mud as such. Only a god could breathe life into it.

SAN FRANCISCO CHRONICLE, SAN FRANCISCO: This is beyond cut-up, and no accident: "A vandal, apparently well versed in Poetry, is slicing through libraries in California's Santa Clara and Santa Cruz counties, chopping out the contents of volumes of modern verse ... Armed with a razor or matte knife, the unknown slasher has gutted books by such well-known modern poets as Philip Levine, David Shapiro, and Philip Booth ... In addition, the slasher also carved up three years' worth of a monthly publication called *Poetry Magazine*." We think there is a wolf among sheep, and he's thinning the herd.

HANS-JØRGENWALLINWEIHE, LILLEHAMMER, NORWAY: "Many of [my poems] are written while climbing in the mountains or being close to nature in other ways. Experiences from Africa, Scandinavia, Russia and North America have inspired me. 'Ladies Dressed for Grand Gala' is inspired by ladies working all along the North Norwegian coastline in fish delivery places—in the pale arctic light of February they are ready for the delivery of thousands and thousands of tons of fish from the big seasonal fishing of cod and pollack." We can relate. This sounds a lot like editing: "Using the knife/ Cod and pollack/ Whatever kind of fish/ Turned into filets ..."

MELODY OWEN, EUGENE, OR: "I am torn between being ashamed of writing poetry and wanting all the attention I can get. Please feel free to tear me apart or ignore me." My dear, surely there are other options. Perhaps we could bite you just a little? "the saint in my toaster" is a turn-on: "she is white, crispy white/ like john wayne's teeth./ only on sundays,/ when she rises above the warm/ orange glow,/ i can see she has something like strawberry jam/ on her hands ..."

SUMMER BONUS: WILLIE SMITH'S SHRIMP SALAD: "Get about two pounds of the biggest cocktail shrimp you can find. You'll also need two fresh lemons, two fresh limes, two bunches of radishes, a large bunch of cilantro, a hunk of fresh ginger root the size of your thumb, eight cloves of garlic, three fresh jalapeno hot peppers (one green, one black-green, and one parrot red is a nice mix) one green bell pepper, one red bell, one orange. Be sure and pick up a couple extra six packs and have the wife drive carefully. When you get home, amble out in the garden and pick some arugula, several leaves of fennel, a sprig of rosemary and any edible flowers Persephone is currently allowing to bloom. And don't forget the five tablespoons of extra virgin olive oil, supplemented by the six-ounce jar of Cara Mia marinated artichoke hearts you shoplifted unbeknownst to your conscious self. Be sure to use all of the citrus ... slice the ginger thin as an honest alibi. Chop the cilantro like a bunch of French counts back in good ole '92. Core the seeds and pulp from the bells. Slice all colors any-whichway, kinda small. Chop the jalapenos no bigger than your average dead roach ... peel the skin from the ginger root, mince into juicy pieces of pure yellow ginger, which you then toss into the bowl. BB gauge capers are optional, and quartering of the fresh radishes *de rigueur*."

DEATH WAITS, TORONTO, ONTARIO: Wait no more upon us, Death. Your devotion to the Portuguese modernist Fernando Pessoa endears you to a reader surfeited by disciples of The Beat Fathers, Allen, Jack, William ... and Buk. Would that young poets read more widely, and postured less familiarly! Pessoa (1888–1935) created a literary milieu peopled entirely by his psuedonyms, or heteronyms, as they were known by him, reasoning that "With such a paucity of literature as it exists

365

today, what can a man of genius do but transform himself—himself alone—into literature? ... what can a man of sensibility do but invent his friends, or at least his companions of the spirit?" (*Always Astonished: Selected Prose*, Fernando Pessoa, City Lights Books, 1988). It is dreary having always to be one's self, and the Self was especially unsatisfactory for Pessoa, who in 1910 described himself this way: "The whole constitution of my spirit is one of hesitancy and of doubt. Nothing is or can be positive to me; all things oscillate round me, and I with them, an uncertainty unto myself." Consequently he created the heteronyms: into one he put his power of dramatic depersonalization, into another his intellectual discipline, while the third, an uneducated shepherd, was given all the emotion Pessoa allowed "neither in myself or in my living. In me there appeared my master," as Pessoa describes the process. Does your own poem, "Re-Birth and Re: Death," herald the appearance of the heteronym "Death Waits"? "I too used to write when I was younger/ poems, stories, songs/ but eventually had to give it up/ move on/ because one day I thought/ no more words, silence, a real poem/ that didn't need words/ to fall back on ..." The lines recall Pessoa's declaration that in men, "hysteria assumes mainly intellectual aspect; so it all ends up in silence and poetry ..."

LISA MOORE, PORTLAND, OR: Isn't it funny how the debasement of the body can result in an elevation of prosody? Your "Poems for Bad Chris" prove that this is so, moving as they do from "you fuck me with disgust, as you might fuck/ a plaintive and slow-eyed cow" ("Pondering Bovine Damnation and Chris") to "God has planted His Word in my belly" ("Haruspication"). An haruspex, according to our *Oxford Concise*, is a soothsayer who divines through the inspection of the entrails of a sacrificial animal, the sacrificial animal in this case being you, disemboweled by lust. To fuck is human; to divine is, well, Divine.

JONATHAN TILL, BLUFF, UT: You mean to say Bubba *isn't* Buddha with the Ds turned backward?

TROY JOLLIMORE, PRINCETON, NJ: "On the street the Cadillac idles impatient/ and gray, and fat like a Buddha" ("January"). That you, Bubba?

BLAKE ROBINSON, WASHINGTON, DC: "Furthermore, the Apples/ stroll with Hercules" ("Small Things").

"Making vast apple strides towards," "The Poems."
(Ted Berrigan, *The Sonnets*, XXXVII).

366

NOAM MOR, BROOKLYN, NY: You must really hate us by now—we lost your poems, what, three years ago? Our mail is deeper than Pandora's box, and twice as dangerous. And now we don't publish the poems, works featuring, incidentally, Pandora, who's apparently a Jewish temptress, cavorting at the beach—no, she's your mother—"She recalls the summer afternoons of my first lost fight." Wouldn't that have been one summer afternoon? No matter. This is such a loving tribute, every mother should have such a son!

C.E. EMMER, BROOKLYN, NY: "I used to think it was sad that, given the inevitable differences in personal taste, everyone will find poems they can't enjoy. So much wasted paper, so many wasted hours! I *used* to think it was sad. Not anymore. When I showed 'Body Bag' to a coworker, he let me in on a little known secret of literature—a poetry transformation process—and gave me a free demonstration which left me completely convinced. The secret? Any flabby poem can be resuscitated with this simple technique: *read it out loud in the style of William Shatner.* It becomes a whole new poem! Corpse readers are instructed to give objective verification to the 'Shatner Process' by testing it out immediately on their most hated poem."

JANE REICHHOLD, GUALALA, CA: This lesson comes to the *Corpse* in the form of "A Letter from Jane," for which we're grateful, illuminating as it does a particularly dark episode in our recent past: "Since your readers seem to find pleasure in the dog fight between Mr. Dorn and Mr. Spitzer, and you yourselves are interested in collaborative poetry, I suggest you look up the old Scottish poetry form of flyting." The definition in *Princeton's Encyclopedia* gives the following: 'FLYTING, fliting. A poetical invective often a kind of intellectual game—in which two poets assail each other alternately with scurrilous, abusive verse, e.g., *The Flyting of Dunbar* & *Kennedie.* The form is especially typical of 16th-c. Scottish poets; despite the excess profanity, flytings have freshness, color and a rich power and are not infrequently superior in quality to English poetry of the same period ... Cursing matches in verse are found in other literature as well, e.g., Greek, Arabic, Celtic, Italian, and of course Provençal (see Tenzone).' "
Jane adds that "the French form died out when it was banned by law because of its excesses. It sounds like something to shoot for." The French, it must be noted, are fond of proscriptions regarding the use of their language. Americans, historically at least, are not so squeamish, our fundamental love of excess giving licence to unprecedented freedoms of speech and unrivalled bad manners. Long live the American art of invective! May it never be absent from these skinny pages.

SCOTT KEENEY, WATERBURY, CT: Reverence for authority and a desperate love of knowledge are the distinguishing features of a dedicated *Corpse* reader:...*I photocopied the E.C. logo and taped it to my wall last semester. And I'm still waiting for another letter from the psychodynamic Clayton Eshelman, just so I can go "Huh?" like I've never gone "Huh?" before. What I mean is that I learn a lot from the pages of E.C. and it's always good to be reminded, even if it is temporarily unsettling, how much I've yet to learn...I'm not being cute here. I don't want to be a writer and often try not to be.* Not cute is a good first step, Scott; indeed, you seem to be embarked on a path of real wisdom. The logos is an equivocal master; many are called, but few are any good. It is better to stick to the study of history or forestry or bacteriology in your interlude at Something-or-Other-State. Things that make you go Huh? are where it's at for developing character. And you've got good instincts: the old odalisque *Corpse* logo makes an outrageously provocative pinup ... interesting company for Betty, Farrah and Heather in the pinup pantheon. She'll be a collector's item if she survives (unsullied) your scholarly devotions. *Carpe cadavre*, man.

JOHN DONNE, LONDON, EARLY 17TH C.: Chicks in poems have always ruled: "I can love both faire and browne,/ Her whom abundance melts, and her whom want betraies,/ Her who loves lonenesse best, and her who maskes and plaies,/ Her whom the country form'd, and whom the town,/ Her who beleeves, and her who tries,/ Her who still weepes with spungie eyes,/ And her who is dry corke, and never cries;/ I can love her, and her, and you and you,/ I can love any, so she be not true."

MELODY HENRY, BROOKLYN, NY: More specifically, "Kim-Sari: eats one scrambled egg with mashed potatoes at 2 AM/ Wears her walkman in one ear all day/ Hates her hair and wears a baseball cap backwards in the house/ Complains of exhaustion/ ...Cries for no reason.../ Looks so much like a boy sometimes people stare..."

RACHEL LEVINE, NEW YORK, NY: "Young Hera looks like Ingrid Bergman;/ velvety doe skin, rose petals and gold" (*Crown Heights*, 1953).

MATTHEW MILLER, LINCOLN, NE: "Here comes the woman/ She's sparkling all right/...You will fuck me,/ she purrs with a deep and justified vanity/ (everyone knew it was her night). There she goes/ a ship making for unknown coasts, a sail/ sinking in the sumptuous silky sea/ a woman named Suzie with bright teeth..." ("American Style").

BLAISE CENDRARS, RIO DE JANEIRO, 1924: "There is no more jealousy fear or shyness/ Our girlfriends are strong and healthy/ They are beautiful and simple and tall/ And they know how to dress/ They are not intelligent women but they are shrewd..." ("South American Women," trans. by Ron Padgett, *Blaise Cendrars Complete Poems*, University of California Press, 1992).

RON KALMAN, CAMBRIDGE, MA: "It's been years/ since I last saw Annie/ in that basement bar/ her sun-bronzed hair/ cropped short/ when she cried/ "You scum"/ and stormed out..." ("Last of Annie").

JEFF HOFFMAN, BROOKLYN, NY: "You'll dream about Amy, in Seattle/ who just got her hair cut..."

STEPHEN ROBERT GIBSON, WASHINGTON, D.C.: "I am following her past the foundry to the piers/ To her long dark car which is parked by the harbor/ To the naugahyde seats and sleet covered windows..." ("At the End of 29th Street").

Okay people, assume the position. '96 doesn't look to have the same potential for pleasure that, say, '69 had. '96 demonstrates a posture of acute alienation: the 9 and the 6 stand back-to-back, facing out and away from each other, a lonely reversal of 69's intimate head-to-tail circle of mutual regard...

The consequences of such inauspicious positioning could be dramatic, particularly for that already ill-favored creature, the poet. Plagued in the best of years by feelings of isolation and sexual frustration, poets in 1996 will achieve peak production of both bad feelings and bad poetry (bad feelings invariably giving rise to bad poetry, and possibly vice versa).

The Bag has proven not to be the deterrent it was once imagined to be, that some in fact feared it *would* be, to the free and earnest expression of Misery and Hope. Though we had hoped that some individuals would opt to express themselves through dance, perhaps, or carpentry, the practice of writing, America's most popular unpaid activity, has prevailed, and the poems in our mail are as many as the galaxies we never knew were there until they fixed the Hubble Space Telescope's defective lens. *Billions and billions.* Enough to make a single entity feel like nothing, nothing, *nothing* in the vastness of creation. Enough to render one *completely* detumescent. We shall endeavor, of course, to keep up.

GEORGE BALMER, BERKELEY, CA: While we are "inundated by texts and manuscripts," a presentation like your *1995 Marketing Plan, Arts & Entertainment*, which includes a recording of your studio

369

performance of Coleridge's *Rime of the Ancient Mariner* ("a recital from memory, rather than a 'reading'"), chapters of your "eco-adventure novel" entitled *Condor Peak*, samples of your "contemplative prose poetry" ("If there are dark clouds—well then, there they are…") and a helpful questionnaire designed to rate your work and solicit comments and contacts…well, such salesmanship distinguishes *itself*, if not the works it represents, from the ordinary. Too bad your expertise as a management consultant in a giant accounting firm has been devoted to perpetuating the *Crime* of the Ancient Mariner, that is, boring young people to death in high school English classes. Your stated mission is "to help spark a revival of the tradition of the dramatic recital of classical poetry" and "to promote poetry as potential 'content' to new media technologists." Strange, because in the photo you include in the plan you look like a fairly young person yourself, leading one to wonder at the weird power of cultural conservatism to find fresh hosts. Stranger still is your apparent lack of adequate market research. Have you been to a poetry reading lately? They're wildly popular, and Populist, and nobody's reciting The Classics. What's really great that is that the stuff that People are reading and performing is gloriously outside the poetry market, whatever that is. Folks seem more interested in making their own rough, yeasty work than in buying the *Norton Anthology of English Poetry* variety. The Internet (new media technology?) is already every poet's playground: perhaps you should create a Classical Poetry home page, do some missionary work / market creation in cyberspace.

LEILA LORING, AMHERST, MA: Didn't homegirl Ms. Dickinson write a poem about a snake? She did love creatures; they make such nimble metaphors. Poets have always written about cats, for instance, presumably because they were around, and of course lady poets Marianne Moore and Elizabeth Bishop were more or less intimate with all sorts of animals, real and imagined. Snakes are the favored non-human subject these days; it's likely your teachers at the U. of Mass., James Tate and Dara Wier, have themselves crafted sensitive meditations featuring reptiles. Regrettably, we've had our fill of light verse about the nasty feeding habits of constrictors.

E. M. CIORAN: "Only a writer without a public can allow himself the luxury of being sincere. He addresses no one: at most, himself."

BOB "THE MAILMAN" DROJARSKI, ROCHESTER, NY: "Leafless trees hang from lifeless skies/ as vultures circle around evictions.// Mountains of snow, dotted with dirt/ melt to water over uncut grass.// Unraked leaf below rotted paper,/ pale garbage and everywhere dogshit.// It sticks to your shoes,/ pants and penetrates your being.// The smell of it in the air,/ Spring is here.// And ten times a day till April/ first from the face of fools/ I hear:// Hey Mailman,/ bet you're glad winter's over./ I nod and press on toward better days" ("Postal Spring").

All hail The Mailman! You're the real hero of the writing biz, you who tote the hopes and dreams of poets by the ton, you who must decipher the scrawled, often nameless s.a.s.e., forward and return and figure postage due, deliver both the letter of acceptance and the dread rejection. Everywhere writers live in fear and awe of you; likewise debtors. So, Bob, we honor you and your dedicated brethren. Thanks for everything. Sorry for all the crap you've been through on account of Art.

TED BERRIGAN: "We are drawn to shit because we are imperfect in our uses of the good" ("Spring Returns").

This seems a natural moment to announce what may be our only hard and fast guideline for submission: Work that comes to our post office box via certified mail, causing us to stand in a long and potentially dangerous line wondering if we are the object of alarming legal action, will not be read by our editorial staff; instead, such submissions will be ransomed for their safe return at a rate of ten bucks a page, payable by check or money order. No joke. This peculiar and abusive practice must be stopped.

DAVID CATRON, DULUTH, GA: "Glutted on the substance/ Of their rotting antecedents,/ Tumescent with plunder,/ The pied cannibals of May/ Erupt, fecund and voluptuous,/ Reeking of salacity/ And promiscuous rapine,/ Drunk with the vernal blaze" ("Les Fleurs du Mail").

ELIJAH CAYAK, ANACORTES, WA: "In July of 1995 ... I sent *Exquisite Corpse* a selection of four new poems. Today the poems came back, in the return envelope I had provided, along with a form rejection. Here's the rub: my poems have not been read. I have a way of folding them so I can tell whether or not they are unfolded and reviewed by the editorial staff ... *Corpse*, you may not know it, but you're dead meat."

Our editorial staff sometimes employ a tantric reading method that does not have as its goal the *unfolding* of the poem; rather, the folded poem becomes the focus of deep meditation, a state facilitated by repetition of the Bag mantra, *there's no place like home ... there's no place like home ... there's no place like home ...* in a process lasting up to twelve complete lunar cycles. It's an exhaustive and exhausting discipline, but powerfully effective: you report that during the months we held the poems, you "recirculated" them and found that two were "quickly" accepted by other publications. So, what's the beef?

Half of your stuff got published. How do you know that these successes are not attributable to our ministrations?

MICHAEL GREGG MICHAUD, LOS ANGELES, CA: Uh-oh. Now is the time for an ignorant editor to practice the discipline of chastisement by mortification, also known as eating crow. Indeed, we agree that Ms. Rosenthal is a "bonehead" with regard to the preparation of mincemeat, and that she was wrong in rejecting the poem "Mincemeat" on the grounds that "mincemeat is a purely vegetarian combo of chopped nuts and dried fruit, not chopped venison." No, she doesn't "feel so smart now." According to Ms. Rosenthal: "I blame my mother. She lied to me many years ago when I asked, before accepting a taste of pie, 'Mother, what's in mincemeat anyway?' She assured me that there was no meat, it was just a deceptive term like sweetbreads, which actually referred to the pancreas and thymus glands of a slaughtered beast, and they weren't sweet at all. Well. I should have checked the *Joy of Cooking* before I dissed a graduate of the Culinary Institute of America and his frontier-woman grandmother, the true subject of The Poem. My only mincemeat recipe calls for ten tons of submissions and a very slow fire. I don't know much about suet and 'venison neckmeat,' but I do know what the Dali Lama said to the hotdog vendor" ("Make Me One with Everything").

JOANNE KYGER, BOLINAS, CA: "I don't believe in any / of your gods or powers / It's all Bullshit/ / I don't even believe / in My powers or gods/ / Her dying words were / Keep the house clean" ("Untitled, but Unmistakably, Mother," 1975).

MARIE A. KAZALIA, SAN FRANCISCO, CA: We opened your envelope on Mothers' Day, and thought we'd forward your challenge to the New Daughters of Lexical Rebirth:

> saying PUSSY into a microphone/ in a bar/ audience/ porno-poetry-reading—/ …I wish she would come-up-with-/ stronger more assured words for what women have/ … two words/ all could use—straight-gay-trans-gender/ Tell men what we want our thing called—/ TWO TERMS/ One slang/ another for more formal writing/ something completely new …

New words can be the perfect gift, but remember: to censor language is human; to extend the lexicon, divine. For a word to lapse into disuse and this be forgotten is okay too, as one hopes will be the case with *snatch, beaver,* and perhaps the most awful, *vagina.* It's also important to remember that the words for what men have are not exactly flattering: *prick, cock, penis* … icky. Maybe, just maybe, to say *pussy* is not "to use a name men made up …" Maybe the words we use (*all* of us) reflect a reasonable fear of primal power, something as scary as God, but way more tangible and far more threatening. So let the girl say *pussy* if she wants to, or *cunt*, or *snatch* if she feels like uttering a frightful name. Let it be a battle cry, if that's what a woman wants. The fact is, words have an organic quality: they are born, they live (for better or worse) and, depending on their usefulness, they thrive or wither. Some words just get tired, or we grow tired of them. Some words, like *nigger* and *kike*, can lie buried for long periods of time and then emerge like toxic waste from a shallow dump, because they are still potent. To forbid a word is to increase its potential power. They die a permanent death only when we no longer need them.

WILLIAM BLAKE: "Welcome, stranger, to this place, / Where joy doth sit on every bough, / Paleness flies from every face; / We reap not what we do not sow.// Innocence doth like a rose / Bloom on every maiden's cheek; / Honour twines arond her brows, / The jewel health adorns her neck" ("Song by a Shepherd," 1787).

But of her cunt we dare not speak (ed.).

EVE BEDNAROWICZ, CHICAGO, IL: "Have you ever wondered what it must be like to be Madonna's baby, cells spawning a dim identity in the shadow of her vain capitalist heart?"

Quite frankly this is something we have never wondered, but now that the question has been asked, our first thought is, what a lucky kid, materially speaking. Certainly we feel no *pity and terror* in regard to the Child's future; surely it will be better off than the children of welfare mothers newly liberated from welfare dependency by the Republican Congress. Madonna's baby can even attend a public school if that's what Madonna wants, because as alien as she may be, she's a U.S. citizen and her kid has the right to become (at least) semi-literate.
    Corpse correspondent Sam Abrams suggests that William Blake's "Holy Thursday" (from *Songs of Experience*) is a fitting tribute to America's "wise guardians of the poor":

> Is this a holy thing to see
> In a rich and fruitful land,
> Babes reduc'd to misery,
> Fed with cold and usurous hand?
>
> Is that trembling cry a song?
> Can it be a song of joy?
> And so many children poor?
> It is a land of poverty!

And their sun does never shine,
And their fields are bleak & bare,
And their ways are fill'd with thorns:
It is eternal winter there.

For where-e'er the sun does shine,
And where-e'er the rain does fall,
Babe can never hunger there,
Nor poverty the mind appall.

God bless the child that's got its own...

Eerily, we recieved a song of another sort; this from *Corpse* patron Lita Hornick, who it must be said has long been generously concerned with the welfare of artists and poets. Here she transports the innocent Blake to Park Avenue:

SONG OF EXPERIENCE

Her husband fell in love with the maid,
And didn't seem to know it.
Lunch at John Giorno's was terrific.
In company, food and conversation.
I ordered daytime and evening clothes from
    Geoffrey Beene.
They are feminine, fashionable and gorgeous.
The president's made it hard to pay my taxes.
I find him coarse and lower middle class.
I dreamed I was mistress to England's Prince
    Charles.
His highness treated me abominably.
Oh, Sunflower weary of time,
Who countest the steps of the sun,
Seeking after the sweet golden clime
Where the traveller's journey is done.

DAYVID J. FIGLER, HENDERSON, NV: "My mother wanted me to tell you that my first name was spelled differently in the issue (in which his work was published) than what she put on my birth certificate..."

Who was it that wrote so insightfully, "all things are tragic when a mother watches?" We're awfully sorry for the mis-identification. To make it up to you, we'll publish your most recent work in this very political Bag:

COLD WAR IS OVER

The cold war has ended
The former USSR now disbanded
This is great.
I knew President Carter's
boycott of the 1980 Olympics
would work.
Eventually.

HAZEL LEE, KAYE BACHE-SNYDER, ANN C. COOPER, ANTONIA GREEN, CLAUDIA LOGERQUIST, BOULDER, CO: Identity is an important issue for most authors, as we have seen, but collaboration would seem to call for some level of selflessness, an understanding that the individual will be subsumed in the interest of the work itself. So it goes against the grain to read the renga "Wildfire Season," "the product of five writers who meet once a week for a freewriting session," with initialled attributions attached to each link. We realize that this is not an uncommon practice, but still it seems wrong, as if the collaboration is fraught with insecurity, or anxiety of attribution. It implies competition, not co-operation, as if no one of you want to take credit for the whole, and might at any time take back her contribution. Undeniably, one-upsmanship is part of the pleasure of collaboration; each line acts as a provocation to the next writer, whether or not the response is consciously competitive; most of us want to be percieved as the best, the most original, the most lyrical, or cutting, or empathetic. Perhaps a new form should be invented, a new game for the poetry olympics: competitive renga, where the object is not to enhance, but to defeat the opposition.

LAST BAG: THE GIFT
Another wistful Autumn is past, and a period of dormancy, of long nights, of rest and restoration has begun. For Nature. For American consumers, however, this once peaceful cold-weather interval has become the designated *gift-giving season*, a time of plenty of credit and very little rest.

One could argue that a poem is a thing created by the poet as a thoughtful gift; meant to be presented, its content carefully selected, its elements formalized (after a fashion), a poem is a package, a token, an offering. Every poem is not, however, the product of a *gifted* poet, that is, one possessing a faculty miraculously bestowed, whose talent is a virtue emanating from heaven, or a *higher power*, whichever you prefer.

Of course, some poems make better gifts than others.

Receiving gifts is a always a risky business. What can you say when your great-aunt Jane gives you green sans-a-belt slacks or a "nice" clip-on tie? Or when your secret Santa at work presents you with a five-gallon drum of cheese-flavored popcorn and a Christian lite-rock CD? *Thanks. That is so thoughtful. I love cheese-flavor.*

A truly great poem, it could be argued, is a gift along the lines of a Trojan horse: sneaky, sophisticated, and loaded with well-armed, highly trained ideas bent on conquest.

Give us a Greek bearing gifts any day.

The golden rule for the recipient of gifts in most cultures is to be *gracious*, a condition commonly understood to mean *nice*. To be *gracious* really means simply to be merciful, if not actually *grateful*. A gift given sincerely should be *graciously* received, no matter how garish, or useless, or banal.

We try, really we do.

But have you never felt a twinge of resentment, a surge of impatience perhaps, when you're forced by convention to thank *graciously* some unfailingly cheap and unimaginative relation for yet another crummy box of Woolworth's handkerchiefs?

Wouldn't it feel great to say, graciously of course, *please don't bother next year*? Well, you can't. To refuse a gift (however polite the refusal, however token the gift) is forbidden by our social contract. Any such action is sure to excite the disapproval of your otherwise *terribly* gracious friends and family members.

It used to be that only the gods were gracious, and people didn't give each other gifts so often. Well, maybe you'd give your girlfriend a rabbit skin, or a pretty rock, perhaps some extra matzoh, but mostly people scrimped and saved and made offerings to the gods.

Offerings were supposed to be made with great humility, and even then the gods weren't obliged to respond *graciously*. They could refuse a gift on the grounds that maybe you didn't seem humble *enough*. They might even demand that you make a *sacrifice*, like an animal or two, or a wife, or your child. Tough customers, the gods. None of this *it's the thought that counts* baloney.

Grace and *mercy* really meant something in those days.

You'd never have offered a god any lame necktie or bottle of Chablis. The three so-called wise men brought the baby Jesus only the most rare and expensive stuff, and he was only the infant son of god. In the ancient world frankincense was more prized than gold. Myrrh, too. Quality stuff. Why don't Christians *really* emulate the wise men?

Times change, of course. Now the Bedouin who roam the biblical desert harvest all the frankincense they can use (the aromatic sap oozes from the bark of a scruffy-looking bush), but its market value has been, shall we say, substantially depressed since the birth of Christ.

The practice of holiday gift-giving in America has little to do with humility, or generosity, or the baby Jesus. It seems that our winter ritual has much more in common with the spirit of *potlatch*, an elaborate feast (big party) at which the host gives away his worldly wealth in the expectation that he will gain in doing so greater social stature. The host may even go into debt in order to give away more smoked salmon and abalone-shell bibelots than he actually owns.

Receipt of these gifts by his guests results in the creation of *obligation*, and reciprocal giving can become increasingly competitive, sometimes leaving even very wealthy families impoverished, and undermining the stability and productivity of the entire village. Definitely a case of too much of a good thing...

Should we feel obliged in some way by the sheer numbers of these many gifts? Must we be gracious in the face of *aggressive, coercive, competitive* giving? Or should we demand a sacrifice?

We'll offer instead this gift of advice: be selfish, be stingy, husband your strength. Put the lumps of coal life has given you under some pressure, and pray humbly for a diamond to form.

Surely, the gods will smile.

LETTERS

BURNS RAPS BAG

Your touch in BODY BAG is getting so gentle it's as if you've grown kind. I dearly hope not. My own venom when I see bad art scares my wife; she figures it's something personal. So I cheer when you're genuinely nasty, indefensible. I still think your typesetter should reserve the en-dash for series and so on, the little uses, and continue to use the hyphen (your ends of lines still have them) for a midtext hyphen. Interesting bodies (in their spaces and substances) in your two *New American Writing* poems. (Laura Rosenthal's Poems Not E.C.'s) It seems to me that Nancy Shaw (coeditor of *Writing* [Vancouver]) does something like it in her excerpted *Scoptocratic* in *Writing* 26. I could mail you a photocopy. First column this issue's BB (Lee Goldstein), either his or your "infractuosity" should be "anfractuosity." I believe the other's not a word. Maybe it's that you've begun, really, to talk to the people, the rejected authors. You've begun to help them. Encouragement replaces rude dismissal. You made my "Short Lines" look awfully good, even funny. I've written another, called "Celluloid," toward Leland Hickman in California,having a rough time now, blast it. I'm pleased to report numbers of my prep-school students have learned lots about power in verse from his recent *Slave Lake Suite*. What a loss, not to have him snarling on the front lines right now. Thanks for lots of good reading in EC, and those contemptible poems on page 4. My female students adored "Fuck Me." I was moved by Keenan's "L & H," Brown's "Stories," even "Eyeglasses." (I lost my Polish relatives in camps.) Nice to see the Terence Winch poems, not quite as plainspoken as his books, or is this not the dead accordionist? Early? Scott Preston is silly, pretending he wants Robin Williams to make pro-Modernist propaganda. That verse couldn't speak to discoveries in those students, and it's lovely and delicate that it's Whitman (no matter what Whitman) the parents and administration can't swallow. There's a place for the verse modernist propaganda tried to annihilate (because it was Father-opposition disguised as Motherloving). But all Preston's heard (from some hip teacher, I think—it looks as if he's vexed that everybody doesn't know this), that "Oh Captain, My Captain" (which he can't quote correctly) is a bad poem. To hell with him. His own prose staggers on two crutches— one, his own taste, which is spavined; two, the sophistication he learned from some Robin Williams type wherever he went to school. Does Preston think Ginsberg and Corso would rather talk to him than to Whitman? I imagine Preston in a supermarket in

379

GERALD BURNS

California, offended that the croissants are not French. Nor were meant to be. Only a jealous man drowns in those adjectives. I teach in a prep-school, approached that film with great caution, and loved it.

BURN BURNS

JEFF JOY

I was surprised, a little, by Gerald Burns' letter in issue 33. His whining about how the *Corpse*'s kindness toward bad art has replaced rude dismissal makes him look incredibly pompous: these glib pronouncements are encased in that letter after all—a letter which serves neither as a model of aesthetic form nor of logical consistency. Or, anyway, I'm not clever enough to see how letter art can so easily be differentiated from that art which Burns is reflexively oozing venom over. Bad art makes Burns scream, and, here he is, screaming about how lovely it is to be indefensible and nasty, and how much he hates Preston for writing nastily about a really bad piece of art (*Dead Poets' Society*). Is the problem that Burns has with Preston's otherwise excellent review simply that Preston was not acting indefensibly or irresponsibly enough? And why does Burns think that "Only a jealous man drowns in those adjectives"? I would say that Preston's dislike of *DPS*, its expensive and contrived fumigation, is well-placed. Equally peculiar is a fit of unintentional irony in which Burns offers that Preston's prose "staggers on two crutches," that his taste is "spavined" and is, furthermore, falsely sophisticated. Bad karma, perhaps? Maybe it is that Burns is simply too exhausted from venting his spleen to hold himself to his own standards. Now, I, too, appreciate the *EC*'s crankiness, but I hardly think that it is indefensible. Rather, this "nastiness" gains force because it is so justifiable. Nastiness can be liberating. Nastiness for the cause of a more desirable global poetry environment is eminently justifiable. On the other hand, indefensible nastiness, by definition, can create nothing good. But I do agree with at least one of the sentiments in Burns' letter: "To hell with him." In my agreement, however, I am careful to render the subject abstractly. How much is bus fare? How many steps must I take on this walk? How many angels are on the head of a pin? To all of these questions, the phrase makes a serviceable cry of emancipation, a reply with a full head of hair. Certainly more useful than all the rhetorical dribble-drabble with which we attack or defend art.

AQUINAS AGAIN

Let me drop this one on you: We are god's pets. Fat cats and dogs in the old man's house. As the rest of the house gets ratty from our claws and urine and spray the old man just feeds more and more wet food to us and we take it. Sometimes we fight. Sometimes we die. But god, even though he kicked us out of the living room, likes to have us around. He likes it when we rub up against him, warm the vacant half of the bed and meow for our food. The other things in creation, the trees and seas, the sun and soil, they are a lot like furniture. We wreck the furniture but god doesn't mind, he likes us. God is not dead. When he is dead no one will be able to open the cans of cat food and we will die. Nietzsche was just a tom cat. Nietzsche was one of god's favorites.

ERAN WILLIAMS

BODY BAG, CONT.

On your wish to see mortal women in Wilma Flintsone's wardrobe: have you forgotten about Nancy Reagan and her single-strapped sequin formalwear collection?

DONALD R. BLUMEN

CORPSE, THE DEVIL

I don't have much time, so I'll be brief. The main reason I've hesitated as to resubscribing to your magazine is that I'm torn as to its content. On the one hand you publish writers like Askari & Creeley, and others whom I find simply outstanding, and then you publish what seems to be outright pornography. I'm not as prudish as that sentence would erroneously indicate; I like my sex and love making (yes, there is a difference) as much as the next guy, but the articles you publish regarding this subject strike me in tones of kitsch. Maybe I'm getting old I don't know. Also, I suppose I should apologize to some extent for my earlier criticisms; after all, it is your magazine, and my democratic decision to buy and read it. And as this seems to be the central thesis of this discussion, I want to let you know that I have decided to subscribe again, because the sections of artful poetry I enjoy, I really do enjoy! But I must tell you there is no way in hell I would keep copies around the house if I had children in it! With this new term, I ask that I be sent a copy of the Nov. 94 issue (I believe that's #51, but I could be mistaken) and have

CHRIS TOLL

my new subscription updated to November of next year to compensate for my request. You're a strange lot, but I gotta' hand it to you, in many ways you kinda sorta really know what you're doing. As the saying goes, "you have to give the Devil his due."

NEW MATH

LEE GOLDSTEIN

Thank you for sending me gratis two copies of EC where I appear in the body bag qua "Math Poet." This does help for my post-adolescent identity crisis, but don't you think that appellation is a contradiction in terms? I mean most mathematicians hate anything near philosophy and mathematicians, if they compose poetry, like to write "bad" or silly poems. This is because mathematicians, better than anybody else realize how attractive stupid thinking is on the planet and mathematicians generally pick some subject, e.g., philosophy, psychology, poetry to be stupid (with conviction) in. For instance, take Stephen Hawking—as a philosopher. Some utilitarian mathematicians are also "stupid" about useless mathematics, and vice versa. My personal stupidity concerns meaning—a leftover from my positivist days. That I pretend meaning in my poems is because, although I am Jewish, I never learned to speak Yiddish. Mathematicians who I know ain't much interested in my poetry it seems (fear of noological contamination, I suppose), and although I can't be certain, I believe I've lost a number of former math professor friends because of these poems. They might, for instance, believe that I am thinking of things which are "oblivionizing" relative to them and thus against their positivist camp, and in an age of polarization in this country, this isn't correct. That for those un-nyches, caught in the middle for any reason, woe to them, for they needs must do the: "danse lethe."

NEO-HOODOO SUPPORT

ISHMAEL REED

I saw a review of *The Stiffest of the Corpse* in the *Village Voice*. Don't let the *Village Voice* shit you. Their record on reviewing books by blacks and others is terrible! They're hypocrites. See my letter about gender supremacists—white feminists who Uncle Tom to anglo men but give us the shaft.

LETTER NOT SENT

Dear *Voice*;
When it comes to assessing misogyny in the works of male writers, the *Voice* employs a double standard. Over the

past few years, black writers like James Baldwin, William Demby, John A. Williams, John O. Killens, Wole Soyinka and I have received a drubbing from your critics for our alleged misogyny, while white male patriarchs receive generous praise, or gentle rebukes for theirs, in a book review which is increasingly beginning to resemble one of those unreadable publications you find in the lounge of some permanent graduate school.

Barry Hannah's *Boomerang* is a racist and misogynist feast, yet your review didn't include the kind of venom accorded black male writers. Mr. Hannah, who writes very well, enjoyed his standard blacks-in-awe-of-Cadillac joke so much that he repeated it (pages 65, 137).

I guess that in a book review managed by feminist good-old-girls, it pays to be a good-old-guy.

WORD BALLOONS: PETROLEUM FUMES

What I really like about your publication is that I don't have to see on half the pages people getting younger and better looking by smoking and drinking while driving next year's Kamiakazi, so my renewal check is enclosed, money and mouths being what they are.

While we're talking, I might as well tell you about the oil spill. It is much worse than you think. When it happened, none of those here knew what to do so they shipped in a lot of experts who turned out to be specialists in rhetoric, and the air became filled with word balloons along with petroleum fumes. Money flowed like wine, and though not much oil was retrieved, coastal bank balances swelled. 18´-20´ skiffs with operator brought/brings $600–$800 a day, and they go out with dipnets and 5-gal. buckets in hundreds and hundreds of square miles of the shit and earn their pay. My wife took the job of boom monitor, which meant that she looked at it twice a day and was paid $600. After three days she quit in disgust. We have little money, but it, like status and power, is a whore, and you might say she wanted to retain her amateur status. What will come of it? Right. The Good Old Boys will stick together, paper will be passed around, and our precious and only world will be further hurt. We accept this for we cannot get along without our precious wheels, in spite of the fact that most people in the world will not ever own an automobile, and they are not all 3rd world anorexics either. We need to turn our thinking around, and to do so we elect Margaret Thatchers and George Whatsiznames. This is not bitterness—I'm just reporting.

And the North Slope crude, two million gallons a day, continues to flow out of the Port of Valdez.

DAVE NIXON

383

THE INNUENDO IS REALITY,
OR, UNMODERN OBSERVATIONS ON DEFINITION

WILLIAM LEVY

During the Gulf War I received correspondence from a publisher in San Francisco and a poet from Alabama both beating their breasts about "fascism" taking over America.

I laughed.

I laughed again when, this autumn, a Midwestern magazine editor wrote me a postcard with the imperative message: "It's becoming more and more fascist out there."

Politically correct rapists? The good genocide? *Quality Time* as the title for a child porn publications?

"O heavy lightness! serious vanity!/ Mis-shapen chaos of well-seeming forms!/ Feather of lead, brightsmoke, cold fire, sick health!"

Although I admit limiting my perusal of the capricious and aggressive daily press to obituaries and the flics on telly—its only non-fiction sections—I wasn't aware that in the States there was only one political organization and all further elections had been cancelled under the beneficent premise, as Mussolini claimed, "Voting has humiliated the nation for decades."

That there was a judiciary with an ideologically directed unitary agenda.

No one told me America had re-introduced obligatory military conscription with a view to taking a flutter with foreign adventures, and that all married women were being asked to volunteer their gold wedding bands toward this effort.

Americans who visit me haven't mentioned they required an exit permit to leave the country.

Or, by "Fascism"—note use of upper case here—is it meant the public transport is inexpensive and runs on time, the Mafia has been crushed, "secondary schools, higher and lower to be mainly classical," the currency stabilized? Really! Is there no shame?

Some folks just can't give up blowing smoke. When I first settled in Holland, circa a quartercentury ago, there was this cute political party, with a small representation in parliament, calling itself *ARP*—Anti-Revolutionary Party. They too had long memories. They too would maybe forget, but never forgive. The revolution they were against was the French one of 1789.

It seems as if this code word "fascist" is being used as name calling merely to demonize one's opponents, freeze dialogue. Stop thought. Trivialize history. Blur distinctions. A kind of naa, naa, naa, naa, naa, naaa; I want twice as much peace as you do. Much the same as others who yelled "Commie" when faced with income tax, gun control, de-segregation. Having quickly exhausted their wit, someone once observed, this kind of person is reduced to raillery. There's nothing worse/ than sticking out your tongue at a nurse.

They are the devil persons. They, the enemy, are "out there."

Recently, in conversation, one well-known American novelist spoke about being "professional" to mean competently performing subservience to an employer—i.e. playing for money, rather than its intended high-minded opposite, to profess and declare one's faith in transpersonal values. How could I be surprised then when she signed on with a sweet-talking Dutch editor who drunkardly, foaming at the mouth, heckled an Allen Ginsberg reading by screaming, again and again: "Get off the stage you filthy kike faggot!"

Not knowing the meaning of words spawns a multitude of maladies.

In a thin, frightened shrill voice, another established NY writer kept refering to "anarchy" as being synonymous with confusion. She was in analysis and couldn't deal with a society without rulers, anarkos.

Is there any forward movement, albeit helical, without precision in terminology? Until 1961 the Jesuits used Latin at conferences for the expressed practical purpose of having continuity of definition. Even the most extreme abstract painters never claimed orange was violet, or green made up from mixing red and black.

Unlike many other long-time *Exquisite Corpse* fans, I enjoyed enormously the change in title. I laughed. Once "Normal" was inserted into the postal address, the command to delete "Exquisite" from the logo couldn't be far behind.

I guess you've heard this one:

What does a dyslexic insomniac agnostic do?

He lies awake in bed all night wondering about the existence of Dog.

THANK YOU FOR LETTING US LOOK AT YOUR WORK

Sometimes you know, as soon as you see someone, that he will play no significant part in your life. We think a similar thing is true for editors. We fear the portions of your work that would make Housman's neckfeathers restless here are few. Where are the lighthouses of your telepath? No new neurorhetorical pathways here, no psychic jumpstarts, only mock introspection. That you could have licked the stamp surprises me; was it your own spit? After reading your work, I feel that to divide authors into those who write to please themselves and those who write to please others is a mistake, for you

P. SCHNEIDRE

seem to be writing to annoy use. There is nothing you have
written that would not have gone without saying. Words
eat from your hand, but only tame ones. In other words,
this may be as far as poetry can go before breaking up into
truth, or packing material.

FEETS DO YOUR STUFF!

ANSELM HOLLO

*The Direction of Poetry: An Anthology of Rhymed and Metered
Verse Written in the English Language Since 1975* edited and with
an introduction by Robert Richman. Houghton Mifflin Company,
Boston, 1988.

Mr. Robert Richman, the editor of this anthology, comes to
us from an alternative universe populated by creatures such as "the
general reader," "unspecialized readers," and "consistent users of
the metrical foot." A former editor for Random House and Harper
& Row, he has caused Houghton Mifflin to publish his favorite
items of "rhymed and metrical verse written in the English language
since 1975." All by himself, he has also written an introduction to
them, by far the most grotesque text in the book.

In his quaint manifesto, Mr. Richman informs us that "after two
decades of obscure, linguistically flat poetry, there has been a decisive
shift. In both the United States and Britain, narration, characterization,
and perhaps most significantly, musicality are showing new vigor."

"Musicality" turns out to consist of the "use of metered language.
This is the principal feature of poetry here, and the central trait of the
'movement' being surveyed in this book.

The movement spearheaded by Mr. Richman—let us call it The
Metered—is now in open revolt against "the free verse orthodoxy that
has reigned for the last twenty-five years in the United States and Great
Britain."

Note the subtle escalation: as Robert Richman warms to his subject, Britain becomes Great, two decades become twenty-five years. No
longer will The Metered let the Obscure Flat Orthodox Establishment
(or OFOE, analogous to ZOG) get away with those "countless critical
judgments, expressed in the sixties and seventies, of the death of metrical
verse."

But sadly, the OFOE's philosophy "has insinuated itself so deeply
into our respective poetic cultures that the entire conception of form has
been corrupted," leading to such decadent mutations as Robert Lowell's
(not to mention Ted Berrigan's) sonnets or John Ashbery's (not to mention Gerry Gilbert's) "unmetrical couplets"—"hybrid verse, in

which the pretense of a traditional form is used without employing any of its technical attributes."

We'll find no such corrupt hybrids here: "the consistent use of metrical foot... unites the poets in this anthology... stress and syllable-stress verse are... the dominant metrical forms the reader will encounter in these pages," and none of the folks who "have an ambivalent attitude toward meter, moving in and out of it in their poems."

I regret to inform all you Amy Clampitt fans that you won't find her here. She just isn't living up to Richman's Metrical Standard: "Many readers view Clampitt as a formalist poet. In truth, Clampitt seldom writes metrically." But that's not all: "just as problematic... is the conflation in many of her poems of 'high' poetic language and a kind of surrealism that was popular in the sixties and seventies."

God, yes, those were hard times. But now, at the onset of the Metrical Millennium, we can blissfully soak in "the headlong rush of strong stresses," "brimming with drama," "appealing and accessible... euphonic affirmation." Some instances:

A woman I have never seen before
Steps from the darkness of her town-house door
—Richard Wilbur

Over the rim of the glass
Containing a good martini with a twist
I eye her bosom and consider a pass
—Anthony Hecht

Back in our silences and sullen looks,
for all the Scotch we drink, what's still between's
not the thirty or so years, but books, books, books.
—Tony Harrison

I am, as much as anyone,
the golden beast who staggers home,
in June, beneath the yearning trees.
—Andrew Hudgins

Always he hoped he might deserve a Plutarch,
Not to be one posterity forgot.
—Donald Davie

This is, of course, unfair. There's some entertaining and unpretentious verse here, e.g. James Fenton's "God, A Poem":

I didn't exist at Creation,
I didn't exist at the Flood,
And I won't be around for Salvation
To sort out the sheep from the cud
(etc.)

Rollicking stuff, sort of like the Intelligent Man's Cowboy Poetry. Elizabeth Bishop, Anne Stevenson, Fleur Adcock, and Daniel Mark Epstein manage to appear unobstrusively metered yet not pompous and even dare light up their lines with the odd flash of intentional humor.

Notable omissions, to this reader's mind, are Stevie Smith—whose work only reached these shores in 1976 with the publication of her *Collected Poems*—and Edward Gorey; but perhaps, like Philip Larkin's executors, they or their representatives found Richman's style a little hard to stomach. A footnote to the introduction informs us that "Farrar, Straus and Giroux ... refused to grant permission to use three of Larkin's uncollected poems in this anthology. This is unfortunate, as Larkin's last poems were to be given a central place in ... *The Direction of Poetry.*" Whatever the reasons for the refusal, one feels it would have pleased the curmudgeon ("bloody pretentious Yankee arseholes").

And while I'm considering "rhymed and metered verse written in the English language since 1975," which I won't be doing much longer, I would like to point out to Mr. Richman one more and truly grave omission—his failure to include, in its entirety, Tom Clark's wonderful sequence *The Mutabilitie of the English Lyrick* (Berkeley, Poltroon Press, 1978), in which Clark boils down and rewrites some perfect gems from that august body of verse:

George Crabbe 1754–1832: Late Wisdom

We've trod the maze of error round,
Long wandering in the winding glade;
And now the torch of truth is found
But alas! from my brain has strayed.

Or:

Walter Savage Landor 1775–1864: Rears

Rears, many vari-shaped rears,
Some of them slung low, & saggy, & some firm, & fine,
Have passed before me over the years,
But none superior to thine.

The back cover of *The Direction of Poetry* quotes May Swenson, a senior participant in this show of strength by The Metered: "It is a good deed to publish such an anthology, signaling the swing away from minimalism and other fads—fads that amount to anti-poetry. Just what we need now."

Well, it's good to know that the Swensons and the Richmans, wherever they may exist, are getting what they need: to this unrepentant minimalist and lover of anti-poetry, most of Mr. Richman's sampling of The Metered has the look, feel, smell and sound of a showroom full of over-priced imitation "period" furniture—with Mr. Hilton Kramer's right-wing kulchural journal (*The New Criterion*, of which Mr. Richman is the Poetry Editor) prominently displayed on the magazine rack in the "reproduction" drawing room.

I guess I'm just not Post-Modern enough, if that term is taken to mean universal acceptance of, and tolerance for, snootily sentimental kitsch. Nor Buddhist enough to view Richman propaganda for these nostalgic neoconservative notions with total detachment: their revisionist and purist tone reminds me too much of the Third Reich's dogmas on Form and Beauty...And rather makes me feel like the protagonist of another rhymed and metered entry in Tom Clark's lovely antidote to this book:

Algernon Charles Swinburne 1837–1909:
The Rebel Against Dogs

Soaring through wider zones that pricked his scars
With memory of the old revolt from dogs,
He reached a middle height, and at the stars,
Which are the brain of heaven, he looked, and sank.
Around the ancient track marched, rank on rank,
The army of unalterable paws.

THE SONNET LIVES

DAVID ZAUHAR

Finally got around to reading Vol 7, #'s 1-5. I liked it again, especially Hollo's review of *It Came from the Tar Pits: An Anthology of Rhymed and Metered Verse Written in the English Language Since 1975*. I found the book in a store last weekend and read Richman's introduction in spite of Hollo's warning about R's use of such concepts as "dominant metrical forms." For Richman and the *New Criterion* in general it seems that poetic meters and parking meters serve the same purpose: regulating where people put things. While doing some random reading and rereading this past week, I found what is probably the best defense of the sonnet in the modern era. It comes from Berrigan's *Sonnets*, and it goes something like this:

xv

In Joe Brainard's collage its white arrow
He is not in it, the hungry dead doctor.
Of Marilyn Monroe, her white teeth white-
I am truly horribly upset because Marilyn
and ate King Korn popcorn," he wrote in his
of glass in Joe Brainard's collage
Doctor, but they say "I LOVE YOU"
and the sonnet is not dead.
takes the eyes away from the gray words,
Diary. The black heart beside the fifteen pieces
Monroe died so I went to a matinee B-Movie
washed by Joe's throbbing hands. "today
What is in it is sixteen ripped pictures
does not point to William Carlos Williams

Berrigan's representational collage sonnet [representational in the old sense of that word: mimetic: in that it recreates on the page the thing it describes, in this case a two dimensional collage from Joe Brainard (someone help me, I'm starting to sound like a fucking language poet)... anyway, if you take this poem and rearrange the fourteen lines so that line one is followed by line fourteen, which is followed in turn by lines two and thirteen, and so on, you get a linear sonnet:

In Joe Brainard's collage its white arrow
does not point to William Carlos Williams.
He is not in it, the hungry dead doctor.
What is in it is sixteen ripped pictures
Of Marilyn Monroe, her white teeth white-
washed by Joe's throbbing hands. "Today
I am truly horribly upset because Marilyn
Monroe died, so I went to a matinee B-movie
and ate King Korn popcorn," he wrote in his
Diary. The black heart beside the fifteen pieces
of glass in Joe Brainard's collage
takes the eyes away from the gray words,
Doctor, but they say "I LOVE YOU"
  and the sonnet is not dead.

The sonnet lives, and it was not killed off by William C. or by anyone else writing in what the *New Criterion* once called "decadent free verse" (opposed I guess to the decadent expensive verse of *NC*). Anyway, Hollo already demonstrated that Richman is a card-carrying Knucklehead so there is no need for me to continue to heap abuse on this man who does for poetry what anthrax does for cattle (oops, forgive me that one last cheap shot).

LETTER FROM NEW HEAVEN

You have to hate it to be able to love it properly. Poetry, I mean. It shows shine (dear Gertrude Stein) only when you approach it "with a fine contempt for it" (dear Marianne Moore). Piety kills. And therefore a toast to Robert Richman's *Direction of Poetry*, which calls itself "an anthology of rhymed and metered verse written in the English language since 1975." For the purity of its piety this book can have few rivals. The introduction indicates Dunce Richman's view that the best poets today are "united in their use of metered language." Then you turn to the contents of the volume, and you find a plentiful amount of free verse. Looks like the editor doesn't know his ass from his trochee. Another beauty is Mary Jo Salter's *Unfinished Painting*. This one is almost too good to be true. "Duty is Truth, Truth Duty," she writes, and that's just one example of her wit, word play, erudition, and cleverness. Really her poems could go on birthday cards, they're so universal, all about the tender feelings a young mother has for her infant daughter, her husband, her dying mother, etc. If you planned to commit suicide, you'd want this poet for a friend, since she'd magnanimously forgive you (see her "Elegies for Etsuko"). That is what is meant by moral depth. I cannot recommend this book too warmly. And life couldn't be better. No more poems about pussy juice, what we want are poems about Emily Dickinson's writing table! Poems we can honestly despise. Pious lime temples of reaming that make us want to commit vandalism. And we do, which is one reason why we write, instead of jacking off in front of the mirror or rubbing oil on the statue's tits, bringing her back to life. Onward!

RUSSELL KOLNIKOV

391

JAMES SCOFIELD

I am a new subscriber, and would be grateful if you would listen to a few comments. First, there is something I like about Laura Rosenthal: She is honest, straightforward, and clearly cares about poetry and the *Corpse*. Keep her, you are lucky to have her. What makes the *Corpse* so readable is a piece like Deborah Salazar's "The Bad News Is the Bad News Is the Same": She too is honest, open—what she shared was very moving. I very much enjoyed "An Evening with Salvador Dali and Dylan Thomas," it was a fascinating peek back into time, a real look at real artists. (When was the last time you read a poem and felt "my skin horripilated, goose bumps all over and hairs bristling, etc…"?) And that brings me to the poems. I am sorry, but as poetry they are usually awful. My concern is that the *Corpse's* commitment may not be to poetry *as an art form*, but to verse that articulates its political and philosophical agenda. That is, today, a universal manipulation of the tradition of poetry. And one of many reasons poetry has lost its memorability, and its power to explore an unseen reality. Perhaps it would be more accurate to place these pieces under the heading: VERSETALK, or, sometimes, VERSEGAB. There is:

"I've been given the finger/ numerous times"

And there is:

"Each night he kneels, each night the Dark kneels with him."

That is what we have lost. There is much to be happy about with *Exquisite Corpse*: There is Laura, a deep concern for this time, a hatred of hypocrisy, much, much caring. May it go on.

EDITOR'S RESPONSE: *We would like to open Mr. Scofield's question to our readers. Is the poetry in the* Corpse *motivated by agendas other than poetry? We think not. Being given the finger numerous times seems to us as lyrically dramatic as kneeling with Mr. Dark, a rather diluted personage since the dissolution of evil and the decidedly milky chiaro-oscuro of the electric night. Mr. Dark is, it seems to us, rather gray these days, and kneelers are vastly outnumbered by finger-givers.*

ON SCOFIELD'S CHALLENGE

I think poets should avoid words like "art," "universality," "enduring," etc. *"Poetry as an artform"* is a particularly lethal mixture. I also think "I have been given the finger/ numerous times" is more lyrical than "Each night he kneels, each night the Dark kneels with him." Kneel for what? To give a blow job? Does anyone kneel for anything else these days? How about: "Each time he gives a blow job, the night kneels with him. The night bites under the neon lights"? Does Claudius trying to kneel and ask forgiveness from heaven have anything to say to our religious sense or is it a cheap shot at creating poetry? I think one should be aware of the phony religiosity (suggestions of humility, repentance, confession, etc.) buried in a line like "Each night he kneels..." A poem should explode assumptions buried, hidden in the poetic aura created by vague, not-quite-believed-in phrasing. Whose line is "Each night he kneels..." anyway?

EDITOR RAPPED, POETRY UPHELD

It is right, and I accept that a critical comment should be thought about and commented on by your readers. That's OK. But your use of the phrase "Mr. Dark," is flippant and condescending. I have no desire to get into a battle with a man and a publication I both like and respect, but that response was not you at your best. The phrase diminishes the line, it diminishes the issue, it diminishes you. The issue is not the line "Each night he kneels, each night the dark kneels with him." But your comment unfairly skews (are you more comfortable with "screws?") the debate in that direction. The issue is not lyricism, or its absence. The issue is should poetry again see its primary vocation as the *intuitive* exploration of reality, and return to a preoccupation with fable, ceremony, passion, and mystery. The use of verse (which does not reach the level of poetry), or lines of prose (broken or not) to articulate the events of the day can be entertaining. It can clarify the political, sociological, psychological issues of our time, but rarely illuminate them. I see in most modern poetry an elaborate version of the occasional poem, and a refusal to move off the surface plane. In good faith these writers want to move closer to the truth; but we come closer to the truth in fiction than in nonfiction, as there is greater liberty for reaching the final circumstance. When poetry limits itself to a grappling with the known, an exploration of the perceived, (rather than an exploration within dimensions of

393

reality not accessible to the reasoning faculty), it fails to realize that this can lead only to denotation, and it's connotation that gets to the unseen reality.

Poetry is mated to the unknown. It has a primal relationship to magic, more a relative of mathematics than prose, in that it is utterly dependent on symbols to realize its nature. We must come back to a deep respect for artifice. For artifice is the tool, the power used to break through the surface tension that exists between the reality of our senses, and that implicated, or enfolded reality waiting for us on a nonmanifest level. Not all poems chosen by *EC* are subject to this concern. However, enough reveal a consistency of theme, tone and style to suggest a predilection if not a prejudice. For what? An ultraliberal perspective on poetry and other matters? Maybe. But that is alright. We all have agendas; but a state of mind that denies any agenda is entirely dangerous. I know; I know how humorless I sound. I love this art. I came to poetry late, its discovery has been the second greatest gift in my life. Not everything lends itself to parody, and the stakes are high in this debate. There is in people an immense hunger for drama, the larger themes, and today's "finger-pointing" poetry adds to our exhaustion. Today many people will choose to die for want of what one true poem would bring them.

REPORT FROM THE FIELD

KAREN CHASE

THIS IS WHAT IT'S LIKE GOING TO A LANGUAGE POETRY POETRY READING. For the first 30 seconds, you go over in your mind whether you're exhausted and that must be why you can't concentrate. You remember you're not tired.

For the second minute, you decide that concentrating will require a great deal of effort, but it's worth it. You tell yourself to muster all your intellectual prowess to understand the poem.

You give up.

For the next few minutes, you notice every detail of each person in the audience—their hair, their sweaters—you weigh whether they like sex, are they students? Et cetera.

This lasts only so long.

You get so bored, you think you will die.

The reader has just informed the audience that her next poem will take 25 minutes to read. You start to have trouble breathing.

a

a

a

the, the, the, the

back
to
wit
hickory
and so James Fenimore

Cooper

5
15
yes
and
adorn

You think of killing her. You think she's killing you. You think of so much murder, you're scared to go to your car in the dark.

NOT ANOTHER FUCKING POETRY READING

I'm tired of all the cults and cabals,
Native American wampum tom tom poems,
Coyote: get fucked; Eagle: bite this.
Black angry word-up whitey's an asshole poems—
Yo Yo your fucking Ma!
Academic epistemology tracts,
Fake avant garde New York School,
Pepsi Cola Museum of Modern Art poems,
Women's odes to fluid cycles,
Gay dick thumping sestinas,
Lost angel poor me juice & junkie rants
Get a fucking job!
Hispanic la raza macho bullshit sonnets,
Revolutionary beret & banderilla posing poems,
Minimalist breathless scentless watercress haiku,
Little old lady lace doily epics,
Yenta cliché and kvetching villanelles.
I'm just tired of poems about poems.
I'm just tired.

JIM TYACK

395

WILLIAM LEVY

Where are all those recent converts to freedom of expression who supported Salman Rushdie? Wanking off, no doubt, in the saloon and looking for another cause allowing them to exercise pseudo-participation. Although writing clearly and vividly is generally considered a virtue, for some reason or other literary mags are afraid of explicit description when it's sexual. Cautiously a Rocky Mountain editor asks me to drop the "reflexive sex" and add more political content. As if there isn't a convergence between our political and sexual vocabularies. Another, from the Mississippi Delta, explains that the action packed erotic story is an "essentially stupid form." But if it's a bad carpenter who blames their tools, then it's a bad writer who blames the form. From the Pacific Northwest they write, "it would be inappropriate ... because the pornographic aspects would bring the whole project into too narrow of a market." What?!? So I have been thrust willy nilly into the wonderful world of sleaze, glossy magazines which pay, but are narrow in their demands, and usually possess a unique combination of being at once both dumb and corrupt. But then I'm an idealist. That is, I'm cad enough to believe—contrarian to consensual reality—that the value of writing comes from what it is and not where it is published. It is humiliating enough to be obliged, by reduced material circumstances, to have to sell one's art without the added ignominy of bragging about one's pimp, or tricks. This winter I received a letter from the editor of *Over 40!* and *Shaving*. At least she was blunt enough to describe what I was forbidden to write. Current taboos are: no anal sex, no piss, no S&M, no B&D, no rape, no underage (no flashbacks to before 18), no rough sex, nothing demeaning to either women or men. When in London recently I mentioned this list to Tuppy "Sex Maniac's Diary" Owens. "Oh, anal sex," she protested, "can be quite lovely. And after all, buggery is the traditional English method of birth control." Xaviera "Happy Hooker" Hollander and I get many giggles from this selection. She, for example, likes her back bitten during sex, and I don't. "Do they think boys and girls get genitals spontaneously on their eighteenth birthday?" she asked. As far as defining "demeaning" goes we could get no funkier than thinking of it vaguely as a form of coercion. Yet, that desire is an incentive to both—to both sex and economics—is certain. And contemporary news and novels are filled with the latter while the former is prohibited. Stories of economic coercion abound. Even the above catalogue of no-no's is not absolute. Paul Bowles' *Collected Stories*, a book that reached the *NY Times* top ten, has a tale of homosexual incest between father and son. In today's climate Jocasta would be a defendant in an *L.A. Law* episode about child abuse. Much of William Burroughs' work has repetitive scenes of pneumatic sodomy and there's an anal rape (murder) as openers in Norman Mailer's novel *Why We Are In Vietnam*. Is Lolita really over eighteen? Therefore, the various censorships accepted and encouraged by the soft-left glossies, stylezines and Sunday supplements are class motivated and elitist. Really not much different from the 19th century. Then—in his shiny volume translation of the *Tales of Arabian Nights*— Sir Richard Burton wrote certain long footnotes in Latin. The NY tabloid weekly *Screw* has been around for twenty years. Although they don't pay much it is a good place for a writer. When they cut things out (usually for reasons of space) they do it carefully and they are willing to publish what most other mags won't. Noted for their vulgarity, they have treated me decently in their start-firsts and my articles have received substantial response. The Penthouse organization is the worst. I've been published, I mean ravaged, by *Forum*, *Penthouse Letters* and *Hot Talk*. With so many different mags, and a deep-penetration national and international distribution system, they tend to dominate the writer's market for erotica. Pity. The contract they ask you to sign would make Faust blush. Moreover, they are a sloppy outfit run by essentially silly people who don't always pay. (Right now they owe me $1000.) And if any of them spent money on a college education they are entitled to a refund. Like so many successful American mags, they have no philosophy and are tolerated because they are not dangerous. In October '88 *Penthouse* cavalierly published a story of mine under someone else's name even though there's a transcribed audio letter in the text (which they left in) with the salutation "Dear Bill." I wrote asking what was going on. The reply I received was the non sequitur of the year. "You are not taking the job seriously."

Another time my story as published was so significantly changed I recognized it as my writing only because this time my name was on it. More embarrassments followed. They had changed the timeframe from the Hooker's Convention (1985) to the Wet Dream Festivals (1970–71). Then they transformed the appearance of the female lead from a tall redhead to a medium-sized brunette. But left in she was much taller than I, thus making me into a geriatric midget. A baroness I know, who is an editor for a major literary publishing house here in Holland, asked me to show her the story. I gave her both the original and published versions. After reading them she said: "Working for *Penthouse* must be every editor's dream, seeing how they make up an entirely new story! Why, for instance, would tall and long-limbed be less attractive than medium height? And is black hair sexier than red?" In most American glossies the editors are just smiling fronts for scowling lawyers who are the final arbiters as to what will be published and how. However, I will not abandon erotics because of criminality and disease anymore than I would abandon God because of Jimmy Swaggart and Company. In the visual arts unclad bodies as subject matter—in movement cojoining without intermingling—has Greek and Renaissance precedents. Psyche, representing soul-mind-spirit, was personified as beloved of Eros. But erotic writing is, has always been, an underground or marginalized genre for expressing the interchangeable gnostic allegories of earthly pleasure and spiritual passion in mystical union.

NOTA BENE: Around Easter '89, the group of editors at *Penthouse* with which I was working were all fired, thus proving (yet again) the efficacy of prayer over litigation.

PUB PUKE POETRY

In England over Christmas, I attended the most unusual poetry reading ever, one that in retrospect continues to amaze me. Gerry Locklin, who had been on an exchange teaching deal in Wales, stopped in London on his way back to Long Beach to give a reading. It was the first event in a series held in the upstairs room of a neighborhood pub in Holborn. But it wasn't very well publicized and only a small group of earnest poetry-lovers came, who sat across the aisle from me and my friends in the little room.

The series organizer, an almost inarticulate youth, shyly introduced Gerry and then retired nearby to a chair, while Gerry started reading his poetry. Suddenly, the sound of puking began, and the young presenter was bent over in his chair, a hand trying to staunch the flow. As Gerry stood there, looking on bemused, unjudging, simply observing the human condition, the poetry organizer staggered out, mouth still dribbling down his sweater, stopping to puke once more in a great wash over the group of young people next to me, and splashing me (which meant almost the whole audience got it). Again he let loose a final flood by the door, as if in farewell. Gerry commemorated the moment by announcing in an awed voice that that was the most unusual response to his poetry he'd ever got.

A while later the young organizer of poetry readings resumed, stammering inarticulate apologies. He dabbed at some of the puddles ineffectually with a paper towel, and sat down again for the poetry reading to resume. The lucky thing was that it was all beer, though I did see a suspicious gob on the jacket of the boy across from me, and didn't smell at all. We couldn't have gone on sitting in that close room if it had been dinner he threw up. But though dazed, nobody seemed fazed, neither the poet, the audience, nor the puker himself. The audience remained perfectly relaxed and genial about it all, as if it was the kind of thing that happened all the time, not even bothering to wipe off their clothes, and they went on laughing and chuckling over Gerry's sassy poems,

and applauded the tapdance he performed in the great tradition of bar-
room performances.

Sure, and it was a reading that will go down in the annals of
poetry, but I thought I'd better get my version in first.

THE LATE WORD

Generation X, Douglas Coupland, St. Martin's Press, New York.

Without admirable intent, the forces of McCulture now and then
stumble in their idiot night against something good. Like Nirvana.
Nirvana is a great grunge band. *Smells Like Teen Spirit*: "Here we
are entertain us, I feel stupid and contagious, a mulatto, an albino, a
mosquito, my libido, yay, yay." I like it, especially with all that
smash-face guitar noise. It gives me hope that maybe life lives after
all. But when the talent scouts go out trying to find the same life on
purpose, they come back with Iron Butterfly. Nevermind.

Generation X is an attempt to find something that's already been
found, not because it's worth finding but because it can be sold to the
"youth market." The novel's cover copy explains, "Finally ... a frighten-
ingly hilarious, voraciously readable salute to the generation born in the
late 1950s and 1960s."

Who wants to be saluted?

Who wants books to be "readable"?

Somewhere, someone whispered Jean Baudrillard's name in St.
Martin's corporate ear. "Ah, the restless youth want books about kids
adrift in the California desert which is a METAPHOR for being mired in
the detritus of American cultural memory."

Yes, this is it, the book in which we find ourselves mired in the
desert!

Generation X is willing to be as square (readable) as it needs to be
in order to convince St. Martin's that it can be its own hip thing. It has
upside down clouds, Lichtenstein-like cartoons in the margin, and
smarmy-smart little mottos everywhere. Like: "nostalgia is a weapon."
"Simulate yourself."

This book makes my heart sink. *Generation X* makes smart and
alive stupid and dead.

» «

CURTIS WHITE

399

Marx's Radical Critique of Capitalist Society, N. Scott Arnold, Oxford University Press, Oxford.

On the other hand, this is a book that seems designed to be neither wanted nor sold. What market is it that pays $40 for an American analytic critique of Karl Marx? In two short years, this book went from being for no one at $40 to being precisely and maybe only for me at $6 at Babbitt's Used Books.

Marx's Radical Etc. is serious, well-written and even witty. It shocked me, this book. Imagine asking the following question in 1990: do the arguments of Marx's writings support his major premise, that capitalism's evils are rooted in its major institutions, thus requiring the eradication of said institutions? I'm disarmed. Charmed. Living in Birmingham, Alabama, Professor Arnold actually thinks it's important to discuss with me, in Normal, Illinois, the possibility that someone is still considering Marx's revolution.

Although Arnold's route is filled with many exciting turns of what Merleau-Ponty called "Adventures of the Dialectic," finally, three hundred plus pages late, Arnold concludes that, no, Marx's argument doesn't sufficiently support its major premise and so post-capitalist society, as imagined by Marx, is impossible. *Dommage!* I could of course do nothing but agree. I did, however, also note that Professor Arnold had once again shown why logic is the enemy of all dreams.

SOBER AT LAST

DANA PATTILLO

I hope you will be kind enough to print the enclosed "Twelve Steps of Poets Anonymous" in *Exquisite Corpse*, as a public service to your readership and the literary community you so ably serve. Addiction has become recognized as one of our society's most besetting problems, and as the editor of a journal such as yours, you already know there are as many—if not more—out of control versifiers, poetasters, and closet rhyme junkies in the general population as there are alcoholics. In fact, dual, or even triple addictions are not uncommon. The Anonymous Program offers hope even to the most wretched of addicts.

THE TWELVE STEPS OF POETS ANONYMOUS

1—We admitted we were powerless over verse—that our lines had become unmanageable.

2—Came to believe that a prosody greater than our own could restore us to syntax.

3—Made a decision to turn our journals and manuscripts over to the care of the editor *as we understood him.*

4—Made a searching and fearless moral inventory of our vocabulary.

5—Admitted to our editor, ourselves, and to another human being the exact nature of our plagiarisms.

6—Were entirely ready to have our editor remove all these defects of narrative.

7—Humbly asked him to remove all our solecisms.

8—Made a list of all the poets we had backstabbed, and became willing to make amends to them all.

9—Made direct amends to such poets whenever possible, except when to do so would hurt our chances of publication or winning grants.

10—Continued to take personally all invective, and when we were backstabbed, promptly squealed about it.

11—Sought through prayer and meditation to improve our social contact with our publisher *as we understood him,* praying only for assurance of his good will toward our work and his power to print it.

12—Having had a rude awakening as a result of these steps, we tried to carry this message to poetasters, and to practice these principles in all our literary affairs.

SERENDIPITY PRAYER

"Muse grant me the serendipity to accept the words I can not change, the courage to change the words I can, and the wisdom to know the difference."

—Dana Pattillo

CONTRIBUTOR NOTES

ANDREI CODRESCU (www.codrescu.com) has edited *Exquisite Corpse* since 1983. He is a poet, novelist, and essayist. His commentaries can be heard regularly on NPR. His film, *Road Scholar*, won the Peabody Award. He teaches at Louisiana State University in Baton Rouge.

LAURA ROSENTHAL is a Louisiana-born poet, editor, and critic. She has written the "Body Bag" column in *Exquisite Corpse* since 1990, and has been a co-editor since 1994. Her poetry has appeared in *New American Writing, Hanging Loose,* and other magazines. She writes on poetry for *The Minneapolis Star Tribune.*

KEITH ABBOTT teaches fiction workshops and "The Contemplative Brush" at The Naropa Institute. Selections from his unpublished novel, *Arfy Darfy Love,* are currently undergoing movie-option negotiations along with his novel *Mordecai of Monterey.* In 1998 he had two solo shows of his paintings, "Buddha Comes to White America" at the University of Colorado, and "Birds Beasts Bugs Buddhas & Baseball" at CDOT in Denver. He has practiced Western and Asian calligraphy for 27 years and Tai Chi Chuan for the past 11 years. Forthcoming publications include an introduction to a Houghton Mifflin edition of Richard Brautigan's early works.

SAM ABRAMS was born, raised and educated in Brooklyn where he walked Walt's streets. He's regularly published in magazines and anthologies but his last book was *The Post American Cultural Congress* (1974). He refuses to change the title of the manuscript he's now circulating, *The Old Pothead Poems: New & Selected,* in spite of publishers' squeaming; 'cause he hopes the title will win him a golden parachute out of academia.

WILL ALEXANDER is a poet, essayist, playwright, novelist, philosopher, and visual artist. He is the author of six books, which include *Asia & Haiti, The Stratospheric Canticles,* and *Towards the Primeval Lightning Field.*

JACK ANDERSON, a poet and dance writer, is a dance critic for the *New York Times* and the author of several books of poetry and dance history. His most recent volume of poetry is *Traffic: New and Selected Prose Poems* (New Rivers Press), which won the 1988 Marie Alexander Award.

NIN ANDREWS is the author of *The Book of Orgasms.* At last notice, she was writing *The Book of Lies* and studying the art of levitation.

ANTLER, Milwaukee, is the author of *Factory* (City Lights), *Last Words* (Ballantine), *Ever-Expanding Wilderness* and *Deathrattles vs. Comecries,* and has work in the new anthologies *American Poets Say Goodbye to the 20th Century; A New Geography of Poets; Eros in Boystown; Reclaiming the Heartland: Lesbian & Gay Voices from the Midwest; What Book!? Buddha Poems from Beat to HipHop* and *Wild Song.*

403

BRENT ASKARI is an actor and writer who lives and works in the Washington D.C. area and Portland, Maine. He has had plays produced in New York and Los Angeles. His first novel, *Not Ready for Prime Time,* was published by Carroll & Graf.

PAUL BAEPLER is the author of *White Slaves, African Masters* (University of Chicago Press, 1999). He has also published fiction in several small journals.

ALIKI BARNSTONE'S book of poems, *Madly in Love* (Carnegie Mellon University Press, 1997) was nominated for the Pulitzer Prize. Her poems have appeared in *Agni, The Antioch Review, Boulevard, Chicago Review, Partisan Review,* and other journals. She is the editor of *A Book of Women Poets from Antiquity to Now* (Schocken/Random House, 1992) and *Voices of Light: Spiritual Poems by Women from Around the World* (Shambhala, 1999).

WILLIS BARNSTONE is a poet and translator from the Greek, Spanish, and Chinese. Among his many books are: *The Other Bible,* translations of Gnostic literature, *The Poetics of Translation, Sappho and the Greek Lyric Poets,* and *Alphabet of Night: Selected Poems, 1948–1998.*

GEORGES BATAILLE was briefly associated with surrealism until he broke with André Breton in the early 1930s to found the College of Sociology. Bataille differed with André Breton in his assertion that culture and humanity were essentially monstrous and could not be contained within any closed philosophical system. His writing reflects his own indigestibility: a whoremonger, drunkard, and librarian by profession.

CONGER BEASLEY, JR. is a professional nature writer, the author of *We Are a People in This World.* He is co-publisher of Woods Colt Press.

CAROL BERGÉ's kitchen window view: past her *Art & Antiques* article on Maria pottery (runes on clay as parallel to Navajo code-talkers) to where friends create quantum cryptography. Rear-view mirror of van: *Light Years: The NYC 1960s Coffeehouse Poets,* anthology she's editing. Eccentric-orbit fiction/poetry/intermix continuum into 71st year.

TREE BERNSTEIN (M. S. Tree) is the publisher and graphic designer for TreeHouse Press and Nest Egg Books. She is the author of *On the Way Here,* fiction (Baksun Books), and *Journal of the Lingering Fall,* a memoir (Dead Metaphor Press). She is also a referee for the Sumo Haiku Heavyweight Championship held sporadically in her home town, Boulder, Colorado.

ANSELM BERRIGAN is the author of *Integrity—Dramatic Life* (Edge, 1999). He currently lives in Brooklyn, but is open to other possibilities.

EDMUND BERRIGAN is the author of *Disarming Matter* (Owl Books, 1999), and *Counting the Hats & Ducks* (Idiom, 1997), & co-author along with Will Yaculik of *A Serious Earth* (Idiom, 1997). He resides where he walks.

MILTON BEYER was born in New York City in 1917. He played a soldier in MGM's *Ben Hur* in 1925. Currently he's a freelance writer and a visiting lecturer at Cornell University and has been a food wholesaler and direct mail creator in Washington, D.C. for 40 years. He's had articles in *Regardies, Cornell Quarterly,* and *Exquisite Corpse.*

DONALD R. BLUMEN lives and works in Nashville, Tennessee.

ROBERT BOVÉ worked as a cattle farm caretaker in W. Virginia, a stage carpenter's apprentice with the New York Stagehands Union, & writer & editor in DC, but now adjuncts English in NYC universities. The pay falls short. Profits from his last poetry chapbook *Nine From Metronome* (Pisces Press) don't, alas, take up the slack.

KAY BOYLE (1902–1992) loved Dubonnet, Paul Robeson, razor clams, and sang "Miss Otis Regrets" like no one else. She was in Paris in the 20's, in New York in the 40's and in jail in the 60's. Her close friends included James Joyce, Man Ray, Picasso, Joan Baez, and Katherine Anne Porter. S.I. Hayakawa labeled her the most dangerous woman in America.

DAVE BRINKS—Provocateur and *guide terroristique* of the American Spoken Language, Brinks says *"the word* is as elemental as earth-air-fire-water." A central figure in the thriving New Orleans poetry world, he co-founded the weekly *Madpoet Express* open reading in 1996, fronts the *Free Speech Orchestra* jazz-poetry project, and operates *Trembling Pillow Press* and *Tsetse* magazine.

Veteran of the San Francisco poetry and film scene, JAMES BROUGHTON's latest collection is *Packing Up for Paradise: Selected Poems 1946–1996* (Black Sparrow Press, 1998). He died at his home in Port Townsend, Washington, on May 17, 1999.

KENNETH BROWN was a Resident Playwright at the Yale Drama School from 1996–69. His play *The Brig* was produced by The Living Theater (1963) and his novel *The Narrows* (Dial Press, 1971) was a Pulitzer Prize nominee.

RONNIE BURK is a revolutionary communist and a surrealist at the end of the Twentieth Century.

GERALD BURNS was born in Michigan, attended Harvard, Trinity College (Dublin), and Southern Methodist University. His books of verse include *Boccherini's Minuet, Letters to Obscure Men, A Book of Spells* [first third] (Salt Lick), and *Longer Poems* (Dalkey Archive). He has authored a collection of essays, *A Thing About Language,* published by S.I.U. Press. Gerald Burns died in 1998.

BECKY BYRKIT works as a music writer and memoirs consultant in Los Angeles. James Tate attempted to take credit for writing her first book, *zealand,* nominated for the Western States Book Award in 1993. Selected for Best American Poetry 1993, Becky's publications include chapbooks *Whoa* (Pearl 1996) and *Solar System for Criminals* (Anaesthetic Popularity Contest Press 1997), manuscript *BirdDog Real,* and a collaborative effort with photographer James Graham and songwriter Al Perry, *Suite: Mary* (PaperBrain Press, 1999).

MAX CAFARD, pre-ancientist philosopher and prophet of surregionalism, lives on a floating island in a dream state. He edits *Psychic Swamp: The Surregionalist Review* and teaches Yat Studies in New Orleans.

JANINE CANAN is the author of ten books of poetry, including *Her Magnificent Body, Love, Enter* and *Changing Woman*. She translated *Star in My Forehead: Selected Poems by Else Lasker-Schüler*, and edited the award-winning anthology *She Rises Like the Sun: Invocations of the Goddess by Contemporary American Poets*. A psychiatrist, she resides in Sonoma, California.

JOE CARDARELLI (1944–1995) was a guiding light of the poetry scene in Baltimore for three decades. He was a teacher at the Maryland Art Institute where he inspired several generations of writers and artists. He was a prolific writer who performed tirelessly, but published only a few small collections of his poetry. A posthumous volume of work is being edited by Anselm Hollo, and should see the light in the year 2000.

HAYDEN CARRUTH was born in 1921 in Connecticut and was educated at the University of North Carolina at Chapel Hill and the University of Chicago. Carruth lives in upstate New York. He has published 29 books, chiefly of poetry but also a novel, four books of criticism, and two anthologies. His most recent books are *Reluctantly: Autobiographical Essays* (Copper Canyon Press, 1998); *Selected Essays & Reviews; Collected Longer Poems; Collected Shorter Poems, 1946–1991* and *Scrambled Eggs and Whiskey* (1996).

KAREN CHASE's poems have appeared (or are forthcoming) in such journals as *The Yale Review* and *The Gettysburg Review* as well as in *The New Yorker* and *The New Republic*. Her work is included in *The Norton Anthology of Poetry*. *Kamimierz Square*, her first book of poems, is coming out from CanvanKerry Press in spring 2000.

TOM CLARK's books of poetry from Black Sparrow Press include *Junkets on a Sad Planet: Scenes from the Life of John Keats* (1994); *Like Real People* (1995); and *Empire of Skin* (1997).

IRA COHEN was born in New York City (1935) to deaf parents and learned to spell on his fingers when he was one year old. He is well known as a photographer and filmmaker and his film *Kings with Straw Mats* of the great Kumbhmela Festival in Hardwar (1986) is finally available from Mystic Fire Video. More infamous than famous when he is not in Budapest or Brussels, he lives in New York City. The unexpected voice awakens us to thoughtfulness.

WANDA COLEMAN was born in 1946 and raised in the Los Angeles community of Watts, famed for its August 1965 Rebellion. She is the author of *Imagoes* (1983), *Heavy Daughter Blues: Poems & Stories 1968–1986* (1987), *A War of Eyes & Other Stories* (1988), *African Sleeping Sickness* (1990), *Hand Dance* (1993), *Native in a Strange Land: Trials & Tremors* (1996) and *Bathwater Wine* (1998), all published by Black Sparrow Press.

RICHARD COLLINS, author of *John Fante, A Literary Portrait* (Guernica Editions), lives in New Orleans.

JACK COLLOM was born in Chicago in 1931 and walked a lot in Salt Creek Woods. He studied Forestry at Colorado A&M, served (swerved?) in USAF. He wrote his first poems in Tripoli, Libya. He worked in factories for 20 years, and got an MA in English on the GI Bill. Collom currently teaches at Naropa where he does much poet-in-the-schools work. The author of 19 books, he has been awarded two National Endowment for the Arts Fellowships.

JIM CORY was born in Oklahoma City in 1953 and has lived in Philadelphia since 1976. He has been a member of the National Book Critics Circle and contributed numerous essays and reviews to newspapers and literary journals. He has published six chapbooks of poems, been a Yaddo and Pennsylvania Arts Council fellow, and co-founded Insight to Riot, a poet's press based in the City of Brotherly Love. Recently he edited a book of James Broughton's poetry entitled *Packing Up for Paradise: Selected Poems 1946–1996* (Black Sparrow Press, 1997).

I.P. COULIANOU was a Romanian-born scholar of religions, a professor at the University of Chicago, and a close collaborator of Mircea Eliade. He wrote *Eros and Magic in the Renaissance,* and other books on Gnosticism, magic, and religion. In May 1991, at age 41, he was assassinated at the University of Chicago by unknown assailants widely believed to belong to the Romanian secret services.

ROBERT CREELEY, born in 1927, held the poetics chair at NYU at Buffalo and has a permanent seat in our Exquisite hearts. Among his many books: *For Love* (1962), *Words* (1967), *A Day Book* (1972), *Memory Gardens* (1986), *Selected Poems 1945–1990.* Black Sparrow Press published the multi-volume Creeley-Olson correspondence.

JOEL DAILEY lives in New Orleans. His most recent works include *Biopic* (Igneus Press, 1999) and the forthcoming *Lower 48* (Lavender Ink, 1999).

RAY DIPALMA is the author of more than 35 collections of poetry, including *Numbers and Tempers, Provocations, Motion of the Cypher,* and most recently, *Letters.* Translations of his work have appeared in Italian, French, Portuguese, Spanish, German, and Chinese. He currently teaches at New York's School of Visual Arts.

BUCK DOWNS lives in Washington, D.C. where he is Senior Editor for Columbion Books. His first collection of poems, *Marijunan Soft Drink,* is forthcoming from Edge Books.

DENISE DUHAMEL's books include: *Exquisite Politics* (with Maureen Seaton, Tia Chucha Press, 1997), *Kinky* (Orchises Press, 1997), *Girl Soldier* (Garden Street Press, 1996), and *How the Sky Fell* (Pearl Editions, 1996). Her work has been anthologized widely in such volumes as *The Best American Poetry* (1998, 1994, and 1993). She has received grants from the Ludwig Vogelstein Foundation and the New York Foundation for the Arts, as well as residencies from Yaddo, the MacDowell Colony, Villa Montalvo, Le Château de Lavigny, and Fundacíon Valparaíso.

RICHARD ELMAN was a novelist, poet, journalist, and published 25 books during his 63 years on this planet, from an account of the war in Nicaraugua (*Cocktails at Somoza's*), to a bitter farce (*Fredi&Shirl&theKids*), to a criminal character study (*An Education in Blood*). But when he died at the beginning of 1998, only one of them, the novel *Tar Beach,* was in print.

CLAYTON ESHLEMAN's most recent collection of poetry is *From Scratch* (Black Sparrow Press, 1998); his most recent translation is Antonin Artaud's *Watchfiends & Rack Screams* (Exact Change, 1995). He is currently completing a 25 year poetic investigation of Upper Paleolithic cave art.

MAGGIE ESTEP's first novel, *Diary of an Emotional Idiot* was published in 1997. She has made two spoken word CD's, *No More Mr Nice Girl* (Imago, 1994) and *Love Is a Dog From Hell* (Mercury, 1997). Her writing has appeared in *Spin, Harper's Bazaar, The Village Voice* and *The New Yorker*. Maggie's second novel, *Soft Maniacs* will be published by Simon and Schuster in October 1999.

CLARISSA PINKOLA ESTES is a poet, storyteller, cantadora, Jungian analyst, and the author of many books, including the best-selling *Women Who Run with Wolves.*

EDWARD FIELD's latest book is *A Frieze for a Temple of Love,* published by Black Sparrow Press in 1998. He won a Lambda Award for his previous book, *Counting Myself Lucky: Selected Poems 1963–1992* (Black Sparrow Press, 1992). He has also edited two volumes of the work of Alfred Chester.

SUSAN FIRER has edited *A Whole Other Ballgame* (Farrar, Straus) writing by women on sports. She teaches at the University of Wisconsin-Milwaukee.

JACK FOLEY's most recent books are *Exiles* and *Dead/Requiem*. His radio show, "Cover to Cover," is heard every week on the Berkeley radio station KPFA. His column, "Foley's Books," appears weekly in the online magazine, *The Alsop Review.*

DAVID FRANKS makes poems on the page, composes poems with music and text, writes songs, and occasionally makes installations. His poetry appears in *American Poets Say Goodbye to the Twentieth Century* (Four Walls), as well as *Left for Dead* and *No Relief* (Hotel Argonne). His music is available on CD as *Musical Words* (Pyramid/Atlantic) and *f,r,o,z,e,n,t,e,a,r,s* (Albion). He has had residencies at the Maryland Institute College of Art, The University of New Orleans, Grambling State & Illinois State University. He lives in Baltimore and may be reached at Franks@charm.net.

BENJAMIN FRIEDLANDER is the author of essays on Charles Olson, Paul Celan, Robert Creeley, and Larry Eigner. His poetry books include *A Knot a Tangle,* and *Anterior Future.*

GLORIA FRYM's most recent book is a collection of short stories, *Distance No Object* (City Lights Books, 1999). She is the author of *How I Learned,* as well as several volumes of poetry. For many years she taught poetry writing to jail inmates. Since 1987, she has been a member of the core faculty of the Poetics Program at New College of California in San Francisco.

GREG FUCHS lives and works in New York City, the city that never lets him sleep (the working title of his current book of poems). His most recent books are *Came Like It Went* (BD Books, 1999) and *Uma Ternura* (Canvas and Companhia, 1998). Look him up next time you are in the City; he wants to photograph you.

JOHN GIORNO's most recent book is *You Got to Burn to Shine* (Serpent's Tail, 1994). In 1965 he founded *Giorno Poetry Systems* which innovated the use of technology in poetry. In 1968, he created *Dial-A-Poem* using the telephone for mass communications. Giorno Poetry Systems has released over forty LPs and CDs of poets working with performance and music, numerous cassettes, videopaks, poetry videos and film.

JILL GONET has published in *The New England Review* and *Exquisite Corpse*.

JIM GUSTAFSON, Detroit's poet extraordinaire, wrote poetry (*Tales of Virtue and Transformation,* among other books), novels (*Discount City*) and essays for Detroit newspapers and magazines. He died in 1997, leaving behind a large unpublished oeuvre and a store of legends.

LAURIE HALBRITTER is getting comfortable in Ann Arbor, a city that has one of every kind of restaurant. Subsisting in the cheapest apartment in town, she writes, paints and curses the marching band during football season. While she may not be able to afford dinner out, there is coffee in Ann Arbor. Everywhere. Several cafes on every block. At three bucks a cup, who can complain?

MARK HALLMAN's collections of poetry include *Plump Testicles and Shared Affections* (with David Bolduc). His short story *Knife, Fork, Fingernails,* was adapted and produced as a play by Reality Check Theater in San Jose, California.

ALFRED STARR HAMILTON: "I'd rather be free than be a poet. I'd rather be free than read and write. I am immune from all church and honorable beliefs. I am that kind of a poet who doesn't do anything else, but poetry. I write free poetry only."

BRIAN CHRISTOPHER HAMILTON is a slam poet in Portland, Oregon. He also writes essays and reviews.

PHILIP HERTER has lived in Mexico City, New Orleans, Los Angeles and New York. He is the author of a play, *Pursued by Happiness* and the novels, *Baby Farm Circus, Felix Easter,* and *The Uptake*.

MICHAEL HEYWARD is co-founder of the Australian literary magazine *Scripsi*. He is the author of *The Ern Malley Affair,* about the celebrated hoax that rocked the Aussie lit scene.

After enriching himself in a multinational corporation, economist ART HILGART now lives entirely for pleasure, producing a weekly theater music program on National Public Radio (*Broadway Revisited*), reviewing jazz for *The Journal of the International Association of Jazz Record Collectors*, teaching musical theater history and jazz history at Kalamazoo College and Western Michigan University, and writing on economics in *The Nation*, religion in *The Humanist*, and whatever in *Exquisite Corpse*.

JAMES HILLMAN was born in Atlantic City, New Jersey in 1926. In 1959 he became the first Director of Studies of the C. G. Jung Institute in Zurich, Switzerland. He is well-known in the field of psychology and founded the movement of thought named "archetypal psychology." A complete bibliography of his books, essays, interviews, and presentations is listed in *Archetypal Psychology: A Brief Account*. His latest nationally acclaimed work, a *New York Times* bestseller, published by Random House, is *The Soul's Code: In Search of Character & Calling*.

ANSELM HOLLO, poet and literary translator, was born in Helsinki, Finland. After sojourns in Germany, Austria, and the United Kingdom, he came to the United States and has lived here for thirty-odd years; for the last ten, he has been teaching at The Naropa Institute's Kerouac School of Poetics in Boulder, Colorado. His most recent books of poems are *Corvus* (Coffee House Press, 1995) and *Ahoe* (Smokeproof Press, 1997).

BOB HOLMAN's most recent CD is *In with the Out Crowd* (Mouth Almighty). His most recent book is *The Collect Call of the Wild* (Holt). His co-edited anthologies are *The United States of Poetry* (Abrams) and *ALOUD! Voices from the Nuyorican Poets Cafe* (Holt) and the digital anthology: *The World of Poetry* (http://worldof-poetry.org). He is a professor of English at Bard College. http://poetry.miningco.com

STOKES HOWELL is the author of the short story collection *The Sexual Life of Savages & Other Stories* (St. Martin's Press). He is co-author (with Laurie Dolphin) of the forthcoming *Evidence: The Art of Candy Jernigan* (Chronicle Books, 1999). He is currently writing a novel.

DAVID IGNATOW was born in Brooklyn, and lived most of his life in New York. He published 16 volumes of poetry and three prose collections. Included in these are *Poems, The Gentle Weightlifter, Say Pardon, Figures of the Human, Earth Hard: Selected Poems, Rescue the Dead, Poems: 1934–1969, Facing the Tree, Selected Poems* (1975), *Tread the Dark, Whisper to the Earth, Leaving the Door Open, Shadowing the Ground, Despite the Plainness of the Day: Love Poems* (1991), *Against the Evidence*, and *I Have a Name*.

LORRI JACKSON (born 1962) was a talented young poet and performer from Chicago. She died in 1990 from a heroin overdose.

STEVE KATZ started the trouble with *The Exaggerations of Peter Prince*, and most recently won the America Award in Fiction with *Swanny's Ways*. Many books of fiction and poetry in between. Screenplays. Small films. Dog wrinkles. Recently he has given up his personage (of which there are many too many) to take on the wings and feathers of the California Condor, (of which there be but a pitiful few).

JAMES LAUGHLIN founded New Directions in 1936. His poetry spanned a period of over sixty years, 1914–1997. The poems printed here are from *James Laughlin Poems New and Selected,* copyright © 1997 by the Estate of James Laughlin. They are reprinted with the permission of New Directions Publishing Corp.

GARY LENHART's books of poems include *One at a Time, Light Heart,* and most recently *Father and Son Night* (Hanging Loose, 1999). He was an editor of *Mag City* and *Transfer* magazines, and *Clinch: Selected Poems of Michael Scholnick.* He also edited *The Teachers & Writers Guide to William Carlos Williams.*

WILLIAM LEVY won an Erotic Oscar for "Writer of the Year 1998" awarded at the Sex Maniac's Ball in London. Recent books include poetry *Billy's Holiday,* as well as essays on art *Politische Pornos: Eine illustrierte Einfuhrung* and *Unser Freund Otto Muhl: Eine Studie zum Kulturschock.*

JAMES LINEBERGER is a poet and screenwriter, living and working in North Carolina.

ADRIAN C. LOUIS fancies himself a tragic figure, now enduring middle age, unemployment, and the winters of the Great Plains. He has written several books and with the help of medications may write several more.

ANNE L. MacNAUGHTON is the project director of the long-running Taos Poetry Circus. A visual artist, organic farmer, teacher and Indian education specialist, she is also a performer and founding member of *The Luminous Animal* jazz-poetry ensemble. Her work has been collected in *The Best Poetry of 1989, The Rag and Bone Shop of the Heart* and *The Ecstatic Moment,* among others. She has also been published in numerous literary journals and magazines.

AMALIO MADUEÑO's work has been published and anthologized since the early 1980's and individual poems are featured on public transit in four cities in New Mexico (the Vehicle Project) and on video featuring poets of New Mexico on KNME TV5 (PBS). He is past president and advisor to the World Poetry Bout Association, which produces the Taos Poetry Circus. He performs continuously in venues around New Mexico including the Taos Poetry Slam and Albuquerque Poetry Festival. Chapbooks include *Two Poems, Fire,* and *An Extra Day of Poetry,* all published by Minor Heron Press.

GERARD MALANGA, poet and photographer, is the author of 12 books of poetry, including his most recent, *Mythologies of the Heart* (Black Sparrow, 1996), and two books of photography, *Good Girls* (1994) and *Resistance to Memory* (1998). Two CDs are scheduled for release in 1999: *Up from the Archives* and *Three Days with My Dog* with the Belgian band, 48 Cameras. He lives in New York.

JANET MASON is an award-winning writer of poetry, fiction, and creative nonfiction. Her two chapbooks of poetry from Insight To Riot Press are *A Fucking Brief History of Fucking* (1993) and *When I Was Straight* (1995). Also a performance artist, she is a member of "Pulsation," a poetry, percussion, tap dance ensemble. She recently completed a creative nonfiction manuscript entitled *Tea Leaves: A Mother-Daughter Odyssey*.

CLIVE MATSON is the author of *Let the Crazy Child Write!* (New World Library, 1998) and *Squish Boots,* his seventh book of poems, which will appear in 1999 from Broken Shadow Publications. He lives in Oakland, California, with his wife, poet Gail Ford, and their son Ezra. He makes his living teaching creative writing.

MICHAEL McCLURE's two most recent books of poetry are *Touching the Edge: Dharma Devotions from the Hummingbird Sangha* and *Huge Dreams* (Penguin/ Viking). He performs his poetry with visionary musician Ray Manzarek. McClure lives with his wife, the sculptor Amy Evans McClure, in Oakland's hills.

SHARON MESMER is the author of the poetry collection *Half Angel, Half Lunch* (Hard Press) and the prose collection *The Empty Quarter* (Hanging Loose). She was the recipient of the MacArthur Scholarship (Brooklyn College), the New York Foundation for the Arts grant, and fellowships to MacDowell and Hawthornden Castle in Scotland. Mesmer teaches writing and literature at the New School and is the English language editor of the Japanese lit mag *American Book Jam.*

MURAT NEMET-NEJAT was born in Istanbul, Turkey, and came to the U.S. in 1959. His forthcoming publications include *A Selective Anthology of Turkish Poetry* (Talisman) and an essay "The Peripheral Space of Photography" (Sun & Moon Press). He is also working on a long poem, "Gol and Miss Kinan's Waters."

RICARDO L. NIRENBERG was born in Buenos Aires, Argentina, in 1939. He taught math at several institutions of doctoral ignorance. He's the author of a novel, *Cry Uncle* (Latino Press, 1998) and various shorter works. Nirenberg edits *Of(f)course,* an Internet literary journal: http://www.albany.edu/offcourse.

Co-founder (with Darrel Gray) of the Actualist Movement, poet and essayist JIM NISBET also writes crime novels. His most recent *roman noir* is *Prelude to a Scream* (Carroll & Graff).

DENISE NOE has been published in *The Brookhaven Buzz, The Humanist, Georgia Journal, Catalyst, Raskolnikov's Cellar, The Lizzie Borden Quarterly, Chrysalis Quarterly, Exquisite Corpse, 'Scapes, The Gulf War Anthology, Light Gauntlet, The Pink Chameleon,* and other places. She is featured in *Here and Now: Current Readings for Writers.*

JAMES NOLAN is a widely published poet, translator, essayist, and fiction writer. His most recent book is *Poet-Chief,* a study of Whitman, Neruda, and shamanism (University of New Mexico Press). He recently returned to his native New Orleans after teaching American literature for many years at the University of Barcelona.

PAT NOLAN has put down roots among the redwoods in Monte Rio, California, where he lives to write. His translation of Philippe Soupault's

412

Comrade appeared in *Poems for the Millennium* (Vol. 1). Most recently he has privately published a limited edition of a four-volume poetry document entitled *Made in the Shade.*

ALICE NOTLEY is the author of over 25 books, of which the two most recent are *Mysteries of Small Houses* and *The Descent of Alette,* both published by Penguin. She lives in Paris.

KIRBY OLSON is a frequent contributor to *Exquisite Corpse.* He is a sometime academic who would prefer to win the lottery and exist in a sleepy suburb of Geneva, but he is currently living with his family and working on a novel in Finland.

JOEL OPPENHEIMER was born in Yonkers, NY, and attended Black Mountain College where he was a student of Charles Olson. He lived among the poets and artists of Greenwich Village, and was a columnist for *The Village Voice* from 1969–1978. His final book, *The Collected Later Poems of Joel Oppenheimer,* includes eleven out-of-print books written between 1975 and 1994, as well as 49 unpublished poems.

WILLIAM PALMER (b. 1952) grew up in Detroit and teaches English at Alma College in central Michigan. At Alma he conducts a service-learning program in which undergraduates lead poetry workshops for inmates at a local prison and for senior citizens. He has published essays and poetry in *Chicago Tribune Magazine, Yankee,* and *The Bellingham Review.* He is married and has three sons.

DANA PATTILLO is the author of two books of poetry by Hang Fire Press: *An Army, with Banners* (1997) and *The Bread of Wolves* (1993). After a fruitful decade in Denver, Colorado, he recently relocated to Tulsa, Oklahoma, where he unexpectedly discovered true love. Mr. Pattillo makes his living as a journeyman scratch baker and cherishes the absurd self image of *ronin* as Pillsbury doughboy. His next book will probably be called *The Homesick Cannibals' Reunion Picnic.*

ROBERT PERCHAN is the author of a book of fiction, *Perchan's Chorea: Eros and Exile* (Watermark). His poems and stories have appeared in recent issues of *The Prose Poem, Libido* and, of course, the *Corpse.* He lives in South Korea.

ROBERT PETERS, prolific poet, dramatist, critic, editor, writer of memoirs, and fiction writer, is also a fine satirist and humorist, as his parodies here show. These pieces are from an epic poem called "The Heniad, or Seventy-Five Ways of Considering the Rooster Mounting His Hen," in the voices of numerous American and British poets. Peters resides in California with his life-partner of nearly thirty years, Paul Trachtenberg, a poet, dictionary maker (*Alphabet Soup*), and professional Scrabble player.

SIMON PETTET is an English poet, long-time resident of New York's Lower East Side. He is the author of the essential *Selected Poems* (Talisman House) and, with Rudy Burckhardt, *Talking Pictures* (Zoland Books). His edition of *The Selected Art Writings of James Schuyler* was recently published by Black Sparrow Press.

HOLLY PRADO's most recent book is *Esperanza: Poems for Orpheus* (Cahuena Press, 1998). A review in *The Women's Review of Books*

(Wellesley College) says "Prado has, more than any other poet I know, the ability to capture and describe the relationship between interior and exterior worlds in a manner that is simultaneously grounded and filled with mystery."

PATRICK PRITCHETT is the author of *Ark Dive* (Arcturus Editions) an elegy for the poet Ronald Johnson. His poems have appeared in *New American Writing, Rhizome, River City, Mirage, Antenym, Bombay Gin, non,* and *Prairie Schooner,* among others. A former development executive in the film industry, he is currently completing his studies in English at the University of Colorado. His book reviews have been featured in the *American Book Review, LA View* and the *Boulder Daily Camera.* He lives in Boulder, CO, with his wife, writer/teacher Barbara Wilder.

RICK PROSE is a boatbuilder and writer who divides his time, with his family, between a forty acre homestead in the woods of Maine and a fifty-year-old sailboat along the coast. He recently finished his first novel *The Yardman's Fall,* for which he figures he'd better find a publisher before starting another.

JAMES PURDY's most recent book is *Gertrude of Stony Island* (William Morrow) and a new collection of stories, *Moe's Villa and Other Stories,* is forthcoming. He currently has two plays running Off-Broadway, *Dangerous Moonlight* and *Down the Starry River.*

PETER RABBIT is a founder of the Taos Poetry Circus. Rabbit performs with Luminous Animal.

CARL RAKOSI is the author of *Two Poems* (1933); *Selected Poems* (1941); *Amulet* (1967); *Ere-Voice* (1971); *Ex Cranium, Night* (1975); *My Experiences in Parnassus* (1977); *History* (1981); *Drôles de Journal* (1981); *Spiritus, I* (1983) *Collected Prose* (1983); *Collected Poems* (1986); *Poems 1923–1941* (1995); *The Earth Suite* (1997), and is featured in *Carl Rakosi, Man and Poet,* edited by Michael Heller (1993).

BRETT RALPH has work in *Rain Taxi.*

ISHMAEL REED is a novelist, poet, essayist, publisher, polemicist, and anthologist. Among his many novels are *The Free Lance Pallbearers* (1967), *Yellow Back Radio Broke Down* (1969), *Mumbo Jumbo* (1972), and *The Last Days of Louisiana Red* (1974). He is the publisher of I. Reed Books, and the editor of three major anthologies of poetry and fiction.

SUZANNE RHODENBAUGH's third chapbook, *The Shine on Loss,* was published in 1998 in the *Painted Bride Quarterly* series. Her essay, "The One Story," came out in the 1999 *Northeast Corridor.* She lives in St. Louis.

EDOUARD RODITI was born in Paris in 1910. He began publishing poetry in 1928 in *transition,* the expatriate Paris periodical to which James Joyce, Gertrude Stein and Hart Crane, among others, were contributing. In 1934, T.S.

Eliot published some of his poems in *The Criterion*. Since 1940, he has contributed to the *New Directions Annuals*, edited by James Laughlin. His books include *Poems 1928–1948* and *The Delights of Turkey* (New Directions), *Emperor of Midnight* and *Thrice Chosen* (Black Sparrow Press), *Magellan of the Pacific* (Faber and Faber) and *Dialogs of Art*.

GERALD ROSEN is the author of five novels including the Sixties classic, *The Carmen Miranda Memorial Flagpole*, *Growing Up Bronx*, and most recently, *Mahatma Gandhi in a Cadillac*, and a non-fiction book, *Zen in the Art of J. D. Salinger*. He lives in San Francisco.

DEBORAH SALAZAR is now a full-time mom to handsome boy genius, Asher. Her poems and essays are widely anthologized and she is a regular contributor to *Natural Jewish Parenting*. She lives in Baton Rouge with professional philosopher Gregg Lubritz (Asher's daddy).

ED SANDERS' most recent book is *America, A History in Verse, Vol. 1 (1900–1939)* (Black Sparrow, 1999). He edits the *Woodstock Journal* and is completing a book-length *Poetry and Life of Allen Ginsberg*.

ELIO SCHNEEMAN was born in 1961 in Italy and died in 1997 in New York City. He grew up on St. Mark's Place on the Lower East Side. In 1978 Ted Berrigan's legendary C Press published a collection of his poems, *In February I Think*. *Along the Rails*, his first full-length collection, was published in 1991 by United Artists Books. Work by Elio has appeared in numerous publications, including *Talisman*, *Transfer*, *Shiny*, *The World*, and in the anthologies *Nice to See You*, *Out of this World* and, most recently, *An Anthology of New (American) Poets*.

ERNIE SEALS has published poems in *Louisiana Literature* and the *New Delta Review*. He currently lives in Baton Rouge, Louisiana.

P. SHNEIDRE lives in Hollywood, California. His English edition of the Bengali poems of Swami Vivekananda, *All of Love*, is available from Vedanta Press. Last year saw the production of *Jesus, a Folk Opera*; two sequels, *Chaitanya* and *The Gospel of Mary Magdalene*, are scheduled for this year. He works as an editor, screenwriter and mystery shopper.

HAL SIROWITZ is the author of *Mother Said* (Crown, 1996) and *My Therapist Said* (Crown, 1998). Both books were translated into Norwegian and became best sellers in Norway. He's a recipient of an NEA Fellowship. He performed on MTV's *Spoken Word Unplugged*, NPR's *All Things Considered* and PBS's *Poetry Heaven*.

DALE SMITH lives in Austin, Texas, and co-edits *Skanky Possum* with his wife, Hoa Nguyen. His book *Texas Crude* was recently published by Blue Press.

MARC SWAN lives on Cape Cod; poems in print and electronic publications in US and abroad, including *Baltimore Review, black dirt, Gallery Zandstraat, Slant, 2River View, Niederngasse*.

WILLIAM TALCOTT has had poems appearing in *Bakunin, Exquisite Corpse, New American Writing, Lingo* and *Processed World*. His most recent work, *Benita's Book*, is a collection of love poems to an audience of one, but voyeurs are invited. He lives in San Francisco.

HUNTER S. THOMPSON is well-known, among other things, for *Fear and Loathing in Las Vegas*, which is the best chronicle of drug-soaked, addle-brained, rollicking good times ever committed to the printed page. It is also the tale of a long weekend road trip that has gone down in the annals of American pop culture as one of the strangest journeys ever undertaken.

Poet of San Francisco, KARL TIERNEY was awarded a 1995 grant from the PEN Center USA West's Grant Program for Writers With HIV/AIDS; he disappeared that same year at the age of 39.

MIKE TOPP currently lives in New York City unless he has died or moved. Some of his books include *Local Boy Makes Good* (Appearances, 1994), *Six Short Stories & Seven Short Poems* (Low-Tech Press, 1997), *Basho's Milk Dud* (Low-Tech Press, 1999) and, with Sparrow, *High Priest of California/Wild Wives* (Beet, 1997).

CHRIS TOLL was the first assistant editor of *Exquisite Corpse*. He is a resident of Baltimore, a poet, and a publisher of the literary magazine *Open 24 Hours*.

NANOS VALAORITIS was born in Switzerland in 1921. He spent nine years in London and ten years in Paris where he was connected with André Breton's Surrealist Group. He taught at San Francisco State University from 1968–1993. He edited *Magazine Pali* in Greece from 1963–1967 and *Synteleia* from 1989–1997. His most recent book is *My Afterlife Guaranteed, Narratives & Poetry* (City Lights, 1990). Nanos lives part of the time in Oakland, California and the other part in Athens, Greece. He's married to American painter Marie Wilson.

THOMAS L. VAULTONBURG is the author of *Poems at the End of the World* (Taproot Press).

IOANNA-VERONIKA WARWICK was born in Poland and came to this country when she was 17. She has been published in *Ploughshares, Poetry, Best American Poetry 1992, The Iowa Review, New Letters, Nimrod, Southern Poetry Review, Quarterly West* (First Prize, 1990 Writers-at-Work Fellowship Competition), *The Prairie Schooner*, and other magazines.

PAUL VIOLI's most recent book, his tenth, is *Fracas*. His work has appeared in numerous magazines and anthologies both here and abroad. Awarded two poetry fellowships from the NEA, Violi has also received grants from the New York Foundation for the Arts, The Fund for Poetry, and The Ingram Merrill Foundation. He teaches at NYC and Columbia.

ELIOT WEINBERGER's books of prose include *Works on Paper, 19 Ways of Looking at Wang Wei, Outside Stories*, and *Written Reaction*. He is the editor of the anthology *American Poetry Since 1950: Innovators & Outsiders*. Among his many translations are Octavio Paz's *Collected Poems 1957–1987*, Vicente Huidobro's *Altazor*, Xavier Villaurrutia's *Nostalgia for Death*, and the *Selected Non-Fictions* of Jorge Luis Borges.

PETER WEVERKA, a freelance writer, lives in San Francisco.

CURTIS WHITE wrote "The Late Word," a review and commentary column, for *Exquisite Corpse* for roughly five years between 1991 and 1995. He is the author most recently of *Memories of My Father Watching TV* (Dalkey Archive Press). He lives in Normal, Illinois.

H. S. WIESNER collaborated with her fiance, I. P. Coulianou, on a number of fantastic stories reminiscent of the fictions of Borges, Eliade, and Eco. At the time, she was a Divinity student at Harvard.

ERAN WILLIAMS has been published in *Wilderness, ONTHEBUS, Reed,* and other magazines. He recently returned from Hungary where he worked for two years as a Soros Teaching Fellow and is currently an instructor in the Linguistics and Language Development Department at San Jose State University.

PATRICIA WILSON was born in Minneapolis, Minnesota on March 25, 1961. She has lived in New Orleans since 1994.

JEFFREY CYPHERS WRIGHT is the author of *Employment of the Apes, Charges, All in All, Drowning Light, Walking on Words* and most recently *Revolutionary Love Gardens Sonnets*, which details his involvement with the endangered community gardens of New York City. He studied with Allen Ginsberg and received his MFA in poetry from Brooklyn College. He is the publisher of *Cover Magazine*, now in its 13th year.

The indefatigable DAVID ZAUHAR was one of the earliest assistants at *Exquisite Corpse*. He is a fiction writer and teacher in Chicago.

Born in the White Mountains, ARIZONA ZIPPER and Susan live on the banks of the Saco with their 5 year old, Lydia Chloe, and a talking parrot. More of her work is forthcoming in *RAW NerVZ HAIKU, NYQ,* and W. W. Norton & Co.'s *Haiku Anthology*.

NINA ZIVANCEVIC, poet, fiction writer, essayist and translator was born and raised in the bomb-ridden Belgrade. She grew up and went to school in England and the US. Presently she lives and works in France at the University of Nancy II. She has published nine books of poetry and four books of fiction.

MISSING IN ACTION:

Donald Blumen

C.A. Conrad

Mark DeCarteret

Joan Fisher

Lee Goldstein

Jeff Joy

Russell Kolnikov

David Nixon

Anthony Robbins

James Scofield

Ravi Singh

Jim Tyack

Printed June 1999 in Santa Barbara & Ann Arbor
for the Black Sparrow Press
by Mackintosh Typography & Edwards Brothers Inc.
Text set in Sabon with heads in Albertus
and New Berolina by Words Worth.
Design by Barbara Martin.
This edition is published in paper wrappers;
there are 300 hardcover trade copies;
100 hardcover copies have been numbered & signed
by the editors; & 20 copies handbound in boards
by Earle Gray are lettered & signed by the editors.